CW00780219

RECOLLECTIONS OF A PROVINCIAL PAST

Domingo Faustino Sarmiento

Translated from the Spanish by
ELIZABETH GARRELS AND ASA ZATZ

EDITED WITH AN INTRODUCTION AND CHRONOLOGY
BY ELIZABETH GARRELS

OXFORD
UNIVERSITY PRESS

2005

OXFORD

UNIVERSITY PRESS

Oxford University Press, Inc., publishes works that further
Oxford University's objective of excellence
in research, scholarship, and education.

Oxford   New York

Auckland   Cape Town   Dar es Salaam   Hong Kong   Karachi
Kuala Lumpur   Madrid   Melbourne   Mexico City   Nairobi
New Delhi   Shanghai   Taipei   Toronto

With offices in

Argentina   Austria   Brazil   Chile   Czech Republic   France   Greece
Guatemala   Hungary   Italy   Japan   Poland   Portugal   Singapore
South Korea   Switzerland   Thailand   Turkey   Ukraine   Vietnam

Published by Oxford University Press, Inc.
198 Madison Avenue, New York, New York, 10016
www.oup.com

Library of Congress Cataloging-in-Publication Data
Sarmiento, Domingo Faustino, 1811–1888.
[Recuerdos de provincia. English]
Recollections of a provincial past /
by Domingo Faustino Sarmiento ; translated from the
Spanish by Elizabeth Garrels and Asa Zatz ;
edited with an introduction and chronology by
Elizabeth Garrels.
p. cm.—(Library of Latin America)
Includes bibliographical references.
ISBN-13: 978-0-19-511369-3 (cloth) ISBN-13: 978-0-19-511370-9 (pbk.)
ISBN-10: 0-19-511369-1 (cloth) ISBN-10: 0-19-511370-5 (pbk.)
1. Sarmiento, Domingo Faustino, 1811–1888.
2. Presidents—Argentina—Biography.
3. San Juan (Argentina : Province).
4. San Juan (Argentina : Province)—Biography.
I. Garrels, Elizabeth.
II. Zatz, Asa.
III. Title.
IV. Series.

F2961.S2413 2004   982'.05'092—dc22   2004016503

9 8 7 6 5 4 3 2 1
Printed in the United States of America
on acid-free paper

My contribution to this book is dedicated to
my son and to my husband,
David and Les Perelman,
and to the memory of two dear friends,
Susanne and Half Zantop
—E. Garrels

This portrait of Sarmiento appears in the original 1850 edition of *Recuerdos de provincia* on display at the Library of the Museum of Sarmiento's Childhood Home in San Juan, Argentina. It is reproduced here with the permission of the Director of the Casa Natal de Sarmiento.

Contents

Acknowledgments   *ix*

Series Editors' General Introduction   *xi*

Biographical Note on Domingo Faustino Sarmiento   *xv*

Chronology of Domingo Faustino Sarmiento   *xvii*

Editor's Note on the Text and Translation   *xxxi*

Introduction   *xxxiii*

Bibliography Cited in the Editor's Note and Introduction   *lxxv*

Select Bibliography   *lxxxi*

About the Editor and Co-translator   *lxxxv*

Recollections of a Provincial Past   *I*

Editor's Notes   *223*

Acknowledgments

My research interest in Sarmiento dates to the early 1980s. In the twenty-odd years since then, I have been generously helped by the support, counsel, and above all, the inspirational scholarship of numerous people, most prominent among them Jean Franco, Diana Sorensen, Tulio Halperín Donghi, Francine Masiello, Mary Louise Pratt, Sylvia Molloy, Doris Sommer, and Adolfo Prieto. Over this period I have received funding for my work on Sarmiento from the Joint Committee on Latin American Studies of the American Council of Learned Societies and the Social Science Research Council (1981), the Levitan Prize for the Humanities and Social Sciences at M.I.T. (1993), and the Dean's Faculty Development Fund administered by Dean Philip Khoury of the School of Social Sciences, Humanities, and the Arts at M.I.T. With regard to this present project, begun in 1996, I wish to thank the following people for reading and commenting on the Editor's Introduction and, in one case, the entire translation: Diana Sorensen, Edward Baron Turk, Pauline Maier, Jeffrey Ravel, and Jean Franco. I also wish to thank Penny Kanouse, Daniel Balderston and Isabelle de Courtivron for their much appreciated practical advice regarding the translation. I am also grateful for the active interest taken in this project by Graham Howard and Sheryl Britig, both of the M.I.T. Libraries, by Elizabeth White, administrative staff to Foreign Languages and Literatures at M.I.T., by David Rumsey, whose wonderful map collection is available to all at www.davidrumsey.com, to

Beatriz O. de Coria, Director of the Casa Natal de Sarmiento, in San Juan, Argentina, for kindly responding to an e-mail from a total stranger, and to my editors at Oxford University Press, Elda Rotor, Catherine Humphries, and Cybele Tom. Several others who also responded generously to requests for information are acknowledged in the Editor's Notes of the present volume. Finally, I am privileged to have enjoyed almost uninterrupted access to Harvard University's Widener Library since 1967. Without Widener's exceptional collection on Argentine literature and history, I could not have done the research for this edition.

Elizabeth Garrels
Lexington and Cambridge, Massachusetts
2004

Series Editors'
General Introduction

The Library of Latin America series makes available in translation major nineteenth-century authors whose work has been neglected in the English-speaking world. The titles for the translations from the Spanish and Portuguese were suggested by an editorial committee that included Jean Franco (general editor responsible for works in Spanish), Richard Graham (series editor responsible for works in Portuguese), Tulio Halperín Donghi (at the University of California, Berkeley), Iván Jaksić (at the University of Notre Dame), Naomi Lindstrom (at the University of Texas at Austin), Francine Masiello (at the University of California, Berkeley), and Eduardo Lozano of the Library at the University of Pittsburgh. The late Antonio Cornejo Polar of the University of California, Berkeley, was also one of the founding members of the committee. The translations have been funded thanks to the generosity of the Lampadia Foundation and the Andrew W. Mellon Foundation.

During the period of national formation between 1810 and into the early years of the twentieth century, the new nations of Latin America fashioned their identities, drew up constitutions, engaged in bitter struggles over territory, and debated questions of education, government, ethnicity, and culture. This was a unique period unlike the process of nation formation in Europe and one that should be more familiar than it is to students of comparative politics, history, and literature.

The image of the nation was envisioned by the lettered classes—a minority in countries in which indigenous, mestizo, black, or mulatto peasants and slaves predominated—although there were also alternative nationalisms at the grassroots level. The cultural elite were well educated in European thought and letters, but as statesmen, journalists, poets, and academics, they confronted the problem of the racial and linguistic heterogeneity of the continent and the difficulties of integrating the population into a modern nation-state. Some of the writers whose works will be translated in the Library of Latin America series played leading roles in politics. Fray Servando Teresa de Mier, a friar who translated Rousseau's *The Social Contract* and was one of the most colorful characters of the independence period, was faced with imprisonment and expulsion from Mexico for his heterodox beliefs; on his return, after independence, he was elected to the congress. Domingo Faustino Sarmiento, exiled from his native Argentina under the dictatorship of Rosas, wrote *Facundo: Civilizatión y barbarie*, a stinging denunciation of that government. He returned after Rosas's overthrow and was elected president in 1868. Andrés Bello was born in Venezuela, lived in London where he published poetry during the independence period, settled in Chile where he founded the University, wrote his grammar of the Spanish language, and drew up the country's legal code.

These post-independence intelligentsia were not simply dreaming castles in the air, but vitally contributed to the founding of nations and the shaping of culture. The advantage of hindsight may make us aware of problems they themselves did not foresee, but this should not affect our assessment of their truly astonishing energies and achievements. Although there is a recent translation of Sarmiento's celebrated *Facundo*, there is no translation of his memoirs, *Recuerdos de provincia* [Recollections of a Provincial Past]. The predominance of memoirs in the Library of Latin America Series is no accident—many of these offer entertaining insights into a vast and complex continent.

Nor have we neglected the novel. The series includes new translations of the outstanding Brazilian writer Machado de Assis's work, including *Dom Casmurro* and *The Posthumous Memoirs of Brás Cubas*. There is no reason why other novels and writers who are not so well known outside Latin America—the Peruvian novelist Clorinda Matto de Turner's *Aves sin nido*, Nataniel Aguirre's *Juan de la Rosa*, José de Alencar's *Iracema*, Juana Manuela Gorriti's short stories—should not be read with as much interest as the political novels of Anthony Trollope.

A series on nineteenth-century Latin America cannot, however, be limited to literary genres such as the novel, the poem, and the short story. The literature of independent Latin America was eclectic and strongly influenced by the periodical press newly liberated from scrutiny by colonial authorities and the Inquisition. Newspapers were miscellanies of fiction, essays, poems, and translations from all manner of European writing. The novels written on the eve of Mexican Independence by José Joaquín Fernández de Lizardi included disquisitions on secular education and law and denunciations of the evils of gaming and idleness. Other works, such as a well-known poem by Andrés Bello, "Ode to Tropical Agriculture," and novels such as *Amalia* by José Mármol and the Bolivian Nataniel Aguirre's *Juan de la Rosa*, were openly partisan. By the end of the century, sophisticated scholars were beginning to address the history of their countries, as did João Capistrano de Abreu in his *Capítulos de história colonial.*

It is often in memoirs such as those by Fray Servando Teresa de Mier or Sarmiento that we find the descriptions of everyday life that in Europe were incorporated into the realist novel. Latin American literature at this time was seen largely as a pedagogical tool, a "light" alternative to speeches, sermons, and philosophical tracts—though, in fact, especially in the early part of the century, even the readership for novels was quite small because of the high rate of illiteracy. Nevertheless the vigorous orally transmitted culture of the gaucho and the urban underclasses became the linguistic repertoire of some of the most interesting nineteenth-century writers—most notably José Hernández, author of the "gauchesque" poem "Martín Fierro," which enjoyed an unparalleled popularity. But for many writers the task was not to appropriate popular language but to civilize, and their literary works were strongly influenced by the high style of political oratory.

The editorial committee has not attempted to limit its selection to the better-known writers such as Machado de Assis; it has also selected many works that have never appeared in translation or writers whose works have not been translated recently. The series now makes these works available to the English-speaking public.

Because of the preferences of funding organizations, the series initially focuses on writing from Brazil, the Southern Cone, the Andean region, and Mexico. Each of our editions will have an introduction that places the work in its appropriate context and includes explanatory notes.

We owe special thanks to the late Robert Glynn of the Lampadia Foundation, whose initiative gave the project a jump-start, and to Richard Ekman and his successors at the Andrew W. Mellon Foundation, which also generously supported the project. We also thank the Rockefeller Foundation for funding the 1996 symposium, "Culture and Nation in Iberoamerica," organized by the editorial board of the Library of Latin America. The support of Edward Barry of Oxford University Press was crucial in the founding years of the project, as has been the advice and help of Ellen Chodosh and Elda Rotor of Oxford University Press. The John Carter Brown Library at Brown University in Providence, Rhode Island, has been serving since 1998 as the grant administrator of the project.

Jean Franco
Richard Graham

Biographical Note on
Domingo Faustino Sarmiento

Domingo Faustino Sarmiento (1811–1888) remains one of the most colorful, controversial, and compelling literary and political figures of nineteenth-century Latin America. An autodidact blessed with prodigious energy and imagination, he fills the century with the influence of his brilliant insights and reductive clichés, his megalomaniac personality, and the irrepressible flow of his fountain pen partnered with the limitless reproductive capacity of the printing press. Always sensitive to his modest provincial origins in an emerging nation whose Atlantic port, expansive export economy, and impressive intelligentsia were fast acquiring continental preeminence, Sarmiento pushed himself to become an omnivore of western culture and a larger-than-life figure consecrated to the transformation of Argentina into a modern liberal capitalist republic. During the exceptionally fertile years of his exile in Chile, from 1841 to 1852, he produced three of the most important literary texts of the nineteenth century: *Facundo* (1845), *Viajes* (1849–51), and the first modern Spanish American autobiography, *Recuerdos de provincia* (1850). He served as president of Argentina from 1868 to 1874.

Chronology of
Domingo Faustino Sarmiento

1811   Domingo Faustino Sarmiento is born on February 15 in San Juan de la Frontera, a city founded by the Spaniards at the eastern base of the Andes in 1562. He is the fifth child born to Paula Zoila Albarracín and José Clemente Sarmiento. Baptized Faustino Valentín, he will assume the name of the family's most beloved saint, Domingo.

           Earlier, on June 17, 1810, news had arrived with the mail from Buenos Aires of the proclamation on May 25 of the provisional governing Junta in that far-off Atlantic port city. On July 7, 1810, an open meeting of the town council proclaimed San Juan's recognition of the authority of the Junta in Buenos Aires.

1816   Sarmiento enters the School of the Fatherland, the first public school in San Juan, in April, the same month that the school is founded. On July 9, at a congress in Tucumán, the United Provinces of the Río de la Plata proclaims its independence from Spain.

1817   On January 18, General San Martín's Army of the Andes moves out of the Argentine city of Mendoza, to the south of San Juan, to begin its campaign to engage the Spanish in Chile. Sarmiento's father is a soldier in this army. On February 12, San Martín defeats the royalists at Chacabuco and enters

Santiago. Sarmiento's father receives the commission to return to San Juan with the news of the victory and a group of Spanish prisoners of war. The town gives him a hero's welcome.

1821/2   Sarmiento travels with his father to the city of Córdoba to become a student at the Seminary of Loreto, but the two return home when the boy becomes ill, frustrating his plan to study in Córdoba.

1823   Sarmiento is not among the ten students chosen at random to receive state scholarships for study in Buenos Aires at the School of Moral Science.

1825   In September, Sarmiento departs with his uncle the federalist priest José de Oro when the latter is exiled from San Juan for participation in the overthrow of the liberal governor Santiago del Carril in July. The two relocate in the neighboring province San Luis, where the uncle preaches in a small rural church and the nephew teaches pupils older than he is to read.

1827   In January, Sarmiento returns to San Juan because the liberal governor has agreed to send him to Buenos Aires to study at the prestigious School of Moral Sciences. The day he returns, the governor is deposed and replaced by a federalist chosen by the powerful caudillo Juan Facundo Quiroga. Sarmiento goes to work in a store owned by an aunt. Around this time, Facundo enters the city of San Juan with his gaucho troops. This is perhaps the only occasion on which Sarmiento actually sets eyes on the fearful caudillo. This year Sarmiento also makes his first trip across the Andes to Chile, in the company of a friend. In Santiago he meets José de Oro's brother and his mother's first cousin Fray Justo de Santa María de Oro, who in 1834 will become the first Bishop of Cuyo.

1828   Sarmiento is named second lieutenant in the Second Company of the Infantry Battalion of the Province of San Juan. He is briefly jailed for refusing to obey an order given to him by Lieutenant Colonel Manuel Gregorio Quiroga, who is also the governor of San Juan.

1829   Sarmiento embraces the political cause of the unitarians. He fights in the battles of Niquivil (July) and Pilar (September). After the unitarian defeat at Pilar, he is placed under house arrest in San Juan between October and March of the following year. During this time, he begins on his own to study French.

1830   Sarmiento, together with a group of other young unitarians, goes briefly into exile in Chile but returns in April when a unitarian becomes governor of San Juan. Sarmiento is promoted to third assistant of the first squadron of the militia in the provincial cavalry.

1831   At the end of March, the unitarian government of San Juan falls, and Sarmiento, in the company of his father, emigrates to Chile. He teaches in a school in Santa Rosa de Los Andes, on the Chilean side of the Cordillera.

1832   Sarmiento goes to teach in the school of the small village of Procuro, two leagues to the south of Los Andes. On July 18, his illegitimate daughter, Ana Faustina, is born. She will be brought up by Sarmiento's mother in San Juan. At the end of this year, Sarmiento relocates to Valparaíso, where he will be employed as a clerk in a store. Here, in Valparaíso, he begins his study of English.

1833   After some time in the port city of Valparaíso, Sarmiento goes to the mining center of Copiapó, in the north of Chile. One of his ex-commanding officers from San Juan, who owns a mine there, gives him a job as a miner. Two years later, Sarmiento becomes a foreman.

1835   Sarmiento becomes seriously ill with typhoid fever and probably depression. His friends apply to the federalist governor of San Juan for permission to allow him to return home.

1836   He returns home to San Juan, where he will work as a teacher.

1838   The young Manuel Quiroga Rosas, who had been linked to Esteban Echeverría's May Association in Buenos Aires, returns home to San Juan with a personal library of the latest progressive books and journals from Europe. He, Sarmiento, Antonio Aberastaín, and Dionisio Rodríguez, all roughly the same age, form a local literary salon, in which they read and discuss these books at length.

1839   On July 9, Sarmiento inaugurates the Santa Rosa School for Girls in San Juan. He will be its director until his imprisonment in San Juan in November 1840. On July 20, Sarmiento brings out the first issue of the first newspaper ever published in San Juan, the weekly *El Zonda,* of which he is the director and the principal writer. The paper will survive for six issues, until August 25.

1840   On November 18, Sarmiento is imprisoned by the government of the federalist caudillo Nazario Benavides. He is almost killed by soldiers on November 18, and the next day he abandons San Juan to go into exile in Chile.

1841   In January, Sarmiento establishes himself in the Chilean capitol, Santiago. On February 14, he anonymously publishes his first article in the Chilean press, in the Valparaíso daily *El Mercurio.* On March 5, he is made editor-in-chief of *El Mercurio.* This year Sarmiento begins his long and close association with Conservative government minister and future Chilean President Manuel Montt. He also meets his cousin Domingo de Oro for the first time. On March 12, in collaboration with De Oro and Vicente Fidel López, he brings out the first of four issues of the *Crónica contemporánea de Sud-América.* Starting on April 14, he founds and directs the political newspaper *El Nacional* in support of the presidential candidacy of the Conservative Party's Manuel Bulnes. (Bulnes begins his first of two consecutive terms as president of Chile in September.)

1842   On January 20, Minister of Public Education Manuel Montt appoints Sarmiento to direct the newly founded Normal School, the first of its kind in South America. On September 10, Sarmiento founds the first daily newspaper in Santiago, *El Progreso.* He directs the paper but does not own it. As director of the Normal School, Sarmiento publishes the book *Análisis de las cartillas, silabarios y otros métodos de lectura conocidos y practicados en Chile* [Analysis of the Primers, Syllabaries and Other Reading Methods Known and Practiced in Chile]. He also founds the Liceo, a secondary school, with Vicente Fidel López.

1843   Sarmiento publishes the autobiographical pamphlet *Mi defensa* [My Defense]. He is named to the Faculty of Philosophy and Letters of the newly founded University of Chile, and before this body, on October 17, he delivers the address "Memoria sobre ortografía americana" [Dissertation on American Spelling].

1844   Sarmiento translates two texts from French into Spanish and has them published. These will be adopted for use by Chile's public elementary schools: *La conciencia de un niño* [The Conscience of A Child] and *Vida de Jesucristo* [Life of Jesus Christ]. Depending on the source, Sarmiento's father dies either this year or in 1848.

1845   In February, in *El Progreso*, Sarmiento publishes "Apuntes biográficos" [Biographical Notes], a short biography of José Félix Aldao, the caudillo priest of Mendoza, Argentina. On May 2, Sarmiento begins the serial publication of *Facundo* in *El Progreso*. At the end of July, he publishes *Facundo* as a book, adding two more chapters. He also publishes *Método de lectura gradual* [A Method of Gradual Reading], adopted by the University of Chile for use in the public schools. The government of Chile sends him on an official mission to study the educational systems of Europe and the United States. He leaves Valparaíso on the steamer *Enriqueta* in October and arrives in Montevideo in December. There he meets Florencio Varela and Esteban Echeverría.

1846   Sarmiento arrives in Río de Janeiro in February and stays there for two months. In May, he arrives at Le Havre in France and goes to Paris, where he remains until September. He visits General San Martín, who has lived in exile in Europe since 1822. Charles de Mazade publishes a very positive and extensive review of the *Facundo* in the *Revue des Deux Mondes* (Paris). Sarmiento travels south to Madrid, where he arrives in October, then on to Córdoba, Sevilla, Cádiz, Valencia, Barcelona, and Palma de Mallorca. In December he goes to Algeria.

1847   In January, Sarmiento returns to France and then proceeds to Italy, where he has an interview with Pope Pious IX in Rome. He travels briefly to Switzerland and Germany and by June is back in Paris. On July 1, at his induction to the

Historical Institute of France, he delivers a speech on San Martín's historic encounter with Bolívar in Guayaquil. At the end of July he crosses the English Channel and takes a train to London. Then he proceeds north to Liverpool, and in mid-August embarks for the United States, where he arrives, in New York, in mid-September. He travels to Canada via Buffalo and Niagara Falls, then on to Montreal. From there he returns to the United States and proceeds to Boston, where he meets Horace Mann and his wife Mary Peabody Mann. He then travels to Philadelphia, Baltimore, Washington, D.C., Pittsburgh, and New Orleans. On November 4, he arrives in Havana, Cuba, where he remains until December 8. From there, he crosses the isthmus of Panama on horseback, and travels by ship down the Pacific coast, stopping in Lima and Arica.

1848   On February 24, Sarmiento arrives in Valparaíso, Chile. On May 19 he marries the widow Benita Martínez Pastoriza, originally from San Juan, Argentina. He adopts her son Domingo Fidel, born in 1845, and goes to live in his wife's house in Yungay, a recently developed suburb of Santiago. Some sources claim that on December 22, Sarmiento's father dies in San Juan, at the age of seventy.

1849   In Santiago, Sarmiento founds the weekly newspaper *La Crónica* (1/28/49–1/20/50 and 11/12/53–1/7/54), and the daily *La Tribuna* (5/1/49–9/13/51). He publishes the book *De la educación popular* [On Popular Education] and the first volume of his travels, *Viajes en Europa, Africa y América* [Travels in Europe, Africa, and America]. He translates and publishes two primers, one on ancient and modern history and the other on physics. In April and again in July, the Argentine dictator Rosas demands his extradition.

1850   Probably in the month of February, Sarmiento publishes *Recuerdos de provincia* [Recollections of a Provincial Past] in the press he operates with Jules Belín, a French printer he had met in Paris. (Belín marries Sarmiento's daughter on July 27.) In March, Sarmiento publishes the book *Argirópolis,* in which he proposes that, after Rosas, the national capitol of

Argentina be established on the island of Martín García. This tract is quickly translated into French and published in Paris. Between September 14 and November 2, Sarmiento publishes the weekly *El Consejero del Pueblo* [The Counselor of The People] to promote the candidacy of Manuel Montt for the Chilean presidential election in 1851. To this end, he also publishes a pro-Montt pamphlet in November. This same month, as national opposition to Montt increases, a group of local socialists briefly take over the town of San Felipe, to the north of Santiago. Sarmiento responds with a pamphlet *Motín de San Felipe i estado de sitio* [San Felipe's Uprising and The State of Siege]. This year he also continues his tireless journalistic campaign against Rosas.

1851   In January, Sarmiento founds the bimonthly review *Sud-América. Política y comercio*. In April he publishes a pamphlet on the Easter Day barracks revolt in Santiago, entitled *Motín en Santiago* [Uprising in Santiago]. In May he publishes another pro-Montt pamphlet. (Montt wins the presidential election in June, and is inaugurated on September 18.) Before embarking from Valparaíso with Bartolomé Mitre, on September 11, to travel to Montevideo, Sarmiento also publishes his *Emigración alemana al Río de la Plata* [German Emigration to the River Plate], with notes by Dr. Wappaüs, Professor of Statistics and Geography at the University of Gottingen, translated from the German by Guillermo Hilleger. On November 2, he arrives in Montevideo and joins the Great Army that Justo José de Urquiza is organizing against Rosas. Sarmiento will accompany the army as official journalist of the military campaign. This year he also publishes the second volume of *Viajes*.

1852   On February 3, Sarmiento participates in the Battle of Caseros outside the city of Buenos Aires, and then enters the city for the first time in his life. On the night of February 4, he goes to Rosas's palace in Palermo, enters the dictator's study, takes pen and paper from his desk, and writes, as a memento for his friends in Chile: "Palermo de San Benito, febrero 4 de 1852." Soon after, he has a falling-out with

Urquiza and leaves Buenos Aires for Rio de Janeiro, Brazil, on February 24. On May 18, he embarks in Rio for Valparaíso. Reestablished in Santiago, he brings out his book *Campaña en el Ejército Grande Aliado de Sud América* [Campaign in the Allied Great Army of South America], which he had begun printing in Brazil. He also publishes the pamphlet *San-Juan, sus hombres y sus actos en la rejeneración arjentina* [San Juan, Its Men and Their Acts in the Argentine Regeneration].

1853   Sarmiento publishes a number of pamphlets, including (between April and May) those that will become known as *Las ciento y una* [The Hundred and One], his polemic response to Juan Bautisti Alberdi's *Cartas quillotanas* [Letters from Quillota]. In September, he publishes *Comentarios de la Constitución de la Confederación Argentina* [Commentaries on the Constitution of the Argentine Confederation]. In August, the government of President Manuel Montt appoints Sarmiento to direct the new official periodical *Monitor de las escuelas primarias* [Monitor of The Primary Schools].

1854   Sarmiento attempts to return to Argentina in January. He is arrested on January 12 in Mendoza and charged with conspiracy. He is absolved of this charge on February 9 and returns to Chile, where he continues his work as a journalist and publisher. He translates and publishes *Exposición e historia de los descubrimientos modernos* [Exposition and History of Modern Discoveries], by the popular French science journalist Louis Figuier. Sarmiento also joins the Freemasonry, to which he will belong for the rest of his life, with the exception of the six years of his presidency, when he will temporarily disengage himself from the fraternal order.

1855   In January, Sarmiento finishes printing (in the press Julio Belín y Cía.) his book *Educacíon común en el estado de Buenos Aires* [Public Education in the State of Buenos Aires], and sends it by ship to Bartolomé Mitre in Argentina. On February 24, he dates the conclusion of his *Memoria sobre educación común* [Thesis on Public Education], written in Chile to be entered in a book competition sponsored by the Uni-

versity of Chile for the best book on Chilean public education. Sarmiento subsequently leaves Santiago, briefly visits
San Juan, and, in May, relocates in Buenos Aires. There he
is named director of the daily newspaper *El Nacional*, and
professor of constitutional law at the University of Buenos
Aires.

1856   *Memoria sobre educación común* is published in Santiago, but
not by Julio Belín y Cía, which by now has ceased to exist.
Sarmiento becomes a councilman in the Municipal Council
of Buenos Aires, as well as superintendent of the School Department of the State of Buenos Aires.

1857   Sarmiento becomes a senator in the Buenos Aires Legislature. His wife and son, Domingo Fidel, arrive from Chile to
live with him.

1858   Sarmiento founds the journal *Anales de la Educación Común*
[Annals of Public Education].

1859   In May, war breaks out between the Argentine Confederation and the State of Buenos Aires. (In September of 1852,
Buenos Aires had broken away from the Confederation,
which in May of 1853 ratified its constitution, thereby legal-
izing the political unification of all the Argentine provinces
with the exception of Buenos Aires.) On October 23, at the
Battle of Cepeda, the Confederation defeats Buenos Aires,
and the latter decides to relinquish its independence and join
with the rest of the country.

1860   In May, Sarmiento is named Minister of War and Foreign
Relations by the new governor of Buenos Aires, Bartolomé
Mitre. He participates in both the convention in which
Buenos Aires proposes amendments to the Confederation's
constitution of 1853, and in the subsequent National Convention, which approves the proposed reforms to the constitution.

1861   In January, Sarmiento steps down as minister and accompa-
nies a military expedition to the interior of the country. In
July, Buenos Aires once more breaks with the Confederation, and on September 17, at the Battle of Pavón, Mitre

defeats the Confederation's forces. In December, Sarmiento goes to Cuyo to set up governments loyal to the victors of the Battle of Pavón. His mother dies on November 21.

1862   Sarmiento arrives in San Juan on January 9 and is elected governor on February 16. In October, Mitre becomes the first president of a unified Argentina. Sarmiento separates from his wife; their son Dominguito is unable to persuade his father to accept a reconciliation.

1863   Sarmiento establishes obligatory primary education in the province of San Juan. The caudillo Angel Vicente Peñaloza, "El Chacho," rises up in La Rioja, which provokes civil wars in Catamarca, San Luis, and Córdoba. Sarmiento declares a state of siege in San Juan. On October 30, El Chacho is defeated at Caucete in San Juan, taken prisoner, and then on November 11, put to death. Many hold Sarmiento accountable, but he denies responsibility.

1864   Confronted by stiff resistance to his political reforms, Sarmiento resigns as governor of San Juan on April 7. President Mitre names him minister plenipotentiary to the United States, as well as to Chile and Peru. Sarmiento crosses the Andes in May and arrives in Santiago. From Valparaíso, he sails to Peru.

1865   Sarmiento acts on his own at the American Congress in Lima and provokes Mitre's displeasure. In April, Sarmiento departs from Peru, sails to Panama, crosses the Isthmus, and embarks for New York, where he arrives on May 15, one month after Lincoln's assassination. Having lost his credentials while en route, he must delay presenting himself to the government in Washington until new copies arrive from Argentina, in November. In the meantime, he travels to Washington, D.C., to watch the review of the returning Army of the Potomac from President Johnson's official stand. From there he visits Richmond and Petersburg, Va. In October, he visits Mary Peabody Mann, Horace Mann's widow, in Concord, Mass. He dines with Emerson, and in Cambridge, he visits Ticknor, Longfellow, and the astronomer Gould at Harvard.

1866   Sarmiento writes and publishes the first biography of Abraham Lincoln in Spanish. He also publishes *Escuelas, base de la prosperidad y la república en los Estados Unidos* [Schools, The Basis of Prosperity and the Republic in the United States]. He writes the *Vida del Chacho* [Life of Chacho], which he will publish together with the *Aldao* and the third Spanish edition of the *Facundo* in New York, in 1868. His son Dominguito dies fighting in the Argentine army in the War of the Triple Alliance against Paraguay.

1867   Sarmiento publishes four issues of the magazine *Ambas Américas* [Both Americas]. He translates Mary Mann's biography of her husband into Spanish and has it published. In June he visits the Universal Exposition in Paris. His name starts to be mentioned as a possible candidate in the upcoming presidential elections in Argentina.

1868   In New York, Mary Mann's English translation of the *Facundo* appears, with translated portions of *Recuerdos de provincia*. In June, Sarmiento receives an honorary doctorate from the University of Michigan, in Ann Arbor. In July, he leaves the United States for Argentina. En route, he learns that on August 16, the National Congress has declared him president of the Republic of Argentina. (He has received 79 out of the 131 electoral votes cast.) He assumes the presidency on October 12.

1869   In January, the allied troops enter Asunción, the capitol of Paraguay; the War of the Triple Alliance is nearing its end. In September, the first national census in Argentina is taken. In October, the Military College of the Nation is created. On December 31, Argentine troops from Paraguay disembark in Buenos Aires and parade through the city.

1870   Ricardo López Jordán, the last of the formidable Argentine caudillos, revolts in the province of Entre Ríos; Urquiza is assassinated, and López Jordán takes control as governor. Sarmiento sends troops, and López Jordán is defeated by the end of January 1871. Taking advantage of the deployment of the army in Paraguay and against the montoneros of López Jórdan, Indian raids increase substantially in the southern part of the province of Buenos Aires. Permanent railroad service is established between Rosario and Córdoba.

1871   More than a thousand public elementary schools are created throughout the country. Telegraphic service is established between Córdoba and Buenos Aires. In Córdoba, Sarmiento inaugurates the National Observatory and the first National Exposition. An epidemic of yellow fever breaks out in Buenos Aires; close to fourteen thousand people die, and for weeks the city is paralyzed.

1872   The trans-Andean telegraph is inaugurated. Sarmiento establishes the Naval Military School in Buenos Aires in October.

1873   In May, López Jordán returns from exile and once again invades Entre Ríos; he is defeated by government forces and flees the country in November. On August 22, in Buenos Aires, Sarmiento survives unscathed an assassination attempt by two Italian brothers contracted for the crime by agents of López Jordán. The National Bank is created, with branches in the provinces.

1874   In August, transatlantic telegraph service is established between Argentina and Europe. On October 12, Sarmiento hands over the presidency to Nicolás Avellaneda. Mitre revolts in arms when he fails to win the presidential election; he is defeated, taken prisoner, and condemned to death, but President Avellaneda will commute his sentence the following year. During Sarmiento's six-year presidency, the number of Argentine children receiving an elementary education has increased more than threefold.

1875   The governor of Buenos Aires names Sarmiento superintendent of schools for the province. Sarmiento is elected national senator for the province of San Juan. He writes for *La Tribuna* and *El Nacional* in Buenos Aires.

1876   Sarmiento publishes the journal *Educación Común* in Buenos Aires. He suffers the first symptoms of heart disease.

1878   Sarmiento resumes the directorship of the newspaper *El Nacional*.

1879   President Avellaneda names Sarmiento minister of the interior. Sarmiento retires from the Senate and from his position as superintendent of schools for Buenos Aires. He resigns as minister after one month.

1880   Sarmiento is named as a candidate for the presidency. He accepts but subsequently withdraws his name from the race.

1881   Sarmiento becomes superintendent of schools of the National Council of Education but resigns from the post the following year.

1883   Sarmiento publishes the first volume of *Conflictos y armonías de las razas en América* [Conflicts and Harmonies among the Races in America].

1884   Sarmiento's grandson, Augusto Belín Sarmiento, edits and publishes the autobiographical text *Introducción a las Memorias Militares y fojas de servicios de Domingo F. Sarmiento, General de División* [Introduction to the Military Memoires and Service Records of Domingo F. Sarmiento, Division General]. Sarmiento travels to Chile with a government commission to persuade Chile, Uruguay, and Colombia to undertake with Argentina the translation into Spanish of selected great books of western civilization. In September, the Argentine Congress passes a law, signed by President Roca, to earmark 20,000 pesos for the publication of Sarmiento's complete works.

1885   In December, Sarmiento founds the daily *El Censor* [The Censor].

1886   Sarmiento publishes the biography of his son *Vida de Dominguito* [Life of . . .].

1887   In May, Sarmiento moves to Asunción del Paraguay, in search of a better climate for his failing health. He returns to Buenos Aires in October.

1888   Sarmiento returns in May to Asunción and dies on September 11. According to his biographer Allison Williams Bunkley, his final words are, "I have written a book three times, and every time I have torn it up. It contained some very good things."

Editor's Note on the Text and Translation

In the prologue to his 1938 edition of *Recuerdos de provincia,* Ricardo Rojas, the dean of Argentine literary historians, suggested that it might be impossible for foreign critics to fully appreciate Sarmiento's writing. While he offered no explanation for this judgment, elsewhere in the same prologue he claimed that as a writer Sarmiento lacked universality. Although I do not agree with the first judgment and dismiss the second as outdated, I can speculate as to what Rojas, an intelligent reader of Sarmiento, had in mind.

Of all of Sarmiento's major texts, no single one demands as much specialized historical and geographical knowledge on the part of the reader as *Recuerdos de provincia.* At any moment in the last one hundred years, even an educated reader from Buenos Aires would have been hard pressed to identify possibly half of the specific names and places that this autobiography contains. *Recuerdos* narrates a history that for the most part takes place in a peripheral backwater of Latin America, a place about which relatively few historical works have been written. Consequently, given that many Argentine readers are challenged to identify the book's lesser-known names and places, it follows that the foreign reader will face an even greater challenge. I offer this explanation to justify the unusual quantity and length of the endnotes that I have felt obliged to provide for this translation, which is, after all, intended for a general, nonspecialized audience. I also admit that, up until now, most readers of this venerable standard of Latin America's literary canon have probably read *Recuerdos*, and indeed made good sense of it, without grasping the historical specificity of many of its names and episodes. The text allows this kind of reading, and I fully recognize its legitimacy. However, I contend that the experience of reading the text can be significantly enriched by greater access to the provincial historical context in which so much of the book's action takes place.

Secondly, the task of reading *Recuerdos,* and especially of translating it to another language, is encumbered by the absence of any so-called definitive, that is, error-free edition of the book in its original Spanish. For the present translation (which is the first complete translation of the text into English), I have consulted the first two editions (from 1850 and 1885, respectively), both of which were prepared with Sarmiento's personal collaboration, and nearly fifteen subsequent ones, including the text's recent digital on-line version. All of these editions include at least a handful of obvious typographical errors, and one or two in particular, which have gone through numerous reprintings, have so many egregious errors as to render whole sentences and even passages entirely nonsensical. I have concluded that the first two editions taken together constitute the most reliable text on which to base a translation. However, I have found that even in these there are at least one or two word clusters that do not make sense. In these very exceptional cases I have, in consultation with native Argentine Spanish speakers who are also specialists on Sarmiento, taken the liberty of giving the recalcitrant words a meaning that I consider logical within their context.

This translation reflects the combined work of two translators and has taken many years to complete. After much back and forth between us, after many disagreements and accommodations, we hope that the final translation can be read and enjoyed as a coherent whole.

Introduction

SARMIENTO'S PASTS AND PRESENTS

I.

A Tale of Two Cities: San Juan and Buenos Aires in the Eighteenth and Nineteenth Centuries

Recuerdos de provincia [Recollections of a Provincial Past] is the best known of several autobiographies by the nineteenth-century Argentinean Domingo Faustino Sarmiento (1811–88). For six years (1868–74), this remarkable man was the president of Argentina, and in that South American country his name has the familiarity of a household word even to this day. Local history books solemnly describe him as the second of three "founding presidents" of the Argentine nation, and far beyond the borders of his native land, he remains one of Latin America's most influential writers as well as one of its more controversial and contested political figures.[1]

Domingo F. Sarmiento was born on February 15, 1811, in Cuyo, the westernmost region of Argentina. Then, and now, Cuyo consisted of three provinces, San Juan, Mendoza, and San Luis. Sarmiento was born in the provincial capital of San Juan, a city of the same name that at the time had a population of roughly three to four thousand inhabitants.[2] This small city, like the somewhat larger and more prosperous city of Mendoza a hundred miles to the south (1810 est. pop.= 7,000), had been founded in the mid-sixteenth century by Spanish explorers who had crossed over the Andes from Chile.[3] Both Argentine cities were situated in valleys long since transformed by the human hand into fertile oases among the eastern foothills of the Andean cordillera. Both had an agricultural economy specializing in wine grapes, and both were dependent on irrigation from nearby rivers fed by the cordillera's melting snow. The capital city of San Juan and its surrounding areas accounted for almost all of the cultural and economic life of the province. The remainder of provincial San Juan was, for the most part, a land of deserts, mountains, and sand dunes, with an arid climate and high temperatures in the valleys, and a rainfall as meager as it was uncertain.[4]

In the *Recuerdos*, which Sarmiento published in 1850 at the age of thirty-nine, he boasted he had been born just nine months after May 25, 1810. On that day a few hundred elite males had proclaimed a patriot junta in the far-off Atlantic port city of Buenos Aires (1810 est. pop.= 50,000). As British historian John Lynch writes, May 25 "was a creole revolution, accomplished by an elite who spoke for the people without consulting them."[5] Although the revolutionary junta claimed to establish self-government until Spain's King Ferdinand VII could be restored to the throne (and although outright independence was not proclaimed until July 9, 1816), May 25 has always been celebrated as the inaugural date of the independence movement in Argentina.

In the early part of the nineteenth century, Spanish-speaking Argentina (or that territory variously referred to as the Argentine Republic or Confederation, or the United Provinces of the River Plate) was roughly equivalent to the northern half of the country that today is the largest in area of Spanish-speaking America and that reaches southward to the Straits of Magellan and the Tierra del Fuego.[6] In 1810, Mendoza and San Luis were the southernmost provinces to the west, while Córdoba in the mid-west, and a considerably smaller Buenos Aires province to the east (which only reached as far south as the Salado River) marked the country's southern boundary eastward to the Atlantic. The immense pampas, a flat expanse of natural grassland the size of Texas and to this day synonymous in the minds of many U.S. readers with Argentina itself, was then mostly Indian territory. Only 10 percent of the pampas was settled by Spaniards and Argentine creoles, although this was changing, as "livestock farming expanded at the expense of the Indians, and the littoral economy became increasingly oriented towards the European market through the port of Buenos Aires."[7]

On opposite sides of the country, the cities of San Juan and Buenos Aires were separated by more than 700 miles of irregular topography, primitive trails made by mules and oxen, and the threat of hostile Indians.[8] San Juan's wine and brandy had to leave for Buenos Aires by mule team due to the unevenness of the route's terrain. Mendoza's route eastward, which permitted the use of the more efficient oxcart, still produced a delay of over a month and a half before its wine could reach the port, where Cuyo's spirits were purchased for local consumption rather than for export across the Atlantic.[9] Much more than dangerous wilderness and extreme distance, however, separated the region of Cuyo from Buenos Aires.

Recently, history has worked overtime to dispel the once common myth of Argentina as the most prosperous and European, and therefore most "modern," nation in Latin America. Before the Great Crash of October 1929, however, Argentina's economic indicators placed it among the twelve most "advanced" countries in the world. Still primarily an agro-export economy, in the mid-1920s it provided 66 percent of the world's exports in corn, 72 percent in flax, 32 percent in oats, 20 percent in wheat and wheat flour, and more than 50 percent in meat.[10] The capital city of Buenos Aires, with a population of 1,500,000 by 1914, had already become "the continent's first metropolis."[11] Yet this apparent prosperity often masked the national reality of what historians have called the "two worlds" or "other Argentinas." As historian Peter Winn writes, "There was another Argentina in the interior, which felt excluded from its fair share of the 'progress' that was so conspicuously on display in Buenos Aires."[12] The relative poverty and "backwardness" of the Argentine interior by the twentieth century responded to a process that, most historians agree, had begun in the late eighteenth century, toward the end of the colonial period.

The San Juan of Sarmiento's birth already took second place to Mendoza in the economic landscape of Cuyo. Although it had begun its existence as the most important Spanish settlement in the region, San Juan had recently entered a decline as a result of the late colonial administrative changes made in South America by the Bourbon monarchy of Spain. Hardly more than thirty years had passed since 1776, when King

Charles III had created the new Viceroyalty of La Plata, and had thereby removed Cuyo from the direct jurisdiction of the Captaincy General of Chile, part of the Viceroyalty of Peru. Before this time, San Juan had prospered as part of a colonial economic network that, from the mid-sixteenth century on, had connected Peru and Chile, on the Pacific, with the Spanish settlements to the east of the Andes. As a whole, this system was organized to produce for and profit from the fabulous silver mines of Potosí in Alto Perú (now Bolivia), as well as to assist, at various points along the routes eastward, in conveying the wealth in silver across the Atlantic to Europe. In the eighteenth century, this economic and demographic structure began to erode, not only as the silver mines yielded progressively less, but as new economic and financial centers emerged in Europe, creating dynamic new global markets for both the consumption and the production of goods.

The creation of the Viceroyalty of La Plata in 1776 (which grouped together major portions of the present republics of Argentina, Bolivia, Paraguay, and Uruguay) and the royal decree in 1778 to end the Seville monopoly and legalize trade among fourteen Spanish and nineteen colonial American ports, including Buenos Aires (whose previous trade in overseas imports and silver exports had been mostly contraband), were a response to these new international pressures.[13] Argentine historian Halperín Donghi writes that the "last decades of the eighteenth century were an epoch of rapid rise for the Littoral region, of only partial and moderate rise, accompanied by painful readjustments for the trade and the craft industry of the Interior, and for the latter's agriculture, one of unalloyed disaster."[14]

After independence and up through the 1830s, conditions in the interior continued to decline, as civil wars, beginning in 1820, brought costly waves of destruction to compound the woes recently produced by the region's shift in economic orientation. Conversely, in the decades following Sarmiento's birth, a thriving cattle business emerged in the province of Buenos Aires, heralded by the establishment of the first salting plants in the 1810s and characterized by the creation, especially from the early 1820s onward, of the economic and social entity known as the *estancia*, that is, the immense privately owned cattle ranch geared for export. Buenos Aires's transformed cattle economy prospered in a new world order in which England's industrial revolution and Cuba's and Brazil's plantation slavery created strong markets for Argentina's hides and salted beef.[15] The opening of the Atlantic port of Buenos Aires to competitive foreign trade not only helped transform what had been a relatively small and primitive settlement into a dynamic and expanding city full of foreigners; it also brought on a deluge, after 1778, of Spain's agricultural exports, including wine, and, after independence, of England's factory-produced textiles, both of which could sell in the eastern Argentine markets at prices far below those of the wines and textiles of Cuyo.[16]

By the early 1840s, civil war in the interior gave way to an uneasy peace imposed from Buenos Aires by a now nationally hegemonic dictator, Juan Manuel de Rosas. As a result of this newfound stability, the central and Andean provinces began to experience some of the distant effects of the prosperity enjoyed since the 1830s by neighboring Chile.[17] In 1845, when Sarmiento wrote and published his most famous book, *Facundo o civilización y barbarie* [Facundo or Civilization and Barbarism], he would lament the general intellectual and economic impoverishment into which all the cities of the Argentine interior had sunk since the mid-1820s. However, he would lay the blame not on earlier free-market reforms or a changed international economy but on the civil wars and what he saw as the barbarous rule of the federalist caudillos, or provincial warlords, who, in his mind, shared Rosas's contempt for progress and civilization. Within the *Facundo,* the year 1825 would stand out, especially for San Juan, as a kind of lost golden age of civic virtue, followed by twenty years of decline and ignorance. Even so, the San Juan—and the Mendoza—of 1845 were relatively better off than other western Argentine provinces, for example, La Rioja and San Luis; "San Juan," Sarmiento wrote, "has grown in population due to its advances in agriculture and the emigrants from La Rioja and San Luis, who flee from hunger and misery."[18] Indeed, six years later, in 1851, when Sarmiento published the second edition of the *Facundo,* he added a footnote praising the "healthy reaction" experienced by his ailing province since the date of the book's first appearance.[19]

Although in the ten years preceding the publication of *Recuerdos de provincia* in 1850, San Juan was starting to know—albeit to a far more modest degree—some of the prosperity experienced since the 1810s and '20s in Buenos Aires, the tone of Sarmiento's 1850 autobiography is elegiac, when not indignant, concerning a contemporary San Juan that the author perceives as poorer and less enlightened than it had been when he was a boy and indeed dramatically poorer than it had been before he was born, during and preceding the colonial childhood of his mother. Metaphorically speaking, Sarmiento's *Recuerdos de provincia,* as the personal success story it is intended to be, is an interesting variation on the generic tale of rags to riches. For example, although the protagonist has attained a sense of material well-being, he measures his riches by the accumulation of so much enriching personal and political experience; these are riches of an intangible sort, which translate into credentials of proven merit and ability, rather than into conspicuous material wealth. However, the truly ironic twist to the conventional tale of success is that Sarmiento's story is written by a poor hometown boy made good, whose once prosperous hometown has itself suffered the inverse fate and gone from riches to rags. Halperín Donghi, perhaps the historian who has written most persuasively on this period of Argentina's past, calls *Recuerdos* an "unforgettable picture" of San Juan's decline, of "that decline of an exceptionally mature style of Colonial life."[20]

Nevertheless, *Recuerdos de provincia,* like Sarmiento's earlier *Facundo,* looks upon San Juan's exclusive agricultural base, one of the objective causes of its decline, as a distinctive feature that grants the province a margin of moral superiority over contemporary Buenos Aires, whose cattle economy Sarmiento detests and considers inimical to the creation of responsible citizenship in a modern democratic state. Despite San Juan's present disadvantage, the long experience of its inhabitants with the cultivation of the soil had earned it, along with its southern neighbor Mendoza, a potential exemplary status with regard to Argentina's future progress. By 1850, Sarmiento's economic, political, and social model for national development was the United States. Especially after his travels in the eastern United States in 1847, Sarmiento idealized this country as a land of small and medium-sized farms tilled by their owners, who, as citizen farmers living on their land, were committed to bringing the institutions of modern civilization—schools, libraries, courts of law, etc.—to their nearby towns, many of which seemed to the South American traveler to change miraculously overnight—so fast was the rate of growth—into dynamic and populous cities, full of technological innovations and bustling with commerce.

In the *Facundo,* the book that established Sarmiento's reputation as a writer and brought him his much coveted recognition in Europe, the author had expounded on the antidemocratic evils of the *estancia* as a mode of production. There Sarmiento denounced an economic enterprise that required vast stretches of natural pastureland but very little human labor, since an accommodating natural environment, especially in the east, provided both feed and acceptable open-air shelter for the abundant herds of wild cattle. Thus, according to Sarmiento's analysis, the *estancia* acted as a disincentive for increasing the rural Hispanic population of a national territory considered to suffer from an extremely limited labor pool.[21] Sarmiento further insisted that the expanding *estancias* grabbed up the land, placing it in the hands of a small and powerful elite, thus discouraging the emergence of farm communities and of the population centers needed to provide them with services.

In the *Facundo*, Sarmiento had also elaborated on the political and social ramifications of both the figure of the *estanciero*, or the rich landowner and cattle rancher, and that of the gaucho, or mestizo cowboy, who was fast losing his eighteenth-century nomadic existence and legendary independence to become a rural peon, or salaried worker.[22] In the decades after independence, the gaucho was coerced into working for the *estanciero* by a number of factors. These included the encroachment of the privately owned *estancias* on the pampas, which had hitherto been a wide-open no-man's land filled with wild horses and cattle and used as hunting grounds by both Indians and gauchos. Another factor was the passage of vagrancy laws, which effectively limited poor rural males to only two alternatives: either work for a *patrón* and thus be documented labor, or be forcibly recruited as a vagrant to serve in the army and protect the frontiers from Indian incursions.[23] As the *estanciero* became the gaucho's *patrón* and, during the civil wars, often his caudillo, these two individuals, of starkly different social class, were bound together in a hierarchical and authoritarian relationship, which could be— and was—used politically and militarily to challenge the authority of centralized and—at least nominally—representative government. The gaucho's dependence on and loyalty to his *patrón* were a threat to modern democracy, which required loyalty to abstractions like "civic responsibility" and "the nation."

Given this, the exceptional status that Sarmiento reserved for San Juan and Mendoza, when generalizing about the Argentine national character in the first chapter of the *Facundo*, was indeed significant:

> The classification relevant to my object, is that which results from the livelihoods of the people of the countryside, for that is what influences

their character and spirit. . . . Now, all the Argentine [provinces], except San Juan and Mendoza, live by the products of livestock and grazing; Tucumán also exploits agriculture; and Buenos Aires, in addition to its herds of millions of heads of cattle, dedicates itself to the multiple and varied occupations of civilized life.[24]

In short, in 1845, Sarmiento had made the claim that San Juan and Mendoza were the only two exclusively agricultural provinces in the country.

Six years later, in a publication dated 1851, Sarmiento would again make the same point, but this time with a minor qualification: "Mendoza and San Juan, as opposed to the other provinces of that State, are exclusively agricultural provinces, with the raising of livestock only entering into their occupations to a very limited degree."[25] One year later (and nine months after the fall of Rosas), Sarmiento would publish a pamphlet titled *San-Juan, sus hombres i sus actos en la rejeneración Arjentina* [San Juan, Its Men, and Their Acts in the Argentine Regeneration]. He began this pamphlet by underscoring the positive social implications of what he presented as the absence of *estancias* and gauchos in his province:

The city of San Juan, situated like Mendoza at the foot of the Andes, is itself almost the entire province. . . . Nature has been stingy with spontaneous gifts in this part of the Argentine territory. Its lands lack the grazing pastures of Buenos Aires, the forests of Tucumán, the navigable routes near the shores of the great rivers. Its population would have degenerated by now into brutishness, had not the need to exercise man's physical and moral strengths been born from that very scarcity of natural resources. In order to work the land, then, the people of San Juan must irrigate it with artificial channels, and they, themselves, must export their products to distant markets. With their industry, they grow the trees to supply the wood required for their civil constructions; artificial pastures, better and more abundant, substitute for natural pastures, and a commerce in search of markets takes its muleteers to different points of America, to Copiapó and Buenos Aires, to Valparaíso, Salta, and Potosí. This idiosyncrasy of the traveling farmer gives to the people of Mendoza and San Juan a marked superiority over the populations of the interior. The gaucho, the horseman of the open country of Buenos Aires, or Entre Ríos, does not exist, literally speaking, in these provinces. Here the inhabitants live in houses by the sides of roads that cross entire valleys and districts, and social relations remain healthy since they are subject to improvement from constant social inter-dependence and from the schooling that travel brings in the inspection of different ways of life. The character of these people is recognizably temperate and good natured. . . .

Where there are no lazy men who live on horseback, where it is necessary to work every day to subsist, the caudillo in the manner of Quiroga, of López, cannot survive. How, then, has Benavides [the federalist caudillo and governor of San Juan from 1836 to 1862] been created? How has he survived? His government has been imported from other provinces; it is the fruit of the Rosas administration.[26]

When Sarmiento pens this contrast between the lazy men of provincial Buenos Aires and the hardworking farmers of San Juan, he is at last in a position to speak from firsthand knowledge. Up until November of 1851, he had never set foot in the littoral of Argentina, much less in the province or port city of Buenos Aires. However, in May of '51, Justo José de Urquiza, both the governor and the richest and most powerful *estanciero* of the littoral province of Entre Ríos, had proclaimed his open rebellion against Rosas. In September, Sarmiento boarded a ship in Valparaíso headed for Montevideo on the Atlantic coast. Once he arrived in November, he quickly signed up to serve in Urquiza's Ejército Grande (Great Army), which was to number 28,000, including *entrerrianos*, unitarians, Uruguayans, and Brazilians.[27] For two months, with the military rank of lieutenant colonel and wearing a European-style officer's uniform that made him stand out among all the American ponchos like a grievously sore thumb, Sarmiento composed and printed the army's official bulletin on an ailing and, by necessity, itinerant printing press.[28] He and the press rode with the army through the littoral provinces of Entre Ríos and Santa Fé as it advanced on the province of Buenos Aires and then on its capital city. For the first time in his life, Sarmiento confronted the Argentine pampas that he had so boldly described—albeit secondhand—in the *Facundo*. And on the day after Rosas's easy defeat at the Battle of Caseros on February 3, 1852, Sarmiento entered the city of Buenos Aires, also for the very first time in his life.

The long-imagined Atlantic port city did not, however, retain the world-traveled Andean provincial for long. Quickly disillusioned by the victorious caudillo Urquiza, Sarmiento abandoned Buenos Aires by the end of the month and traveled to Río de Janeiro in neighboring Brazil. From there he boarded a ship to return to Chile, his home in exile since 1841. By October, he had already reestablished himself in Santiago, where he produced the above-cited pamphlet on San Juan in the publishing house that he owned and operated with his son-in-law.

II.

Recuerdos de provincia: *The First Modern Spanish American Autobiography?*

Until recently, it was accepted wisdom among critics of Spanish American literature that the autobiography was a rare bird within the literary fauna of the Spanish-speaking New World. In 1966, Argentine critic Adolfo Prieto rejected this notion as false in the case of Argentine literature, and more recently, his compatriot Sylvia Molloy has done the same for Spanish American writing as a whole. Molloy suggests that this habitual blind spot may well be a factor of the inability or unwillingness of critics to accept Spanish American autobiography on its own terms. If critics approach this genre with expectations derived from reading, or reading about, European autobiography, they usually come away disappointed, having found something that deviates from the canonical autobiographies of the European tradition. For Molloy, then, the critical oversight has partly been a matter of misreading.

In one of her early essays on the subject, Molloy claims that Sarmiento's *Recuerdos de provincia* is the "founding text" of the genre of Spanish American autobiography. There she uses its date of publication, 1850, to mark the beginning of a specifically Spanish American tradition to which many important writers will subsequently contribute.[29] She describes the instances of self-writing that occurred before 1850 as precursors, that is, as part of "the genre's prehistory."[30] For her, to count as an autobiography, a text must display, as indeed *Recuerdos* does, a literary self-awareness: It must see itself as part of a rhetorical tradition of models. (In Sarmiento's case, Rousseau, Lamartine, and Benjamin Franklin are a few of the explicit models that he acknowledged.) In addition, it must betray at least a suspicion "that autobiography is less directly referential than it aspires to be," that is, that the first-person identity represented in the autobiographical text is a constructed one, one that the writer consciously chooses to project and, thus, one that inevitably contains elements of fiction.[31]

Prieto, who asserts that there has been an abundance of autobiographical writing in both nineteenth- and twentieth-century Argentina, pushes the genre's beginnings back to the immediate aftermath of May 1810. If he and Molloy disagree on the genre's date of origin, they nonetheless agree that the Spanish American autobiography is the product of a historically determined crisis of identity. Prieto speaks of the profound contradictions arising from the clash between conservative—indeed decidedly aristocratic and antidemocratic—social customs and attitudes inherited from the colonial past, and the new political circumstances and liberal ideologies of the independence movement.[32] The tensions generated by these lived contradictions as well as the suddenly overwhelmingly political content of public opinion—that ideological creature of the eighteenth-century democratic revolutions in France and North America that sought to replace the passive subjects of absolute monarchy with a public of thinking citizens—help explain why so many activists who participated in the political changes of the day felt the need to write about themselves and to justify their actions before this new and distinctly modern social tribunal. Thus, self-justification and self-defense against the gossip and slander of one's political enemies were principal motivations behind the emergence of a new and public form of self-writing in the Spanish America of the early nineteenth century.

While other less specifically political motivations would come to complicate and enrich later autobiographical writing, this original need to seek the reader's approval would continue, according to Molloy, to characterize the genre and distinguish it from other traditions. Thus, Molloy insists that readers' discomfort with Spanish American autobiography as a genre does not fully account for its marginalization and critical neglect. On the contrary, the texts themselves communicate their own discomfort to the reader, their own ambivalence about drawing attention to the self through a literary form.[33]

In colonial literature, first-person narratives (of which there were many) were generally addressed to a privileged reader, such as the king of Spain or the viceroy (the king's direct representative in the New World), or a religious superior, who might also be one's confessor. In addition, these narratives tended to be written for a specific purpose: to attain recognition for services rendered, to seek forgiveness and regain favor. While the relationship between writer and reader could be extremely delicate and even dangerously strained, their relative social positions were clearly understood by both.[34] The dramatic regime change that independence brought about destroyed this long-established and stable pact between writer and reader, as the latter was replaced by a new reading public that, in fact, was often more ideal than actual. In a world suddenly politicized through and through, where social issues and questions of power were so urgent and so passionately debated that other areas of life came to be seen as secondary, the notion of writing about the self, or even writing for pleasure, could appear suspect. Molloy notes that until fairly recently, "[f]iction—telling for the pleasure of telling—was still tentative . . . ; an utilitarian view of literature—literature at the service of any ideology, be it revolutionary or supportive of the powers that be—was firmly ingrained in writers' and readers' minds alike."[35]

The independence movement aggravated questions of identity, both individual and national, that still have not been laid to rest. Molloy insists that in Spanish America, the "ideological crisis" unleashed by the wars of independence and their aftermath, which was also "a crisis of authority," has led to an enduring "preoccupation with national identity" that is "undeniably present in Spanish American self-writing." Though the nature of the crisis changes with time and circumstance, there is "an ever-renewed scene of crisis" that is "necessary to the rhetoric of self-figuration" in Spanish America.[36]

Furthermore, in the early examples of this relatively recent, postcolonial genre, Molloy identifies a recurrent desire on the part of the male writer to render his story "part of a more important History in the making." Often, this results in a metonymic identification between the autobiographer and his emerging nation. Molloy singles out the same instance cited earlier where in *Recuerdos de provincia* (Chapter 15), Sarmiento boasts of having been born nine months after May 25, 1810, the inaugural date par excellence in the patriotic narrative of the birth of the Argentine nation. Such self-conscious dating, she insists, "unambiguously establishes a genetic, quasi biological link between Sarmiento and his newly independent country." Molloy finds this gesture to be emblematic of the fact that this particular form of self-identification receives greater emphasis in Spanish American autobiography than in its European counterparts.[37]

Midway through *Recuerdos* (as measured in pages and not in chapters), Sarmiento begins "My Education" (Chapter 15), as follows:

> Here ends the colonial history . . . of my family. What follows is the slow and arduous transition from one mode of being to another, the life of

the nascent Republic, the struggle of the parties, civil war, proscription, and exile.

He concludes this first paragraph by establishing the link between his life and that of the entire South American continent:

> ... in my life, ..., I seem to see portrayed this poor South America, thrashing about in its nothingness, making supreme efforts to spread its wings and at each attempt lacerating itself against the irons of the cage that keeps it imprisoned.

Further on in the same chapter, Sarmiento writes:

> Through my mother, I was inclined towards the colonial vocations; through my father, I was infused with the revolutionary ideas and concerns of the time; . . . .

These "contradictory influences" (Sarmiento's own words) and the "slow and arduous transition from one mode of being to another" of the chapter's first paragraph eloquently capture the historically determined crisis of identity that both Molloy and Prieto acknowledge as a fundamental catalyst for Spanish American autobiography.

III.

Mi defensa: *Sarmiento's Earliest Public Act of Self-Writing*

Recuerdos de provincia was not Sarmiento's first public act of self-writing. In 1843, a younger man of thirty-one, unmarried and only two years into his second and longest Chilean exile of nearly twelve years, published a pamphlet in five folio installments on the subject of his past and present life. Its unequivocal objective was to defend its author against the libelous leaflets and newspaper of a Chilean named Godoy. Sarmiento claimed that the otherwise undistinguished Godoy, whose brother, a Chilean consul in San Juan, had known the Argentine exile back home, had been bent on destroying his reputation ever since his arrival in Santiago in 1841.

According to Prieto's criteria, *Mi defensa* would qualify as an autobiography. It is an individual's first-person life story presented to the public in self-defense against unrelenting calumny; it is an urgent move to save the public writer's social capital and thus, quite literally in Sarmiento's case, his livelihood. On the other hand, *Mi defensa* would not meet the criteria that Molloy requires for authentic autobiography: It displays no sense of belonging to a literary tradition and absolutely no suspicion that it might have much in common with fiction. Its explicit rhetorical premise is that the first-person writer is telling the truth, the best he can, to set the public record straight, and the text, in its entirety, is structured to address the specific accusations made by Godoy. In fact, when the pamphlet announces that the defendant has already begun legal action against his detractor in the courts, it defines its function as subordinate to a larger, very pragmatic, and focused strategy to discredit Godoy and his lies.

Reproduced in all editions of Sarmiento's *Obras completas* [Complete Works], *Mi defensa* is always included in the same volume as *Recuerdos de provincia*, where it occupies a scant twenty-three or so pages in comparison to the nearly two hundred pages of the author's second autobiographical text. However, *Mi defensa* is not only much shorter than *Recuerdos*; it is also much less ambitious. In it, for example, Sarmiento never makes the claim, as he does in *Recuerdos*, that he might be a historically representative individual whose trajectory serves to illuminate contemporary South America, an idea that owes no small debt to Hegel's world-historical persons, Victor Cousin's great men, and Thomas Carlyle's heroes.[38] Also, while *Mi defensa* is single-minded in its focus, *Recuerdos* is centrifugal, meandering, and heterogeneous. In addition to a biography of the self, it offers the reader the well-developed stories of at least ten other people dating as far back as the sixteenth century. Indeed, it is this heterogeneous and digressive quality that stylistically places it closer to the author's other major literary works—*Facundo* (1845), *Viajes* [Travels], I (1849) and II (1851), and *Campaña del Ejército Grande* [Campaign of the Great Army] (1852)—than to its autobiographical predecessor *Mi defensa*.

To claim, as I have, that *Mi defensa* sticks efficiently to its practical goal and, also, that it never self-consciously enters the terrain of literary autobiography is not to say that it forsakes literary fiction as a source of rhetorical ammunition. In fact, to render his case more sympathetic, Sarmiento as first-person speaker initially assumes certain characteristics of the romantic hero: He is the newcomer, a conspicuous and strangely successful upstart, the mysterious foreigner who has provoked universal curiosity as to his unknown origins. As he begins to dispel this mystery by divulging his past, which is shown to be honorable—and not criminal, as his detractor has insisted—he takes on the equally romantic and even melodramatic persona of the innocent victim, unjustly persecuted by his enemies and cruelly treated by fate. Also, he is young, solitary, passionate, and confrontational, and these qualities are central to his persona throughout.

Indeed, age and its conventional trappings are fundamental rhetorical markers that consistently distinguish the first-person speaker of *Mi defensa* from that of the later *Recuerdos*. The youthful writer/protagonist approaches the conclusion of *Mi defensa* undiminished in his defiance:

> Everyday I irritate susceptibilities and cultivate the desire to find actions in my conduct that condemn me. I should be more prudent; but in terms of prudence, I am like those great sinners who leave their repentance for their final hour. When I am forty years old, I will be prudent; for now I'll be as I am, and nothing more.[39]

In contrast, the first-person in *Recuerdos,* though capable of frequent indignation and aggressiveness, speaks from the perspective of a mature, self-confident, and far more prudent man who is, after all, about to turn forty.

He is the respected and established middle-aged public servant, and consequently his ambitious claim to being representative acknowledges a conformist side as well as an exceptional one. In fact, in *Recuerdos,* the protagonist's immediate family is apparently so unremarkable for his social position that he hardly even speaks of it. This is in marked contrast to the treatment of the protagonist's immediate family in *Mi defensa.* There he takes pains to point out that although young and unmarried, he is, and has been since the early age of fifteen, the dominant male of a male-headed household that subverts the traditional hierarchy of the patriarchal conjugal family:

> From the early age of fifteen, I was the head of my family. Father, mother, sisters, servants, everything was subordinated to me, and this dislocation of natural relations has exerted a fatal influence on my character. I have never recognized any authority but my own; however this . . . [subversion] is

founded upon justifiable reasons. Since that early age, care for the subsistence of all my relatives has weighed upon my shoulders. It remains there still, and never has a burden been carried more gladly.[40]

In a now classic essay, historian Tulio Halperín Donghi has convincingly argued that the man who was to outlive his presidency by fourteen years to die at the age of seventy-seven had early on in his career, that is, before the defeat of Rosas in 1852, "offered two extreme versions of his social origins, both destined to reappear in attenuated form throughout his life."[41] Halperín is referring here to the starkly different self-portraits found in *Mi defensa* and *Recuerdos de provincia*. He points out that in *Mi defensa*, the author presents himself as the archtypal "self-made" and self-making man. His origins are poverty and social obscurity; his native province is "poor and backward," with a local tradition "whose provincialism and extreme simplicity" are "unmitigated flaws."[42] In *Recuerdos*, by contrast, Sarmiento paints himself as the deserving scion of a long and noble tradition of eminent public servants. He belongs to a poor but respectable branch of several of the pedigreed first families of San Juan, a city with a proud colonial past. Hard work and self-discipline are still decisive in this second narrative account of his accomplishments, but these qualities are now the logical product of his noble breeding and not the exclusive fruit of a prodigious will rebelling against fate.

IV.

Recuerdos de provincia *as the Idealized and Nostalgic Portrait of a Colonial Family*

In the preface to *Recuerdos de provincia*, titled "To My Compatriots Only," Sarmiento's stated objectives are deceptively modest. He calls the 1850 autobiography an "*opúsculo*," that is, a small and even trivial work. He says it owes its "existence to circumstances of the moment, which, once past, [will] be understood by none." In short, just as he had done in the "Introduction" to *Mi defensa*, he explains this act of self-writing as "justified by necessity," the "inevitable" response of any good man and patriot to a serious act of libel that both dishonors and vilifies his good name.

Thus, it comes as no surprise that the writer opts for legal language to defend his right to a "hearing." This rhetoric of the courtroom invokes the inalienable rights of man to a fair trial by jury, an appropriate ideological authority for a mid-nineteenth-century patriotic liberal democrat, which is indeed what Sarmiento was. However, the writer then proceeds to invoke a second and very different kind of authority when he surprisingly announces he will summon his ancestors to testify on his behalf.

This evocation of the memory of those relatives "who earned their country's regard" unequivocally legitimates the authority of the aristocratic ideology of birth and blood. Once this more archaic authority is foregrounded, the individual ceases to be sovereign, and sovereignty devolves instead upon the family, understood as genealogy. In this latter, more traditional system, a person's rights and social respect are both inherited and guaranteed by the rights and respect earned and thereafter maintained by the merits of one's forefathers (and even of the occasional foremother). Sarmiento's 1850 autobiography literally includes a family tree, which the author calls the book's "index" (to be read as "table of contents") and which traces backward from himself—through his parents and grandparents, to a great-grandfather born at the beginning of the eighteenth century—and branches outward to include aunts, uncles, and cousins, some quite distant and some only related by marriage, but most of them claimants to social prestige. To accommodate the tensions between individual and family, as well as between democracy and the republic, on one hand, and aristocracy and the colony, on the other, Sarmiento feels obliged to coin the paradoxical phrase "*nobleza democrática*" [democratic nobility].

The family that Sarmiento portrays in *Recuerdos de provincia* is the extended patriarchal family, which, according to historian Peter Winn, was "the basic institution of Spanish American creole society," that is, of the majority of the elite during the colonial era.[43] Given the enormous distance from the center of empire, the colonial administration was often arbitrary and unreliable in its interpretation and enforcement of the law. Relatively weak state institutions thereby created a vacuum of power and authority that was filled by competitive groupings of extended elite families. These took responsibility for protecting their own economic interests by relying on the active support of trustworthy relatives strategically placed in local *cabildos* (colonial municipal councils) and in the church and state bureaucracies, and by extending the reach of their patron and client loyalties through the formation of family alliances built on arranged marriages within their class. Like many of the social structures and attitudes inherited by the newly independent American nations from the colony, the institution of the elite extended family continued to be a powerful force after independence, and in a new political reality marked by war and social upheaval, it could offer a haven of relative stability to its privileged members.[44]

Yet in spite of the insecurity and dislocations of these years, throughout the decade of the 1840s our writer remained optimistic. He insisted that a great social revolution was afoot. Like many of his contemporaries elsewhere in the western world, he placed the beginning of this presumably global though protracted transformation (which in the same decade Marx and Engels would identify specifically as the revolution of the bourgeoisie), back in time, in the seventeenth century. By the eighteenth century, this revolution had erupted in France with the momentous political events of 1789.[45] Indeed, stressing the universal course that this revolution would inevitably take, Sarmiento was to describe the second French Revolution, of 1848, as "the patrimony of the human race."[46]

On the first anniversary of the abdication of King Louis Philippe and the proclamation of the Second French Republic, which lasted from February 1848, to December 1851, the expatriate Argentine journalist published a newspaper article in Chile, in which, writing as a republican of the Americas, he hailed this latest French affirmation of the republican form of government. Republicanism, as distinguished from democracy (the object of a considerably more critical treatment in the article), belonged to the "same force that for three centuries has been destroying bad systems just when they believe themselves most secure," and that "in the end will conclude with the glorious work of assuring for the moral world the laws of justice that reign in all the other works of God."[47] As a summary of the principles proclaimed by the Second French Republic, Sarmiento pointed to "the right to life for all men, and the renunciation of the ancient shedding of blood, be it in the name of justice, in the name of religion, or in the name of politics."[48] He then went on to abjure violence, in principle, as a means to an end (in spite of the fact that, in his later political career in Argentina, he would not necessarily always do so in practice).

In 1849 and still in exile, Sarmiento condemned political violence not only because strategically he sought to assign a monopoly on its practice to Rosas and other Spanish American caudillos whom he labeled "barbarians." During his recent tour of Europe (1846–47), he had been alarmed by the signs and talk of class warfare, and lately this alarm had been compounded by press reports of the French workers' rebellion, in June of '48, against the conservative turn taken by the government of the Second Republic. To his already entrenched fear of the destructive power of the Hispanic American masses, viewed by him as intoxicated since independence by the rhetoric of democracy, he now added his dismay at the specter that was haunting Europe. (*The Communist Manifesto*, written in German in January of 1848, had appeared in French translation, in Paris, shortly before June of the same year.) In particular, Sarmiento shuddered at the appeal that the specter of communism might have, in the none too distant future, even in his remote South America, which he (not unlike Marx) viewed disparagingly as an economic and social backwater among the Christian nations, due to its double legacy of miscegenation and Iberian indolence. Educàte the children of the poor to be citizens, he warned toward the end of his article; "time is running out; tomorrow will be too late."⁴⁹ "Be careful not to say, in the name of political ideas, that the insignificant struggles of industry are a war between the *rich* and the *poor*. . . . Educate [the] reason [of the poor], or that of their children, in order to avoid the chaos that well-meaning but poorly understood ideas can bring about on a none too distant day."⁵⁰

Within this article, titled "Revolución francesa de 1848" [*French Revolution of 1848*], Sarmiento took special care to include France's defiant workers swayed by Communist ideas within the generic fold of barbarism:

> . . . the violence, disorders, and shedding of blood that today afflict all the countries of the Earth, do not come from the republicans. . . . [but from] the barbarians which all societies contain within them . . . ; because barbarism alone sheds blood and oppresses.⁵¹

The same year (1849), Sarmiento published the book *De la educación popular* [*On Popular Education*], in which he was to raise this observation to a general law of human evolution. According to this law, humanity softened its customs and developed a greater repugnance to violence and bloodshed to the extent that it became civilized by the progress of science.[52] Other aspects of this law included the future assimilation, on the part of the poor, of the social customs and values of the rich. In other words, this law predicted the eventual homogenization of ideologies and social practices by means of an observable global movement toward uniformity in dress, work ethic, perception of civic responsibility, and family life. As envisioned by the mid-century South American writer, in full agreement on this point with the "ideologists of the era of triumphant bourgeois liberalism: say from 1830 to 1880" (to use the words of British social historian E. J. Hobsbawn), "civilization" marched onward toward the universal creation of republican citizens schooled in reason, order, and discipline, that is, toward the universalization of bourgeois ideology and social practice.[53]

Thus, the ideal model of the family toward which Sarmiento saw all of humanity slowly and unevenly moving was the smaller, more nuclear family of the European and Anglo-American bourgeoisie. Republican citizenship and capitalist free trade and freed labor defined "man" as an individual male social subject, liberated from traditional corporate constraints and thus empowered to make his own life—to become a self-made man—by taking up a career now open to talent and of his own free choice. The more nuclear family of the bourgeoisie, as opposed to the patriarchal extended family of the aristocracy, was the place where ideally the education, or creation, of this self-motivated and self-interested individual was to begin. Thus, the redefinition of the elder male, from autocratic patriarch to loving head of the household, and the redefinition of wives from legal wards of the *paterfamilias* to the heart of the household, angel of the hearth, homebody, and first and most crucial educator of the future (male) citizens of the republic.[54]

It was indeed to this model of the modern male-headed bourgeois family that Sarmiento himself had recently sought to conform, when, at the age of thirty-seven, he contracted marriage for the first time, in May of 1848. He had married a widow and gone to live in the house built by her first husband in Yungay, a recently developed suburb of Santiago. With the couple lived the widow's young son whom Sarmiento forthwith adopted (thus turning his probable biological son into his acknowledged legal heir). Also, to the house in Yungay, the impatient newlywed quickly summoned from San Juan his aging mother and his illegitimate daughter, Ana Faustina, who had been born some seventeen years before. Thus, Sarmiento's young three-year-old son, Dominguito, was to receive the maternal attentions of three female homebodies, including those of the living exemplar of the author's openly proclaimed ideal of republican motherhood, his very own mother, Paula Albarracín de Sarmiento.[55]

Is there not a contradiction between the real-life modern and bourgeois family he had so recently constituted for himself and the literarily constructed traditional and aristocratic family to which he laid claim and paid homage in his autobiography of 1850? Is there not a curious inconsistency between the family with whom he shared his daily life while he was writing his *Recuerdos* and the family invoked in the book itself, in which his immediate family was alluded to only once or twice, and then, indirectly and in passing? The imagined textual family of *Recuerdos*, so different from his current household, is, quite simply, the calculated public version of a personal mythology that, in the years between 1848 and 1850, Sarmiento had powerful reasons to want to create.

V.

The Ideal of Public Service and the Didacticism of Auto/Biography

In the same essay cited above, Halperín Donghi writes:

> In *Recuerdos*, the urban culture that Sarmiento from the start identified with civilization has discovered an unexpectedly rich past; and loyalty to that past, very much alive among its prominent heirs [among whom the author now proudly includes himself], serves as the discriminating criterion.[56]

That is, loyalty to what, in 1850, Sarmiento idealized as a characteristic wedding of wealth and enlightenment during colonial times had come to serve him as the criterion he would now use to discriminate between mere wealth, no longer a necessary companion to enlightenment and intelligence, and civilization, the possession of which, he maintained, bestowed the right to govern. One of the consequences that Sarmiento ascribed to the federalist regime that had held sway in San Juan since the late 1820s was the catastrophic impoverishment of the established elite families. If federalist caudillo and provincial governor Nazario Benavides was now the richest man in San Juan, Sarmiento reasoned, he was nonetheless ignorant and barbaric. According to Halperín, from 1848 on, Sarmiento would never accept that the distinction between rich and poor, the criterion for social differentiation that was becoming dominant in Argentina in the mid-nineteenth century, could or should outweigh the distinctions between enlightened and ignorant and between civilized and barbarian. Rather, Sarmiento would now insist on seeing a long-standing commitment to enlightened public service as part of a positive legacy of the colonial elite. Thus, he would begin his evolution toward pessimism when, in the post-Rosas era, between 1861 and 1863, he returned to San Juan as governor, only to be disillusioned by the selfishness, corruptibility, and outright opposition to his politics manifested by the oppressed heirs of the colonial elite—the *gente decente*—whom he believed he had come to restore to power. In the years that followed, Sarmiento's disappointment with this group, to which in *Recuerdos* he had taken such great pains to prove that he belonged, would only increase. He would come to view the heirs of the bygone elite as traitors to their historical mission because of their refusal to live up to what the author now saw as the disinterested example of their colonial forebears.

The autobiography of 1850, then, seeks to make the case that its author is the worthy scion of an illustrious colonial family committed to enlightened public service. The self-made man from nowhere, the ambitious romantic hero of mysterious or dubious origin, has become the continuation in the present of a long and distinguished familial past. Consistent with its far more individualist perspective, *Mi defensa*'s first chapter (placed after an introduction that justified the writer's act of going public) begins by challenging its readers to take a long, hard look at who its author is. The ensuing narration of self commences with the words, "I was born in an ignorant and backward province. . . ." In contrast, the narration of the author's birth in *Recuerdos* is postponed until Chapter 15, far into the middle of the book. The first half of the 1850 text is filled with numerous biographies of the author's forebears, who are meant to prefigure the virtues—and the quirks—of the author himself, explicit protagonist of the book's concluding half. The remembrance of things past reaches back well beyond the birth and even the mythically endowed conception of our hero (presumed to have occurred, the reader will remember, on May 10, 1810) to resurrect the anecdotes, and in some cases the biographies, of the hero's ancestors, his mother, his teachers, his friends.

This gallery crammed with the miniatures of loved ones dead and alive is the necessary antechamber through which the reader must first pass in order for the grand self-portrait at the end to be fully intelligible. Sarmiento tells us in the preface (or dedication) of *Recuerdos* that he has a predilection for biography. It is the handmaiden or even midwife of history. At the conclusion of the book he revisits this theme when he insists that, "The biography is the most original book that South America can produce in our time, and the best material that one can provide for the writing of history." He claims that the *Facundo* and these *Recuerdos de provincia* belong to the same genre, thus erasing with a single stroke the difference between third and first-person life narratives.

Early on in his journalistic career and one year before the publication of his first autobiograpy in 1843, Sarmiento had published a short newspaper article in which he defined biography as the compendium of historical facts most accessible to the majority of readers and the one that provides them the clearest and most direct instruction.[57] Biography, in this view, popularizes history and makes it didactic. Biography inspires the reader to imitate or reject the exemplary virtuous or villainous life it presents. It facilitates the reader's understanding of the complexities of history:

> The biography of a man who has played a great role in a given epoch and country, is the summary of contemporary history, illuminated with the animated colors given off by the national customs and habits, the dominant ideas, the tendencies of civilization, and the special direction that the genius of great men can imprint upon society.[58]

The same article contains a recipe for writing biography, one which the author will follow a year later in *Mi defensa*, then in the *Facundo* in 1845, and then again, in 1850, in the second half of *Recuerdos*. In this recipe, the reader witnesses the birth of the hero, and then attends him in his childhood games, his studies, and his domestic life. The reader watches as the hero reaches the age when he can pass out through the door of the parental home into the public sphere beyond. There the hero will participate first as a spectator, then as an instrument, and finally as a principal actor upon "the stage of the activity, the struggles, and the trials that prepare and produce the great events, the social revolutions, and the progress of humanity."[59]

As a close reproduction of this recipe, Chapters 15 through 17 of *Recuerdos* (a mere three chapters out of twenty-three but a good third of the entire book) narrate the life of the autobiographical hero. (The final six chapters of the book, which are extremely brief, constitute what the author calls his service record, a kind of curriculum vitae.) Chapter 15, "My Education," presents the hero's birth and childhood. Chapter 16, "Public Life," narrates the experiences of the very young man who now operates in the public sphere, first as a spectator and then, almost immediately, as an instrument. Chapter 17, "Chile," the last long narrative chapter of *Recuerdos*, deals with the most recent decade of the author's life, during which, except for two years and five months spent traveling abroad (between October 1845, and February 1848), the hero has resided in Chile. In this chapter, the still youthful protagonist evolves from being an instrument of history to becoming a principal actor upon its stage.

VI.

Public Servant in Chile and Aspiring President of Argentina

The chapter entitled "Chile" begins with the story of Sarmiento's inauguration as a public writer in his new country of residence. Likewise, it narrates how the young man, having already essayed a number of careers by necessity, discovers in journalism the one that perfectly suits his temperament and talent. The very first sentence foregrounds the act of writing, in particular two youthful acts that unfold within the chapter to produce the mature author's self-confident and, so he claims, universally acknowledged identity. Both initial acts of writing occur when Sarmiento is twenty-nine years old, the first, the political graffiti "On ne tue point les idées," in Argentina, where he is about to become an exile, and the second in Chile, where he has now become a foreigner. His inaugural article as a foreigner, published anonymously and under the guise of a fictitious first-person who presents himself as an aging Chilean veteran of the wars of independence, appears in Chile's only daily newspaper at the time, *El Mercurio* of Valparaíso, four days before its author's thirtieth birthday. Nine years later, when Sarmiento writes Chapter 17 of *Recuerdos* and reaches by its conclusion a narrative present that corresponds to his lived, historical present (he is now writing about himself as he is while he writes), he is close to celebrating his thirty-ninth birthday. The self-image of this mature writer, who writes and then rushes to publish his second autobiography, has undergone an important transformation during the ten years he has been away from home, that is, away from San Juan on the other side of the Andes. Indeed, during the last third of Chapter 17, Sarmiento tells us he is narrating "one of the most active, turbulent, and perhaps fruitful phases of . . . [his] life"—1842 to the present.

How does the writer describe what he has now become? He portrays the person he was during the early years of this most recent phase of his life as a "young man," "fervent in battle" against the many detractors who used his status as a "foreigner" to his detriment. At last he has ceased to be a foreigner. He has "triumphed completely" over local hostility to outsiders, for now "the word *foreigner* is banned from the [Chilean] press." "By acclamation," he writes, "I am declared a good and loyal Chilean."

Moreover, he is no longer the unknown writer who hides away "in the bare room under the Arcade": "it seems to me an established fact that I have won the public's entire confidence." He has matured and acquired prudence, as well as experience in life and experience in politics. Just two years later in his book *La campaña del Ejército Grande* [The Campaign of the Great Army], Sarmiento will place himself atop the proverbial eminence of age to preach about the young:

> I sympathize with many, almost all of the principles that young men show they profess when, for sincere and reasoned love of republican ideas, they sign on to all the oppositions; but from there to the organization and government of a country, there is an abyss. Dedicated to militant politics from my earliest youth, I have grown gray in its study. . . .[60]

It is the latter, his experience in and his study of politics, that Sarmiento especially wants to emphasize. Argentinean by nationality, he nonetheless makes it clear that since his arrival in Santiago, he has been active in Chilean politics, and from the outset, has associated spontaneously and deliberately:

> . . . with the party in Chile in which Montt, . . . and so many other distinguished young men are active. . . . Movement in ideas, stability in institu-

tions, order to be able to agitate all the better in politics, the government in preference to the opposition, this is what may be deduced from my writings with respect to my preferences.

Earlier in Chapter 17 Sarmiento narrates how in 1841 he had been approached by the Chilean Liberal Party, known as the *pipiolos*, who had tried to enlist him in their ranks. Openly identified with the liberal opposition to Rosas in his own country, he had nonetheless chosen not to side with the Chilean Liberals but rather to lend his services to one of two candidates from the governing Conservative Party. His reasoning had been a model of realpolitik. Rosas accused his liberal opponents of being anarchists dedicated to the overthrow of orderly government; thus, it would be unwise to be seen as forever in the opposition. Besides, Sarmiento reasoned, it looked as though the Conservatives were going to win reelection, which indeed they did. Such arguments convinced the Argentine liberal to agree to write for the Conservatives in the upcoming electoral campaign, and, after the Conservative victory, to remain the close collaborator of Conservative leader Manuel Montt, a minister in the new government. Years later, in 1850, while Sarmiento was preparing his *Recuerdos* for publication, he was also busy churning out electoral propaganda for his friend and mentor Montt, who the following year would himself become president of the nation. Indeed, Chapter 17, titled "Chile," includes campaign rhetoric for two presidential hopefuls, and one of them is clearly the Chilean Montt, who merits his own brief and flattering portrait in Sarmiento's packed portrait gallery in prose, *Recuerdos de provincia*.[61]

Sarmiento's identification with conservative politics in Chile (which he insisted were often really liberal and progressive) may partially account for the more conservative tone and content of *Recuerdos* when compared to the earlier *Facundo* and *Mi defensa*. But it is also a fact of the author's life, one that he finds useful in furthering the personal ambitions to which he now openly admits. In the *Facundo* of 1845, he had presented the unitarian General José María Paz as the man destined to deliver Argentina from the stronghold of Rosas. Now in *Recuerdos*, Sarmiento offers himself as the ultimate public servant, the man to face down Rosas and take his place. *Recuerdos* is the calculated narrative of a champion of order, a statesman, who because of his several pasts, each admirable in itself, embodies the logical link between the past and the present, tradition and change, provincial life and an acquired familiarity with the modern mores of capital cities in both the New World and the old. Sarmiento presents himself as an ideal solution to a national presidency, a man versed in international politics, in the practices of national government, and in the perspectives of the provinces and the periphery. True, his east-coast compatriots will see the fact that he has never set foot in Buenos Aires, nor anywhere else in Argentina east of Córdoba, as a liability for his presidential aspirations. (The ambitious Sarmiento must still wait two years to behold Buenos Aires.) However, the western provincial from San Juan is convinced that he can present himself as equal to any possible candidate from Buenos Aires, on the Atlantic coast, in part because of his exceptionally privileged access to the center of national power and politics in Chile, on the Pacific coast.

Recuerdos de provincia is in large part Sarmiento's apologia and implicit public relations stunt for a future presidential campaign in Argentina that by 1850 had already begun to gather momentum. The book plays off Santiago against Buenos Aires nearly as much as it does Cuyo against the Argentine littoral. In both cases, the oppositions are manipulated far more subtly than are those aggressively promoted between the righteous Sarmiento and the infernal Rosas and between enlightened civilization and regressive barbarism. Yet the fact that Sarmiento seeks to contribute to shaping the political futures of both Argentina and Chile cannot be considered immaterial to the shaping of this book.

VII.

The Publication, Distribution, and Immediate Reception of Recuerdos de provincia

Unlike the *Facundo*, which before coming out in book form had been serialized in Santiago's recently founded daily, *El Progreso*, *Recuerdos de provincia* initially appeared as a book.[62] It was published in early 1850 by the Santiago printing house of Julio Belín & Co.[63] Sarmiento had met the young printer Jules Belín in France in 1846 and had invited him to come to America and join him in setting up a printing business. Belín accepted, arrived in Chile in May of '48, and by the end of the year the two, plus a third partner, were the owners and operators of Julio Belín & Co. This press, which in July of 1850 literally became a family affair with

Belín's marriage to Sarmiento's daughter, would, until 1854, publish the writer's books and pamphlets as well as several newspapers and magazines that he founded and directed during this period. In short, Sarmiento, in his persona as publisher, brought out his own autobiography *Recuerdos de provincia*, the fruit of his persona as writer, and he did so with the collaboration not only of his soon-to-be son-in-law but also, it should be noted, with that of fellow Argentine exile Juan María Gutiérrez (1809–1878), who, like Sarmiento, was to play a major institutional role in Argentina's future and who at the time was employed by Julio Belín & Co. as a proofreader and occasional translator.[64]

When *Recuerdos* appeared, Sarmiento distributed a few copies to friends in Santiago, but sent most copies of the book across the mountains to Argentina. Since Rosas would remain in power until 1852, *Recuerdos* could not circulate openly in the author's homeland, much less be offered for sale in Argentine bookstores. Yet, as had occurred with the author's *Facundo* of 1845, *Recuerdos* would be smuggled in and read in Argentina and then smuggled out again and read in Montevideo and beyond. In fact, in May of 1850, the Buenos Aires newspaper *La Gaceta Mercantil* [The Mercantile Gazette] reproduced two intercepted letters that Sarmiento had sent to fellow exiles, one of them to Vicente F. López, and the other, unaddressed, either to Juan Bautista Alberdi or to Bartolomé Mitre, the latter of whom, like Sarmiento, would also become president of Argentina in the second half of the nineteenth century. In both these letters the author wrote, part jokingly, part boastfully, about his soon-to-appear autobiography. To López, he wrote that although *Recuerdos* constituted a panegyric to himself, people would have to forgive him his daring because the book contained so many good things worth telling. In the other letter, Sarmiento characterized *Recuerdos* as a new *Facundo*, whose "hero," he said, would be the vicissitudes of his own life, linked to the memory of the "great names" of the Republic. In this new book, he announced, he would take on Rosas, man to man, making the dictator look like a petty chieftain and presenting himself as the rival candidate for political leader of Argentina.[65]

However, once they were able to read the published book, a number of Sarmiento's peers in the scattered Argentine exile community did not forgive him his daring; indeed, they could not condone what they considered the audacity of writing publicly about oneself. Like the author, they, too, saw *Recuerdos* as a panegyric, but considered it in bad taste and a political mistake. One of the harshest criticisms was to come from his erstwhile friend Juan Bautista Alberdi (1810–84), originally from Tucumán but an important member, along with Gutiérrez, Vicente F. López, and Esteban Echeverría, of both the Literary Salon and the May Association in the Buenos Aires of 1837–38. Posthumously considered one of the most brilliant if not the most brilliant intellectual of his generation, the young Alberdi had settled in Valparaíso in 1843, and had actively collaborated with the many Argentine exiles in Chile, including Sarmiento. However, he became Sarmiento's political adversary after the defeat of Rosas in 1852, when the two men parted ways over how best to organize the nation. Their exchange of letters on this subject was published for all to read in 1852. In Alberdi's third letter, he addressed Sarmiento in the following terms:

> Your *Recuerdos de Provincia* is your biography, not a book about politics. In writing a book about yourself, you haven't been able to learn anything more than what you already know. This work is not a service rendered to the Argentine Republic, and I doubt that it is to you, either. It is the first example we have in our country, so rich in notable men, of a republican who publishes two hundred pages and a family tree to narrate his life, that of all his relatives and even of his servants.[66]

Earlier, shortly after the publication of *Recuerdos*, Esteban Echeverría (1805–51) had penned an equally unfavorable opinion of the autobiography in a letter addressed to Alberdi. Echeverría, who in literary histories is credited with introducing European romanticism to Hispanic America and with catalyzing the artistic and political rebellion of the Argentine Generation of 1837, had met Sarmiento only once, when the Cuyan provincial on his way to Europe had visited the large Argentine exile community in Montevideo, in December of 1845. In a letter dated June 12, 1850, Echeverría wrote:

> Sarmiento is going crazy. Rosas has achieved his goal; he has inflated . . . [Sarmiento's] vanity to the point of making him believe he is his most formidable enemy outside the country, and also his rival candidate for power.[67]

Author and readers alike were quick to see *Recuerdos* as electoral propaganda intended to position Sarmiento for the presidency of a new

Argentine Republic, after the fall of Rosas and the Confederation. Two years before the end of the Rosas regime, Sarmiento was optimistic about his prospects for imminent presidential success.

Argentine history, however, had a different narrative prepared. Sarmiento would have to wait sixteen years beyond the fall of Rosas to become president of Argentina. In the meantime, after his break with Urquiza, he would return for two and a half years to a Chile now governed by President Manuel Montt, then relocate to Buenos Aires, where he would remain for seven. There he would serve as editor-in-chief of *El Nacional*, an important newspaper that to this day is still published in Argentina. His record of public service would expand to include the positions of head of the school department, senator, and minister of government and foreign relations. Between 1862 and 1864 he would reside in San Juan as the controversial and strong-handed governor of the province.

In March of '64 he would be named minister plenipotentiary to represent, before the governments of Chile, Peru, and the United States, the new provisional national government of Argentina, established under Mitre in 1862. On May 15, 1865, he would arrive in New York, just a month and a day after Lincoln's assassination, which itself had followed, by a matter of days, Lee's surrender at Appomattox and the end of the Civil War.

As soon as Sarmiento arrived in New York, he wrote to Mary Peabody Mann, Horace Mann's widow. He had met the intellectual couple during his earlier visit to the States in 1847, when he had traveled to Boston to study public education in Massachusetts. With this letter, a correspondence began between the two that was to last until Mary Mann's death. Sarmiento visited Mrs. Mann several times during his second stay in the United States, which this time lasted three years. She introduced him to her friends in Concord and Cambridge, to Emerson, Longfellow, and Ticknor. The latter two men were professors of Spanish at Harvard, where, in a reception for Sarmiento, Ticknor gave a public reading from his own English translation of passages from *Recuerdos de provincia* and proclaimed its author one of the masters of the Spanish language.[68]

Still in the United States, Sarmiento received news from Argentina that there was a move at home to make him a presidential candidate in the upcoming election of 1868. Once again, Sarmiento chose book publication as a way to campaign. He published the first biography of Abraham Lincoln in Spanish *(Vida de Abrán Lincoln)*, which he composed with excerpts from existing biographies that he then translated into Spanish and to which he added his own introduction. (According to his biographer Ricardo Rojas, Sarmiento intended to use the example of Lincoln's conduct during the Civil War to justify his own strong measures as governor of San Juan.[69]) In 1867 he translated and edited, for a Hispanic audience, the *Life of Horace Mann* written by Mary Mann and published in Boston just two years before. Sarmiento considered his own work as an educator to be one of his greatest civic achievements, and the association in print of his name with that of the world-famous pioneer in public education was, to say the very least, timely.

Perhaps most interesting of all in this round of politically motivated publication was the first English version of Sarmiento's *Facundo*, which he personally helped Mary Mann translate and edit, and which appeared, published by Hurd and Houghton, in New York in 1868. Indeed, that same year—Sarmiento's election year—the third Spanish edition of the *Facundo* also appeared in New York, published by Appleton. Since his first trip to France, in 1846, the author had used his *Facundo* as an intellectual calling card, to open doors and gain admittance to the circles of the international intelligentsia and power elite. This card had worked before, and Sarmiento was eager to play it again, this time to gain recognition and respect among the North American reading public for the soon-to-be-inaugurated president of Argentina. As had been his practice since the *Facundo*'s second Spanish edition (Chile: Julio Belín & Cia., 1851), Sarmiento, in 1868, produced two heavily abridged and politically sanitized versions of his famous work. Both the English and the Spanish texts of 1868 lacked the first edition's Introduction, Chapters X and XI of Part II, and various other entire paragraphs, all materials that Sarmiento had long since viewed as no longer politically expedient, given the changing historical circumstances and his expanding political ambitions. The 1868 Spanish version also included Mary Mann's highly promotional "Preface" to the English translation, as well as the author's two other portraits of villainous provincial caudillos, *Aldao*, first published in Chile in 1845, and *El Chacho*, written in the United States in 1866 and published for the first time in this edition. The English translation of the *Facundo* included Mary Mann's "Preface," in which she went to great lengths to insist that Sarmiento deeply admired the federalist government of the United States. It also included numerous and even some fairly long excerpts that Mary Mann had translated from *Recuerdos de provincia* and inserted in her extended "Biographical Sketch of the Author" at the end of the volume. This English edition was a book clearly intended to present Sarmiento in the best possible light to a North American public. Appropriately, the translator's "Preface" begins as follows:

> Since the translation of this work by Colonel Sarmiento was begun, the tide of events has carried its author to the proudest position before his country which any man since San Martín, the hero of its independence and of the independence of some of its sister Republics, has ever occupied. . . . Colonel Sarmiento, after an absence of seven years, . . . has by an almost unanimous movement been made the candidate *par excellence* for the Presidency of the Argentine Republic. . . . [70]

This very moment, as she writes the "Preface," the votes for Sarmiento's election are being counted; "doubtless," she adds, "before these pages see the light, the favorable result will be confirmed."

Confirmed it was, and Domingo F. Sarmiento was at last able to fulfill this particular and most potent political dream. His old enemy Rosas, the direct inspiration and necessary foil for what nearly all readers consider his two best literary works, *Facundo* and *Recuerdos*, had been absent from the Argentine political scene since 1852. Sarmiento's great muse, whom he would never see in the flesh, not even once, had long since gone into exile in faraway England. Ironically, the two would never be physically united until 1989, when President Carlos Menem would have the dictator's remains repatriated to Argentina and buried in the same cemetery in Buenos Aires where Sarmiento had been laid to rest a hundred years before.

A year earlier in 1988, on the occasion of the centenary of Sarmiento's death, Argentine novelist Ricardo Piglia wrote in an inspired essay that, "After the fall of Rosas, Sarmiento can no longer write."[71] He meant "write literature," great literature. If, as Piglia would have it, exile and the impossibility of dedicating himself entirely to politics gave Sarmiento the necessary space and freedom to write his greatest works, the responsibilities of practical politics as well as its language, by upsetting the earlier balance, exacted their toll on Sarmiento's writing during the second half of his long existence. Sarmiento would continue to write until his death (He would even leave behind an unfinished book), but the chemistry of Rosas and exile that had produced his greatest writing would be gone.[72]

Piglia writes, "the best Argentine writer of the nineteenth century becomes President of the Republic," and he calls this writer "the founder of Argentine literature."[73] The figure of the president, the nation builder, synthesizes the second half of Sarmiento's life, but it is the founder of the nation's literature and its best writer of the century who gives us his life story in *Recuerdos de provincia*.

NOTES

1. The other two were Bartolomé Mitre (1862–68) and Nicolás Avellaneda (1874–80). The three are referred to as the "founding presidents" because their three presidencies cover the period from the provisional establishment of a national government, with its provisional capital in Buenos Aires, in 1862, and the definitive federalization of Buenos Aires as the national capital in 1880. This last date is generally used to mark the final constitution of the nation and the definitive formation of the state. Between 1852, after the defeat of the dictator Rosas, and 1862, Argentina was the scene of intermittent civil war between the province of Buenos Aires and all the other provinces, which were organized into a single confederation.

2. It seems unwise to speculate about a figure more precise than this estimate, since the censuses taken in Argentina in the eighteenth and early nineteenth centuries employed different political divisions from those used in more recent ones. For example, in the censuses of Cuyo of both 1777 and 1812, the unit of measurement was the *comandancia de armas*, a military district that was equivalent in size to the parish. The *comandancia de armas* of San Juan included the city of San Juan as well as Jáchal and Valle Fértil. Jáchal, a village of perhaps 684 in 1777, appears on the map to be roughly equidistant from San Juan to the north as Mendoza is to the south; it took a person on mule or horseback, the only possible means of transport, two days and two nights to travel from San Juan to Jáchal. (See Carmen P. de Varese and Héctor D. Arias, *Historia de San Juan* [Mendoza: Ed. Spadoni, 1966] 49, 105.) Natalio Botana, however, gives a figure of 3,000 for the city of San Juan in 1811. Based on the censuses of 1777 and 1812, Horacio Videla estimates that in 1810 the city proper of San Juan had a population of 4,000. (See Botana's very useful introduction, "Vida y obra de Domingo Faustino Sarmiento," to the *Obras completas*, I, by Domingo Faustino Sarmiento [San Justo, Buenos Aires, Arg.: Universidad Nacional de la Matanza, 2001] xv, and Horacio Videla, *Historia de San Juan*, II [Buenos Aires: Academia del Plata,

1972] 139.) In 1869, during the second year of his presidency, Sarmiento ordered the first official general census taken in the history of the young nation.

   3. Videla, *Historia de San Juan,* II, 140.

   4. According to the official government website on tourism in San Juan, currently only about 10 percent of the province's surface of 92,789 square kms. is suitable for intensive agriculture, while two-thirds of the province is covered by mountains. (The capital city of San Juan, situated in the fertile Valley of Tulún on the banks of the San Juan River, belongs to the agricultural 10 percent.) For the province as a whole, the average annual precipitation is 92.7 mm. "San Juan, Argentina—Ubicación geográfica y datos generales," La página oficial de turismo de San Juan, available at http://www.ischigualasto.com/, accessed December 8, 2001.

   In Vol. I of his *Historia de San Juan,* published in 1962, Horacio Videla described the province of San Juan as having a rigorous climate with dramatic differences in temperature. In a study of the city of San Juan's climate between 1901 and 1950, which Videla reproduces, the average annual maximum temperature recorded was 46.3 C, or a little over 113 F, the hottest months being December, January, and February. Freezing temperatures were recorded between April and October, with the coldest months being June and July; the average number per year of days with freezing temperatures was 33.4. The average number of days with precipitation per year was 21, and with electric storms, 22. The average annual precipitation was 92.7 mm. (Videla put the average annual precipitation for the province as a whole at 52 mm.) The nonnavigable San Juan River, the largest in Cuyo and also in the entire northwestern section of the country, has produced serious flooding as well as draughts when the river's water level had receded drastically. For the nineteenth century, Videla reported serious floods for the years 1817, 1828, 1833, 1888, and 1894 (Sarmiento was living in San Juan during the first two); he reported serious draughts for 1842, 1859, 1861, 1889, and 1898. *Historia de San Juan,* I (Buenos Aires: Academia del Plata, 1962), 35–53.

   5. John Lynch, *The Spanish American Revolutions, 1808–1826,* 2d ed. (New York: W.W. Norton, 1986), 56.

   6. According to Nicolas Shumway, the term "Argentina" only received official sanction in 1826. Nicolas Shumway, *The Invention of Argentina* (Berkeley: University of California Press, 1991), 47. Contemporary Argentina measures one million square miles and some 2,300 miles in length, and is "four times larger than Texas, five times larger than France." James Scobie, *Argentina: A City and A Nation,* 2d ed. (New York: Oxford University Press, 1971), 3, and David Rock, *Argentina 1516–1987: From Spanish Colonization to Alfonsín,* 2d ed. (Berkeley: University of California Press, 1987), 2.

   7. Lynch, *The Spanish American Revolutions,* 59. In Argentina the "littoral" refers to an area comprised of four provinces situated on the shores of the great rivers that empty into the Río de la Plata [River Plate], a huge estuary that flows

into the Atlantic. The four littoral provinces are Buenos Aires, Entre Ríos, Corrientes, and Santa Fé.

8. Today, if one travels by national routes overland, the trip between San Juan and Buenos Aires is 785.5 miles or 1265 kms. long (PrincipalesCiudades.htm, http://www.caminosargentinos.com/Rutas/Distancias/distancias, accessed November 16, 2001). The official website of the provincial government of San Juan places the distance between San Juan and the city of Buenos Aires at 1150 kms., or roughly 714 miles (http://www.sanjuan.gov.ar, December 8, 2001).

9. Samuel Amaral, "Free Trade and Regional Economies: San Juan and Mendoza, 1780–1820," trans. Patricia Jepsen, ed. Jonathan C. Brown, in *Revolution and Restoration: The Rearrangement of Power in Argentina, 1776–1860*, ed. Mark Szuchman and Jonathan C. Brown (Lincoln: Nebraska University Press, 1994), 138.

10. Elizabeth Garrels, *Mariátegui y la Argentina: Un caso de lentes ajenos* (Gaithersburg, MD: Ediciones Hispamérica, 1982), 37. In a recent article from the *New York Times* on the web, Larry Rohter wrote that, "Early in the 20th century . . . [Argentina] was the seventh richest country in the world, with a per capita income ahead of those of Canada, France, the Netherlands, Italy, Japan and Spain and not far behind that of the United States.

Today, the average Argentine income is less than a quarter of America's, and 40 percent of the country's 37 million people live below the poverty line." Larry Rohter, "Argentina Paying Heavily for Squandering Blessings," http://www.nytimes.com/2002/02/08/international/americas/08ARGE.html, accessed February 9, 2002.

11. Peter Winn, *Americas: The Changing Face of Latin America and the Caribbean,* 2d ed. (Berkeley: University of California Press, 1995), 106.

12. Winn, *Americas,* 133. "Two Worlds" is a chapter title in Scobie, *Argentina.*

13. Amaral, "Free Trade and Regional Economies," 125. Around 1620, in response to pressures applied by the merchants who profited from the trade route between Panama and Lima, the Spanish crown reduced Buenos Aires's legal exterior trade to one ship per year from the Spanish port of Seville. See Scobie, *Argentina,* 53.

14. Tulio Halperin Donghi, *Politics, Economics and Society in Argentina in The Revolutionary Period*, trans. Richard Southern (Cambridge: Cambridge University Press, 1975), 5.

15. John Lynch, *Argentine Dictator: Juan Manuel de Rosas, 1829–1852* (Oxford: Clarendon Press, 1981), 14–15, 19–23.

16. For a dissenting opinion on the impact of Spain's late-eighteenth-century free trade policies on Cuyo's wine exports, see Amaral, "Free Trade and Regional Economies."

17. Tulio Halperín Donghi, *Historia contemporánea de América Latina*

(Madrid: Alianza, 1969), 203. An English translation of this important history appeared in 1993 (*The Contemporary History of Latin America*, trans. John Charles Chasteen [Durham: Duke University Press]); however, this translation was edited for a North American audience, and it does not include the cited reference to the effects of Chile's prosperity.

18. Domingo F. Sarmiento, *Facundo o civilización y barbarie* (Caracas: Biblioteca Ayacucho, 1977), 71. All translations appearing in this volume from the *Facundo* are my own. (Until the late fall of 2003, there existed only a single, incomplete, and dated English translation of the *Facundo*, entitled *Life in the Argentine Republic in the Days of the Tyrants* and done by Mary Mann in the nineteenth century. [See Bibliography Cited in the Introduction and in The Editor's Chapter Notes]. Shortly before the completion of the materials for this edition of *Recuerdos*, the first complete English translation of the *Facundo* was published: Domingo Faustino Sarmiento, *Facundo: Civilization and Barbarism*, trans. Kathleen Ross and intro. Roberto González Echevarría [Berkeley: University of California Press, 2003]. Time did not allow me to take advantage of this latest translation.)

19. Sarmiento, *Facundo*, 71–72.

20. Halperín Donghi, *Politics*, 15.

21. One must keep in mind that the common nineteenth-century characterization of Argentina as underpopulated and thus largely a desert, meaning "deserted," did not count the unassimilated Indian population that remained beyond the control of the state. These Indians, estimated at about 100,000 in 1869, when the national census placed the total national population at 1,800,000, did not in effect constitute an available labor pool for national projects. Scobie writes that at the time of independence, the total population of Argentina was probably around five hundred to six hundred thousand: "Of this figure probably 30 per cent were Indian and 20 per cent were Negro and Mulatto. The remainder were creole and mestizo . . ." (*Argentina*, 31). It is unclear, however, whether this 30 percent represents only peaceful Indians living within the Christian frontier or also those living beyond it. By the late nineteenth century, dramatic changes in the Argentine economy together with massive European immigration and a genocidal military campaign to eliminate the Indians, known as the "Conquest of the Desert" (1879–80), had contributed to a complete demographic transformation of the country. Indians and blacks largely disappeared; those who remained, however, were erased from the national consciousness, as official Argentina made the choice to see itself as white and European.

22. See Lynch's excellent discussion of these ramifications in "The River Plate Republics," *Spanish America after Independence, c.1820–c.1870*, ed. Leslie Bethell (Cambridge: Cambridge University Press, 1987), 314–26.

23. As early as 1815, the government of Buenos Aires proclaimed an important

vagrancy law that, according to Enrique Barba, turned the poor and unemployed rural population into servants and the *hacendados*, or *estancieros*, into "hardly less than feudal lords." Enrique Barba, "Unitarios y federales," in *Buenos Aires: Historia de cuatro siglos*, I, 2d ed., ed. José Luis Romero y Luis Alberto Romero (Buenos Aires: Altamira, 2000), 246.

24. Sarmiento, *Facundo*, 29.

25. Sarmiento, *Emigración alemana al Río de la Plata*, in Obras completas, XXIII (2001), 126. The translation is mine.

26. *San-Juan, sus hombres i sus actos en la rejeneración Arjentina. Narración de los acontecimientos que han tenido lugar en aquella provincia ántes i despues de la caida de Rosas.—Restablecimiento de Benavides i conducta de sus habitantes en masa con el caudillo restaurado.—Tomada de fuentes auténticas i apoyada en documentos públicos.* (Santiago de Chile: Imprenta de Julio Belín i Ca., 1852), 11. This document is not included in Sarmiento's inaccurately named *Obras completas* [*Complete Works*], and I have seldom seen it referred to. For that reason, I allow myself to quote at length from this illuminating and relatively unknown pamphlet, a copy of which I discovered in Harvard's Widener Library. (The translation is mine.)

To identify Quiroga (who is Facundo Quiroga, the protagonist of Sarmiento's 1845 book), López, and Benavides, see Editor's Note 1 for "To My Compatriots Only," Note 4 for Chapter 10, and Note 6 for Chapter 5, respectively.

27. "*Entrerrianos*" is the Spanish term for people from the Argentine province of Entre Ríos. "Unitarians" *(unitarios)* did not belong to a political party in the contemporary sense. The unitarians were an identifiable political coalition or group in the 1820s opposed to federalism as a viable model of political organization for the Argentine nation. In contrast to the federalists, who favored localizing authority, the unitarians advocated centralizing power in a single, unitary national government. In terms of policy, they espoused a brand of elitist or undemocratic liberalism, favoring free trade, secular education, the abolition of traditional corporate privileges enjoyed by the Catholic Church and the military, harsh vagrancy laws, and limited suffrage based on property-ownership. When Rosas came to power in 1829, many of the unitarians went into exile, where they remained committed to their cause.

28. The nineteenth-century poncho, which constituted the soldiers' uniforms on both sides of the conflict, was identical to the South American ponchos of today.

29. Sylvia Molloy, "At Face Value: Autobiographical Writing in Spanish America," *Dispositio* IX, nos. 24–26 (1984): 1–2.

30. Ibid., 2.

31. Ibid., 5–6.

32. Adolfo Prieto, *La literatura autobiográfica argentina* (1966) (Buenos Aires: Centro Editor de América Latina, 1982), 30–35.

33. Sylvia Molloy, "The Unquiet Self: Spanish American Autobiography and the Question of National Identity," in *Comparative American Identities: Race, Sex, and Nationality in the Modern Text*, ed. Hortense J. Spillers (New York: Routledge, 1991), 26–27.

34. Ibid., 28.

35. Molloy, "At Face Value," 17.

36. Molloy, "The Unquiet Self," 28–29.

37. Sylvia Molloy, *At Face Value: Autobiographical Writing in Spanish America* (Cambridge: Cambridge University Press, 1991), 82, 230.

38. Hegel's world-historical persons are discussed in Georg Wilhelm Friedrich Hegel, *The Philosophy of History* (1832), trans. J. Sibree (New York: Dover, 1956), 31; Victor Cousin's great men, in M. Victor Cousin, "Lecture X," *Course in The History of Modern Philosophy*, I, trans. O.W. Wight (New York: D. Appleton and Co., 1852), 193–210 (these lectures were originally delivered in Paris in 1829–30); and Thomas Carlyle's heroes in *On Heroes and Hero-Worship* (1841) (London: Oxford University Press, 1935).

39. D. F. Sarmiento, *Mi defensa* (1843), in *Obras de D.F. Sarmiento*, III (Buenos Aires: Félix Lajouane, 1885), 23. (The translation mine.)

40. This translation of a passage from *Mi defensa* is taken from Tulio Halperín Donghi, "Sarmiento's Place in Postrevolutionary Argentina," in *Sarmiento: Author of A Nation*, ed. Tulio Halperín Donghi, Iván Jaksic, Gwen Kirkpatrick, and Francine Masiello (Berkeley: University of California Press, 1994), 19–20.

41. This is the article cited above in Note 40.

42. Ibid., 21.

43. Winn, *Americas*, 54–55. "Creoles" were the American-born white descendants of Europeans. During the centuries of colonial rule, people from Spain, known as "peninsulars," continued to arrive and enjoyed a certain advantage over creoles within the state and church bureaucracy. However most of the colonial elite as well as a good portion of the middle sectors (i.e., lesser officials and shopkeepers) were creole. This whole group shared a common social ethos, which earned them inclusion in the blanket category of "*gente decente*" [decent folk], as opposed to the vast majority of the population, the racially mixed "*pueblo*" [common folk]. Shared characteristics of the "*gente decente*" included Europeanized dress and strictly controlled female sexuality as an essential guarantee of family honor. What bound this group together most was their claim to social and legal legitimacy, their birthright to possess and exercise authority based on their membership in and their loyalty to a patriarchal extended family.

44. Lynch, "The River Plate Republics," 327.

45. Domingo Faustino Sarmiento, "De las biografías," *El Mercurio*, March 20, 1842, in *Obras completas*, I (Santiago de Chile: Imprenta Gutenberg, 1887), 180.

46. Domingo Faustino Sarmiento, "Revolución francesa de 1848," *La Crónica*, February 25, 1849, in *Proyecto y construcción de una nación (Argentina 1846–1880)*, ed. Tulio Halperín Donghi (Caracas: Biblioteca Ayacucho, 1980), 59. (The translation is mine.)

47. Ibid., 57.

48. Ibid., 58.

49. Ibid., 59.

50. Ibid.

51. Ibid.

52. Domingo Faustino Sarmiento, *De la educación popular* (1849), *Obras completas*, XI (Buenos Aires: Imprenta de Mariano Moreno, 1896), 45.

53. Thus the nation itself was but "the stage of evolution reached in the mid-nineteenth century." It would be superseded by "the unified world of the future." E. J. Hobsbawm, *Nations and Nationalism since 1780: Programme, Myth, Reality* (Cambridge: Cambridge University Press, 1990), 38–39. One year before publishing the *Recuerdos*, Sarmiento had published the first volume of his *Viajes*, in which he had written, "And is it not undoubtedly beautiful and consoling to imagine that one day not very far away all the Christian peoples will be a single people, united by railroads and steamships, with a postal service linked up from one end of the earth to the other, with the same dress, the same ideas, the same laws and constitutions, the same books, the same objects of art? This may not be very soon; but it is moving forward and it will reach its mark, in spite of, not the unique character of different peoples, in which I do not believe, but the level of culture in which the species finds itself, in different parts of the earth." Domingo Faustino Sarmiento, *Viajes por Europa, Africa y América, 1845–1847, y diario de gastos*, ed. Javier Fernández (Buenos Aires: Colección Archivos, 1993), 123. (The translation is mine.)

54. For a more detailed account of Sarmiento's ideal of motherhood and the family, see Elizabeth Garrels, "Sarmiento and the Woman Question: From 1839 to the *Facundo*," in *Sarmiento, Author of a Nation*, ed. Tulio Halperín Donghi, Iván Jaksic, Gwen Kirkpatrick, and Francine Masiello (Berkeley: University of California Press, 1994), 272–93.

55. Regarding Sarmiento's father, José Clemente Sarmiento, there is disagreement as to the date of his death. Some authors claim he died in San Juan on December 22, 1844, while others place the event in 1848.

56. Halperín Donghi, "Sarmiento's Place in Postrevolutionary Argentina," 21.

57. "De las biografías," originally published in *El Mercurio* of Valparaíso on March 20, 1842, and collected in *Obras completas*, I (Santiago de Chile: Imprenta Gutenberg, 1887), 178–80.

58. Ibid., 178. (The translation is mine.)

59. Ibid., 179.

60. Domingo Faustino Sarmiento, *Campaña en el Ejército Grande Aliado de Sud América*, ed. Tulio Halperín-Donghi (Mexico: Fondo de Cultura Económica, 1958), 27. (The translation is mine.)

61. Toward the end of his life, in 1880, Sarmiento, now past-president of Argentina, would publish an obituary of his Chilean friend and past-president of the neighboring republic. In this obituary, Sarmiento would pay Montt the extraordinary compliment of having been "the only man of government who has founded a State in America." Now more pessimistic than ever about the results of nation building in Argentina, Sarmiento called Chile, "the first felicitous effort to constitute a government in this America," that is, Latin America as opposed to Anglo-America. Anticipating the question of how Montt had accomplished this, Sarmiento wrote, "Don Manuel Montt constituted the government of Chile following the plan for a republic that was the least democratic possible, with the object of preserving for the richest and most cultivated class their legitimate influence in government." Domingo Faustino Sarmiento, "Necrología de don Manuel Montt," *El Nacional* of Buenos Aires, September 23, 1889, in *Obras completas*, III (San Justo, Buenos Aires: Univ. Nac. de la Matanza, 2001), 251–52. (The translation is mine.)

62. *El Progreso*, Santiago's first daily newspaper, was founded in September of 1842. It was owned by the powerful Conservative Vial family, and, from the first issue, its editor-in-chief (or *redactor*) was Sarmiento, who held this position until his departure for Europe in 1845. Like the more established *El Mercurio* of Valparaíso, *El Progreso* received sizeable subsidies from the Conservative government.

63. Regarding the dates of composition and publication of *Recuerdos*, as well as its distribution, I follow Raúl Moglia, "La redacción de *Recuerdos de provincia*," *Filología* 7 (1961): 176–79.

64. Years before in Buenos Aires, Gutiérrez had distinguished himself among his contemporaries as an important member of the foundational 1837 Literary Salon (Salón Literario) and of Esteban Echeverría's 1838 May Association (Asociación de Mayo). Gutiérrez would remain one of the most important intellectuals of his generation, later known as the Argentine Generation of 1837. He would come to be recognized as the first serious practitioner of literary criticism in Argentina as well as the first *rector*, or president in the modern sense, of the University of Buenos Aires, which had originally been founded in 1821.

65. These letters were summarized in the third person by the Argentine scholar Antonio Zinny and published posthumously in the early twentieth century. See Antonio Zinny, *La Gaceta Mercantil de Buenos Aires, 1823–1852 (Resumen de su contenido con relación a la parte americana y con especialidad a la Historia de la República Argentina)*, III (Buenos Aires: Talleres Gráficos de la Penitenciaria Nacional, 1912), 326–28.

66. Juan Bautista Alberdi, *Cartas sobre la prensa y la política militante de la República Argentina* (Buenos Aires: Ediciones Estrada, 1945), 104–5. (The translation is mine.)

67. Ana María Barrenechea, "Carta de Sarmiento a Rugendas," *NRFH* XXXVI, no. 1 (1988): 409. (The translation is mine.)

68. Ricardo Rojas, *El Profeta de la Pampa: Vida de Sarmiento* (Buenos Aires: Losada, 1945), 369.

69. Ibid., 481.

70. Mary Mann, "Preface," to *Life in The Argentine Republic in The Days of The Tyrants' or Civilization and Barbarism*, by Domingo F. Sarmiento, L.L.D., trans. Mrs. Horace Mann (1868) (New York: Hafner, n.d.), iii–iv.

71. Ricardo Piglia, "Sarmiento the Writer," in *Sarmiento: Author of A Nation*, ed. Tulio Halperín Donghi, Iván Jaksic, Gwen Kirkpatrick, and Francine Masiello. (Berkeley: University California Press, 1994), 127. This collection includes papers delivered at a conference on Sarmiento at the University of California at Berkeley in October 1988.

72. This was *Conflicto y armonías de las razas*. The first half was published in 1883, but the second half, left incomplete, was published posthumously.

73. Piglia, "Sarmiento the Writer," 142, 138.

Bibliography Cited in the Editor's Note and Introduction

Alberdi, Juan Bautista. *Cartas sobre la prensa y la política militante de la República Argentina.* Buenos Aires: Ediciones Estrada, 1945.

Amaral, Samuel. "Free Trade and Regional Economies: San Juan and Mendoza, 1780–1820." Translated by Patricia Jepsen and edited by Jonathan C. Brown. In *Revolution and Restoration: The Rearrangement of Power in Argentina, 1776–1860,* edited by Mark Szuchman and Jonathan C. Brown, 124–49. Lincoln: Nebraska University Press, 1994.

Barba, Enrique. "Unitarios y federales." In *Buenos Aires: Historia de cuatro siglos,* I, 2d ed., edited by José Luis Romero and Luis Alberto Romero, 245–60. Buenos Aires: Altamira, 2000.

Borges, Jorge Luis. "Prólogo." In *Recuerdos de provincia,* by Domingo F. Sarmiento, 9–14. Buenos Aires: Emecé, 1944.

Botana, Natalio R. "Vida y obra de Domingo Faustino Sarmiento." In *Obras completas,* I, by Domingo Faustino Sarmiento, xiii–xliii. San Justo, Buenos Aires: Universidad Nacional de la Matanza, 2001.

Bunkley, Allison Williams. *The Life of Sarmiento.* Princeton: Princeton University Press, 1952.

Bushnell, David. *Reform and Reaction in the Platine Provinces, 1810–1852.*

Gainesville: University of Florida Monographs, Social Sciences #69, University Presses of Florida, 1983.

Campobassi, José S. *Sarmiento y su época. I. Desde 1811 a 1863.* Buenos Aires: Editorial Losada, 1975.

Collier, Simon. Introduction ("Jotabeche and His World"). In *Sketches of Life in Chile, 1841–1851,* by José Joaquin Vallejo ("Jotabeche"), translated by Frederick H. Fornoff, xiii–xxxv. New York: Oxford University Press, 2002.

Collier, Simon and William F. Sater. *A History of Chile, 1808–1994.* Cambridge: Cambridge University Press, 1996.

————. "From independence to the War of the Pacific." In *Chile Since Independence,* edited by Leslie Bethell, 1–31. Cambridge: Cambridge University Press, 1993.

————. "Chile." In *Spanish America after Independence, c. 1820–c. 1870,* edited by Leslie Bethel, 283–313. Cambridge: Cambridge University Press, 1987.

Coluccio, Félix. *Diccionario de voces y expresiones argentinas.* Buenos Aires: Editorial Plus Ultra, 1979.

De Varese, Carmen P and Héctor D. Arias. *Historia de San Juan.* Mendoza: Ed. Spadoni, 1966.

Garrels, Elizabeth. "Sobre indios, afroamericanos y los racismos de Sarmiento." *Revista Iberoamericana* LXIII, nos. 178–179 (January–June 1997): 99–113.

————. "Sarmiento and the Woman Question: From 1839 to the *Facundo.*" In *Sarmiento, Author of a Nation,* edited by Tulio Halperín Donghi, Iván Jaksic, Gwen Kirkpatrick and Francine Masiello, 272–93. Berkeley: University of California Press, 1994.

————. *Mariátegui y la Argentina: Un caso de lentes ajenos.* Gaithersburg, MD: Ediciones Hispamérica, 1982.

Granada, Daniel. *Vocabulario rioplatense razonado,* I, II. Montevideo: Biblioteca Artigas, 1957.

Halperín Donghi, Tulio. "Sarmiento's Place in Postrevolutionary Argentina." In *Sarmiento: Author of a Nation,* edited by Tulio Halperín Donghi, Iván Jaksic, Gwen Kirkpatrick, and Francine Masiello, 19–30. Berkeley: University of California Press, 1994.

————. "Economy and society." In *Spanish America after Independence, c.1820–c.1870,* edited by Leslie Bethell, 1–47. Cambridge: Cambridge University Press, 1987.

————. *Politics, Economics and Society in Argentina in The Revolutionary Period.* 2d ed. Translated by Richard Southern. Cambridge: Cambridge University Press, 1975.

————. *Historia contemporánea de América Latina.* Madrid: Alianza, 1969.

Hobsbawm, E. J. *Nations and Nationalism since 1780: Programme, Myth, Reality.* Cambridge: Cambridge University Press, 1990.

Jaksić, Iván. "Sarmiento and the Chilean Press, 1841–1851." In *Sarmiento: Author of a Nation*, edited by Tulio Halperín Donghi, Iván Jaksić, Gwen Kirkpatrick, Francine Masiello, 31–60. Berkeley: University of California Press, 1994.

Knight, Franklin. *Slave Society in Cuba during the Nineteenth Century.* 2d ed. Madison: University of Wisconsin Press, 1977.

Lynch, John. "The River Plate Republics." In *Spanish America after Independence, c.1820–c.1870*, edited by Leslie Bethell, 314–75. Cambridge: Cambridge University Press, 1987.

————. *The Spanish American Revolutions, 1808–1826.* 2d ed. New York: W.W. Norton, 1986.

————. *Argentine Dictator: Juan Manuel de Rosas, 1829–1852.* Oxford: Clarendon Press, 1981.

Masiello, Francine. *Between Civilization & Barbarism: Women, Nation, and Literary Culture in Modern Argentina.* Lincoln: University of Nebraska Press, 1992.

Moglia, Raúl. "La redacción de *Recuerdos de provincia.*" *Filología* 7 (1961): 176–79.

Molloy, Sylvia. *At face value: Autobiographical writing in Spanish America.* Cambridge: Cambridge University Press, 1991.

————. "The Unquiet Self: Spanish American Autobiography and the Question of National Identity." In *Comparative American Identities: Race, Sex, and Nationality in the Modern Text*, edited by Hortense J. Spillers, 26–39. New York: Routledge, 1991.

————. "At Face Value: Autobiographical Writing in Spanish America," *Dispositio* IX, nos. 24–26 (1984): 1–18.

Mörner, Magnus. *Race Mixture in the History of Latin America.* Boston: Little, Brown, & Co., 1967.

Operé, Fernando. *Historias de la frontera: El cautiverio en la América hispánica.* México: Fondo de Cultura Económica, 2001.

Piglia, Ricardo. "Sarmiento the Writer." In *Sarmiento: Author of a Nation*, edited by Tulio Halperín Donghi, Iván Jaksic, Gwen Kirkpatrick, Francine Masiello, 127–44. Berkeley: University of California Press, 1994.

Pinilla, Norberto. *La generación chilena de 1842.* Santiago: Editorial de la Universidad de Chile, 1943.

Prieto, Adolfo. *La literatura autobiográfica argentina* (1966). Buenos Aires: Centro Editor de América Latina, 1982.

Rock, David. *Argentina, 1516–1987: From Spanish Colonization to Alfonsín.* 2d ed. Berkeley: University of California Press, 1987.

Rodríguez Pérsico, Adriana. *Un huracán llamado progreso: Utopía y autobiografía en Sarmiento y Alberdi.* Washington, D.C.: Colecciones INTER-AMER, Secretary General of the OAS, 1993.

Romero, Luis Alberto. "Sarmiento, testigo y testimonio de la sociedad de Santiago." *Revista Iberoamericana* LIV, No. 143 (April–June 1988): 461–75.

Sarmiento, Domingo Faustino. *Facundo: Civilization and Barbarism.* Translated by Kathleen Ross and Introduced by Roberto González Echevarría. Berkeley: University of California Press, 2003.

————. *Emigración alemana al Río de la Plata.* In *Obras completas,* XXIII, 113–30. San Justo, Buenos Aires: Universidad Nacional de la Matanza, 2001.

————. "Los emigrados" (posthumous). *Obras completas,* XIV, 249–83. San Justo, Buenos Aires: Universidad Nacional de la Matanza, 2001.

————. "Los mineros," *El Nacional,* April 14, 1841. In *Obras completas,* I, 30–33. San Justo, Buenos Aires: Universidad Nacional de la Matanza, 2001.

————. "Necrología de don Manuel Montt," *El Nacional* (Buenos Aires), September 23, 1880. In *Obras completas* III, 249–52. San Justo, Buenos Aires: Universidad Nacional de la Matanza, 2001.

————. *Viajes por Europa, Africa y América, 1845–1847, y Diario de gastos (1849–51).* Edited by Javier Fernández. Buenos Aires: Colección Archivos, 1993.

————. "Revolución francesa de 1848," *La Crónica,* February 25, 1849. In *Proyecto y construccion de una nacion (Argentina 1846–1880),* edited by Tulio Halperín Donghi, 57–60. Caracas: Biblioteca Ayacucho, 1980.

————. *Recuerdos de provincia.* Edited by Susana Zanetti and Margarita B. Pontieri. Buenos Aires: Centro Editor de América Latina, 1979.

————. *Facundo o civilización y barbarie* (1845). Caracas: Biblioteca Ayacucho, 1977.

————. *Campaña en el Ejército Grande Aliado de Sud América.* Edited by Tulio Halperín-Donghi. Mexico: Fondo de Cultura Económica, 1958.

————. *Los caudillos: El General Fray Félix Aldao. El último caudillo de la montonera de los llanos: El Chacho.* Buenos Aires: El Ateneo, 1928.

————. "De las biografías," *El Mercurio,* March 20, 1842. In *Obras de D.F. Sarmiento,* I, 178–80. Santiago de Chile: Imprenta Gutenberg, 1887.

————. "Ernesto: drama de don Rafael Minvielle," *El Progreso,* February 15, 1843. In *Obras de D. F. Sarmiento,* II, 107–13. Santiago de Chile: Gutenberg, 1885.

————. "El diez i ocho de setiembre de 1845," *El Progreso,* September 18, 1845. In *Obras de D.F. Sarmiento,* II, 323–26. Santiago de Chile: Imprenta Gutenberg, 1885.

————. *Mi defensa* (1843). In *Obras de D.F. Sarmiento,* III, 1–23. Buenos Aires: Félix Lajouane, 1885.

————. *San-Juan, sus hombres i sus actos en la rejeneración Arjentina. Narración de los acontecimientos que han tenido lugar en aquella provincia ántes i despues de la caída de Rosas.—Restablecimiento de Benavides i conducta de sus habitantes en masa con el caudillo restaurado.—Tomada de fuentes auténticas i apoyada en documentos públicos.* Santiago de Chile: Imprenta de Julio Belín i Cía., 1852.

———. *Life in The Argentine Republic in the Days of the Tyrants; or, Civilization and Barbarism* (1868). Translated by Mary Mann. New York: Hafner Press, n.d.

Scobie, James R. *Argentina: A City and a Nation.* 2d ed. New York: Oxford University Press, 1971.

Shumway, Nicolas. *The Invention of Argentina.* Berkeley: University of California Press, 1991.

Verdevoye, Paul. *Domingo Faustino Sarmiento, Educar y escribir opinando (1839–1852).* Buenos Aires: Plus Ultra, 1988. (An earlier version in French was published by the author in 1963.)

Videla, Horacio. *Historia de San Juan,* I–IV. Buenos Aires: Academia del Plata, 1962–76.

Weinberg, Félix. "El periodismo en la época de Rosas." *Revista de Historia* (Buenos Aires), no. 2 (2nd trimester, 1957): 81–100.

Winn, Peter. *Americas: The Changing Face of Latin America and the Caribbean.* 2d ed. Berkeley: University of California Press, 1995.

Zinny, Antonio. *La Gaceta Mercantil de Buenos Aires, 1823–1852 (Resumen de su contenido con relación a la parte americana y con especialidad a la Historia de la República Argentina),* III. Buenos Aires: Talleres Graficos de la Penitenciaria Nacional, 1912.

Select Bibliography

RECOMMENDED EDITIONS OF WORKS BY SARMIENTO

Campaña en el Ejército Grande Aliado de Sud América. Edition, Prologue, and Notes by Tulio Halperín-Donghi. México: Fondo de Cultura Económica, 1958.

Facundo: Civilization and Barbarism. Translated by Kathleen Ross and introduced by Roberto González Echevarría. Berkeley: University of California Press, 2003.

Facundo: Civilización y barbarie. Prologue and Notes by Susana Zanetti. Madrid: Alianza Editorial, 1988.

Facundo o civilización y barbarie. Notes and Chronology by Nora Dottori and Silvia Zanetti and Prologue by Noé Jitrik. Caracas: Biblioteca Ayacucho, 1977.

Facundo. Critical edition by Alberto Palcos. La Plata: Universidad Nacional, 1938. Also the augmented reedition by Alberto Palcos. Buenos Aires: Ediciones Culturales Argentinas, 1961.

Obras completas. 52 volumes. Introduction by Natalio R. Botana. San Justo, Buenos Aires: Universidad Nacional de la Matanza, 2001.

Recuerdos de provincia. Prologue by Susana Zanetti and Margarita B. Pontieri and Notes by Margarita B. Pontieri. Buenos Aires: Centro Editor de América Latina, 1979.

Viajes por Europa, Africa y América, 1845–1847, y Diario de gastos (1849–51). Edited by Javier Fernández; includes critical contributions from various authors. Buenos Aires: Colección Archivos, 1993.

RECOMENDED PROLOGUES TO EDITIONS OF *RECUERDOS DE PROVINCIA*

Ara, Guillermo. "Estudio preliminar." Buenos Aires: Editorial Kapelusz, 1953, 13–37.

Borges, Jorge Luis. "Prólogo." Buenos Aires: Emecé Editores, 1944, 9–14.

Ghiano, Juan Carlos. "Prólogo." Buenos Aires: Sur, 1962, 7–23.

Rojas, Ricardo. "Nota preliminar." Buenos Aires: Librería y Editorial de La Facultad, 1938, 9–18.

Zanetti, Susana and Margarita B. Pontieri. "Prólogo." Buenos Aires: Centro Editor de América Latina, 1979, i–viii.

FURTHER READINGS ON SARMIENTO AND *RECUERDOS DE PROVINCIA*

Altamirano, Carlos and Beatriz Sarlo. "The Autodidact and the Learning Machine." In *Sarmiento, Author of a Nation,* edited by Tulio Halperín Donghi, Iván Jaksic, Gwen Kirkpatrick, and Francine Masiello, 156–68. Berkeley: University of California Press, 1994.

Anderson Imbert, Enrique. *Genio y figura de Sarmiento.* Buenos Aires: Editorial Universitaria de Buenos Aires, 1967.

Barrenechea, Ana María. "Sobre la modalidad autobiográfica en Sarmiento." *Nueva Revista de Filología hispánica* XXIX, No. 2 (1980), 509–19.

Botana, Natalio R. "Vida y obra de Domingo Faustino Sarmiento," *Obras completas,* I, by Domingo Faustino Sarmiento, xiii–xliii. San Justo, Buenos Aires: Universidad Nacional de la Matanza, 2001.

Bunkley, Allison Williams. *The Life of Sarmiento.* Princeton: Princeton University Press, 1952.

Garrels, Elizabeth. "Sobre indios, afroamericanos y los racismos de Sarmiento." *Revista Iberoamericana* LXIII, Nos. 178–179 (January–June 1997): 99–113.

———. "Sarmiento and the Woman Question: From 1839 to the *Facundo.*" In *Sarmiento, Author of Nation,* edited by Tulio Halperín Donghi, Iván Jaksic, Gwen Kirkpatrick, and Francine Masiello, 272–93. Berkeley: University of California Press, 1994.

Halperín-Donghi, Tulio. "Sarmiento's Place in Postrevolutionary Argentina." In *Sarmiento: Author of a Nation,* edited by Tulio Halperín Donghi, Iván

Jaksić, Gwen Kirkpatrick, and Francine Masiello, 19–30. Berkeley: University of California Press, 1994.

Jaksić, Iván. "Sarmiento and the Chilean Press, 1841–1851." In *Sarmiento: Author of a Nation,* edited by Tulio Halperín Donghi, Iván Jaksic, Gwen Kirkpatrick, Francine Masiello, 31–60. Berkeley: University of California Press, 1994.

Molloy, Sylvia. "The Unquiet Self: Mnemonic Strategies in Sarmiento's Autobiographies." In *Sarmiento: Author of a Nation,* edited by Tulio Halperín Donghi, Iván Jaksic, Gwen Kirkpatrick, Francine Masiello, 193–212. Berkeley: University of California Press, 1994.

———. *At face value: Autobiographical writing in Spanish America.* Cambridge: Cambridge University Press, 1991.

———. "The Unquiet Self: Spanish American Autobiography and the Question of National Identity." In *Comparative American Identities: Race, Sex, and Nationality in the Modern Text,* ed. Hortense J. Spillers, 26–39. New York: Routledge, 1991.

———. "At Face Value: Autobiographical Writing in Spanish America," *Dispositio* IX, Nos. 24–26 (1984): 1–18.

Piglia, Ricardo. "Sarmiento the Writer." In *Sarmiento: Author of a Nation,* edited by Tulio Halperín Donghi, Iván Jaksic, Gwen Kirkpatrick, Francine Masiello, 127–44. Berkeley: University of California Press, 1994.

Rodríguez Pérsico, Adriana. *Un huracán llamado progreso: Utopía y autobiografía en Sarmiento y Alberdi.* Washington, D.C.: Colecciones INTER-AMER, Secretary General of The OAS, 1993.

Romero, Luis Alberto. "Sarmiento, testigo y testimonio de la sociedad de Santiago." *Revista Iberoamericana* LIV, No. 143 (April–June 1988): 461–75.

Verdevoye, Paul. *Domingo Faustino Sarmiento, Educar y escribir opinando (1839–1852).* Buenos Aires: Plus Ultra, 1988. (An earlier version in French was published by the author in 1963.)

About the Editor and Co-translator

Elizabeth Garrels is professor of Spanish and Latin American Studies and Head of Foreign Languages and Literatures at the Massachusetts Institute of Technology. She is author of *Mariátegui y la Argentina: Un caso de lentes ajenos* (1982), *Las grietas de la ternura: Nueva lectura de Teresa de la Parra* (1987), and co-editor of *Siete ensayos de interpretación de la realidad peruana*, by José Carlos Mariátegui (1979). She has also published numerous articles on Sarmiento and the Argentine Generation of 1837.

Asa Zatz's first translations were from German, of two plays by the Austrian dramatist Ferdinand Bruckner. Born in Manhattan, Zatz returned to his native land after a brief sojourn of some thirty-three golden years in Mexico that fit neatly into his rigidly unstructured life. His professional career there was ushered in with the translation of *The Children of Sanchez* for Oscar Lewis, whose translator he remained for Lewis's other major works over the following twenty years. Since his return home, Zatz has confined himself almost exclusively to a wide variety of Latin American literature, including works of: Cardoza y Aragón, Bartolome, Carpentier, Eloy Martínez, Fuentes, Ibargüengoitia, García Márquez, Galeano, José Luis González, Sábato, Sarmiento, Vargas Llosa, and Valenzuela, among others, with a foray into the Spanish of Spain with Valle Inclán's *Three Barbaric Comedies*.

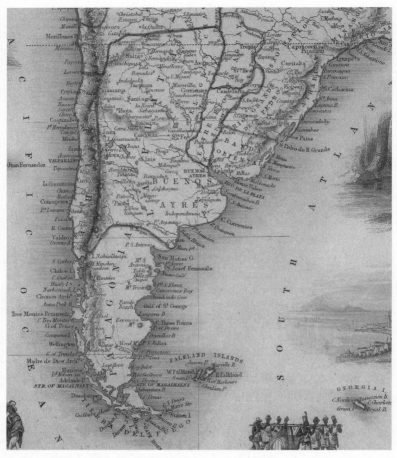

R. M. Martin's and J. F. Tallis's 1851 atlas map of South America, *The Illustrated Atlas, and Modern History of the World Geographical, Political, Commercial & Statistical*. The map is a detail of Chile, Argentina, and the Banda Oriental (Uruguay). Image No. 0466066, courtesy of the David Rumsey Map Collection, www.davidrumsey.com

RECOLLECTIONS OF A
PROVINCIAL PAST

Contents

To My Compatriots Only   5

Genealogy of a Family from San Juan de la Frontera in the
Republic of Argentina   9

1. The Palm Trees   13

2. Juan Eugenio de Mallea   16

3. The Huarpes   22

4. The Sons of Jofré   27

5. Mallea   31

6. The Sayavedras   35

7. The Albarracíns   36

8. The Oros   46

9. Fray Justo Santa María de Oro   59

10. Domingo de Oro   70

11. The Historian Funes   92

12. The Bishop of Cuyo   115

13. The Story of My Mother   120

14. The Parental Home   132

15. My Education   144

16. Public Life   167

17. Chile   186

18. Daily Newspapers and Periodical Publications   205

19. Pamphlets   208

20. Biographies   212

21. Books   214

22. Translations   218

23. Institutions of Learning   220

To My Compatriots Only

The printed word, like the spoken, is limited in its range. The following pages are purely confidential, addressed to no more than a hundred people, and prompted by personal considerations. In 1832, I wrote a letter to a boyhood friend in which I committed the indiscretion of calling Facundo Quiroga a common thief.[1] Today, all of Argentina, the Americas, and Europe agree with me on this point.[2] At the time, my letter was turned over to a dishonorable priest, who was president of a Chamber of Representatives. My letter was read out loud before the full assembly, a motion was made for my exemplary punishment, and they had the impudence to turn the letter over to the offended party, who more impudent even than his flatterers, insulted my mother, called her odious names, and promised her he would kill me whenever and wherever he should find me.

This incident, which made it impossible for me to return to my native land, *forever,* were it not that God disposes of human affairs in a way quite different from the designs of men, this incident, I was saying, repeats itself sixteen years later, with consequences, it appears, all the more alarming. In May of 1848, I also wrote a letter to a former benefactor, in which I also committed the indiscretion, I am proud to say, of having characterized and condemned the Rosas government in accordance with the dictates of my conscience, and this letter, like the one of 1832, was passed on to the very man against whom this judgement was pronounced.[3]

What followed is now common knowledge to all Argentineans. The governor of Buenos Aires published the letter, lodged a complaint against me with the Chilean government, and accompanied the diplomatic note and letter with a circular to the governors of the Confederation; the government of Chile replied to the request, Rosas sent a reply, circulars were once more dispatched, responses arrived from the governors of the interior, and the system of publicizing all those stupidities that, more than just a government, dishonor the whole of the human race, continued, and it seems that the farce will continue still, with no one able to foresee the outcome. The press of all the neighboring countries has reprinted the publications of the Buenos Aires government, and, in those thirty or more diplomatic notes that have been exchanged, the name of D. F. Sarmiento has unfailingly been coupled with the epithets of "infamous," "filthy," "vile," "savage," and variants of this fund of insults that seem the national coin, along with others that the provincial governors, in their infinite wisdom, have been able to discover, such as "traitor," "idiot," "lunatic," "degenerate," "pervert," "pigheaded," and so forth.[4]

I am characterized in this fashion by men who do not know me, to people who hear my name for the first time. The slander emanates from the highest reaches of public office, the Argentine newspapers reprint it, endorse it, and further darken it, there being no secret that the press in that country has but one handle, and this is held by the government; those who would avail themselves of the press as a means of defense encounter nothing but prickly thorns, the epithet of "savage," and arbitrary reprisals.

And, yet, my name is vilified by my countrymen; that is how they see it always written, and that is how, through the eyes, it imprints itself upon the brain; and, should anyone by chance wish to doubt the truth of those demeaning epithets, he does not know what to say in my defense, for he neither knows me, nor is aware of anything about me that is positive.

The desire of all good men not to be underestimated, the zeal of the patriot to stand high in his compatriots' regard, has motivated the publication of this opuscule that I herewith abandon to its fate, with no other justification than the merit of its intent. An arduous task it is, no doubt, to speak of oneself, to call attention to one's good qualities, without prompting disdain, without calling down opprobrium, well-deserved at times; but it is even harder to tolerate dishonor, to swallow insult, and to permit that modesty be complicit in our detriment. I have not wavered for a moment in choosing between such opposite extremes.

My defense forms part of the voluminous protocol of notes of the various Argentine governments in which my name is the object, and the motivation, contemptible. My response, which is registered in No.19 of the *Crónica*, my protest, in No. 48, and this opuscule must be read by those who would not judge me without a hearing, for such is not the way of decent men.⁵

My *Recuerdos de provincia* are no more than what the title implies. I have evoked reminiscences, resuscitated, so to speak, the memory of my relatives who earned their country's regard, rose to high rank in the hierarchy of the Church, and honored American letters with their works. I have been drawn by fondness to my province, to the humble home in which I was born; flimsy boards, no doubt, like those upon which in their helplessness the shipwrecked seize, but which allow me to remind myself that there are moral, lofty, and delicate sentiments within me, and so I take pleasure in encountering them close at hand, in those who preceded me, my mother, my teachers, and my friends. There is a democratic nobility that is unable to cast a shadow upon anyone, imperishable, that of patriotism and talent. I am proud to recognize in my family two historians, four representatives to the congresses of the Argentine Republic, and three high dignitaries of the Church, along with other servants of the nation who show me the noble path they followed. In addition to this, I have a predilection for biography. It is the most appropriate cloth for imprinting good ideas; he who writes it performs a kind of judicature, punishing vice triumphant, heartening virtue constrained. There is something in it of the fine arts, which from a piece of rough marble can bequeath to posterity a statue. History could not move forward without drawing from it its notable personages, and ours would indeed be very rich in characters if those able to do so were to gather, in good time, the information that tradition preserves about contemporaries. The lay of the land has on occasion revealed to me the physiognomy of men, and these indicate almost always the turn taken by events.

The family tree that follows is the index of the book. The names that appear in it are linked to mine by ties of blood, education, and examples followed. The details of my life are hidden in the shadow of those names, with some of them intertwined, and the honorable obscurity of mine can be illuminated by the light of those torches, without fear of their revealing stains better left concealed.

With neither pleasure nor foreboding, I tender my compatriots these pages inspired by truth and justified by necessity. Having read them, you may destroy them, for they belong among those many publications that owe their existence to circumstances of the moment, which, once past, none would understand. Are they deserving of dispassionate criticism? What am I to do? This was an inevitable consequence of the epithets of "infamous," "perverted," "evil," lavished on me by the government of Buenos Aires. Against defamation, even the attempt to defend oneself is a stigma!

Geneology of a Family from San Juan de la Frontera in the Republic of Argentina

DOMINGO DE ORO[ii]
Secretary of the Argentine Legation, close to Bolívar. Delegate to the Constitutional Congress of 1826. Advisor to López and Rosas. Agent of the Quadrilateral Treaty. Author of *El tirano de los pueblos argentinos* [The Tyrant of the Argentine People], El Mercurio Press, 1840. Editor of *Crónica Contemporánea* [Contemporary Chronicle], Santiago, 1841; of *La Epoca* [The Epoch], Bolivia, 1846.

JOSE ANTONIO DE ORO.[iv]
Government minister, 1827.

MIGUEL DE ORO[iii]
Descendant of the Conquistado‍ Capt. Don José de Oro.

PRESBYTER JOSE DE ORO[v]
Chaplain of the No. 1 Chasseurs of the Andes. Delegate to the National Convention, 1827. Government minister, 1829.

ELENA ALBARRACIN[vii]
Patroness of the Convent of Sai‍ Dominic.

FRAY JUSTO DE SANTA MARIA DE ORO[vi]
Provincial of the Recoleta Dominica of Chile. Delegate to the Congress of Tucumán, 1816. General of the Dominican Order, 1818. Bishop of Thaumaco and later Bishop of Cuyo, 1830.

TRANSITO DE ORO[viii]
Founder of the Santa Rosa Boarding School for Girls , 1839.

DOMINGO F. SARMIENTO
Member of the University of Chile, of the Historical Institute of France, of the Agricultural Society of Santiago, of the Society of Professors of Madrid, of the American Sericultural Society; founder of the Chilean Teachers' College, 1842; author of *Civilización y Barbarie* [Civilization and Barbarism], *Viajes por Europa, Africa y América* [Travels in Europe, Africa, and America], *Educación Popular* [Popular Edcation]; founder of and contributor to the *Zonda, Mercurio* [Mercury], *Nacional* [National], *Progreso* [Progress], *Crónica Contemporánea, Heraldo* [Herald], *Crónica, Tribuna* [Tribune]; author and translator of a series of texts for use in elementary education, adopted by the University of Chile.

PROCESA SARMIENTO
Artist, pupil of Monvoisin.[xvi]

BIENVENIDA SARMIENTO
Principal of various schools for girls.

PAULA AND ROSARIO SARMIENTO
Workers in embroidery, weaving, etc.

PAULA ALBARRACIN[xiv]
Weaver, dyer, knitter, and embro‍derer.

JUAN PASCUAL ALBARRACIN
Secular Dominican friar, priest ‍ the Conception.

JOSE MANUEL EUFRASIO DE QUIROGA SARMIENTO[xv]
Doctor, presbyter, priest, dea‍ and current Bishop of Cuyo.

JOSE CLEMENTE SARMIENTO[xvii]
Militia captain, was present ‍ Chacabuco.[xviii]

MASTER FRAY REMIGIO ALBARRACIN[ix]

MASTER FRAY JUSTO ALBARRACIN[x]
A dwarf. An altar built in proportion to his height was preserved for many years.

FRAY MIGUEL ALBARRACIN[xi]
Doctor of theology, author of *Tratado de Filosofía* [Treatise on Philosophy] and a work on the *Milenario* [Millennium]. He was called before the Inquisition of Lima, judged, and absolved.

PEDRO ALBARRACIN[xiii]

BERNARDINO ALBARRACIN[xii]
Maister of the Campe.

CORNELIO ALBARRACIN

MARIA ANTONIA IRARRAZABAL[xix]
Founder of the shrine of Santa Lucía.

ANTONIA IRARRAZABAL

JOSE DE LA CRUZ IRARRAZABAL
Of Santiago de Chile.

JUANA MORALES

ABBOT DON MANUEL MORALES[xxi]
Jesuit, author of *Historia de Cuyo y Observaciones sobre la Cordillera y llanuras de Cuyo* [History of Cuyo and Observations on the Cordillera and Plains of Cuyo], cited by Molina, *Historia natural y civil de Chile* [Natural and Civil History of Chile].[xxii]

JOSE IGNACIO SARMIENTO[xx]

JUAN LUIS FUNES
Militia Captain in 1811, relieves the Spaniards of their command of the troops.

TERESA FUNES

JUANA ISABEL FUNES

DR. DON GREGORIO FUNES[xxiii]
Dean of the Cathedral of Córdoba, rector of the University. Delegate to the Congresses of 1811 and 1819. Author of *Ensayo sobre la historia civil del Paraguay* [Civil History of Paraguay], translator of Daunou, editor of *Argos*, etc.[xxiv]

DR. AMBROSIO FUNES

JOSE FUNES

1

The Palm Trees

Not long ago, there were three solitary palm trees standing a few blocks north of the Plaza de Armas in the city of San Juan. Now, only two remain, rising above the crests of the dark-green orange groves and tracing their plumes of whitish leaves against the blueness of the sky, like those illustrations of the feather headdresses worn by American Indians. The palm tree is an exotic growth in that part of the eastern slopes of the Andes, like all the luxuriant vegetation that, intermingling with the scattered buildings of the city and its surroundings, tempers the summer heat and lifts the traveler's spirits when, crossing the neighboring barrens, he catches sight in the distance of the city's white towers sketched in over the green line of vegetation.

However, the palms did not come from Europe as did the orange and the walnut trees. They were émigrés that crossed the Andes with the conquistadors of Chile, or arrived shortly after in the baggage of Chilean families. If, in the earliest times, when the city was still a village, the streets were roadways, and the houses makeshift huts, he who planted one of them at the doorstep of his dwelling was pining for the land he had left behind, like Abd-al-Rahman, the Arab King of Córdoba, he might have addressed it thus:

> You, too, are a foreigner here,
> illustrious palm tree;

> The sweet breezes of Algarve caress and
> kiss your crown,
> Taking root in the rich soil, you raise
> your crest to the sky;
> Sad tears would you weep were you able
> to feel as I.[a]

Those palms had caught my attention ever since I was very young. Certain trees grow with secular slowness, and in the absence of written history, serve on no few occasions as a reminder and monument to memorable events. I have sat in Boston under an oak in the shadow of whose foliage the Pilgrims deliberated on the laws they would give the New World they had come to settle.[2] The United States sprang from there. The palms of San Juan mark the spots in the new colony that were first cultivated by the hand of the European.

The buildings in the neighborhood of those palms are threatening to collapse, with many of them already demolished and few rebuilt. It can be surmised from the names of the families who lived there that it must have been the first barrio to be populated in the rising city; in the three square blocks that contain those ancestral trees are the dwellings of the Godoys, Rosases, Oros, Albarracíns, Carrils, Maradonas, Rufinos, old families who composed the original colonial aristocracy. One of those houses, which now gives asylum to the youngest of the palm trees, has an ancient and dilapidated front door, with hollows in the lintel where leaden letters were once imbedded, and in the center the emblem of the Company of Jesus. In the same block and facing another street, stands the Godoy house, where there hangs a Roman portrait of a Jesuit Godoy, and where among some old papers was found, when an inventory of the family property was made, a portfolio containing manuscripts with this description: "This file contains the *Historia de Cuyo* [History of Cuyo] by the Abbot Morales, a topographical and descriptive map of Cuyo, and Mallea's *probanzas.*"[*] At some point I happened upon this

---

[a] *Historia de la dominación de los árabes en España* [History of the Arab Domination in Spain], Vol. 1, Chapter IX, by Conde. [Author's Note]

[*] *"Probanza"* is a legal term for "proof" or "evidence." Such proofs were documents that had to be presented to the proper royal authority for certification by anyone aspiring to a position within the Spanish colonial administration in the Americas.—Ed.

legend, and I yearned to see that history of my province I had so hoped to find. But, alas, the portfolio contained but one lone manuscript, that of Mallea, dated 1570, ten years after the founding of San Juan! Later on, I read in the *Historia natural de Chile* [Natural History of Chile], by the Abbot Molina, describing rare stones that can be found mixed with clay in the Andes, that the Abbot Don Manuel de Morales, "a keen observer of the province of Cuyo, his homeland," had made a detailed study of those same stones in his work entitled: *Observaciones de la cordillera y lla-nura de Cuyo* [Observations on the Cordillera and Plains of Cuyo].[b]

Here, then, is the scanty and deteriorated fund of historical evidence that for many years I was able to gather regarding the earliest times in San Juan. Those ancient palm trees, the Jesuit inscription, and the nearly empty portfolio. But one of the palms is at the Morales home, the leaden inscription identifies a Jesuit monastery, and the meaning of the portfolio's legend was now, for me, finally made clear. Searches for the ancestral documents are under way in Rome and Bologna, and I do not lose hope of one day making them public.[*]

[b] *Compendio de la historia geográfica, natural y civil de Chile* [Compendium of the Geographic, Natural, and Civil History of Chile], Vol. 1. [Author's note]

[*] In the original Spanish, "ancestral" is "*abolengo*" ("lineage") used as an adjective. Sarmiento is talking here about his own lineage, but this is only made clear if one consults the "Genealogy," which in the first edition of 1850 appeared on a separate fold-out between the preface and the first chapter, "The Palm Trees." In the "Genealogy" Sarmiento indicates that Juana Morales was his paternal great-grandmother and that she was related to the Abbot Don Manuel Morales, a Jesuit and the author of the *History of Cuyo* and *Observations on the Cordillera and Plains of Cuyo*. Just as the narrator Sarmiento plays the detective in this chapter and successfully solves the mysterious identity of the Abbot Morales, he forces his readers to read like detectives and match the clues he provides with information found in the "Genealogy," in order that they too may explain for themselves the legend on the portfolio.

In 1885, the editor of the second edition of *Recuerdos*, the Chilean Luis Montt, added a footnote to the last sentence of Chapter 1, in which he indicated that he had discovered the slightly incomplete work of the Jesuit Morales among the manuscripts of Abbot Molina, and that subsequently he had persuaded the Chilean government to purchase Morales's work for the National Library of Chile.—Ed.

2

· *Juan Eugenio de Mallea*

In the year of Our Lord 1570, that is, 280 years ago, "in the city of San Juan de la Frontera, Don Juan Eugenio de Mallea, *vecino* of said city, appeared before His Honor Don Fernando Díaz, His Majesty's Judge of First Instance, in the form and fashion most befitting his right, and said: that, having to present certain witnesses in order to make a *probanza, ad perpetuam rei memoriam,* he requested and pleaded that the witnesses he presented before His Honor, after being duly sworn, be questioned and examined under said oath following the set of questions contained at the end, and that what they declared and put forward be signed and sealed by the court clerk, and that His Honor, using his authority and jurisdiction, have it delivered over to him, Don Juan Eugenio Mallea, so that he could pursue justice, and before all else, that he summon and request the presence of the officials of this city at the administration of the oath and questioning of the said witnesses, so they might speak and object as they deemed pertinent."*

* *"Vecino"* (neighbor) is a colonial term that, in the early years of colonization in the Argentine interior, referred to the Spanish residents of a city who were considered white and who had full rights of citizenship. These were the original European settlers and their legal descendants, who formed the small upper class. The term *"vecino"* was opposed to that of *"morador"* (dweller) used to designate most of the nonwhite inhabitants, who, as distinguished from the *vecinos,* did not enjoy full rights. By the second half of the seventeenth century, however, when more Spaniards were increasingly arriving in the Americas, being white no longer guaranteed a person the status of *vecino* or upper class. Also, in the pattern

The *probanza* dated and presented, and there being no further witnesses to take the stand, and "having exhausted the municipality's supply of paper," Mallea went to the city of Mendoza del Nuevo Valle de Rioja to continue the judicial procedure. The witnesses who appeared in San Juan to be questioned before the court clerk, Diego Pérez, were: Diego Lucero; Gaspar Lemos, administrator and treasurer of the city; Francisco González, prosecutor of the Royal Tribunal; Gaspar Ruiz; Anse de Fabre; Lucas de Salazar; Juan Contreras; Hernando Ruiz de Arce, tax collector and inspector; Hernán Daría de Sayavedra; Juan Martín Gil; Diego de Laora; an individual named Bustos; Juan Gómez, an islander; and two others. From the tenor of the replies to the twenty-four questions of the interrogation, and with some reading between the lines, the history of the first ten years of the founding of San Juan emerges, as well as the fascinating biography of the *hidalgo* Don Juan Eugenio de Mallea, who had been Judge of First Instance and was, at the time, Auditor of the Royal Treasury and Royal Standard-Bearer, housing the colors and maintaining men and horses at his personal expense.* Setting aside the irritating style and verbosity of the notarial profession, I will outline in brief the proven facts that come to light in said investigation. Most of the *vecinos* of San Juan who testify have known Mallea for sixteen years and have fought with him in the campaigns of southern Chile, Mallea having come from Peru with General Don Martín Avendaño in 1552.

In 1553, the year the death of Pedro Valdivia came to pass, Mallea was attached to the Imperial Forces under Francisco de Villagra, who played such a distinguished role in the Arauco wars.[1] Aware of the disastrous condition in which Concepción had been left after the Tucapel debacle, the commander repaired with his men to that city, put its affairs in order, and set out anew on a campaign with 180 men, among them Mallea, who was involved in the unhappy expedition of Mariguiñu Hill, known since

---

of settlement that characterized the Atlantic coast of Argentina, which was very different from the more traditional pattern of the interior, the early *vecinos* were in fact predominantly mestizo, and yet they considered themselves, and were considered by others, creole and upper class. (See Scobie, *Argentina,* 46, 51, 54.)—Ed.

* "*Hidalgo*" is a title of the ancien régime, that is, of the legal hierarchy that characterized European society and its colonies before the eighteenth- and nineteenth-century liberal-democratic revolutions. Early on "*hidalgo*" was a term that in principle was common to all Spanish nobles, but by the sixteenth century it was used to designate the lowest level of nobility in a four-tier system.—Ed.

that time as Villagra Hill in commemoration of the disaster. He went to Concepción immediately after and was later assigned to the repopulation of Villarica. In 1556, he removes to Valdivia together with Don García Hurtado de Mendoza, until in 1558 he sets out with the 150 men who had been under the command of García, with Captain Jerónimo de Villegas, to repopulate Concepción, which had been abandoned since Villagra's defeat.² He is a *hidalgo*, and he was always seen among the captains; he had served for twenty years at his own expense "with his arms and horses and had carried out all that was expected of him, as a staunch and capable subject of His Majesty," until, married in San Juan to the daughter of the chief of Angaco, named Doña Teresa de Ascensio, who brought him a rich dowry of gold pesos and gave him various progeny, he was finally in debt for pesos in gold, his wife's wealth having been swallowed up by the cost of supporting his retainers and household in the king's service, and having received no tribute from the Indians who in Mendoza had been allotted him in *encomienda* and who, after the establishment of San Juan, fell within the limits and jurisdiction of this latter city.*

---

*"*Encomienda*" was a royal grant of trusteeship, to a Spanish conquistador, of a group of Indians residing in a specific place. Typically, at the time a new Spanish settlement or "city" was founded, all the Indians belonging to the preexisting local indigenous communities were apportioned among the principal Spaniards. The receiver of the *encomienda*, the *encomendero*, had the right to demand tribute and labor from the Indians granted him. The Spanish crown, anxious to avoid the development of landed feudalism in the New World, retained dominion over the territory itself and did not grant or sell large extensions of land to private owners until the seventeenth century, when the *hacienda* replaced the *encomienda* as the major rural institution for the private accumulation of wealth.

Encomienda in Argentina, although not formally abolished until Independence, was, by 1620, no longer viable as a source of coerced labor due to the rapid decline of the native population, which in relative terms had never been large. David Rock writes that, "while the Indian population of central Mexico at the time of the Spanish conquest may have been as high as 25 million, no more than 750,000 Indians—and quite possibly only half that number—lived in what became Argentina" (Rock, *Argentina, 1516–1987*,1). (Scobie estimates 300,000 Indians in the Argentine area in the early sixteenth century [Scobie, *Argentina*, 36].)

Furthermore, *encomienda* only made economic sense in those places in Argentina where there were concentrations of sedentary agricultural Indians, whom the Spaniards had already proven elsewhere that they were able to subjugate. Thus, in the area around Buenos Aires, where the Indians were nomadic hunters who successfully resisted subjugation, the institution of *encomienda* never took root to any significant degree. (See Scobie, *Argentina*, 36–40, 45, 51, and 56.)

In the year 1560, Captain Pedro de Castillo crossed the snow-covered mountain range to eastern Chile with one hundred troops and founded the city of Mendoza del Nuevo Valle de Rioja, for so it is called in the records kept in that city in 1571 by the notary public Don N. Herrera.³ According to the statements of witnesses, it appears that they distributed in Mendoza the inhabitants that they found there, it being reasonable to presume that Mallea received some from the lagoons of Guanacache, which explains why the Indians he acquired would later fall within the limits of San Juan. Shortly thereafter, General Don Juan Jofré left Mendoza with a band of men to explore to the north, and, in fact, discovered several unnamed valleys, one of them presumably Tulún, in which, having gone back to Mendoza and returned a short while later, he founded the city of San Juan de la Frontera [Saint John of the Frontier]. The similarity of Tulún, Ullún, and Villicún, names still used in the area, seems to suggest that these, together with the Valley of Zonda, were the ones that "were densely populated with natives and apparently contained very fertile land," which is indeed the case. In 1561, under Don Rodrigo de Quiroga's administration in Chile, General Don Gonzalo de los Ríos crossed into the province of Cuyo with new troops to put down an Indian rebellion. After the city had been laid out, the Huarpes, who inhabited it, rose up, and the land was pacified once more.⁴ Three leagues to the north of the city is a place called Tapiecitas, because of the remnants

---

Finally, the *encomendero* Mallea's marriage to the daughter of the chief of Angaco reflects two policies of the Crown that found a measure of compliance among its New World subjects. One was a 1556 instruction issued by Cardinal Cisneros, as regent of Castile, expressing that Spaniards should marry the daughters of the indigenous chiefs when they were the successors of their fathers. (Under *encomienda*, the chiefs, or caciques, were theoretically allowed to continue to govern their people, and were given the rank of "hidalgo.") Another policy, articulated in 1539, ordered the *encomenderos* to marry within three years or, if married, to send for their wives in Spain. The penalty for failure to comply was loss of their *encomiendas*. During the sixteenth century, or at least probably most of it, the mestizo offspring of Spaniards married to Indians were accepted as creoles, or Spaniards born in the New World, and the first generation of mestizos born after Spanish settlement was frequently recognized by their Spanish fathers even when they were born outside of marriage. As time passed in a settled area, however, more and more of the mestizos were illegitimate, and Catholic disapproval of illegitimacy led to the appearance of legal restrictions against them as a group. See Magnus Mörner, *Race Mixture in the History of Latin America* (Boston: Little, Brown, and Co., 1967), 27–28, 37–38, 41–44.—Ed.

of a fort, the ruins of which were still discernible some twenty or thirty years ago.* Its existence in that place seems to account for the name of San Juan de la Frontera, since the Indians of Jachal and Mogna were not subdued. In fact, their last chief lived until 1830, when he died at an age of over 120.

That General de los Ríos, having returned to Mendoza from his campaign, learned through an Indian prisoner about a remote country in whose mountains there was gold so abundant, that of course the imagination of the Spaniards baptized it with the name of *Nuevo Cuzco*.[5] The expedition in search of that El Dorado went from Mendoza to San Juan, and all those able to muster horses set out in quest of the golden fleece. Don Juan de Mallea "departed with his followers and many horses." They marched, following their Indian guide, along a route that twisted and turned. Their rations soon began to dwindle, and one morning they awoke to the new day's trek to find that the Indian had disappeared. They were in the midst of a wilderness with no water and no idea how to find their way back to the colonies. After indescribable privations, the frustrated contingent arrived in San Juan, disgusted and disheartened, with fifteen of their group having perished from thirst and starvation. And how strange!, the tradition of this event lives on among us to this very day, and not a decade goes by that an expedition isn't organized in search of the heaps of gold that are still waiting to be discovered and that the early settlers sought in vain when their food ran out, or when the Indian guide slipped away, just as they had come across one of the clues given in the *derrotero*. Since it was the obsession of the conquistadors to find gold everywhere in the same abundance as in Mexico and Peru, the poetic fantasy of the colonies, the popular myths, are concentrated throughout America in written legends known as *derroteros*. Whoever possesses one of these mysterious itineraries keeps it jealously hidden away in the hope of embarking one day on a pilgrimage fraught with uncertainty and danger but rich in expectations of a fabulous find. There are three or four of these in San Juan, the best known being that of the *Casas Blancas* [White Houses] in which, after overcoming infinite difficulties, which are only lacking, to be true Arabian tales, in frightful dragons and immense giants who block the way and must be vanquished, one will find, after negotiating the ascent of an extremely high and rugged

---

*The word "*tapiecitas*" means "little mud walls."—Ed.

mountain, the coveted *Casas Blancas,* from whose ceilings hang, in guanaco necks, bags of gold nuggets that they say were left there hidden by
the ancients, and from which many of the nuggets have spilled and lie
scattered on the ground because, so the *derrotero* says, the hide of those
necks has all but rotted away. I can picture the first settlers of San Juan,
few in number in the early years, lacking all of life's comforts, under a
scorching sun, and settled upon arid and unyielding soil that gives no
fruit save that wrenched from it by the plow, discontent with their meager conquest, those who had seen the treasures of the Incas, anxious to
move on, and discover that vast territory which, from the eastern slopes
of the Andes, allows one to presuppose a limitless horizon beyond. The
dubious directions proffered by some Huarpe, perhaps from the
Hualilán or Carolina mines, sufficed to attract groups of conquistadors
condemned to dig ditches to irrigate the soil, with those hands trained
for the musket and the lance. Tillers of America! You should never have
left gay Andalusia, its vast olive groves and its vineyards! The location of
most American cities reveals the dominant obsession of the time. All are
way stations to facilitate passage to the countries of gold; few are on the
coast in places favorable to commerce. Agriculture developed under the
belated impulse of necessity and disillusion, and its harvests found no
outlet in the distant corners so far-removed from the ports and their
cities.

3

The Huarpes

The Huarpes, undoubtedly once a great and numerous nation, inhabited the Tulún, Mogna, and Jachal valleys and the Guanacache plains. According to the *probanza*, the land was "densely populated with natives" at the time of the conquest.

The historian Ovalle, who visited Cuyo sixty years later, refers to a grammar and a Christian prayer book in the Huarpe language, of which no vestiges remain among us but the above-mentioned place names, and Puyuta, the name of a barrio, Angaco, Vicuña, Villicún, Guanacache, and a few others. Woe to the nations that fail to march forward! If only their worst fate were that of remaining behind! It took no more than three centuries for the Huarpes to be wiped from the roster of nations. Woe to you, indolent Spanish colonists! In even less time you have seen yourselves reduced from a confederated province to a village, from a village to a settlement, from a settlement to an uninhabited wilderness. You once counted among you the wealthy, such as Don Pedro Carril, owner of lands that stretched from Calle Honda to Pie-de-Palo.[1] Now all these rich men are poor! Scholars like the abbot Don Manuel Morales, who wrote a history of his native land and *Observaciones sobre la cordillera y las llanuras de Cuyo* [Observations on the Cordillera and the Plains of Cuyo]; theologians like Fray Miguel Albarracín; statesmen like Laprida, president of the Congress of Tucumán; governors like Ignacio de la Rosa and Salvador M. del Carril.[2] Today you no longer even have schools, and the prevailing level of barbarism is on display, for all to see, in the very men who govern you. Beyond general ignorance, there is yet another step, general impoverishment, and you have taken that one, too. The step that follows is obscurity, and then communities quickly disappear, and no one knows when or where they went!

The Huarpes had cities. Their ruins can still be seen in the valleys of the cordillera. Near Calingasta, on a spacious plain, more than five hundred houses of circular design still stand, with porticos facing east, all scattered in disorder and looking like those horns that our country folk play by making a steel reed vibrate with their finger. In the Valley of Zonda, on White Hill, are painted rocks, crude remnants of the forerunners of fine art; outlines of guanacos and other animals, human footprints sculpted in stone, as though they had been stamped in soft clay. Often out of the flanks of sand dunes and mounds of earth there appear painted clay pitchers filled with carbonized corn, which old maidservants believe is gold, enchanted to mock the white man's greed. This does not negate the fact that in the Huarpe city of Calingasta, a pair of crude plates of solid gold were found that had been in service for many a year and, because they were so pretty, had never been melted down; thus was their fortune until a passer-by bought them for a peso each and sold them later in Santiago to Don Diego Barros for their weight on the goldsmith's scale.

Those nations lived by fishing on the lagoons of Guanacache, whose shores their descendants the Laguneros still inhabit, disdaining to mix with outsiders; doubtless they also survived by cultivating corn in Tulún, today San Juan, as is suggested by a canal, now gone but still discernible, running from the Albardón and capable of bringing water from the river as far as Caucete. More recently, they hunted and fed on guanacos, which graze in herds on the grass of the foothills. To this day, tradition conserves the laws and rituals of the national hunt that the Huarpes conducted once every year. Nothing has changed in the ways of the Huarpes but the introduction of the horse. "A *corregidor* and captain-general of the province of Cuyo," writes Father Ovalle, "told me that as soon as the Huarpe Indians sight the deer (guanacos), they approach, and then pursue them at a lope, keeping them always in sight, not letting them stop or eat, until a day or two later, they tire and give up, making it easy for the Huarpes to catch them, and then the hunters return, bearing the prey to their homes, where they celebrate with their families . . . making soft and smooth jackets from the skins, which are very warm and most welcome in the winter."[a][*]

In the early months of spring, when the guanacos are preparing to enter the cordilleras, watered and replenished by the runoff from the thawing frosts, the word spreads in Jachal, Huandacol, Calingasta, and the other inhabited areas, as to the day and meeting-place for the start of the great hunts. The sturdy young men and youths hasten there on their best horses, duly trained for this fiesta, in which they hope to distinguish themselves and be rewarded with slain guanacos for their horsemanship, their accuracy in throwing the bolas, and the surefootedness and speed of their mounts. On the appointed day, the horsemen arrive in groups upon a spacious plain where a meeting is held to appoint the judge of the hunt, who is the most experienced Indian, and to draw up the plan of operations. When he gives the order, the docile and obedient party divides into groups that he assigns, which separate and gallop away in different directions, some to seal off the entrance to a ravine, some to drive the guanaco herds towards the plain where the roundup will occur. Two days later, the dust clouds raised by the fleeing herds mark the approach of the anticipated moment. The huntsmen disperse, and four pairs of bolas, as light as are needed to rope guanacos, are set to whirling with consummate skill and grace all at the same time around the horsemen's heads. The guanacos take flight in panic, the horses charge off, without the rider loosening his reins, for fear that his mount could roll over, which is sometimes fatal (but which the Indian gaucho avoids, though he be sure of landing on his feet, for fear of falling behind). When the best riders are in a position to throw, four pairs of bolas are released from a single hand, binding several guanacos together, one after another. As the horse continues to race, four more pairs of bolas replace those already used, and thus the skillful huntsman can assure himself of ten, fifteen, and even more guanacos in the chase. If his supply of bolas is used up, he immediately leaps to the ground to kill the prey and disentangle the cords. Remounting his excited steed, he dashes off after the dust cloud, the yelling huntsmen and the neighing

---

[a] *Histórica relación del reino de Chile* [Historical Account of the Realm of Chile], by Alonso de Ovalle, 1646. [Author's note]

[*] *Corregidor.* A sixteenth and seventeenth-century colonial magistrate. Rock writes that after 1563, "Cuyo was administered separately by a *corregidor*, who remained subject to the captain-general of Chile until 1776" (Rock, *Argentina, 1516–1987*, 15). Here the *corregidor* and the captain-general are the same person.—Ed.

horses, until he succeeds, if he can, in taking position. One or two mishaps from falling are not uncommon. The hunters return to claim their animals, which each one recognizes by the bolas that ensnare them. If a dispute should arise, which is rare, since each one's property is inviolable, the judge of the hunt makes a decision to which there is no appeal. The groups then disband to return to their homes. The women eagerly await the guanaco hides whose silken fleece they can already envision in ponchos of different colored stripes, to say nothing of the savory meat that will fill their larders, the primordial concern of every housewife. The children delight in sporting with a baby guanaco caught by the huntsmen, while the joyous young men tell the endless story of the mishaps of the hunt, of how they fell and how they then recovered.

Another Huarpe custom survives, an offspring of the ancient and exhausting chase on foot. I will repeat what the historian Ovalle observed in his time, and the informed reader will spare me the task of explaining it. "I must not fail to tell of a most unusual God-given talent possessed by these Indians for tracking down lost or stolen things. I will describe one such instance that took place in Santiago de Chile to which many were witness. A certain man who found some orange trees missing from his grove called in a Huarpe, who took the man from one place to another, up one street and down the next, until finally he stopped with him in front of a house, and finding the door closed, the Indian said to the man, 'Knock and go in. Your trees are here.' The man did so and found his orange trees. Many such things they do everyday that are much wondered at, tracking with great assurance whether over smooth stones, or through grass, or water."[b]

Illustrious Calibar! Your stature is not in the least diminished from that of your grandparents! The celebrated tracker from San Juan, after having used his science to recover many a stolen article for its owner, and after having allowed prisoners to escape from jail, as happened with my cousin M. Morales, who failed to cover the tracks that Calibar had promised not to find, has retired to die in Mogna, the land of his tribe, leaving to his sons the glory of his name. His fame has reached Europe through a feuilleton in the *Revue de Deux Mondes,* which reprinted the paragraph on the "Rastreador" [Tracker] in *Civilización y Barbarie.* Thus, Calibar has left behind a more lasting memory in Europe than have the barbarities of Facundo, the perverse white man who is unworthy of fame.

[b] Ibid. Ovalle. [Author's note]

Have you, perchance, seen those little baskets in a variety of shapes that contain the sewing kits of our young girls, those baskets that are sometimes closed at the mouth in the form of an onion, or, on the contrary, wide open like a bell, the edges cleverly finished and gaily colored, and picked out with variegated tufts of wool? These baskets are remnants of Huarpe handicraft that still exist in the lagoons. In Ovalle's time they were used to hold drinking water, so tight was the weave of the soft and lustrous yellow straw that grows on the banks of the lagoons of Guanancache. Poor lagoons, whose destiny it was to have served, better than those of Venice, to connect their distant shores, ferrying back and forth, in schooners or in boats with lateen sails, the products of industry and the fruits of the land! The Huarpe still floats his bulrush rafts, to cast his nets for the bounteous trout; the white man, made brutish by the use of the horse, parades along the shore of the lakes with his mules, packed full like those of a Spanish smuggler, and if you should speak to him of canals and steamships like those in the United States, he will laugh at you, content with himself and believing that you are the fool out of touch with reality! And yet, in Pie-de-Palo there is coal, in Mendoza, iron, and between those distantly separated points undulates the placid surface of the meandering lakes, rippled by grebes playfully trailing their partially webbed feet in the water. Nothing is lacking there, save the genius of man, save intelligence and freedom. White men degenerate into Huarpes, and it is now a lofty claim to public admiration, to know how to throw bolas, to wear *chiripá*, or to track a mule![3]*

The idea that the Jesuit Ovalle set in motion, in the Spanish realms, about the blessings of San Juan's privileged soil, is still, two hundred years later, an unheeded cry, a sterile desire. . . . "There is no doubt that, if 'foreigners' should begin to arrive, this land will become one of the richest in the Indies, since in view of its great fertility, nothing is called for but people to work it and reap the benefits of the great abundance of its fruits and harvests."[c] Oh, my poor homeland! You, on the contrary, are at war to drive away the "foreigners" who will surely come; and you cast out those of your children who offer you good counsel!

---

* *Chiripá.* A gaucho legcloth. For futher discussion of the word "*chiripá*," see Note 6, Chapter 8.—Ed.

[c] Ovalle, *Histórica relación,* book II, ch. VI. [Author's note]

4

The Sons of Jofré

Whence do the men come whom we see distinguished in our times, in ministries, legislatures, presidencies, professorships, and the press? From the mass of humanity. Where will their children find themselves in times hereafter? Among the broad mass of the people. Here is where to find the first and last page in the life of each of our contemporaries. Those ancient, privileged castes that traversed centuries counting the number of their ancestors, that immortal name called Osuna, Joinville, or Orléans, has now fortunately disappeared.[1] How the human multitude has had to purify itself in order to bring forth candidates who are named Pitt, Washington, Arago, Franklin, Lamartine, Dumas, and who are noblemen of their country and even kings of the world, without their elevation having cost a single sigh of pain![2] The old colonial families have disappeared in the Argentine Republic; in Chile, they still cling to the land and resist at the level of oblivion, which waits to swallow them up.

Captain Juan Jofré had left a dazzling trail of his merit and deeds of valor in the conquest and civil history of Chile. In 1556, the town council of Santiago, alerted to the general uprising of Indians plotted by Lautaro, ordered Juan Jofré to enter the territory of the Promaucaes with thirty soldiers, and to proceed fully armed to wherever the outbreak should occur; the captain achieved his objective, and gained time to take precautionary measures and prepare for a more decisive campaign.[3]*

Such prowess accorded him great fame and prestige, for on July 9 of the same year, the town council of Santiago, decreeing that the feast day of this saint, as the patron saint of the capital, should be a solemn holy day, appointed Juan Jofré Standard-Bearer, with the charge of presenting, on the saint's feast day, the royal banner that bore upon it the city's coat of arms emblazoned in gold and topped with an image of the apostle on horseback.[4] The ceremony took place on the twenty-fourth of the same month, with the councilmen announcing from a window to the standard-bearer in the street: *"We deliver over to Your Grace, Señor Standard-Bearer of this City of Santiago del Nuevo Extremo, this standard, in the name of God and H.M., our King and natural sovereign; and of this city, and of its council, its courts, and its regiment, so that with it you may serve H.M. whenever called upon to do so;* and said Captain Jofré replied that *he was receiving it with that understanding and he promised to do it and to comply,* and he received it on horseback; and they all departed together with other gentlemen to accompany him to the main church, where they heard vespers, and when finished, they remounted and rode through the streets of this city until they arrived at the Captain's house, where the standard remained."[a] The extent of his influence and eminence in the complex dealings of the time may be seen in the fact that, as mayor of Santiago in 1557, Don Juan Jofré received orders to convoke the town council on May 6, before which were presented the official appointment and powers of Don García Hurtado de Mendoza, who, after his installation as chief justice, named Diego Araya to the post of mayor, not without complaint of injustice to Jofré, who was deposed.

I knew the last descendant of Don Juan Jofré, founder of San Juan.[5] In

---

* "Promaucaes" was a term used by the Spaniards to refer to Indians who lived between the Nuble River and the Bío Bío, in what is today Chile. This area included the site of Concepción. According to Robert Charles Padden, the Spaniards used this term to differentiate these indigenous peoples from those they called the "Pincunche," a term they used to designate non-Mapuche Indians living within what they considered Mapuche territory but to the north of the Mapuches. Padden, "Cultural Adaptation and Militant Autonomy among the Araucanians of Chile," in *The Indian in Latin American History: Resistance, Resilience, and Acculturation,* ed. John E. Kicza (Wilmington, DE: Scholarly Resources, 1993), 69–88.—Ed.

[a] Gay, *Historia de Chile* [History of Chile], Vol. I, chapter 28. [Author's note]

1820, Don Javier, a portly and ostentatious gentleman, was a worthy scion of his illustrious grandfather. His house adjoined the town hall, as was usual in the colonies, when the prison and the governor occupied the same frontage on the main square. The revolution of independence found him alive, and the two—the revolution and Jofré—embraced each other, as the latter presided over the solemn inauguration of the new era in his spacious salon, decorated with elegant stucco moldings, the work of architects of distinction who used to make their way into the colonies, and who even emerged among the Jesuits. This salon, given an air of solemnity by damask drapes suspended from gilded poles, was used for the inauguration of the provincial representatives. Its walnut chairs and its crimson velvet sofas have been used until recently for all important political ceremonies, but these, like so much else, have succumbed to mistreatment and bureaucratic neglect. This same salon is at present a billiard room, after having been adapted for use as a theater. Before, a sturdy poplar stood at the northern edge of the spacious grounds, which the axe of greed perchance did not respect. It was the father of those millions of poplars that make civil construction so practical and cheap; it was the first immigrant of its species to take root in San Juan. Ten blocks to the west of the main square there is an obelisk, or pyramid, which today lifts its truncated top in the middle of an uninviting open space. Twice I have seen two or three cows seeking refuge in its shade from the scorching sun. That pyramid is the tomb of the revolution, dead in its infancy, already a ruin thirty years after being erected. It also serves as a signpost for Don Juan Jofré's property and as a symbol of his patriotism. In the summer evenings of 1816, when the hot, dry breeze whipped around the face, bathing without refreshing it, my mother would stroll with us children through the tree-lined promenade at whose center the pyramid stood. From it, two diagonals radiated outward to the edges of a square, flanked by charming poplars, at whose feet there extended rows of white lilies and pink roses. Four pilasters, serving as pedestals for statues, marked the four corners, and I don't know what confused notion I remember of a labyrinth of alleys and circles in various directions. I can still sense the cool, perfumed breeze and see the groups of lanterns that threw off their light amid the foliage of the trees. The pyramid was the work of the Spanish engineer Díaz, about whom many amusing anecdotes remain in the history of the war of independence, and it was intended to commemorate the expedition of the liberating army to Chile.[6]

In 1839, one of Don Javier Jofré's heirs laid claim to the land where the public promenade had been, alleging that the conditions and purpose for which the land had been given no longer held. Since there was no objection on the part of the government, the interested party asked the minister, in my presence: "And what about the '*pírame*,' señor?" What he meant to ask was: What should be done with that monument? To which the minister replied with boundless generosity, "As for the '*pírame*,' you can knock it down!"

This is what I heard! A few days later I wrote an article in *El Zonda* entitled *"La Pirámide"* [The Pyramid].⁷ That was the first time that the imagination's fantastic fictions served to mask the indignation of my heart. Those barbarians have still not destroyed it; they would have had to start demolition from the top, and they probably couldn't figure out how to erect a scaffold.

5

Mallea

The Spanish families that subsequently established themselves in San Juan took revenge on the *hidalgo* Mallea through the sons of the Indian queen of Angaco. They called them mulattos! And I have seen Mallea's descendants still fighting this calumny passed on from fathers to sons.[1] My mother, who is not aware that Don Juan Eugenio de Mallea served at his personal expense with his own arms and horses, tells me that Don Luciano Mallea was well-versed in genealogies and maintained that his family was mestizo of pure and noble blood.[2] That old fellow was the archetype of the Spanish colony, a sort of poor but austere patriarch, sententious in speech, as well as a poet, who had an adage or a verse for every occasion. Societies that do not think live by moral tradition, and the book of proverbs resides scattered about among the old folks. Thus the elderly Mallea, in modulated tones, would unfailingly say to the betrothed young men:

> Marry and you'll have a wife
> To distrust, be she comely,
> To abhor, be she homely,
> To obey, be she of means,
> To support, if she hasn't got beans;
> Marry and you'll have a wife.

When he heard a respectable person giving voice to coarse expressions, he would say, chiding him with sarcasm: "It's not the snot that one sees but the spot from which it hangs."[a] This calls to mind the time I saw an important Chilean personage grimace with disgust upon reading in an official communication the following words: "*revolting*," "*infamous*," "*vile*." That man was not seeing the snot but the place from which it hung.[3]

Another offshoot of Mallea must have settled in Mendoza, for the father of Don Alejo Mallea, now governor of that province, was a descendant of his and, like him, bore the name Juan Eugenio. In fact, the present-day representatives of the royal standard-bearer came into our family through Doña Angela Salcedo, wife of Don Domingo Soriano Sarmiento, and Don Fermín Mallea, husband of Doña Mercedes. As a widow, Doña Angela entrusted me with her husband's business and her son's elementary education. In my absence, a slave of hers, a rebellious one, denounced her as a unitarian, the proof being that she had a few bags of silver coins hidden away in a hole.[4] The police and the minister of interior affairs arrived to investigate; and these high officials of the confederate state, irresistibly attracted, seduced by those pieces of eight . . . filled their pockets in the presence of the innocent victim of the robbery. This time, Facundo, the looter of towns, was disgusted by his henchmen, and fifteen years later, Benavídes repaid a part of the theft, out of an impulse of shame that does him honor.[6]

Don Fermín Mallea, to whom I allude in my *Viajes*[Travels] when I speak of the ruins of Pompeii, came to a most wretched end.[7] His death, in 1848, was caused by the courts; and the judges, clerks, and notaries, who all shared equally in the blame, will one day pay for it in the ignominy of their sons: in them, in the prevailing ignorance, in the ineptitude of the judges, in the unbridled passions that a wicked system that, already bearing crime written on its brow, abets rather than contains, by heading all its decrees with the sacramental "*Death to . . .*"; that on issuing the decree, spews forth slander like a leper's spittle: "*savage*," "*filthy*," "*villainous. . . .*" Ah! You will pay for it in your children, immoral people, debased victims, accomplices all in the evil that descends from on high! My uncle Fermín was a difficult person with a harsh personality. I was much affected by it in my youth; but these quirks of character

---

[a] "A snot swings from his nose." Quevedo. [Author's note][5]

did not tarnish certain most laudable endowments of the heart. He took on a clerk by the name of Oro, who was gentleness incarnate, and so hardworking and honest, that Mallea, in recompense, made him a partner in the shop they jointly managed. The years went by, and the business prospered. Mallea would withdraw funds for his own use, and not the slightest cloud ever disturbed the harmony that resulted from the extreme disparity of their characters. One day they had to balance the accounts, and it came to light that the entire business belonged to the clerk, since this is what corresponded to his share of the profits. Mallea tore his hair, cursed a blue streak, and denied the evidence; but the figures were there, deadly and inflexible. Mallea had drawn out over a ten-year period such and such an amount, and the young man hadn't touched a penny! And here is where Mallea's stubbornness came into play. From the balance he turned to an auditor, from the auditor to the courts and the execution of writs, and from there to exasperation, wire-pulling, and interminable legal wrangling. Oro's easy-going, sweet nature was unable to withstand such a cruel ordeal. He deeply loved Mallea, and that delicate plant began to droop on its withered stalk; spiritual hypochondria was followed by physical prostration, and sickness, by death; for the poor fellow died of sorrow, of seeing the injustice done him by his boss and benefactor. The doctors performed an autopsy, and assure they found the heart completely dry!

Mallea, while he was pursuing that unfortunate suit, one month prior to the young man's death, had stopped leaving his house; he would speak of his business to everyone he saw, and could be discovered at any moment, bemused, adding up sums, whose numbers he traced with a finger in the air. Feuds and disputes in provincial cities are, as everyone knows, grist for the gossip mills; and under a system of government that admits of no public life, in which it is the better part of wisdom to hold one's peace, domestic matters occupy the public's attention, and fill, in place of newspapers, discussions, political parties, projects, ideas, and laws, the idle hours of the most serious individuals.* The death of young Oro

---

*In the original Spanish, the first noun in this sentence is the plural form of "*feudo.*" Normally, this word is not a cognate of the English "feud," which is the word chosen here to translate it. "*Feudos,*" however, appears not to be a typographical error; in fact, Sarmiento uses it again, in a context where the English translation "feud" is also justified, in the fifth paragraph of Chapter 8, "Los Oro." After considering all the evidence at my

shook the foundations of the entire city. When a long procession of mourners was wending its way to the graveyard with the hearse, the vehicle creaked, broke down, and the coffin had to be lowered at the very doorstep of the unfortunate Mallea, who at that moment was frantically engaged in pursuing the fatal calculation that had brought him to his present confusion. With horror in their eyes, the bystanders set upon muttering epithets like "God's punishment!", while the judges, who had with their own ineptitude produced this outcome to a simple numerical question that in six years they had found impossible to resolve, were also carrying on about believing in a divine Providence that punishes our misdeeds. So that's how it is in that place: Crime is not a crime if an official commits it! From that moment on, the last remnant of reason abandoned Mallea, and weeping night and day, and scribbling on paper with no rest whatsoever, he grew disfigured, wracked by doubt, always adding up his sums to make them clear, howling when his tears ran dry, until he expired after a torment of many years' duration, which was made worse by the love and regard he felt for the young man on whom he had looked as a son, and by his own basic decency; for in this whole sad affair, there was nothing involved but stubbornness of character, and passions run amok, which the injustice and ineptitude of the judges neither knew how nor wished to restrain.[8]

---

disposal, I have concluded that *"feudos"* may well be an Anglicism perhaps coined by Sarmiento himself, whether consciously or unconsciously, I cannot say. In a later chapter of *Recuerdos*, we read that he began studying the English language early on (1833) during his first exile in Chile. By 1850, he had visited both Great Britain and the United States, and had remained in the latter for close to two months. Even though Sarmiento would later reside in the United States as a diplomat between the years 1865 and 1868, as far as I know, he would never claim to speak the English language well.—Ed.

6

The Sayavedras

In the barrio of Puyuta there was once an ancient pine tree whose trunk now supports the chancel of the church of Los Desamparados [The Destitute], the only public structure built in these barbaric times and a model of ignorance of the rules of architecture, which one day will be visited with amazement by more enlightened generations. I met the last two descendants of the soldier who bore this name; one of them was sentenced to death for murder. The other, known as the Indian Sayavedra, of gigantic stature and a fierce soul, was a bandit by trade in Mendoza and San Juan and was called, due to his reputation for brutality, into the Federation's service when Lavalle landed in 1839.[1] He was to threaten me with his lance in the main square on November 18, 1840, calling me "*savage*," and six years later he was put to death for the crime of murder.[2] Thus, the bellicose characteristics of the grandfathers degenerate into vandalism when societies decline and are degraded. Woe to the children who are receiving their education in the school of "*Death to . . .* " and of violence![3]

7

The Albarracíns

In the middle of the twelfth century, a Saracen sheik named Al Ben Razin conquered and gave his name to a city and to a family that later became Christian.[a] M. Beauvais, the celebrated French sericulturist, ignorant of my maternal surname and not having seen me in a burnoose, remarked that my physiognomy was completely Arab; and, since I pointed out to him that, their name notwithstanding, the Albarracíns had green or blue eyes, he replied in support of his idea that in the long series of portraits of the Montmorency line, the characteristic familial type appeared every fourth or fifth generation.[1] In Algiers, I was surprised to find such a resemblance in the physiognomy of the Argentine gaucho and the Arab, and my *chauss* flattered me by saying that at first sight everyone would take me for a true believer.[*] I mentioned my maternal surname to him, which struck a chord, for it was a common family name among them; and, as a matter of fact, I am pleased and gratified by this genealogy that makes me a presumptive relative of Mohammed.[2] Be this as it may, the old Albarracíns of San Juan took such pride in their noble lineage, that for them the son of the house of Alba would have been, at very best, a nobody.[3] An aunt of mine, almost a beggar, used to

[a] *Diccionario geografico histórico* [Geographic-Historical Dictionary], article on Albarracín. [Author's note]
[*] A "*chauss*" is a civil servant acting as a guide.—Ed.

arrive at the house from her land in Angaco astride a dreadful-looking, broken-down nag, bearing huge saddlebags stuffed with vegetables and chickens, cursing out Don So-and-So who had failed to greet her because she was poor. A review would then follow of the wretched man's four lineages, in which the second or third generation was sure to include a mulatto on one side and a cross between an Indian and a negro on the other, who in addition was excommunicated. I, however, have found the Albarracíns at the brink of the common grave of the impoverished and nameless masses. Besides that aunt, there was another brother of hers, an idiot, whom she supported; my uncle Francisco made his living treating horses, which is to say, being a veterinarian without knowing it, just as M. Jourdain had written in prose without suspecting it.⁴ As for my mother's other eleven brothers and sisters, several of their children now wear the poncho and go barefoot, working as peons at a real and a half a day.*

Still and all, this family has occupied a place of distinction during the Spanish colony, and has produced eminent and illustrious men who have worn the mortarboard and the miter, and have honored letters in the halls of learning, and on the rostrum of congresses. The Albarracíns are distinguished, even among the plebeians, by their green or blue eyes, as I said before, and by their prominent, thin and high-bridged, though not aquiline, noses. They are noted for transmitting from generation to generation intellectual aptitudes that would seem to be organic, signs of which have appeared in four or five generations of Dominican friars, ordained priests, and which culminate in Fray Justo de Santa María, bishop of Cuyo.⁵ The heads of this family founded the Convent of Saint Domingo in San Juan, and to this day the family preserves the patronage and keeps the feast day of the saint, whom we have all come to call Our Father.† There is a Domingo in each of the branches into which the family is divided, just as there have always been two or even three Dominican friars among the Albarracíns at any one time. One of my mother's brothers, Don Juan Pascual, was a secular priest of the Conception, an excellent theologian and a dyed-in-the wool unitarian; and until the convent was closed in 1825, the choir always contained a representative

---

*The "real" was a silver coin worth about U.S. $0.10.—Ed.

† The word "convent," both in English and Spanish, can refer to male as well as female religious houses. Here it refers to a male house.—Ed.

of the patronal family of the Order.[6] It is well known that in those Middle Ages of the colonization of America, letters found refuge in the convents, a friar's hood being the recognized symbol of wisdom, a talisman, perhaps, for protecting the mind against all heretical thought. It didn't, however, entirely protect the mind of the celebrated Fray Miguel Albarracín, whose glorious memory has been preserved to this day as the pride and joy of the convent.

There are strange manias that obsess the human spirit in given epochs; curiosities of thought that arise, one knows not why, as though present conditions signaled the need to gratify them. Following upon the philosopher's stone that gave rise to chemistry in Europe, came the famous question of the Millenium, in which an important figure like Saint Vincent Ferrer was made to appear the fool.[*] Various have discoursed on the Millenium: noteworthy among them the Chilean Lacunza, whose work was recently published in London. Long before him, Doctor Fray Miguel had brought his wisdom to bear on the arduous problem; monastic tradition had it that Fray Miguel was divinely inspired, so vast was his knowledge. The folio he produced on the subject was examined by the Inquisition of Lima, the author summoned before the Holy Office, accused of heresy; and, much to the consternation of his brothers, he repaired to that distant tribunal to answer the fearful charge.

The Inquisition of Lima was a phantom of terror that Spain had sent to America to intimidate "foreigners," the only heretics it feared; and, lacking sympathizers of Judaism and heresy, from time to time the Inquisition would bait some aging *beata* who claimed to be in holy congress with the Virgin Mary through the intercession of angels and seraphim; or some other such woman, less refined, who preferred commerce with the fallen angel.[†] The Inquisition would pretend not to notice for a long time, it would lie in wait, and when the reputation for sanctity or bedevilment had ripened into sufficient notoriety, it would pounce upon the hapless, moonstruck woman, bring her before the Holy

---

[*]The "question of the Millenium" was a pseudo-mystic belief, dating from the high Middle Ages, that proclaimed the end of the world and on occasion verged on heresy. It assumed various manifestations in France, Germany, and the north of Italy.—Ed.

[†]One of the colloquial meanings of the Spanish word "*beata*" is "female religious fanatic."—Ed.

Tribunal, and after a lengthy and scholarly trial, make of her all-too-human flesh an agreeable and lively wick for the flames, to the deep satisfaction of the communities, workers, and higher clergy, who attended the ceremony by the thousands.

Documents exist in Lima of a number of trials of autos-da-fé, among them a very notable one against Angela Carranza, a native of the city of Córdoba del Tucumán, who moved to the city of Lima around 1665 and began to acquire a reputation for saintliness and for being in grace with God. Eight years later she gave herself over to writing her revelations, claiming to have been assisted and inspired by the doctors of the Church. These writings came to comprise 7,500 pages, in the form of a diary, until the month of December 1688, when they fell into the hands of the Inquisition of Lima, which found them heretical and blasphemous. Locked up in the Inquisition's dungeons on December 21, 1688, she was subjected to a trial that lasted for six years, at the end of which she was condemned to "appear as a penitent in a public auto-da-fé, bearing the green candle, a rope around her neck, and then to be confined in a cloister for a period of four years." This sentence was executed on December 20, 1693, as attested to in an account published in Lima by the Royal Printing Office in 1695. The woman's name is still remembered in every town in Peru, and the aforesaid description of the auto-da-fé, in which she is discussed, is one of the strangest books ever published in Lima.

This *beata*'s great crime was to have become deeply and mystically infatuated with two gentle personages of our Christian history: Saint Ann and Saint Joaquim, whom she describes in full detail. Our Lady Saint Ann was "very beautiful, rather fully fleshed, thick-lipped, hands very pale. And Saint Joaquim, with coarse features and a large nose, although an old man, did not arouse repulsion in his wife for he was clean and well dressed. The issue of the Lady Saint Ann's pregnancy were Christ and Mary, but Christ as Mary's head; and when Christ was born of Our Lady Saint Ann, Joachim and Ann were also reborn; and when Saint Ann fed the Holy Virgin of her milk, Jesus Christ also sucked; and from the breasts of Saint Ann sucked only Christ and Mary, but the first who sucked was Jesus Christ."

After the *beatas* came the "foreigners," of whom, among others, was one Juan Salado, a Frenchman, who was burned at the stake for no other rational cause than the novelty of being French, a *rara avis* in the colonies at the time, and an object of hatred among the Spanish people.

However, as always happens with absolute and iniquitous powers, in Lima, among the victims of the Inquisition, there once fell a relative of Saint Ignatius of Loyola who, accused of being a practicing Jew by his servants who wanted to rob him, died in prison, and the holy tribunal had him buried in secret. With the passage of time, however, one of the servants died, and on his deathbed he confessed to his villainy, and the Inquisition offered to make reparations to the corpse, which was exhumed for that purpose. One can get a good idea of the horribly puerile customs of the time from the following extracts of the sentence of acquittal: "Don Juan de Loyola Haro de Molina, a native of the city of Ica where he obtained the honorable positions of maister of the campe of the battalion, and several times that of mayor, having the first vote in his illustrious city council and regiment, slightly older than 60 years of age, unmarried, who, while a prisoner of this holy office, died. He came forth to the ceremony, in the form of a statue, and dressed as an innocent, all in white and with a palm in its hand, he was read a decree of absolution that acquitted the deceased of the crimes of *heresy and Judaism*, of which he had been accused by malicious conspiracy and false calumny. The good name, reputation, and prestige he enjoyed before imprisonment thus restored, it was ordered that he be taken out in the company of two important personages named by the holy tribunal so that they could sponsor him in the procession of prisoners, and, when the ceremony in the church was being prepared, that the statue be placed amidst the most highly esteemed of the assemblage; and rescinding all confiscations and sequestrations of his real estate and wealth, that everything be returned in accordance with the inventory taken at the time they were confiscated; and that, should his brothers, nephews, and relatives wish to parade the statue through the most transited public thoroughfares, upon an elegantly accoutered white horse, they might do so on the day following the ceremony, in which the ministers of the holy tribunal were to carry out the penalty of lashes that was administered to each prisoner; and that in consideration of the body having been buried secretly under orders of the holy tribunal in a chapel of the church of the Saint Mary Magdalen, a convent of Saint Dominic, they might exhume it in order to carry out last rites, removing him to the place that with his last wishes he chose for his burial; and that confirmation of this act be sent to his brothers and relatives, so that the calumny suffered should not at any time constitute a hindrance to their obtaining the most distinguished posts, be they political, or employment with the holy office, the Tribunal honoring them with the pardons deemed proportionate to vouchsafing the innocence of the aforesaid Don Juan de Loyola, deceased. His sponsors were Don Fermín de Carvajal, Count of Castillejo, and Don Diego de Hesles Campero, Brigadier of His Majesty's Royal Armies and Official Secretary of His Excellency, Señor Count de Super Unda, Viceroy of Lima."

Describing this unusual rehabilitation, a writer originally from Lima says: "In the procession of the holy office from its headquarters to Saint Dominic . . . two lackeys in opulent livery carried a statue, which, bearing on its breast a sign, elegantly engraved on a silver plaque, displayed the full name of the innocent Don Juan de Loyola, who, falsely accused of the heinous crimes of *heresy and of being a practicing Jew*, died in 1745 while a prisoner of this holy tribunal, even though shortly prior to his demise, the iniquitous conspiracy of false calumny had already begun to come to light. The statue was dressed in a robe of *white lamé*, the color that symbolizes innocence, decorated with the finest Milanese gold-appliqué work and diamond buttons, and picked out with numerous jewels of great price, which further enhanced the beauty of the cloth. In one hand, the statue held a palm, insignia of Loyola's triumph, and in the other his cane, its handle of gold inlaid with precious stones, in honor of his having obtained the distinctions and eminent posts of maister of the campe of the cavalry, and several times that of mayor in the city of Ica, of which he was a native, being a member of the most illustrious House of Loyola, in the village of Azpeitia of the province of Guipúzcoa."[b]

In like fashion, the scourge of the poor confederation, when he can no longer find any *savage* unitarian to hand over to the holy office of the Mazorca, seizes upon a Camila O'Gorman, an unborn child, and a priest living in sin, to have them killed like dogs, in order to revive, from time to time, the terror lulled to sleep by the abject submission of debased peoples.[8] Brutal despotism has never invented anything new. Rosas is the disciple of Dr. Francia and Artigas in their atrocities, and the heir of

---

[b] Account of the unusual auto da fé held in the Church of Saint Dominic on October 19, 1749, etc., by Don J. Eusebio Llano Zapata, an author who has written many other interesting works; he traveled extensively in Europe and America, and the fact that he was born and brought up in Lima is not widely known. [Author's note]

the Spanish Inquisition in his persecution of enlightened men and for-eigners.[9] The three have brutalized Paraguay, Spain, and the Argentine Republic, leaving behind them a legacy of ignorance and shame for years and even centuries to come. Close to a hundred years ago, the French moralist La Bruyère wrote: "Neither art nor science is needed to exercise tyranny, and the policy that only consists of spilling blood, is extremely limited and without refinement; it inspires us to murder those whose life is an obstacle to our ambition; and a man born cruel does that without difficulty. This is the most horrible and the crassest way to stay in power or to elevate oneself."[c]

What more can we now say about Rosas, that pathetic imitation of an old man, with a few brutalities of his own invention? Tiberius ordered that a red ribbon be placed on his portrait and, as Tacitus relates, citizens were lashed in the streets of Rome two thousand years ago if found not wearing the emperor's effigy on their chest. The Inquisition had its pro-scriptive catch phrases, such as *"heretics," "Judaizers,"* like the *"savage* uni-tariarns" of today; and so unmistakable is the filiation of these ideas, that Colonel Ramírez has called me a "Jew" in order to curry favor with the Argentine Inquisitor.[10] Wretched Spaniards!

I return to the learned Fray Miguel Albarracín, who was summoned to appear before that fearful tribunal, perforce to justify audacious doc-trines that he had pronounced regarding the Millenium. Fortunately, the friar was, so they say, eloquent like a Cicero, whose language he pos-sessed without par; profound like a Saint Thomas; subtle like a Duns Scotus; and with God interceding and, I suspect, with neither him nor the Inquisition understanding one iota of all that hodgepodge of conjec-tures about a prophesy that forecasts a change in the fate of the world, he emerged triumphant from the battle, amazing his judges, who were also of the Dominican Order, with those treasures of scholastic sophistry of which he made ample ostentation and display.[12] What is worth noting is that a few years after he produced his writings on the Millenium, the South American revolution of independence broke out, as if that theo-logical itch had been just a hint of the commotion to come.

My uncle Fray Pascual, seeing that I was a bright lad and eager to learn, explained Lacunza's work to me, telling me with indignant pride: "Study this book. It is the work of the great Fray Miguel, my uncle, and

[c] *Les Caractères,* by La Bruyère, Vol. i, p. 232. [Author's note][11]

not of Lacunza, who robbed him of the credit, removing the manuscript from the Inquisition's archives, where it was deposited." He then proceeded to show me the reference that Lacunza makes to a work on the Millennium by an American author whom he dared not cite. Afterwards, I have thought that family vanity made my uncle unjust with poor old Lacunza.

The maister of the campe Don Bernardino Albarracín is said to have come from Esteco, the sunken city, in the surrounding areas of which the family owned hundreds of leagues by royal grant, and which was later inherited by one Señora Balmaceda, a surname that has disappeared today but that has provided the name for a bridge and, on the maternal side, a governor for San Juan.[13] The son of the maister of the campe, Don Cornelio, married the daughter of Don José de la Cruz Irarrázabal, of Santiago de Chile, a family extinct there as well, which has left to posterity the church of Santa Lucía, founded and endowed through the munificence of Doña Antonia Irarrázabal, and the feast of the Sweet Name of Mary, the sponsorship of which is still maintained by a branch of our family. The houses of the Sweet Name, now rundown for having served to quarter troops, because of their size, once served as the sumptuous residence of the wealthy and powerful Doña Antonia, who, not having children, used to be visited regularly by my mother or other of her nieces.

There are details so curious in colonial life that I cannot proceed without mentioning them. The family was attended by noisy groups of black slaves of both sexes. In the guilded bed chamber of Doña Antonia, two young slave girls would pass the night watching over her slumber. At mealtime, a six-piece orchestra of male slaves played sonatas on violins and harps to liven the feast of their masters; and at night, two female slaves, after taking the chill off her bed with silver bed warmers, and perfuming the rooms, proceeded to divest their mistress of her petticoats of rich brocade, damask or *melania* that she used at home, where her pretty little feet wore silk stockings with slashes of color, which she sent by the basketful to be darned in the homes of her less-favored relations. On grand festive days, precious fabrics embossed in gold, still preserved in chasubles at Santa Lucía, lent luster to her figure, which, wreathed in clouds of Holland lace, was set off all the more brilliantly by enormous topaz earrings, coral chokers, and the rosary of aventurines, precious coffee-colored stones flecked with gold, and which, divided into groups of ten by bars of gold twisted into spirals and big as hen's eggs, reached almost to her knees, ending in a large wooden cross that had touched the Holy Places of Jerusalem and that was mounted in gold and encrusted with diamonds.[14] Still found in the old estates are elaborate garments and decorations of that era that dazzle the poor inhabitants of today, and allow the more knowledgeable among us to suspect that there has been a decline. Doña Antonia frequently went riding on horseback, preceded and followed by slaves, to check on her vineyards, the old trunks of which are still to be seen in the chantries of Santa Lucía.

In the house, once or twice a year, a strange activity would take place. The heavy doors to the street, studded with enormous copper nails, would be closed shut, and both patios would be sealed off from each other, in order to keep the children and the servants out; then, my mother tells me, the black woman Rosa, cunning and curious like a monkey, would whisper the news to her: "There's a *sunning* today!" Cautiously placing a small ladder under a window that faced the patio, the crafty slave lifted up my mother, still but a slight child, taking care that very little of her head showed, in order that she might spy on what was going on in the big patio. My mother, who is truth incarnate, tells me that, large as it was, the patio was covered with hides upon which they had laid out in the sun a thick layer of blackened pieces of eight so as to rid them of their mold; and two old Negroes who were the custodians of the treasure moved from hide to hide carefully turning the sonorous grain. Patriarchal customs of those bygone times, in which slavery did not corrupt the good qualities of the loyal Negro![15] I have known Uncle Agustín, and another black, Antonio, a master mason, who belonged to the estate of Don Pedro del Carril, the last man of enormous wealth and power in San Juan, who together, until 1840, held two bars of gold and several bags of coins in safekeeping for their master's family. It was the mania of the colonials to hoard peso upon peso, and to take pride in doing so. In San Juan people still talk of caches of silver buried by the old-timers, a popular tradition that recalls the past opulence, and not even three years ago, the storehouse and patios of Rufino's vineyard were excavated in search of the thousands that he was said to have left and that at his death could not be found. What could have happened, oh you colonials, to the fortunes of your grandfathers? And you, federal governors, military scourges of the people, could you amass, by squeezing dry, by torturing an entire city, the sum of pesos that only sixty years ago was enclosed in a single patio belonging to Doña Antonia Irarrázabal?

I have been astounded in the United States to see one or two banks in every town of a thousand souls, and to know that there are millionaire property owners everywhere. In San Juan, not a single fortune remains after twenty years of confederation: the Carrils, Rosas, Rojos, Oros, Rufinos, Jofrés, Limas, and many other powerful families lie prostrated in poverty, and descend day by day into the mass of the destitute. The Spanish colonies had their way of life, and they got along well under the king's indulgent tutelage; but you people, convinced that the least qualified is the one who governs best, have invented kings with long roweled spurs who just dismounted from the colts they were taming on the *estancias.* The wealth of modern nations is the exclusive issue of cultivated intelligence. It is fomented by the railroads, steamships, machinery, the fruits of science; they give life, liberty for all, free movement, the postal service, the telegraph, the newspapers, debate, in short, liberty. Barbarians! You are committing suicide; in ten years time your sons will be beggars or highwaymen. Consider England, France, and the United States, where there is no *Restaurador de las leyes* [Restorer of the Laws], nor stupid *Héroe del desierto* [Hero of the Desert], armed with a whip, a dagger, and gang of wretches to shout and put into effect the slogan of "Death to the *savage* unitarians," that is to say, those who no longer exist, and among whom there were so many distinguished Argentineans![16]

Have you heard, re-echoing throughout the world, any names other than those of Cobden, the wise English reformer; Lamartine, the poet; or those of Thiers and Guizot, the historians; and always everywhere, on the rostrums, in congresses, the government, savants and not peasants or rude herdsmen, like the ones you, at your own peril, have endowed with absolute power?[17]

8

The Oros

Doña Elena Albarracín wedded Don Miguel de Oro, the son, according to family tradition, of Captain Don José de Oro, who came over to the Conquest upon the cessation of the Great Captain's wars in Italy.[1] She brought him a dowry of worldly treasures and the patronage of Santo Domingo, which is still conserved among their descendents; and if two generations did not prove false the reputation for intelligence that ran in the Albarracín blood, on Don Miguel's side their children were endowed with a passionate imagination, bold characters, and such vigor in spirit and action that even the women of that house are distinguished by their extraordinary attributes, in which ambition and thirst for glory go hand in hand. Don Miguel had a brother, a cleric, who was mad; one of his daughters, a nun, is mad; and the presbyter Don José de Oro, my teacher and mentor, had such strange quirks of character that, sometimes to excuse his actions, people would attribute the extravagances of his youth to the madness that ran in the family. Chaplain of the 11th Regiment of the Army of the Andes, a first-rate horseman, companion in brawls and escapades of the celebrated Juan Apóstol Martínez, the cassock not stopping him from wearing the battalion uniform and the long saber of the period, he had the sufficient audacity to fling a handsome wench across the rump of his horse at the entrance of a dance, and draw his scimitar and slash the face of the boldest swain, if the fellow got the strange idea to take it amiss.[2] His companions in roistering have assured me that in such capers there was more knavery and mischief than real debauchery.[3]

My earliest years are linked to the home of the Oros by all the ties that make of a child an adopted member of a family. My godmother, and the wife of Don Ignacio Sarmiento, my uncle, was the matron Doña Paula, gentle in nature, like a dove, equally grave and affectionate, like a queen, and a prototype among us of the perfect mother. Don José, the presbyter, took me from school to his side and taught me Latin; I accompanied him in his exile in San Luis, and, as teacher and pupil, we felt so much love for each other, we had so many conversations, he talking and I listening with rapt attention, that, if all were merged into one single conversation, I deem it would produce a speech that would take two years to deliver. My intellect was molded under the impression of his, and it is to him that I owe my instincts for public life, my love of country and freedom, and my consecration to the study of my native land, from which I have never been distracted, not by poverty, exile, nor long years of absence. I emerged from his hands with my mind fully formed at the age of fifteen, reckless like him, insolent toward absolute rulers, chivalrous and vain, truthful like an angel, with notions about many things, and laden with facts, recollections, and stories about the past and of what was then the present, which fitted me afterward to pick up with ease the thread and spirit of events, to be inspired by a passion for good, to speak and write bluntly and forcefully, without the exercise of journalism finding me devoid of resources for the prodigality of ideas and thoughts that it demands.[4] Except for the turbulent activity of his youth, for I have always been reserved and timid, his entire soul transmigrated into mine, to the point where my family in San Juan, on seeing me take off in flights of rapture, would say, "That's Don José Oro himself talking"; for even his mannerisms and the inflections of his high and resonant voice had rubbed off on me. All the while I lived with him I considered him a saint, and am glad of it, since for that reason he was able to transmit his sage counsel to me, and its efficacy was not impaired by the doubt that a contrary example can inspire. As a bearded man, I learned his story from the hearsay of others. He was a horse breaker of renown, who vied in prowess with Don Juan Manuel Rosas, and for the fiesta of the *acequión* he would descend from the mountains where he had his ranch *Los Sombreros*, riding a colt, his legs shielded by *guardamontes* that allowed him to negotiate ravines and marshes and to withstand the tall, dense nettles that make travel in our countryside so difficult.* He retained his physical energy into old age, and once I saw him seize a hulking Spaniard and send him rolling on the ground ten yards off. He was daring and took pride in his boldness, was fond of weaponry, and always carried a brace of pistols on his saddlebow. He dressed like a *paisano*

Acequión: Margarita B. Pontieri, author of the most useful set of textual notes in all of the many Spanish-language editions of *Recuerdos* that were consulted for the preparation of this edition, describes "*acequión*" as a traditional annual fiesta in Cuyo that celebrated the life-giving power of water. *Acequia* in Spanish means "irrigation ditch"; the noun suffix *ión* acts here as an aumentative. In the first edition of *Recuerdos* (1850), the word appeared as *Acequión*, but was changed to the lower case in the second edition of 1885. In Sarmiento's later work *El Chacho: Ultimo caudillo de la montonera de los llanos. Episodio de 1863*, the author refers several times to a small settlement named Acequión, to the east of the city of San Juan. See Note 40 in Domingo F. Sarmiento, *Recuerdos de provincia*, ed. Susana Zanetti and Margarita B. Pontieri (Buenos Aires: Centro Editor de América Latina, 1979), 230.

   "Ranch"—In the Spanish original, the text says "hacienda de ganados," but here the unmodified word "ranch" has been used, since in Spanish "ganado" can refer to either "ganado mayor" (cows, bulls, oxen, mules, horses, etc.) or "ganado menor" (sheep, goats, pigs, etc.), and in the case of San Juan in the 1810s and '20s, it would be unwise to assume, without further information, that Oro's ranch was dedicated to cattle. During the colonial and early independent periods, both kinds of *ganado* were raised in San Juan, but, as opposed to the littoral, progressively characterized by its cattle culture, it was "ganado menor" that predominated throughout the Argentine interior (Halperín, *Politics*, 13). In fact, a local report written in June of 1835, ostensibly to promote economic cooperation among San Juan, Mendoza, and San Luis, suggests that at this time, the raising of *ganado* of either kind was was not a major economic activity in San Juan. During the hegemony of Juan Facundo Quiroga in Cuyo (1827–1835), most of San Juan's commercial traffic was in the direction of Buenos Aires, and its most direct route was via San Luis. According to the report, San Juan and San Luis were mutually dependent because San Luis provided San Juan (and Mendoza) with *ganado*, but in turn provided a consumer market for the products of the other two provinces (De Varese and Arias, *Historia*, 211–213). Also, in the first half of the nineteenth century, the cultivation of alfalfa pasture, for grazing by herds of *ganado* raised elsewhere and in transit to remote markets, was slowly emerging as a new model of livestock economy in San Juan (Halperín, *Politics*, 16). Videla describes the province of San Juan as lacking in the appropriate natural characteristics for *ganadería*, that is, livestock production (I, 1962, 69).

   "*Guardamontes*"—In *El Chacho: Ultimo caudillo de la montonera de los llanos. Episodio de 1863*, Sarmiento provides a good definition of the word: "At the base of the Andes are two cities, San Juan and Mendoza, which do not modify with their luxuriant agriculture, except for a few leagues around their circumference, the aspect of flatland, occupied in part by sand dunes, in part by lagoons, and to the north covered by thorny forest, *garabato* and *uña de león* [plants], that rip both clothes and skin, if these make contact. These thorns, curved with a jacket, and did not read the breviary, by special dispensation from the pope.* He loved to dance with a passion, and he and I have gone astepping every Sunday of an entire year, joining in *contradanzas* and *pericones* in San Francisco del Monte, in the Sierra de San Luis, in whose chapel he was priest and where he would call together, in the evenings after the daily homily, the local lasses, white or dark-skinned, for they come in every shade and are as pretty as young Dianas, with the idea of civilizing them a bit, because no improper thought was ever entertained in the course of these innocent pastimes.† I cannot say that he never kicked up his heels in his youth, for that is none of my concern. He was profoundly scornful of society, from which he fled, and was not to be seen in the city except on the feast day of Santo Domingo, or in the

---

or grown together like darts, would leave a passing man hanging like Absalom, if the branch did not give way to his weight. The peasants who inhabit these flatlands carry, when mounted, a parapet of hide on both sides of their horse, which covers their legs and rises sufficiently to let them lie down flat and cover their body and face behind the parapets' wings" (Domingo Faustino Sarmiento, *Los Caudillos: El General Fray Félix Aldao. El último caudillo de la montonera de los llanos: El Chacho* [Buenos Aires: El Ateneo, 1928], 83–84).—Ed.

* *"Paisano"*—Refers to a person who lives in the rural areas of Argentina and in accordance with traditional customs. Unlike the word *campesino* (peasant), it does not refer specifically to the kind of labor one performs or to his or her insertion in the social hierarchy. Rather, it stresses that a person has been born or brought up in the countryside and follows the traditional practices of his or her rural area. It is not a synonym of *gaucho*, but at times is used in its place. In the case of José de Oro, a landowner, dressing like a *paisano* would suggest that he dressed according to what elsewhere Sarmiento called the "American" and not the "European" or "civilized" fashion. In other words, he would not wear the contemporary bourgeois suit for men, which the mature Sarmiento called "universal" and in which he almost always insisted on being photographed, except when he was posing in a military uniform. In the nineteenth century, there were typical regional costumes for both the poor and the well-off, but male *paisanos* of both statuses would have worn a poncho and a *chiripá*. The *chiripá* was a quadrangular piece of cloth wrapped around the waist and sometimes used as a skirt, but often it was drawn between the thighs and reattached to the waist in the back and used in place of trousers. The definitions of *paisano* and *chiripá* are based on Félix Coluccio, *Diccionario de voces y expresiones argentinas* (Buenos Aires: Editorial Plus Ultra, 1979), 67, 148, and Daniel Granada, *Vocabulario rioplatense razonado*, I, II (Montevideo: Biblioteca Artigas, 1957), I, 217; II, 127–28.—Ed.

† *"Contradanzas"* and *"pericones"*—Popular dances. The *pericón* is an Argentine dance executed by even numbers of couples. The dance is interrupted from time to time so that one of the dancers can recite a stanza of poetry or make a witty remark, to which his or her partner must respond.—Ed.

pulpit. He once told me that by 1824 he had preached seventy-six sermons; and since I wrote down three or four of them for him, I can attest
to his concise oratory, replete with good sense and elevated ideas, expressed in a fresh language, and without that tiresome apparatus of
Latin quotes and biblified words. Gentlemen, he would say when he
began his sermon, addressing his audience from the back of the pulpit,
where he remained motionless, with his arms across his chest, to avoid
the hand waving of the ceremonial, and he would deliver his oration in
the tone of a conversation, similar to the system that Mr. Thiers has introduced with such brilliance in the French assembly.5 One time, while
dictating to me a sermon on Saint Raymund, he recalled an incident of
his boyhood when he had been trapped under an adobe wall that had
collapsed on top of him, and in order to set him free, it had been necessary to break up the wall by pounding on it with a spade while he was
still underneath. He was saved by the ironclad bones that framed his
body, positioned face down on top of his hands and feet, and the intercession of Saint Raymund, who was invoked by his sobbing mother,
upon whose heart resonated every blow of the spade, in fear that her
beloved son would be split wide open, while the brawny rascal shouted
from below: "Keep pounding, I'm still alright!" As he recalled this miracle on the part of the saint, a sob of gratitude made his voice break,
while he went on dictating to me; my eyes misted over, and heavy
teardrops fell on the paper, blurring the words and making it impossible
for me to continue, until a great, wrenching sob from him caused me to
follow suit, and hearing this, he held out his arms to me, and we wept
together for a long while, until he said, "Let's leave the rest of the work
for tomorrow. . . . We're acting like children!"

His way of imparting ideas to me would have done credit to the greatest of teachers. We kept a notebook, entitled *"Diálogo entre un ciudadano
y un campesino"* [Dialogue Between a Citizen and a Peasant], which I regret having lost not long ago. I was the citizen, and he, with his knowledge of Spanish grammar, made comparisons with the Latin, pointing
out to me the differences. Declinations other than those of Nebrija were
our topic, and a study of the laws of conjugation was followed by that of
regular verbs that I formed upon the roots.6 My questions and his an-
swers began, day by day, to fill the diary, and, while still studying the
rudiments, I soon began to translate not Ovid or Cornelio Nepos, but a
geography book by the Jesuits. I read it out loud to him, almost always in
the shade of some olive trees, and more than for Latin, I developed a lik-

ing for the history of nations, which my teacher would enliven with digressions on the geographical content of the translation. And so, I forgot Latin and restudied it several times, but ever since childhood, my favorite subject has been geography. We spent the time in varied conversations, and from these some useful point always remained fixed within my memory. All accidents in life provide food for thought of some sort or another, and I could feel my horizon expanding visibly from day to day. On one occasion he said to me, "Hand me that book on the chest of drawers." In reaching for it, I bumped the piece of furniture, causing the beautifully carved crucifix upon it to shake and the crown of braided hemp upon its wooden hair to slip down and come to rest upon its shoulders. "What happened to Our Lord?" he asked in a soft voice. "I was getting the book, and the chest of drawers. . . ." "That doesn't matter," he replied, "explain to me what happened and why." I did so, and he added: "What you just saw took place in Chile one time when there was an earthquake," and he told me the story of the *Señor de Mayo* [Lord of May], with comments that would have seemed sacrilegious to the ordinary believer, quoting to me provisions of the Council of Trent regarding ignoble images and the authenticity of miracles and the *legal* basis, so to speak, for being required to believe in them.[7] Not many years ago, in commenting on a play, I added, without realizing it, some sentence or other that alluded to the nun Zañartu.[8] What an outcry this provoked in Santiago! Denunciations rained down thick and fast upon my head because of the *slander,* and even a leading churchman put in his two cents' worth against *the scandalous outrage.* Where in the devil, I asked myself, dumbfounded, did I come up with this accursed story? As best as I could remember, it was something my Uncle José had told me, but which I thought was based on the authority of *res judicata* [prior adjudication] of a hundred years ago. I kept my explanation to myself and, as I withdrew, fired back deserved broadsides at my adversaries.

Don José took it upon himself to purge all harmful preoccupations from my budding young spirit, and so will-o'-the-wisps, hobgoblins, and the souls of the dead disappeared, after lingering doubts and even resistance on my part. One night, we were alone in our solitary room in San Francisco del Monte, and in the church next door there was, lying in state, the body of a woman who had died of dropsy; "Go, Domingo," he said, "and fetch me my missal from the sacristy. I must consult a *speibus* in it that contradicts Nebrija." I had to enter by the church door, walk past the coffin surrounded by candles and take one, or resign myself to being swallowed up in the dark canyon of the building, and enter the sacristy. I was sweating buckets at the church door for a good long time, taking one step forward and then backward, until vanquished by that fear that, in stimulating itself redoubles its power, I refused to enter, and turned back, tail between my legs, to confess to my uncle that I was afraid of the dead. I was resolved, like a braggart put to the test, to bear the shame of humiliation, even of scorn, when I noticed my uncle's placid face through a window, so tranquil as he slowly puffed out a long plume of smoke just drawn from his cigar. At the sight of that noble countenance, I felt so unworthy that I turned, went back into the church, passed by the corpse, and propelled now by the sentiment of honor and no longer by fear, I felt around for the book, and came out holding it on high as though I were already saying to my teacher: Here's the proof that I'm not afraid. On the way back, however, it seemed to me from a distance that there was not sufficient room to squeeze by the corpse without risk of the dead woman grabbing me by the legs. This grim thought unnerved me for a moment, and circling the coffin, with my body and eyes turned toward it and my back brushing against the wall, moving sideways and then backward in order not to lose sight of it until I gained the doorway, I emerged from that adventure safe and sound, and my uncle received the book, looked up what he wanted, and found it. But in all his life he never knew of the perils that had shaken my spirit in those six minutes. I had been contemptible, great, heroic, and cowardly, and had passed through the fires of hell, so as not to feel unworthy of his approval.

Don José de Oro's history is one I can reconstruct from memory. He studied in Chile and was ordained there, and I am familiar with almost all the vicissitudes of his life in school. As a young priest, fervent, and a gaucho, he was driving mules to Salta when the reconquest of Chile offered a worthier outlet for his fiery young manhood.[9] He took part in the battle of Chacabuco and ministered last rites under heavy fire to a number of the mortally wounded.[10] In France, I was never able to get San Martín to discuss his grievances against the cleric Oro, but the two had clashed, and the Oros were put in prison as supporters of the Carreras, or rather, as enemies of San Martín and Don Ignacio de la Rosa, his lieutenant in San Juan.[11] He harbored deep rancor toward them and always spoke to me of their feuds. However, something very serious must have happened, for later, when we met again, Don José had been shut up for years in his vineyards, having no contact with others, and cut off from involvement in public affairs. During the enlightened administration of Don Salvador M. del Carril, he was appointed representative of the provincial junta, and his presence was enough to put an end to a serious matter that had been debated for a long time and that had stirred up the public, which crowded around the doors and windows of the Jofré drawing room, where the meetings were being held.[12] The matter at hand was the rescinding of the tithe on holy oils, the toll we pay at the entrance to life; and the cleric Astorga, who had been an *unreconstructed Goth*, was then a *fervent Catholic,* and was later to be a *firebrand federalist,* was stirring up the fanaticism of the very same poor whom reformers were seeking to relieve of the burden of that tax, in precisely the same way that the barbarians now apply the epithets of *savages* and *foreigners* to those who wish to return these same poor to their place among civilized peoples.* The presbyter Oro, as soon as he was sworn in, took the floor, separated the religious issue from the purely financial one, confounded Astorga, who sat scratching his chair with his contracted fingers, and the tithe on holy oils was abolished, and so it remains to this day.

Later, Don José left the party of the progressive men of the time, who numbered in the hundreds, and had a falling out with Carril, not so much over liberal ideas as over hurt feelings. I have heard tell of an incident from that time, which exhibits the strange mixture of lofty attributes and the most inexplicable extravagances. At the *Tapón,* a dammed-up stream belonging to the Oros, a gathering was under way, the purpose of which was to sound out opinion regarding the Carta de Mayo [May Charter].[13] Carril and half of San Juan were there, but Don José had not been invited, and in retaliation, he undressed at home as if for a ·bath, and, completely nude, got on his horse, and rode off to the *Tapón,* where, in view of the guests, he dove into the water; he took a leisurely swim, and springing agilely onto the back of his black horse that emphasized his forms, white and taut like those of an athlete among the ancients, he proceeded to return home, ignoring those who called out after him. I do not vouch for the authenticity of the tale, since I never saw him do anything extravagant.

---

* "Goths" [*godos*] was the derogatory term used by pro-independence creoles to refer to Spanish and creole royalists during the Wars of Independence (1810–1824).—Ed.

Such incidents drove him into the federalist party of the time, which included among its ranks respectable and enlightened men.

Doctor Don Salvador María del Carril was the eldest of Don Pedro de Carril's offspring, a graduate of the University of Córdoba, an outstanding disciple of the celebrated Dean Funes, imbued with the spirit of Rivadavia, and reflecting, in the haughtiness and elegance of his manners, the culture of the time and the nobility of his family.

His words were few, precipitated, like those of the leader who feels under no obligation to give explanations to underlings, accompanied by sudden movements and impatient, disdainful gestures. Carril was the generous aristocrat who, in granting rights to the masses, seemed convinced beforehand that they were incapable of appreciating the gift, and he took little care to make the gift acceptable. "Be free," he told them in the *Carta de Mayo*, "for you are too unfit for me to take you as slaves." And he was right! The Spanish settlers have shown the same sentiment as the old emancipated Negroes, who preferred slavery under the master's roof, shunning a freedom that would have required them to think for themselves. Carril dictated so fast that his scribes had trouble keeping up with him, an indication of the clarity and force with which his ideas followed one upon the other.

The influence he wielded in San Juan bordered on fascination. The populace en masse had faith in his talents and wisdom, and every reform he introduced was accepted in advance and backed by public approval. So great must his popularity have been in the early days of his administration, and so painfully aware his adversaries of their own limited numbers, that in order to oppose ratification of the Carta de Mayo, they circulated petitions among the women.[14] The lofty organizational measures he proposed did, however, produce discontent, and a garrison of fifty men, barely enough to cover the watch, rebelled and removed him from command. Carril and his supporters emigrated to Mendoza, from whence a division came and put down the uprising. Then an incident took place that demonstrates the noble school to which he belonged. On the eve of the battle of Las Leñas, he called all his followers together in his tent and explained to them the need to defray, out of their own pockets, the costs of the expedition, which would be reimbursed by the National Treasury.[15] However, those unseasoned spirits, blinded by victory and chafing with resentment at the injustices, exactions, and brutalities suffered, preferred to impose fines upon those neighbors who were implicated in the uprising of July 26.[16] The overwhelming majority voted

Carril down, and not wishing to be compromised, he relinquished command. Those who turned a deaf ear on his counsel and let themselves be carried away by the heat of the moment have lived to regret it! The measures of persecution of those days were later avenged by horrible reprisals, and all, with few exceptions, subsequently atoned for their original mistake.

Don Salvador María was appointed minister of the treasury by Rivadavia and proved himself equal to the demands of the post. He resigned along with Rivadavia, until, with the December 1st Revolution, he was again appointed minister by the provisional government, and followed the fortunes of his party.[17] He married in Mercedes, in the Banda Oriental, went into business for a time, resurfaced in 1840 with Lavalle, as commissioner for the Argentineans in Montevideo; he attended the conferences held on the island of Martín García with the commanders of the French squadron; he was later appointed quartermaster general of the Army, and if Lavalle had followed his advice, the revolution would have taken a different course.[18] He now lives in Brazil, in Santa Catalina, respected by all who know him.

San Juan owes to him the establishment of its one printing press, no longer in use after twenty-four years of relentless service; the creation of an *Official Registry;* the survey of the city's land; a public promenade; and an unsuccessful attempt to write a charter that would have designated and regulated the branches of government.[19] He surrounded himself with the province's most distinguished men, of whom there were many at the time; and the period of his administration was, without a doubt, San Juan's most brilliant. Today, his name is forgotten, like that of Laprida, Oro, and so many other men of genius of whom that province should be proud.[20]

Five families of Carrils, all of them headed by Don Salvador María's brothers, are now permanently settled in Copiapó, Santa Catalina, and Coquimbo, and, among them, they have managed to amass in exile a fortune bordering on half a million pesos; the family home in San Juan has served until this year as the episcopal palace, and the substantial assets of the former head of the family, Don Pedro, the richest man in San Juan, have been depleted and squandered in a distribution that remains unsettled after twelve years, as a consequence of ineptitude, laziness, and ignoble passions. The vineyards in the legacy occupy sixty-six square blocks, and the uncultivated lands lie sideways in a line seven leagues long from Low Street to the slopes of the Pie-de-Palo.

After the battle of Las Leñas, in which his side was defeated, Don
José de Oro emigrated to San Luis, and I went to join him soon after,
abandoning the engineering studies I had begun.[21] We loved each other
like father and son, I wanted to be with him, and my mother gratefully
approved. Some traces of our residence in San Francisco del Monte
must have remained there. We introduced flowers and vegetables, which
we cultivated, spending hours on end crouched around our firstborn, a
single-petal wallflower. We founded a school attended by the two Ca-
margo "boys," twenty-two and twenty-three years of age, respectively,
and we had to expel one other pupil because of his insistence on wanting
to marry a very pretty white girl, whom I was teaching to spell. I was the
schoolmaster, the youngest of all, for I was fifteen years old; but, as far as
the formation of my character was concerned, I had been a man for at
least two years, and woe to anyone who dared think he could overstep
the line between pupil and teacher on the basis of having bigger fists!
The chapel was off by itself in the midst of the fields, as happens in the
countryside of Córdoba and San Luis. Having had three months of engineering study, I drew up the plan for a village, the main square of
which we made triangular in order to make the most of a small piece of
canvas; we marked off a street, and if memory does not fail me, a Señor
Maximiliano Gatica worked on constructing the sidewalk. We tore
down the facade of the church that had been struck by lightning, and
built the ground floor of a tower and a choir of sturdy pillars of carob,
crowned with a natural *garabato*, found in the forest, which made three
arches, the center one higher than the others, on which I carved this inscription in large block letters: "*San Francisco del Monte de Oro, 1826.*"* By
what strange combination of circumstances was it that my first venture
in life should be to found a school and to lay out a town, the very same
efforts that are now revealed in my writings on *Educación popular* [Pop-
ular Education] and immigrant colonies?[22]

I used to wander about in the afternoons when it came time to fetch
wood; and in the neighboring forests, I would follow the course of a
stream by stepping along the stones; I would penetrate to the innermost
solitary recesses, accustoming my ears to the echoes, the soughing of the

---

*"*Garabato.*" In Argentina, *garabato* is the name for diverse bushes whose many
branches have thorns resembling hooks. See Note 5 above, on the word "*guardamontes.*"
—Ed.

palm trees, the hissing of snakes, the songs of the birds, until I came upon the hut of some *paisano,* where, recognizing me as the priest's protégé and the teacher at the little school, they would lavish attention on me. Toward evening I would return to our solitary chapel laden with my bundle of firewood and the cheeses or ostrich eggs given me by these good people. Those solitary excursions, that rough backland life among rustic folk, combined, however, with the cultivation of the spirit through the lessons and informal talk of my teacher, while my body was developing in the open air, in touch with the sadness of those places, left a profound impression upon my spirit, and I am constantly reminded of the physiognomies of those people, the sight of those fields, and even the smell of the vegetation of the palm trees in full leaf and of the red *peje* trees so spectacular and fragrant. Back home in the evenings, I would listen to a certain Ña Picho telling tales in the kitchen about witches, and then return later to my uncle's side to talk about what had happened, to read a book with him, and to prepare the next day's lessons.* One morning, a relative of mine appeared to take me back to San Juan, from where I was to be sent to Buenos Aires to be educated at government expense. My uncle let me make my own decision, and I dashed off the most indignant and poignant letter to my mother ever to have issued from the pen of a fifteen-year-old lad. Everything in it was, of course, pure nonsense! My father soon came for me, and then there was nothing more to be said. We parted in sadness, my teacher and I, without a word between us, he taking my hand and looking away so I would not see his tears. Ah! When we met on his return from the Santa Fe Convention, to which he had been named delegate in 1827, I was . . . a unitarian! The mind that he had developed with such care had seen the light, and on one occasion when we touched on the subject, he saw that I had deep, logical, and reasoned convictions, deserving of respect. After that, we met as friends; subsequently, when I was a grown man and a lieutenant in the army, I would visit him at night in his vineyard, where I spent the pleasantest of hours at his bedside listening to him talk, as he lay prostrate, given over to reminiscing freely. Once, I found him so downcast that I wondered for the first time whether in that moment his reason was clear. Later, I learned that the vapors of wine were enlivening that monotonous existence, in order to lift his spirits when the body flagged. During the time

* "Ña" is a common contraction of "Doña" in popular speech.—Ed.

we lived together, I never saw any signs of exceptional elation, even though he drank wine in moderate quantities, and in San Juan, this is an illness that carries off hundreds of people. As they grow old, disenchanted with life, without hope, without emotions, without theaters, without movement, for there is neither education nor freedom, many of them retire early to their vineyards. Loneliness and spiritual emptiness bring on boredom, this calls them to drink, as an antidote, and they end up withdrawing from society and giving themselves over to misanthropic, solitary, and permanent inebriation.

Don José de Oro died in 1836, as he had lived, the son of nature, the peasant, as he liked to style himself in the "Dialogue" with me. He slept behind closed doors in winter, and under the open sky in summer. He bolted from bed at three in the morning in all weathers, and his cough, familiar to everyone, was audible in the silence of the night, as he wandered about the vicinity of his vineyards. Never did the sun catch him abed. As the end drew near, he retired to the cordillera where he had his hacienda, to breathe the purer air, and he died, surrounded by a few family members, blessed by all, and with scarcely any pain. The goodness of this most exceptional and strange man exceeded all known bounds. He was warned one time that his overseer was stealing from him, to which he replied, laughing: "I know, but what in the devil am I to do? The scoundrel has a slew of kids, and if I fire him, they'll starve." When he was a minister in the government of Don José Tomás Albarracín in the year 1830, a forced contribution of six oxen payable in three days was levied on my mother, on account of me. My uncle José had signed the implacable order, and when my mother was at her wit's end, unable to figure out how she could come up with six oxen, she who had nothing to eat, the minister came into her house, saying, "Now, don't be foolish, you mustn't cry; half an hour ago a messenger left to bring down eight fat young bulls from my hacienda Los Sombreros, which they'll deliver to you so you can pay the contribution and stock up on provisions for the winter." More recently, Facundo demanded of her a contribution of clothing; and when the good priest heard of it, he arrived with his own wardrobe of trousers, jackets, and cloaks, and contrived to convert them into half a dozen uniforms for soldiers.

9

Fray Justo Santa María de Oro

Among those rascals, rowdies, and pranksters who were Don Miguel's sons, Justo, the eldest, stood out in contrast for the evenness of his temper and the tranquility of his contemplative soul. As a boy, he was relentlessly harassed by his brothers José and Antonio. They would pummel him with pillows when he was trying to sleep, pee in his boots when he was about to get up, and vex him every which way all day long, laying traps for him, accusing him to their stern mother of pranks they themselves had played to get him in trouble.

The child Justo had been given his name in order to assume the mantle of his uncle, Fray Justo Albarracín, who was the shining light of the monastery of Saint Dominic and the pride of the family at the time the lad was born. In those days, when aristocratic families were duly represented in the cloisters, the firstborn Oro was foreordained to carry on under the Dominican aegis the uninterrupted chain of family scholar-priests. He, of course, proved himself a worthy successor to his forebears and was sent to continue his studies in Santiago, then the capital of the provinces of Cuyo, where, at the age of twenty, having distinguished himself for his talent, he was already teaching theology.[1] He was ordained at twenty-one by dispensation of the pope, Pius VI, and then went on to the Dominican Recollect in pursuit of monastic perfection. His attributes of character, knowledge, and demeanor must have been considerable, since after he had been in their order for only a few years the Recollects requested him for their lifetime director, and the general of the order in Spain approved this petition.

The new prelate let himself be borne aloft by the creative spirit of his genius. The hacienda Apoquindo, which was community property, was supposed to be turned into a branch of the Dominican Recollect, and in order to obtain the necessary permits, or to have the general of the order accept his plans, he made a voyage to Spain, the Europe of those times, where the revolution of independence caught him by surprise. Like Bolívar, like San Martín and all those who felt themselves strong enough to act, he hastened to join his people, disembarked in Buenos Aires, spoke out in favor of the revolution, saw his family in passing, returned to his monastery in Chile, and after lending his support to the patriots until 1814, emigrated to the United Provinces when the Spanish regained control of Chile.[2] Appointed delegate to the Congress of Tucumán for the province of San Juan, together with the distinguished Laprida, who was elected President, he had the honor of signing the Act of Declaration of Independence of the United Provinces, and of participating in all the bold acts of that Congress; his was the motion adopted by the Congress to acclaim Saint Rose of Lima patron saint of America and defender of the South American independence.[3]

The reconquest of Chile opened the way for him to act again in the theater of his original honors, enhanced now through the prestige accorded him by his participation in the decisions of the Congress of Tucumán, which, at a distance, induced a kind of awe because of their solemnity and decisiveness. In 1818, he resolved one of the most serious problems that was retarding the progress of events. The religious orders, split into royalists and patriots, were responsible to the deputy general of the order, installed in Spain; and this could impair the friar's popular influence with respect to the progress of the revolution that was still not firmly entrenched. The provincial Fray Justo de Santa María declared the independence of the province of San Lorenzo Mártir of Chile in the Order of Preachers, as the Chilean patriots had declared the civil and political independence of the nation, indeed, as he himself had signed the act of emancipation of the United Provinces. Upon reading the capitulary documents of the governing council of the Order of Preachers, it is evident that they have been inspired by the genius of the Congress of Tucumán. "Fray Justo de Santa María de Oro—they say—Professor of Sacred Theology and humble prior and provincial of the same province. Venerable Fathers and dearest brothers: In accordance with the immutable principles of reason and natural justice, Chile declared its freedom given by the Creator of the Universe, decreed by the order of human events, and confirmed by the grace of the Gospel. In defiance of the ambition and fanaticism of the former Spanish throne, Chile shattered the chains of its enslavement, demolished all the ties that bound it to the sad condition of a colony, and, following the designs of Providence, declared itself a sovereign State, independent of all foreign domination. Claiming its freedom and in the exercise thereof, it constituted the higher branches of government that are to regulate and guide the nation to its prosperity.

"The church has, in every era, followed the advances of civilization and the aggrandizement of empires in support and sustenance of national independence. . . . From the time a state regains its liberty, all jurisdiction exercised by prelates of another land with respect to the secular and regular clergy is nullified. This reverts to the Supreme Pontiff. . . ."

Upon a foundation as solid as this, the independence of the Province of Santiago was declared, with all the powers of the deputy general of the order being invested in the same Fray Justo, provincial of the Dominican Recollect.

The monastery had, thus, conferred all that it could in honors, posts, and titles. Doctor Fray Justo Santa María de Oro needed a new horizon; a miter would sit well on the brow of the prior, provincial, and general of the order. Leo XII was then at work renewing relations interrupted by the revolution, between the Apostolic See and the American colonies. Wise policy seemed to suggest that he curry favor with independent America in order to exonerate the Apostolic See of the charge of complicity and connivance with the Spanish Crown. The for-so-many-reasons worthy delegate at one of the American congresses was, therefore, a candidate for the episcopate, which would give credibility to the Holy See's good intentions. Father Oro was aware of this, and he had agents in Rome who attended to his affairs. In 1827, I came recommended to him by his brother Don José, as a member of the family; he received me kindly, and at our second meeting, introduced me to his projects, describing all his accomplishments in order that I might fully satisfy the curiosity of his relatives on my return to San Juan. Indeed, bulls were not long in arriving that named him bishop *in partibus infidelium,* under the title of Thaumaco.[4] Cienfuegos invested him in San

Juan in 1830, soon after which he was made bishop of Cuyo by Gregory XVI who, for that purpose, separated this province from the bishopric of Córdoba.

This establishment of a new bishopric impelled Oro to take up the pen once more to clear the way of obstacles that threatened to interfere with his plans. At that time, the capitular priest for the vacant see of the Córdoba Cathedral was Doctor Don Pedro Ignacio de Castro Barros, former delegate to the Congress of Tucumán and titular priest at the main church of San Juan, the same one that was to be elevated to the status of cathedral. Since 1821, when he had been designated titular priest, the successive provincial governments had prevented him from taking up his functions, in order to escape the evil designs of that caudillo of fanaticism. The one who, as suffragan, officiated in his place was presbyter Sarmiento, today the Bishop of Cuyo, for whom bulls were on the way, elevating him to the eminence of dean of the new cathedral. Doctor Castro Barros, whether out of ambition or stubbornness, refused to recognize the papal bulls, summoned a meeting of the city council of Córdoba, and through illegal maneuvers, that even went so far as to cast doubt on the authenticity of the bulls, submitted a petition to the ecclesiastical tribunal to desist from carrying out the separation already ordered and implemented. Bishop Oro sent a pamphlet to be printed in Chile.[a] Doctor Castro Barros has published his appeal, so as to lend it authority, together with a panegyric of the late medieval Spanish saint Vincent Ferrer.[b] In the documents published by the Bishop Oro, there is to be found this sentence from the communiqué of the Governor of San Juan, dictated by Bishop Oro himself: "For which reason the government warns Señor Don Pedro Ignacio Castro that it considers the claims put forward in the note of August 15, which is addressed to it from Córdoba, an offense against religion, the unity of the Church, obedience to the Roman Pontiff, and the consideration due this Government of San Juan, and it issues this categorical reply with a reserve copy for the secret files of this administration." Barros's note, which was answered in this way, had been an attempt to subvert civil authority, as he

---

[a] *Defensa de la Vicaría Apostólica, etc.* . . . . [Defense of the Apostolic Vicariate, etc. . . .], impugned by the diocesan judge of the vacant See of Córdoba. Printed in Santiago de Chile, 1831, National Press, by M. Peregrino. [Author's note]

[b] Buenos Aires, 1836. Argentine Press. [Author's note]

had been able to do in Mendoza, in order to oppose the decision of the Apostolic See. Paragraph 31 of Bishop Oro's rebuttal makes this point categorically: "The objection has also been raised that the papal brief in question lacks the opinion of the secular authority, and for that reason it is said to be *essentially a national matter, which belongs exclusively to the general congress;* the Governors of Cuyo are urged to protest the bull; His Excellency of Córdoba's influence is sought by aggrandizing the eminence of the office he holds; and by reminding the other Excellencies that they are *charged* with the same duties."

Lastly, he adds in note (d): "Señor Castro Barros wrote proposing an agreement between that ecclesiastical court and the Apostolic See, without anything of importance coming to pass. On August 6, he proposes to the chapter that they pursue this matter with the governorships of Cuyo (no copy of has been remitted of this letter); he suspends the former due to the compliance of the city council on July 25; he alarms the said governors with his official documents of solicitation inciting them to disobey the Apostolic See; he issues in printed form to the public his advice to resist the Holy Father. . . ."

These intrigues on the part of Doctor Castro Barros were fatal to his ambition. He received notice a year later that his name had been placed on the blacklist of the Roman Curia, as a priest in rebellion against papal authority and thus unauthorized to perform any priestly function for the rest of his life. *At his own expense,* Castro Barros sent the cleric Allende, his friend, to Rome to plead his case, but in vain; all doors were shut to Allende's approach, and he was compelled to return to America without a word of consolation for his friend, blasted by the lightning bolts of the Church. From that time on, Doctor Castro Barros gave himself over to the most extreme ultramontanism, spent over five thousand pesos reprinting every pamphlet he could find against the royal right of patronage, in defense of the Jesuits, of the defunct Inquisition, and any absurdity that could suggest his desire to ingratiate himself to papal authority, the recognition of which he had sought to impede when such recognition was detrimental to his particular interests.[6] In 1847, when I was in Rome, influential persons in the Roman Curia asked me about Castro Barros, reiterating the irrevocable interdiction hanging over him and which would continue to hang over him until the day he died. Castro Barros's main works of atonement are *Triario literario o tres sabios dictámenes sobre los poderes del sacerdocio y del Imperio, reimpreso en Buenos*

Aires, a expensas del doctor Castro Barros con el loable objetivo de que se salve su recíproca independencia [Literary Triplet or Three Wise Judgements on the Powers of the Priesthood and the Empire, reprinted in Buenos Aires at Doctor Castro Barros's expense for the praiseworthy purpose of preserving their mutual independence]; *Restablecimiento de la Compañía de Jesús en la Nueva Granada, reimpreso a solicitud del doctor Castro Barros, con notas suyas* [Restoration of the Company of Jesús in Nueva Granada, reprinted at the request of Doctor Castro Barros, with his own notes], which say: "The Popes, the Inquisition, the Company of Jesus, and all religious institutions have always been impugned and reproached by heretics, infidels, and other enemies of the Catholic religion." "All the more reason why the Jesuits will be the Pope's grenadiers [*granaderos*] in Nueva Granada . . . ," an absurd pun, to which Béranger's phrase may be added: *les capucins sont nos cosaques* [the Capuchins are our Cossacks]; "None of this is to the liking of today's philosophers because they say there is no God, Heaven, or Hell. Oh, what brutes!"[7] These and other outpourings of the ambitious priest condemned by the Church earned him the honors of saintliness upon his death in Chile, and one of his panegyrists ended up exclaiming: "Were I not concerned about anticipating the Church's decision, I would seek the protection of Saint Pedro Ignacio Castro."[8] However, since saints cannot be created without the beatification of the Church, we may be sure of not having to kneel before one of the idiots who, through their fanaticism, personal ambition, intolerance, and hypocrisy, have spilled the most blood in the Argentine Republic. I left off writing his biography in order not to interfere with his admirers' aims, but I take the liberty here of setting forth the truth regarding matters of a purely domestic nature that concern my family.[9]

After having been named and consecrated bishop, Fray Justo devoted himself to the multiplicity of creations accessory to the cathedral he had erected, and in the implementation of this task that occupied his every waking moment, he displayed the strength of character and persistence of purpose that make great plans come to pass. In an obscure province, devoid of resources, he set about establishing a cathedral, a conciliar seminary, a school for the laity, a monastery open to the education of women, a choir of canons endowed with sufficient revenues; and Fray Justo undertook all this at the same time with such confidence in his resources and such a clear conception of the end result that he might have been thought to possess treasures, notwithstanding the fact that he was almost always short of funds to pay his peons' wages. He wanted to build a tabernacle though he lacked the necessary model or the artist to make one; but he had everything else, the idea and the will, which are the real plan and artist. And so, he called upon me, considered by him and his family an ingenious lad, and, haltingly, in poorly executed drafts, copying the capital of a column out of a book and even consulting Vitruvius, we finally managed to design our tabernacle on its Doric columns with a dome like Diogenes's lantern, so that an even more incompetent carpenter might proceed to execute that imperfect sketch.[10] But, oh, the tabernacle was destined to serve as the dossal for a humbler object of worship. I first used it on the catafalque built for his funeral rites and upon which there stood, symbolizing the two major phases of his life, the statue of Liberty holding the Declaration of Independence, and that of Religion with the Bull that had consecrated him bishop, both of them expressions of good will more than of art, in honor of a life that was so full, yet so prematurely cut short. All his works were very near the point of completion, when he was surprised by death; and as he was expiring, he said to the notary who was acting as his scribe: "Hurry, for I have few hours left, and we have much to write." And, in fact, at that supreme moment, he was giving instructions on the completion of the convent church, how it should be covered with wood, the funds and materials he had set aside, his correspondence with Rome, the idea for an adornment for the construction of the choir, the disposition of certain moneys owed him by the Dominican Recollect, family details, his will, thus projecting his entire soul and mind beyond the temporal limit of death; and as he said to the dean who was with him at the end, "My heart is with God, but I need my wits about me here, to arrange for the continuation and completion of my works." Death interrupted that dictation, leaving a sentence unfinished . . . !

His instruction was vast for his time. He had learned French, Italian, and English; he was a profound theologian, that is, a philosopher; and from his frequent chats I was able to infer that his ideas ranged, without overstepping licit bounds, beyond what was called for by his position. The outstanding quality of his nature was tenacity, temperate at the same time that it was persistent. He knew how to wait, never losing heart nor sight of his object in the face of mounting problems. If he was applying for a necessary concession, he would test his influence for obtaining it; when discouraged, he would apply for a different one that led to the same end, and then seek the first under a different guise. Ten more years of life would have brought advances to San Juan through Bishop Oro's efforts that all its many governments have been unable to provide. Quiroga obstructed his founding a school; and death, his completing the educational convent; and since he owed his importance entirely to his breadth of knowledge and keenness of intellect, he would have brought all that will power to bear upon the task of spreading education. Bishop Oro died prematurely, at sixty-five years of age, having spent his entire life in the arduous ascent that, from being a humble friar of a convent, took him to the rank of bishop; such is the luck of many worthy men born under an ill-fated star, who have to erect, piece by piece, all the scaffolding of their own glory, create their theater, and train its audience, so that they may forthwith make their appearance. How many times is a work destroyed, which must then be started all over again! How many days and years spent in confronting an obstacle that blocks ones path!

The convent he sought to establish revealed the elevation of his sights, and the results of a long experience, aided and enriched by study of the real needs of his time. Nuns' vows would not be compulsory except for a certain number of years, upon the termination of which, the women could return to civil life if they so desired, or renew their vows for another given period. The convent would be a refuge and, at the same time, a house of public education. It was to be established by a sister of his, a nun at the convent of the Roses in Córdoba and who now has returned to San Juan . . . mad.

Some years later, I undertook with Doña Tránsito de Oro, the bishop's sister and worthy scion of that family so richly endowed with creative talent, to bring to fruition part of Fray Justo's vast plan, taking advantage of the completed cloister to found the boarding school of Santa Rosa, a patriotic appellation he gave to the convent and which we took care to perpetuate. The only daughter of Doña Tránsito, one of my teachers, was a girl who, from her earliest childhood, showed extraordinary intellectual gifts. Fray Justo, having met me in Chile in 1827, and being very pleased at finding me well versed in geography and other academic subjects, subsequently wrote to his sister telling her to entrust her daughter's education to me, and from my acceptance and the results obtained, there emerged full-blown the entire educational program, and the project of the boarding school of Santa Rosa, which we inaugurated on July 9, 1839, to commemorate the declaration of independence, in which Fray Justo had played a part, and to make the school's public examinations a provincial civic celebration, since Laprida, the president of the Congress of Tucumán, was our compatriot and even a relative of mine.

In his speech inaugurating the school, which appears in No. 1 of *El Zonda,* the late lamented Quiroga Rosas, in commenting on the scene, said: "The first voice to be heard was that of the young director, Don Domingo Faustino Sarmiento, who read the act of independence, to which the assemblage listened in mystical silence. He, himself, then delivered the following address, modest in its form, vast in its scope: 'Señores: a classical day for the nation, a day dear to the heart of all good people, has arrived to fulfill the expectations of those citizens who love civilization. The idea of forming an educational institution for young women is not altogether mine. An illustrious man whose image presides over this scene [the Bishop's portrait was hanging in the hall] and whose name belongs doubly to the annals of the Republic, had already laid the foundations of this important advance. Out of his ardent love for his country, he conceived this idea, great like those he materialized, and those that an untimely death left merely sketched out. Furthermore, I have been the interpreter of the wishes of the thinking portion of my country. An educational institution was a need that urgently called out to be met; and I indicated the means; I judged that the time had come and I offered to bring it about. In short, *Señores,* I converted the idea and the general interest into my own idea and my own interest, and the only honor I deserve is for that alone.'"[11]

That school whose cornerstone we laid at the time lasted two years and yielded enviable fruits. Oh, my school, how I loved you! I would have laid down my life on your doorstep to guard your entrance! I would have given up all other avocations to add years to your existence! My plan was for a generation of girls to pass through your classrooms, to receive them at the entrance, tender plants formed by nature's hand, and return them, their spirits sculpted by study and ideas in the likeness of the Roman matron. We would have let the fevered passions of youth subside, and come together once more in the afternoon of life to lay out the road for the emerging generation. *Mater familias* one day, wives, you would have retorted to the barbarism fanned by the government: Do not cross my threshold, for your foul breath would blot out the fire of civilization and morality entrusted to us twenty years ago.[12] And one day, that repository, incremented and multiplied by the family, would overflow and exude into the street, releasing its soft exhalations into the atmosphere. My Lord, is it possible that we must make a religion of the endeavor to preserve the remains of culture in the Argentine people, and that the desire to educate others should take on the appearance of a vast, calculated plot? In my mature years, intelligence's innocent illusions return to me in the early manifestations of their power, and I still believe in everything that youthful inexperience made me believe in then, and I still hope.

Our leave-taking was solemn and tender. Six or eight sixteen-year old girls, ingenuous and delicate as white lilies, charming as kittens frisking about their mother, visited me so that I might hear them recite their lessons at the last refuge proffered me by my country in 1839, the prison where I was being readied for death, humiliation, or exile; and, in that foul, crumbling dungeon, its walls covered with crude figures and inane inscriptions scrawled by untutored inmates, six girls, the flowers of San Juan, the prides of their families, and the future promises of love, recited by the light of a candle, set on a brick, their geography, French, arithmetic, and grammar lessons, and displayed their drawings of the past two weeks. From time to time, an ugly rat that was making its leisurely way across the floor, certain of not being bothered, would provoke repressed shrieks from those hearts susceptible to impressions like the sensitive mimosa. At first, tears of compassion had brimmed over in those eyes destined at a future time to provoke storms of passion; and once the class was ended, and the teacher's gravity put aside, they gave themselves over to that endless bubbling chatter, eager, curious, irrepressible, rambling, which renders angelic and saintly the effusions of a woman's heart. Candies sent the prisoner by lady friends caught the attention of various pairs of greedy eyes, and upon receiving the signal that they could help themselves, they fell to, like a flock of little birds, talking, eating, laughing, with white necks stretched over the dish, from whose center ivory fingers disappeared by the minute, escaping with a tidbit. They sang me a quartet from the "Tancredo" that I enjoyed immensely and took leave of me cheerfully, filled with renewed desire to continue their studies.[13] We have never seen one another since then! Nor will I ever again see them, in the same way that I carry them in my mind as images of nubile ingenuousness opening to chaste emotions, like the calyx of the flower that receives the evening dew. They are now wives, mothers, and the abrasions of life will have left their mark on skin as velvety as that of the apple yet untouched by the hand of a man, and the loss of innocence will have wiped from their countenances the curious and presumptuous expansiveness that shows by its very self-assurance at times, that it scarcely even suspects there are passions in the soul that require only a spark to set them aflame!

10

Domingo de Oro

The eldest son of Don José Antonio de Oro, brother of the presbyter and the bishop, is Domingo de Oro, whose name is familiar to all men active in the public life of the Argentine Republic, of Bolivia, and of Chile, and of whom Rosas has written: "He is an air pistol that kills without a sound," and whom the Argentineans have been unable to classify since they see him emerging on every page of the history of the civil war, sometimes in bad company, and almost always steeped in the mystery that foreshadows intrigue. Since he inspires no terror, for deeds of blood have always been foreign to his nature, people distrust him from a distance, promising themselves to shun his irresistible seductions, the beguilements of this Mephistopheles of politics. And, yet, Domingo de Oro could wager that he would be able to emerge safe and sound from the lair of a tigress with a litter of cubs, should tigers be susceptible to the allure of the human voice, to suave, affable eloquence, unembellished, insidious, if it may be said, like spirits that, in attacking the brain, benumb it fiber by fiber and deliver over the will in shackles. Such sorcery was used with equal success on Bolívar and Portales, on Rosas and Facundo Quiroga, on Paz and Ballivián, on *unitarios* and *federalistas,* on friends and enemies; and in cabinet meetings, in drawing rooms and in more public social gatherings, Oro's words have resounded—unique, overpowering, attractive—luring in a circle of listeners, prevailing over antipathies, artfully stroking objections in order to strip them of their trappings and, thus, in leaving them naked, make them look foolish.[1] Oro, held in low esteem by all who have only known him through hearsay and beloved by everyone who has had close contact with him, is not the most profound of thinkers, nor the most capable politician, nor the most knowledgeable of men; he is simply the most attractive fellow, indeed, the most beautiful example of virility that nature has managed to produce in America. Oro is the live word itself, endowed with all the fortuities that are beyond the scope of oratory to invent. I have studied this inimitable model, followed the thread of his discourse, uncovered the structure of his phrasing, the machinery that underlies the magical fascination of his words. His methods are simple, but the execution is as artistic, as distinctive of the master as the brush stroke of Raphael, or the more rapid stroke of Horace Vernet.[2] The nobility of his visage contributes greatly to the effects of his dialectic, much as does the set design of the Paris opera to "Robert le Diable."[3] His considerable height, carried with ease and grace, is already in conflict with the idea of art or embellishment in the spoken word: His long oval face, dark-complected though pale, is suffused for moments with the emotions of smiles that pour from his accentuated and charming mouth, like the perfume of the word that is about to open its bud, like the twilight tones that precede moonrise, inviting all those present to be merry. At the same time, his eyes glowing with generosity, liveliness, and skepticism give that happy, playful physiognomy an air of melancholy that doubles the fascination of a forehead that has encroached prematurely upon the upper part of the cranium, shiny and clean as though it had never grown hair. And so, one seems to be listening to a sage, to an old man who, though bowed by the bitterness of disillusionment, laughs with pity and pain that there should be so much to laugh about in this life.

This, then, is one of Oro's deep secrets; the others concern his delivery and are no less successful. He pronounces his words clearly, slowly modulating each one with the finesse of a miniature, with a painstaking quality that is so much the product of patient and persevering study that it has ended up becoming second nature. The passion, the fervor of a scorching reply will never precipitate the sentence, leave a comma unacknowledged, a phrase not rounded out, even in so simple a matter as giving orders to his servant. If he challenges the idea of another, Oro adopts it, embraces it, and holding it in his arms, he presents it to the one who gave it issue, asking affectionately, if a different phrasing would not suit it better, if he would not recognize it as his child with this or that birthmark removed, and the father, bewildered, begins to reject his offspring, and to cherish and adopt the one Oro considers legitimate; if he agrees, he does so in such a manner that the other's thought takes on the force of an axiom, of a result confirmed by his experience with people and things; if he argues a point, he listens with interest to the retorts, with countless benevolent smiles, until his adversary's fatuousness causes him to take the floor, and then, if the matter is not worth discussing nor his opponent convincing, he leads the conversation away to a distance of a thousand leagues, through endless byways, as though the digressions were involuntary, sowing the way with the wittiest quips and funniest jokes; for Oro is aware of all the absurdities that have occurred in America and has at his fingertips the language's entire repertory of devices for provoking laughter; anecdotes of infatuated friars, of complaisant cuckolds, of decrees and laws promulgated by fools, with a repertoire of racy tales for the entertainment and solace of both the callow youth and the confirmed bachelor, which would make of him always a companion worth so much per minute of frolic, in which he invites the neophyte to partake, with an off-color exclamation worthy of a sergeant, calculated to put everyone at ease, relieved of all shyness and inhibition.

This man, so splendidly endowed, has paved the way for Don Juan Manuel Rosas and dropped him with a crash the day he embarked upon a course of pointless violence that, even today, he cannot leave behind; he has fought beside the caudillo López, been the favorite of Bolívar, the friend of General Paz, has taken part in the most sensational events of the Argentine Republic, and today, if I am not mistaken, he manages a foundry where he struggles with louts who grind metals, just as he struggled all his life with louts who, as generals, governors, and caudillos, ground down and demolished whole populations.[4] It is not his acts that these populations have not forgiven him, but his superiority. We always avenge ourselves by speaking ill of our masters, and Oro pays for the moments of fascination he involuntarily produces with the distrust he provokes, because nobody really considers himself as small and as stupid as he proved to be at his side, but rather because there must have been, on the part of the faker, deceit and manifest fraud, the exact nature of which, however, cannot be explained.

In view of his gift of self-expression, Oro would surely be notable among the young notables of Europe. I have seen young men, recently emerged from the most cultured circles of Madrid society, agape at the exquisite distinction of his demeanor, rendered ever more provocative by the American, Argentine, gaucho coloration that Oro lends his polished manners, without ever letting them descend to the level of vulgarity; for Oro, scion of one of San Juan's most aristocratic families, has wielded the lariat and *bolas*, and has carried around his favorite knife, like the best of gauchos. I once saw him, torch in hand, at a Corpus fiesta in San Juan, wrapped in his poncho, but with the folds artfully draped.⁵ These predilections acquired through his contact with the masses of horsemen in Corrientes, Santa Fe, Córdoba, and Buenos Aires, have gone to his head and evolved into a political system, of which there is still hope, even today, that he may be cured. However, these gaucho predilections of his are a complement without which the glitter of his words would have lost half their spell; the poise acquired in his rubbing elbows with the most eminent men of his time, his knowledge of men, his keenness of judgement precociously developed, and the gifts he already possessed from nature, take on that romantic coloration imparted to American life by the distinctive features of its land, its pampa, its semi-civilized customs. Oro has established the model and prototype of the Argentinean of the future: European to the most arcane subtleties of the fine arts, American to showing a mustang who is boss, Parisian in spirit, pampa in energy and physical prowess. I met Don Domingo de Oro in Santiago de Chile in 1841, and such was the idea of his superiority that I had brought with me from the Argentine Republic that, when I published my first article in Chile in *El Mercurio,* I sent a friend undercover to the soirée that Oro frequented to deduce from his expression the effect that reading my article produced on him. Had he disapproved of my piece, found it vulgar or ridiculous, *c'en était fait,* I would have lost, for a long time, my natural aplomb and my confidence in the integrity of my ideas, the only quality that can make a writer. My friend returned after a couple of hours of anxious expectation on my part, calling out to me from a distance: "Bravo! Oro applauded." I was a writer, then, and have since proved it, up to a point. Afterward, I saw in him one of his most distinctive gifts. Contrary to many, Oro, as I emerged from my obscurity, allowed the modest evaluation he had made of my potential at the beginning to grow. I believe that one day he began to think, without manifesting anything but pleasure and indulgence, that I already came up to his chin, and that he would come to persuade himself that I continue without shame the career he has abandoned, without this conviction causing him either chagrin or displeasure.

Oro's life is proof of the way I understand his rare eloquence, the achievement of a rich and splendid nature. His political character is at all times the same, and despite the many apparent contradictions of the various phases of his life, the unity of intent is such that it constitutes a most logical sequence of acts.

Oro counts his years with the nineteenth century. His childhood went by without those constraints that weaken the will to act and are a product of the very endeavor to educate the intelligence that must direct it; a little Latin in San Juan, a smattering of algebra and geometry in Buenos Aires, and a familiarity with French, account for all the riches he had amassed by the time he was nineteen, when political life erupted in his face, and launched him into a series of acts that were to determine the course of his future. His uncle, the presbyter Oro, had incurred the displeasure of San Martín's supporters. Before very long, the whole Oro family found itself involved, and when the Mendizábal revolt broke out, Oro, at age twenty, was the intermediary between that rebel officer and San Martín in proposing an agreement, which, signed in Mendoza by Colonel Torres, now living in Rancagua, San Martín refused to ratify.[6] On Oro's return to San Juan, he found a second revolt in progress, of the No. 1 of Chasseurs of the Andes, and, having approached the rebels, he was taken prisoner and exiled by the government to Valle Fértil or Jachal.[7] However, the new complexion taken on by the uprising, as it changed instigators, reconciled the government of San Juan with Oro.

In 1821, no sooner did San Juan find itself free of rebels than a new danger, unforeseen, made it long for the support of those brave deserters from the army of the Andes, misled by intrigues that came from afar: Don José Miguel Carrera was launching his campaign to pass over into Chile to avenge the exclusion of his band and the death of his brothers.[8]

Carrera, driven by vengeance, appeared in the tent of Ramírez, Artigas's *montonero* lieutenant; he touched that remnant of noblesse that is never wanting in the soul of the brigand, and from among his horsemen he took his trail guides, and from his camp fire the torch with which he was to cross the pampa, setting the grasslands afire to create a horizon of flame and smoke that would advance overland with him, as far as the snow-covered peaks of the Andes in the West, which he intended to scale with his horsemen.⁹* The *montonera*, like an avalanche of heartless men, fell upon the towns of the Argentine countryside, slaughtering the herds, plundering the dwellings, abducting the women; and from the mayhem of the orgy lit up by the burning fields and roofs, both victors and vanquished went forth, men and women, possessed by the same frenzy of pillage and bloodletting of which many of them had so recently been victims. The women fought in the combats like furies; and, I know of an incident in which a single *montonero*, taking on one extremity of an army unit that was lined up waiting for orders, put it to flight by dint of killing off, one by one, the corporals at the end.

The terror of the populace lingers on in local tradition; along the roads one can still see the bleached skeletons of the cattle wantonly sacrificed with that exquisite sense of evil that spurred on those pirates led by a heroic Morgan who had locked away his heart to keep from hearing the cries of the victims and the consternation of the cities.¹⁰ But, for those cities, the Chilean patriot and his feuds with San Martín were overshadowed by the fearsome reputation of the *montonera*. Carrera, in fact, so that he might cross the pampa in safety, became an Argentine and assumed the national coloration in its blackest hue. Imposing forces from San Juan and Mendoza advanced to face him and were destroyed at Río IV, and retreating, they stoked with their gruesome accounts of the atrocities committed by Carrera's *montonera*, the terror that already preceded his name.¹¹ Carrera would have occupied San Juan and Mendoza, the two towns that hold the key to the Andes, without their own forces being sufficient to save them, had it not been for Oro who, in a moment of inspiration, hit on a good idea, and the general panic seized upon it as the only possible salvation; Oro, himself, was assigned to put it into effect by going in search of Urdininea and eight other officers, all

---

Montonero. An adjective (or noun) indicating a combatant belonging to a *montonera*, a band of irregular soldiers under the command of a rural caudillo. The *montonera* as a form of warfare appeared in the Río de la Plata with the Wars of Independence, in which successive patriotic governments were forced to call upon *hacendados* to provide men and provisions (i.e., cattle) for the war. This militarization of the countryside gave considerable power and prestige to those *hacendados* and/or *estancieros* who successfully led their men (often their own laborers) in battle; this prestige could raise such *hacendados* to the political status of caudillos. *Montoneros* wore the clothes of the gaucho rather than the uniform of a regular soldier.—Ed.

Bolivians, who were in La Rioja, and entreating them to come and organize the resistance.[12] Urdininea agreed, and the despair of that disconsolate province gave way to exultation; all males capable of bearing arms came forward regardless of class or age. Urdininea brought with him the military science that had been lacking at Río IV, and all believed themselves saved. As one of my childhood recollections, I remember the extravagant and diminutive figure of Rodríguez, which made an impression on us boys. This was the Rodríguez who was found murdered on the beach in Buenos Aires and whose death remains a mystery among the many that eventually will be solved by time, which reconstructs and illuminates history.[13]

Carrera came within six leagues of San Juan; a Chilean soldier by the name of Cruz, who crossed his path in the Majadita, briefed him on the new course that things had taken, and he changed direction, marching instead on Mendoza, through arid fields that destroyed his horses and resulted in his capture by the enemy. To San Juan fell the most inglorious aspect of warfare, to round up prisoners, who, by a vengeful decree, were condemned to death, along with all who had accompanied Carrera, whether officers, friends, or advisers. One of those who had the misfortune to be taken prisoner was Urra, Carrera's secretary, a young man of twenty-eight, gifted with most unusual talents, highly educated and, what was quite uncommon then, in possession of many languages. More than his merits and his youth, what weighed in his favor was the very cause he had followed, for it came out that, far from having taken part in the crimes of the *montonera*, which were horrible, he had used his influence to put a stop to many of them. Oro launched a campaign to save the life of that unfortunate young man who had won the sympathy of the entire population; the priesthood interceded for him, as well as the very troops who had fought in the campaign. But God save us from governments and men counseled by fear; they are implacable toward the vanquished. Urra was executed at night, at the far end of some old walls, like that most estimable Duke d'Enghien.[14] For hours, Oro's life hung by a thread because he had swayed the troops in Urra's favor, and he was not free of danger until he had left his province far behind, to embark on that novelesque pilgrimage that is yet to end. He visited Córdoba, where he was pursued by the threats of his enemies; he went to Buenos Aires, where Agrelo made him move on to Corrientes; and there, at the side of General Mansilla, governor of the province, he put the finishing touches on his special physiognomy, glossing over the aristocratic background of his heritage with the patina derived from his close contact with Argentine cattlemen.[15] Oro had seen the *montonera* rise up once again, on its native grounds, so to speak, in the still fresh tracks of Artigas and Ramírez; there, for the first time, he was confronted with the provinces' hatred for the *porteños,* a hatred of pure social breakdown and disorder, but which was later to become such a powerful political instrument; there he was to educate himself by serving the party of the cities in the futile struggle against the *montonera,* and from there to arrive at the deep-seated conviction that it was hopeless for men of European culture to oppose those titans of war, who were destined to win; a conviction he was to maintain at least until 1842, when we argued this point at length, and which, as far as I know, he holds to this day.* Separated from Mansilla's command, Oro became the secretary of one Sola, governor of the gaucho party, with whom he, as was to be expected, could never get along, since it was impossible to put a stop to the stupid willfulness of those children of nature, who, from Artigas down to the last village chieftain, share the ideas of Harun ar-Rashid in matters of government.[16] In that period, however, young Oro had another youth from Buenos Aires living in his house, also a gaucho, and one whose name was to become known, although in a most unhappy manner, by all the peoples of the world. This young cattleman with whom Oro became acquainted at the time was a certain Don Juan Manuel Rosas.

However, from the dusty obscurity into which he had been thrust in Corrientes by the *montoneras* of the interior and the Brazilians and Uruguayans who instigated them, Don Domingo de Oro had captured the attention of Rivadavia's government, which went out of its way to promote the fortunes of all those men whom it saw distinguishing themselves on the political horizon. Rivadavia's intention was to send a legation to Bolívar, whose name was aspiring to eclipse that of the Argentine Republic, and for this diplomatic mission he chose General Alvear, the most brilliant military officer of the time; Doctor Díaz Vélez; and Don Domingo de Oro, as secretary.[17] The Argentine legation arrived at Chuquisaca, and as for Oro, he was considered by Bolívar, Sucre, Miller, Infante, and Morán a worthy example in diplomacy of the Argentine youth whom they had seen represented in war by Necochea, Lavalle,

---

* "Porteño" is the name for inhabitants of the port city of Buenos Aires.—Ed.

Suárez, Pringles and so many other brilliant and wild young men, always the first in battle, the first with the ladies and, should the occasion arise, never the last in a duel, a bacchanal, and the dissipations of youth.[18] Bolívar and Sucre, successively, competed for the hours of that conversation, pleasant as a morning in spring, sparkling and effervescent as a bubbling goblet of champagne, already nourished with the vitality that comes from the experience of risk, from the difficulties overcome in the stormy political life of the Argentine Republic, a sun that withers the delicate plant but ripens and gives flavor to the fruit that matures early in the wellborn.

His mission having failed, Oro was posted as secretary to the legation in Lima; and even before assuming this new appointment, he received dispatches naming him secretary of the delegate who was to be sent to the Congress of Panama, which likewise never took place.

He had still not returned to Argentina, when he was appointed delegate for San Juan to the Constitutional Congress, which he nevertheless did not attend.[a] From those beginnings of Oro's political and diplomatic career, there remained the general impression that he was clear-sighted on all matters, and that his word was a power that could be used to oppose the material forces beginning to multiply around the Rivadavia presidency.

In Santiago del Estero Oro found letters from Rivadavia's ministers ordering him to San Juan to organize the resistance against Facundo Quiroga.[19] Facundo had already made his entrance into San Juan, for lack of a man who, like Oro, could point out the weak side of the political situation and shore it up. Nevertheless, he went on to Córdoba and Mendoza, where he discovered the very friends of the government conspiring with the Aldaos.[20] He sent on to Buenos Aires a statistical breakdown of public opinion and of the different interests involved, but no subsequent action materialized to indicate that his advice had been taken to heart. The presidency fell, and in that closing scene of one of the most brilliant chapters in Argentine history, Oro once again saw his family in San Juan, but by now he had aged, for since his departure seven years had passed, and his physiognomy had been transformed by that patina which contact with famous men and great events leaves on the human face.[21]

---

[a] As set forth in a document drawn up in San Juan on July 18, 1828, naming him deputy-elect for the province of San Juan. No. 18 of the *Official Registry*. [Author's note]

Oro returned to Buenos Aires when Dorrego, his acquaintance and traveling companion of a year before, was head of the government.[22] Dorrego was the realization of the political idea that Domingo de Oro had gleaned from his long apprenticeship in Corrientes, and that his travels throughout the provinces had only confirmed, government by the enlightened on behalf of the caudillos; but men of principle do not govern on behalf of what destroys those principles; governments in America are approved or reproved by the nation's enlightened minority, wherein political life resides. Beyond this terrain, government bears no resemblance to that of Christian peoples: Everything opposing it is dismantled or exterminated; Artigas had done just that, Facundo did just that, and later Rosas did just that. Oro was mistaken, as was Dorrego, and Oro had to move quickly to put his finger on the spot that was already starting to bleed. Behind Dorrego, the constitutional and enlightened lie, was Rosas, the awful truth, which was covered up by the forms and names of the political parties. Oro was no sympathizer of the fallen party, nor had he made up his mind to support Dorrego, who called him a few days after he arrived in Buenos Aires to serve in a ministry, which he refused to do for the time being, although he accepted another post later in the Ministry of War, under the express condition that he not have to write in the political press. He resigned that position at a moment when his personal sympathies for the majority of public figures were beginning to incline him toward coming out for the unitarian party. He took over a press, that of the *Río de la Plata;* as editor, he published the first issue of *El porteño,* an opposition newspaper, and would have published *El granizo* if his editors had agreed to give him carte blanche.

Rosas was then Commander General of the Countryside, and he was put in charge of establishing the new frontier, and of the *Negocio pacífico* [Peaceful Negotiation], an agreement reached with the savages, in accordance with which, in exchange for a certain government subsidy, the barbarians would occupy specific places while submitting to government jurisdiction. Rosas sought out Oro, whom he had met in Corrientes, to take charge of the accounting for that negotiation, and Oro accepted in the belief that this would save him from the decision that, by their very nature, the political parties were imperiously demanding of all men of note. But Rosas was already at work bringing the frontier to the main square of Buenos Aires, and Dorrego feared less the opposition of the

supporters of the Congress and the Presidency, which he had dismantled, than the open rebellion of the Commander General. Oro used his
influence to avoid or postpone the rupture. Dorrego wanted to separate
Oro from Rosas's side, for fear that to his adversary's shrewdness and
tenacity, would be added the sagacity and clearsightedness of the young
man whose capability he had had occasion to appreciate before; Rosas,
meanwhile, insisted on keeping him at his side, certain of having found
what until then he had been lacking, a civilized veneer for his designs. In
this tug of war or, as Oro once put it, "between those two millstones," he
sought to protect himself by taking advantage of the occasion offered
him by the government to go hence to Corrientes and use his influence
to prevent a revolution that was brewing at the instigation of Rivera,
who meant to take over that province.[23] Oro had complete success in his
mission, although the problem resurfaced later on. He controlled the situation momentarily, until new complications rendered all efforts in vain.
He drew back to Santa Fe, from where, reunited with Mansilla, he once
again derailed the revolution, until, taken over by Sola, that former Governor of Corrientes, the situation entered its true terrain, the exclusion
of all political thought, the satiation of selfish passions.

In Santa Fe, Oro drew up a plan for the exploitation of state-owned
forests and went to Buenos Aires to set up a company for that purpose..
Buenos Aires was in turmoil at the moment, and he wrote to his friends
in Santa Fe of the tremors he felt underfoot and of the rumors foreshad-
owing the crisis. December 1st was merely the explosion of the forces
that until that moment had been repressed.[24] Oro's behavior at that
supreme moment was sublime in its frankness, boldness, and misjudg-
ment. Now that we are gathered in exile, expelled by the same hand,
both those who supported the revolution and he who fought against it,
he can convince himself that the effort, despite its having been well-
intentioned, was not for that reason any less mistaken. Oro came from
the provinces and was in contact with all the forces of disorganization;
he had compared them and gauged their impact; the December 1st Revolution did no more than galvanize all their energies and bring them to
the surface. Oro fought the attempt; once consummated, he rejected the
deed, and in the Plaza de la Victoria, in the midst of those people intoxicated with the presence of the army, before two thousand citizens
packed around him, astonished at such daring and such eloquence, and
before Salvador María del Carril, surrounded by those soldiers who, fin-

gering their mustaches and leaning on their imperial swords, smiled with pity at those who dared gaze upon their lances, he delivered the most eloquent, the most desperate protest against that revolution that seemed to be the end of all past evils and that, according to him, was nothing but the precursor of all the calamities yet to come.[25] Carril spoke to him of rights violated, of violence committed, and Oro, in response, detailed the acts of violence, the crimes and evils yet to be committed, as proof of what was the dominant, irrefutable fact. Oro was not defending the justice of the incriminated procedures, but the ineffectiveness of the means adopted to get rid of them. Dorrego was defeated, executed; and on December 14 in the café of La Victoria, and amid the victors, Oro again insisted on his theory, qualifying as murder that act that for the moment seemed to belie his former predictions. He maintained that the governors were not the cause but the effect of an evil that had been eating away at the Republic since the days of Artigas; that this evil had spread little by little throughout the entire Republic; that the elevation of Dorrego to the government of Buenos Aires was the complement of its victory and its takeover of the Republic; that even though it now seemed that the revolution was putting in question that earlier decision to elevate Dorrego, actually, his death only served to provoke the true victor; that now that the gaucho element had been let loose, it was going to do what it had not done before; that it would behead the party that contained the greatest number of enlightened and wealthy men, and it would plunge us into barbarism; that it was necessary to fight against the revolution in Buenos Aires before it ignited in the interior and the desolation spread throughout the nation.

Oro presented this version of the question to me in 1842, and I was undoubtedly the most well-disposed to understand it since I had been studying the same problem for many years, and indeed in *Civilización y Barbarie* I attempted to provide a solution, one which all the parties have adopted and which is now gaining supporters in Europe and thus scattering the cloud of obscurities raised by the cunning of Rosas. This theory will yield its fruits quite soon, since the chronic disease has produced its last results; its end is not as far off as one might think. The only point on which Oro and I disagreed was the possibility of having set the course of public affairs in a new direction. Dorrego had trampled the political edifice by seeking support from the disorganizing forces of the interior; if the enlightened minorities and the army, repository until then of the traditions of the independence, did not attempt an effort, they and Dorrego would succumb in the presence of the Commander of the Countryside, the Artigas of the south of Buenos Aires; if the capital withdrew into itself, as in 1820, the enlightened men of the provinces would be abandoned to Quiroga and the rest of the barbarians, who knew neither charity nor justice, and just as Dorrego had coordinated and disciplined those brute forces, so the friends of the presidency were everywhere in evidence and could not break the fatal chain that linked them to Buenos Aires. What they did in 1829, then, was fatal, logical, and necessary. They had to play the last card, a tradeoff for combating evil no matter how profound that evil might be.[b]

They did not succeed because they were not supposed to succeed; they needed men to head the army who were less valiant and arrogant and more knowledgeable about the matter at hand; they needed time and good fortune; they needed to have evil itself triumph, so it could produce all its horrors and sterility; they needed twenty years of Rosas's administration to teach the people to understand where the system leads that Artigas introduced, that Facundo continued, and that Rosas completed; in fact, Oro needed to come to hate and detest *caudillismo,* whose brutal indiscipline he thought he could restrain, so that today, from the last of Rosas's men to the highest of unitarians, we might all be in agreement on a single sentiment, and this is, that gauchos and enlightened men, indeed all of us today, need protection and security against violence and terror.

Don Domingo de Oro, free of any involvement with the revolutionaries, known to the caudillos, left Buenos Aires in February of 1829, and met with López, of Santa Fe, to lend him his counsel, since his triumph was to Oro as clear as the light of day.

In Rosario, he was to meet Don Juan Manuel Rosas, the predestined tyrant of Buenos Aires. At the time, Oro counted for more than he; Rosas was disconcerted, indecisive, and Oro gained his trust. Rosas was afraid to approach López, who had an implacable aversion to him, and Oro smoothed the way. At Oro's request, Rosas was given a high rank in López's army, but without duties; and, when the old animosities rekindled in the gaucho from Santa Fe and he was ready to dismiss Rosas at

---

[b] This doctrine was expertly expounded by Don V. F. López, in a series of articles in *El Progreso* of Santiago. [Author's note]

any moment with curses, Oro was then his godfather and his protection. There are things that men with no real merit do not forgive when they come to power. Woe to him who has seen them insignificant, humbled, and subjugated! Woe to those who have seen them tremble! Better for them to run a thousand leagues away, for they will never be forgiven! What hatred Rosas professes for Oro!

The vicissitudes of the campaign are of no concern here. The defeat at Puente de Márquez gave Oro a chance to enter Buenos Aires alone and to meet with the ministers and urge them to save themselves through a treaty with López.[26] There was still time; but the unitarians were not yet convinced of their impotence. After his final efforts to persuade them, Oro returned to his camp to finalize the victory of his side. General Paz had been more fortunate in Córdoba than Lavalle in the Buenos Aires campaign, and Oro, going forward with his system, set his eyes on General Paz from that moment on. This was, on his part, but the necessary incorporation of fact into the mass of victorious facts that confronted him everywhere. Paz, strengthening his position in Córdoba, was still a bulwark against the barbarism of the interior led by Quiroga; Paz, then, was a barrier it was advisable not to destroy; an anchor that was still in place. Oro was sent to Córdoba, and although Paz and Oro could not agree on what was at the bottom of the crisis, they respected each other from that time on, and their relationship has remained close to this day.

Under these circumstances, Lavalle yielded in Buenos Aires to the pressure of the rural element that, with its thousands of men on horseback, had smothered, rather than conquered, the army in the battle at Puente de Márquez. Oro's counsel prevailed now, but impelled by the victory and the arrogant Revolution of December 1st, he had been content with a surrender that guaranteed the lives of the unitarians and the military officers. Oro arrived in Buenos Aires when Rosas was in power, that same Rosas he had taken under his wing in Rosario and talked out of his plan to emigrate to San Pedro in Brazil. Governor Rosas displayed all the concern of a friend for his protector; and yet, Oro began to realize that in that frigid soul, cold like the belly of a snake, there was no human feeling whatsoever. Oro was everything to Don Estanislao López, from under whose wing Rosas had emerged, and Rosas in Oro respected merely that power he was waiting to subdue. After the battle of Puente de Márquez, López and Rosas had endorsed a political plan suggested by Oro, which was based on respect for the lives, property, and freedom of the defeated party, a plan in which Oro followed his system of containing the winner of a race just within the finishing line. Rosas's subsequent actions have demonstrated the sincerity with which he endorsed that plan, the obligations of which he has, of course, sought to ignore.

In 1830 the governors of the four littoral provinces met in San Nicolás de los Arroyos, and Oro was invited to attend this meeting by López and Rosas. Ferré attended for Corrientes; an envoy whom I do not remember from Entre Ríos; and that most unfortunate Maza, who later had his throat slit within the very chambers of the House of Representatives in Buenos Aires, and whose docility was better suited than Oro's to the secret designs of the foul creature.[27] In that congress of four governments, it was decided that a confidential mission should be sent to General Paz, and Oro was entrusted with the task. The notes were prepared under Rosas's influence, and Oro refused to serve as their bearer if they were not modified. López, Ferré, and Oro worked in unison, and in good faith wished to end the war, while the scarcely dissimulated aim of Rosas was to prolong the war, cause problems, and gain time. In this conflict, López and Ferré insisted that Oro accept the mission, for fear of its falling into less well-meaning hands; this he did at last, succeeding in modifying in part the notes and instructions. Oro, enjoying the full confidence of General Paz in Córdoba, sought only to prevent Rosas from quietly sabotaging the proposed compromise. Oro next prepared a meeting among Rosas, General Paz, López, Ferré, and others; he notified the latter, but in order to prevent the meeting from being derailed, he kept Rosas in the dark until the appointed time drew near. Nonetheless, the plan was leaked, and General Paz received an anonymous warning that he was to be killed at the meeting. Rosas sent agents to López with the same information. Nonetheless, he pretended to lend his support to the project, but he postponed its implementation, provoking disputes with the government of Córdoba, until the provinces of Catamarca and Salta invaded Santiago del Estero; and once the *status quo,* which had created a basis for the compromise, was broken, although this transpired much to the regret of General Paz and without his participation, all attempts at negotiation were suspended.

From this moment on, Don Domingo de Oro abandoned all political initiative. The tunic of the Argentine Republic was to be played for like a stake in a dice game, and it no longer mattered to him who the winner might be. The calamity he wanted to avoid had been consummated in spite of his efforts. From then on, he travels the warring provinces, well received in all because he is now extraneous to the issues at stake. He goes to Buenos Aires and Santa Fe, returns to Córdoba en route to San Juan, and gives General Paz an insidious message from Rosas, but saying, like Ulysses to Telemachus: "Take heed that you be not deceived by my words." Those two exiles, the last sincere and well-intentioned men who were to leave the field of Argentine politics, to give way to the extermination of a party, conversed sadly about the past and about the future of the struggle. Paz, already worn down by discord (1831) and the lack of resources, understood his situation. His duty was, he said, to die fighting, it being impossible for him to abandon to the knife those whom Rosas intended to wipe out by the thousands.

After a few months' residence in San Juan, Quiroga seizes control of Mendoza, and Oro, not wanting to be taken for a unitarian, waits for the caudillo to enter so that he can slip away discreetly. He has with Quiroga, the terrible Facundo, a clamorous meeting, and this other barbarian thinks, like Rosas, that he has found in him the complement he needs; but Oro no longer expects anything from the release of those brutal passions, and he sets out for Chile. Quiroga overtakes him in Uspallata, beseeching him to return and take charge of the office of secretary of the government. This he formally refused, returning, however, so as not to give the impression that his departure was an escape, at which point he was commissioned by the government to present a formal claim in Chile for the arms and horses taken out of the country by the emigrés. This occasioned a meeting between Oro and Portales, which began under the most threatening conditions for the former, and ended in peace and cordiality.[28] He returned at once to San Juan, under circumstances in which Quiroga was preparing the expedition against Tucumán; they saw little of each other; he then proceeded to Buenos Aires and visited Rosas at his camp at Arroyo del Medio, where Rosas, in order to deceive him about that which neither could any longer be deceived, put him up in his own tent. They saw each other again later in Buenos Aires, and this time they broke off for good in an unequivocal and formal manner. The *Gaceta* published a decree that rescinded all the guarantees of which the officers of Lavalle's army had been assured in the capitulation of Buenos Aires.[29] Oro had seen Rosas coming to this point, but he still doubted that he would be cynical enough to formalize in a public document that flagrant violation of a treaty. Unable to control himself, Oro tore the *Gaceta* to shreds in the presence of many observers, erupting in imprecations against the scoundrel. Rosas heard about it, and feigning serenity by dissembling behind that icy mask the volcano of bloody and vengeful passions that constantly gnaw away at him, tried to entice him to a reconciliation. General Mansilla was charged with asking Oro that he meet with Maza to that end; Don Gregorio Rosas also interceded, without receiving any response from Oro other than his reiterated public protest against the perverse acts of the man who had betrayed his hopes.[30] This act was on his part a justification before his own conscience and before history, of the sincerity of his intentions on adopting the cause of the caudillos. The day Rosas launched his new policy was the day Don Domingo de Oro announced to the world that he was no accomplice in any of the acts of bloody madness that could be seen in embryo in that decree. Oro has been the only federalist among those who elevated Rosas who has not been prostituted, stained, and degraded by allowing himself to be swept along with the current of events; the only man of principles who has said: up to here is my work, from now on I publicly wash my hands, preferring to be a victim rather than an accomplice. A sublime effort of conscience to remain pure in the midst of the mud that was going to fall upon everyone!

A doubt has often assailed my spirit, and that is, what direction would the December 1st Revolution have taken if Don Domingo de Oro had espoused rather than combated it, if, in fact, he had been able to win the government over to his conviction, which the Decembrists did not share, regarding the strength of the caudillos to resist. As for López, he would have induced him to retire to his tents in Santa Fe; Rosas would not have emerged so soon without López and without him, and Oro already understood his situation well enough to be able to disarm, peacefully, the destructive machine that Rosas was preparing in the Campaign of the South; with Buenos Aires secured, Santa Fe tranquil, and Córdoba occupied by Paz, the Republic was saved; but the hypothesis is illusory, and one should not ask for conditions that are impossible to meet.[31] In such a case, the December 1st Revolution would not have taken place, and thus it is not possible to guess the direction that things would have assumed.

Oro's subsequent life is already that of a failing light, of a lost existence. Oro, to exist, needed a homeland and a government with European forms, and in the chaos of barbarism and violence that begins from that time on, his political talents, his eminently diplomatic character, his brilliant eloquence, were all bound to make him the target of distrust, of jealousy, and of persecution. The unitarians could not forgive him for having defeated them; the barbarians, for refusing to sanction their crimes. Where, then, could he find a place even to repose in obscurity and inaction?

Oro returned home to San Juan, secretly affected by an illness of the spirit that he took pains to conceal. Oro feared an attempt on his life, and was on guard. Facundo returns from Tucumán, treats him well for a time, and then suddenly becomes somber. Oro passes over into Chile in 1833, conscious of whence the plots proceed that threaten his life. In Chile, he is beset both by the suspicions of the government and by those of Santa Cruz, each one considering him an agent of the Argentine caudillos.[32] In 1835, upon his father's death, he returns to San Juan to claim his inheritance and, with the aristocratic magnanimity of one who had done so many things without ever touching the spoils of the conquered, he exchanges, without inventory, his parents' vineyards, storerooms, and farm implements for a ranch that grows alfalfa pasture. Yanzón, then in power in San Juan, a barbarian who nonetheless had a decent heart, wanted to turn the government over to Oro, unaware that he was living under the knife of Rosas's proscription. In fact, letters from Rosas soon arrive denouncing him to the caudillos. Oro accepts a cabinet post, and then something happens that has lent support to the first charge against him. Colonel Barcala was given asylum in San Juan, and Oro had guaranteed Yanzón of his good behavior.[33] Barcala hatches a conspiracy in Mendoza, is betrayed and discovered, and the priest Aldao calls for his extradition, by virtue of the quadrilateral treaty recognized by those governments. A patrol suddenly appears in San Juan; Barcala's letters are intercepted and leave no room for subterfuge of any kind; Barcala does not try to escape, and Yanzón, who wants to avoid a rupture with all the federal governments, and Oro, who is not a unitarian, hand over Barcala, who is executed by firing squad in Mendoza, accusing Oro of involvement in his conspiracy. Oro becomes suspect to Yanzón, he is tried, condemned, absolved on appeal, and banished.

Don Domingo de Oro arrived in Copiapó in 1835. At *La Puerta* many notable Argentineans were gathered, who heard him paint the picture of all the horrors that were to follow upon Don Juan Manuel Rosas's rise to absolute power.[34] I recall some of his words: "America is going to shudder in fear; the Inquisition in its darkest days has not produced such spectacles. The minds of those who have already seen Quiroga and others, will be unable to grasp what is to be seen henceforth. I know this vicious fiend; he has no heart, nothing moves him, his face never betrays any sign of the hunger for vengeance that gnaws at his sides: he can be talking to you about trifles, while selecting the spot on your neck where the knife he is preparing will enter. You are going to see him soon; not a single man of any importance will be left alive, above all, not a single officer in the army; I have seen him give the order to kill twenty-seven prisoners in San Nicolás, enjoying himself the while, like a tiger gorging on blood. . . ."[35] Some months later the news arrived in Chile of the slaughter of eighty Indians in the Plaza del Retiro, and everyone repeated it instinctively: Oro said it; murders in the homes, prisoners decapitated; and everyone repeated in horror: Oro predicted it in *La Puerta* in 1835![36] These arguments were also reproduced by Oro in the press.

From that time onward, Oro becomes just another of the exiles in Chile; he shares their feelings, he lives with them, but without their hope, for he does not believe that the lethargy is over, the inertia that has seized the moral energy of the populations immobilized by the enormity of the evils they have suffered; a tragic apathy into which the spirit falls that has seen the germ develop, grow, spread, and blanket, as if with leprosy, the entire Republic.

In 1840, Oro penned these notable words in Chile: "Nature granted Don Juan Manuel Rosas a robust constitution, which his labors as a cattle rancher and a farmhand completely developed, equipping him to do justice in more than one respect to the enormous role he has taken on. His manner, when among men who enjoy his confidence or those whose sympathy it interests him to cultivate, is pleasant, and when you speak to him, his face assumes an expression of attention and seriousness that is gratifying; but, in his dealings with other men, one sees a crudeness of manner and coarseness of language consistent with a certain taciturn air that seems in him characteristic. In these instances, he rarely looks at the person to whom he is talking and if he does so intermittently with rapid movements of the eyes, it is to gauge the effect of his words. Other than that, no involuntary sign ever reveals the affect of his soul; and no one, to look at him, would suspect the meanness of the brutal passions that seethe within his breast. But, although he possesses the capacity for dissimulation attributed to Tiberius, his face, normally flushed, turns pale with fear in a moment of danger, not that he lacks the courage to face it, when the situation is unavoidable or extremely urgent.[37] It is true, though, that afterward his faculties become disordered, and he lapses into a certain state of befuddlement, or one bordering on stupidity. Rosas is frugal in his eating habits and austere to an extreme, which was the case even before he became tormented by the fear of being poisoned. He is thoughtful, reflexive, hard-working like few others. He has no religious or moral ideas, and all the faculties of his soul are subordinated to the passion of absolute power and the passion of revenge, the two dominant qualities of his nature. In the history of the New World until our time, there has not been a tyrant as calculatingly brutal and cruel as Rosas. The feverishness with which he works degenerates into mad, ferocious extravagance in his moments of rest and distraction."

This thought, worthy of La Bruyère, belongs to Oro: "Those who do not know Rosas will be inclined to think that this sketch is exaggerated. . . . Humankind instinctively rejects the notion that such beings can exist; and the improbability of the horrors of which they have been guilty and which should necessarily bring universal hatred down upon them, puts truth into question and becomes a protective refuge for the depraved."[c38] A most beautiful thought this is, and one that has been borne out over the last twenty years. America and Europe have doubted the truth for a long time; history arrives, however, on the heels of deeds; and when the passions, interests, and opinions of the moment have subsided, it will present to the attention of an astonished world the blackest page in the annals of human criminality. Not a single deed among a thousand will escape being verified, clarified, authenticated, and the truth, the terrible truth, will put an entire generation to shame. "Truth is not buried with the dead; it survives popular adulation and fear of the powerful, which are never sufficient to stifle the clamour of the blood; truth seeps out from dungeons and even from the grave."[d]

In his wanderings, Oro went to Bolivia where the government of General Ballivián sought his counsel.[39] The last piece of advice he gave him was to relinquish power if he did not wish to wait for it to be

---

[c] *El tirano de los pueblos argentinos* [The Tyrant of the Argentine People]; Valparaiso, 1840. This is a different pamphlet from that written by García del Río with the same title in the *Museo de ambas Américas* [Museum of Both Americas], 1843. [Author's note]

[d] *La Rusia en 1838* [Russia in 1838] by the Marquis de Custine. [Author's note]

snatched away from him by the sad revolution, the one that is working away at Bolivia now, very similar in its disorganizing power to that other one he had studied in its cradle and had followed until loosing sight of it. Oro's behavior, as well as that of other Argentine emigrés, moved General Ballivián to exclaim from his refuge in Valparaiso: "Were it not for the generous abnegation of these Argentineans, I would have ended up cursing the human species."

Having escaped this revolution and sought asylum in Tacna, Oro felt himself embraced from behind in the port of Arica, in 1848, by someone trying to be recognized by the sound of his voice alone. Freed from the grasp to satisfy his curiosity, he turned around, and then we could embrace anew, he who was stretching his wings for the third time to launch himself on the uncertain waters of exile, I who was returning from travelling the world, to re-enter Chile, whence I had departed in the opposite direction; and in friendly conversations on the warm benches of the steamship, as we watched the deserted American shoreline slip by on the horizon and sank our gazes into the ocean's deserted surface, I gleaned from his lips half the information that makes up these memoirs and that complements what I already possessed. Oro is beached like an empty hulk abandoned who knows where; while I continue on with no definite route, no fixed destination, yielding to impulses that move me forward.

The last news I have had of him is contained in the following letter:

"Señor Don Domingo F. Sarmiento, Copiapó, November 6, 1849. My esteemed friend: I have received a copy of your book *Educación popular* [Popular Education]. The nature of your *Crónica* had already caught my attention by its tendency to convert into practice, into deed, theories that continue to be discussed. It seems to me that you conceived your newspaper as a machine for getting people to work in the sense of industry and of the mechanical and material movement. Your book is the machine for applying the same impetus to the intellectual movement, which I would call the *intellectual and moral industry*, which will, in good time, increase with its force the elasticity of the material and industrial movement.

Your book has so aroused my former sentiments of philanthropy and patriotism, that my past illusions have almost been revived, to the point of making me believe in the future happiness of our countries. I will not tell you how many dreams passed through my head! They have been the life movements of a corpse induced by galvanic stimulation. Discouraged and skeptical, I came to have a moment of faith, in the enormous good that the instruction derived from reading your book would bring us. But the exaltation has passed, and I am left only with extreme admiration for your efforts, great sympathy for the generosity and loftiness of your sentiments, very keen and most abiding affection for your person, and no hope whatsoever that such noble, generous, and wise efforts will be crowned by success. Yours, Oro."

11

The Historian Funes

This exercise is at least of interest for its examination of the notable individuals of various families, because as the generations pass, one sees how the principal personages are gradually transformed, how the garb of events in which they dress themselves changes, and how they come to present, almost in their entirety, the various phases of history. If, for example, we consider the Albarracín family, starting with Fray Miguel, Fray Justo de Santa María, and Domingo de Oro, we see the following elements: the convent, theology, the Millennium, the Inquisition, voyages to Spain, the declaration of independence and Bolívar who brings it to a close, the civil war, the caudillos, Rosas, and exile. Three generations have sufficed to consummate these deeds, three individuals have reflected them in noteworthy and significant acts. There is a moment, just as there is a person, that marks the midpoint between the colony and the Republic. All notable men of that epoch are like Terminus, the god of the ancients with two faces, one looking toward the future, the other toward the past.

Dean Funes was a distinguished example of this truth. The priesthood was, as befitted the situation of the Spanish colonies, the theater in which his career was to unfold. Trained by the Jesuits, he forever held them in special regard, notwithstanding the various changes his ideas later underwent; it was to them that he owed his penchant for letters, which, even within the priesthood, they alone cultivated with profit. A few years after presbyter Don Gregorio Funes was ordained, family affairs or the thirst for knowledge took him to Spain in the final years of the reign of Charles III, a time when Spanish letters were cultivated with great care.[1] In Spain, he received a doctorate in civil law and, thanks to the elevated position of his family and to his own recognized merit, he was awarded an honorary canonry as a distinction to carry back with him to his native land. Córdoba was then the colonial center of enlightenment and the fine arts. Its university and lecture halls shone brightly; its various monasteries were populated with hundreds of monks; the religious processions provided the city with colorful pageantry, lent an aura to worship, authority to the clergy, and prestige and power to its bishops. Canon Funes came from the court, had studied in Alcalá, enjoyed contact with the learned, and in addition he brought back treasures of science in a personal library as rich as it was select, such as had never been dreamed of in the University of Córdoba. The eighteenth century was thus introduced *in toto* into the very heart of the colonies. From that moment on, the prestige of his learning must have been immense; there is no better proof of this than the hostility of the magisterial canon of Córdoba, later bishop of Paraguay, Don Nicolás Videla del Pino, who saw in the honorary canon a dangerous rival for the higher favors of the Church. From then on a sometimes muted, sometimes vociferous struggle ensues between the two canons, which has political consequences, the first not failing to stand in the way of the latter on various occasions to divert him or to obstruct his advancement.

With the elevation to bishop of Córdoba of Sr. Don Angel Moscoso, son of a distinguished family of Arequipa, upon the transfer of Bishop San Alberto to the metropolitanship of Charcas, Canon Funes, despite the magister Videla, was appointed judge of the ecclesiastical court, vicar general, and governor of the bishopric. In that theocratic administration, the office of vicar general was, as in our day, a ministry of internal affairs, which gave legitimacy to reputations being made, and the means whereby they could be justified with deeds, bringing them within the confines of the bishopric. Funes was the supreme arbiter in ecclesiastical matters while Moscoso was alive, and after his death, elected dean of the cathedral, he continued to govern the diocese for a few years more while the office of bishop remained vacant. He did so without fear of possible rivalry, since Videla had already been appointed bishop of Paraguay.

When Charles III died, Funes delivered a funeral oration that must have done much to enhance his literary prestige. Rich in erudition from the works of the most celebrated French writers that he alone possessed, and filled with ideas of a different order from the limited ones that circulated in the colonies, the sacred orator was able to rise to the occasion, paying tribute in grandiloquent terms to the royal decrees that had made the dead king's reign so worthy of praise. He spoke of free trade in the colonies with the aplomb of a financier, describing the distress of his vassals in words that were, unfortunately, not his own.[2]

Another congratulatory sermon on Charles IV's accession to the throne, and various court cases in which he defended Señor Moscoso before the royal tribunal of Buenos Aires, and which went on appeal before the Supreme Council of the Indies in Spain, were more than enough to give him a colossal reputation that reached beyond the borders of the viceroyalty.

But another dispute, much in the spirit of the times, was to provide the wise dean with material for new undertakings, a vast field for his activities, putting into his hands a powerful weapon he had been trying for a long time to secure. With the expulsion of the Jesuits, the *Colegio* and University de Córdoba, where he himself had acquired the first rudiments of knowledge, had been turned over temporarily to the Order of Franciscan monks, who in the cultivation of the sciences followed most closely the expelled brethren. Belonging to this order was the celebrated Father García, whom in 1821 or 1822 I heard preach a May 25th sermon, in the presence of Bustos, the governor of Córdoba, that left the listeners astounded with the incriminations that the patriotic friar hurled at the governor from the pulpit, recalling the revolt of Arequito in his review of the progress of the revolution.[3] I can remember the structure of the bit of oratory to which I refer, which began this way: "May 25, 1810! A day to remember!" etc., "May 25, 1811!", and he went on concretizing the historical events until, on reaching the year 1820, he shifted from praise to attack, describing the sun that shone during the month of May that year as if ashamed of the deeds it had witnessed. The people in the cathedral looked at each other; I could see Bustos, toying with the tassel of a velvet cushion on the table upon which the missal lay before him, while the implacable friar, invested with the doctoral insignia of both laws, continued to thunder at the powerful official, upon whom he kept his gaze steadily fixed.

The secular clergy of Córdoba had many years before claimed for it-self the administration of the curriculum, gone before the viceroys, and appealed to the Spanish court, which after twenty or thirty years of dis-pute between the two clergies, issued a royal edict ordering that the ad-ministration of teaching go to the secular clergy. But royal edicts had little force in getting the powerful and influential friars to give up the su-perintendence they had exercised for so many years, the loss of which also threatened to dim the glory of the seraphic order. Córdoba was di-vided into factions, the monasteries followed the friars, the students ral-lied their families behind their teachers, and governors and even viceroys, won over by Franciscan intrigues and influence, proved laggard and ineffectual in enforcing the royal decrees. "The monastic spirit," says a document I have before me, "Aristotelianism, and the various *virtual and formal* distinctions of Saint Thomas and Duns Scotus, had perme-ated the courts, the soirées of the ladies, and even the workshops of the artisans. With few exceptions, the clergy were friars, the youth were choir boys, and all society a convent." I still know some Cordovans who have maintained the zeal of their grandfathers. The prevailing spirit at the University of Córdoba was such that the Franciscan administration kept under surveillance, vilified, and even punished any unfortunate youth who preferred to study civil law rather than the theology of the time, which sought to explain by essence and form, the natural questions that chemistry has now resolved by affinity and crystallization.

Dean Funes took an active part in the controversy; he boldly made two trips to Buenos Aires to demand compliance with the royal edicts; but the new provisions obtained met with delaying tactics on the part of Don Victorino Rodríguez, governor of Córdoba, who was under Fran-ciscan influence and an enemy of Funes for reasons of literary envy and familial grudges.

In the year 1806, after the reconquest of Buenos Aires, Liniers, a friend of Funes and an enlightened Frenchman, assumed the the post of viceroy.[4] Nevertheless, new orders were issued in confirmation of the previous ones, the initial neglect of which prompted their reissuance in 1807, with instructions for Doctor Ambrosio Funes, the Dean's brother, to notify the governor that if they were not implemented within three days, he would be removed from office in accordance with the attached written order to that effect. The governor understood, and immediately gave the secular clergy, in the person of Dean Funes, possession of the rectory of the *Colegio* of Montserrat and the chancellory of the University of Córdoba, in December of 1807. Thus, the Middle Ages had waged the fiercest of battles to prevent its being dispossessed of the guardianship of souls; forty years of struggle; the royal order disobeyed; five consecutive orders of execution ignored; without ceding ground until a son of France headed the viceroyalty. The learned city has not been so resistant in recent times, when their former doctors have been supplanted in command by sons born of the cattle country!

Regenerative ideas, then, had stormed that citadel of the colonies. Doctor Funes, in accepting the duties he had so coveted, gave evidence of the purity of his intentions by refusing the income that accrued from them and by using it to endow a chair of mathematics, which was inaugurated with Liniers's authorization, despite official orders to the contrary from the Spanish court.

This first step taken made abundantly clear the new direction that the conspiracy of the American spirit was going to give to university studies under Funes's influence. The dean then prepared a program of studies that, after being sent to the Spanish court for authorization, was subsequently prescribed for the other universities in America. "There being no need," he says in his *Ensayo Histórico* [Historical Essay], "to defer to the barbarism of gothic times, to which the precepts of the ecclesiastical ministry subjected students in the form of four years of obligatory scholastic theology, it was proposed to give more discipline to the intellectual man. In addition to introducing the study of mathematics and improving the subjects in the major schools, it was sought at the same time to promote the cultivation of the fine arts and the rebirth of good taste. It is undeniable that under this method, education has necessarily made great strides and the tree of knowledge promises good fruits."[a]

Education ceased to be theocratic in approach and degrading in its discipline. Instead of the Aristotelian philosophy of Goudin and the theology of Gonet and Polanco, more modern authors were introduced as texts, replacing scholastic theology with the dogmatic theology of Gott, Bergier, and others; the moral of Antoine; and the natural of Brison, Sigaud de la Fond, Almeida, and the most modern authors known at the time. Chairs of mathematics, experimental physics, and canonical

---

[a] *Ensayo Histórico de las Provincias del Paraguay* [Historical essay of The Provinces of Paraguay], Vol III. [Author's note]

law were established, subdividing into two the chair that until then had covered Roman law and Spanish civil law. At his own expense, Funes established classes in geography, music, and French within the *Colegio* and, as if he wished to draw attention to the importance he attached to these disciplines, reputed at the time to be unworthy of a scholar, the dean of the cathedral and the governor of the bishopric, the favorite of the viceroy, and the chancellor of the University, in person attended and taught them!

The fame of the salutary revolution spread throughout all of America. Viceroy Liniers sent his three sons to take classes under the profound thinker; two youths from the Philippines quickly followed; General Córdoba registered his son, who has since figured so prominently in Spain; a young Roman, Arduz, who has subsequently served in the magistracy in Bolivia; and hundreds of Americans from Peru and Paraguay, Montevideo and Chile, followed them. What the revolution in intellectual thought produced for the liberty of the Argentine Republic, for letters and the law, the Argentine reader will appreciate by passing in review the following names of other similar disciples educated under the inspiration of Dean Funes.

Don Juan Cruz Varela, the most rigorous of the Argentine poets in his time, who was fortunate enough to remain original without deviating from the great models.[5] He is the Quintana of the Río de la Plata; and so, just as the latter rejuvenated Spanish poetry, calling for independence and singing the invention of the printing press, so Varela introduced new themes worthy of the modern muse, intoning sublime odes to acts of public beneficence, to projects of social reform and, in particular, castigating fanaticism, an enemy he attacked relentlessly during his entire life.[6] He was a delegate to the congress which was supposed to meet in Córdoba in 1816; secretary of the Buenos Aires Congress until its dissolution; chief officer of one of the government ministries. He published many newspapers during the administrations of Rodríguez, Las Heras, and Rivadavia: *La Centinela* [The Sentinel], *El Tiempo* [The Times], *El Granizo* [The Hail], and, during the time of Governor Dorrego, whose reactionary course he attacked with lampoons that all Argentineans conserve in their memory as models of humor and Attic wit, he published the *El Patriota* [The Patriot] from the dungeons of the police force's central prison, after having saved his life thanks to the steadfastness of his spirit.[7] He died in exile in Montevideo while at work on a verse translation of the *Aeneid*, the first two cantos of which he left completed and polished with his characteristic meticulousness.

Doctor Ansina is another of Dean Funes's worthy disciples, one of the most brilliant members of the legal profession in Buenos Aires, as he has demonstrated in his defenses of the Yañezes, accused of murder, of Colonel Rojas, and of the government's right to the Malvinas [Falkland] Islands occupied by the British. He was professor of law at the University until 1840, when, imprisoned and about to be turned over to the Mazorca, his wife, the daughter of Dr. Maza, president of the House of Representatives and of the Supreme Court of Justice and murdered by Rosas in the very chamber of the House, rescued him from the prison ship where he was being held, and fled with him to Montevideo. He has defended notorious cases in both courts of the Plata.[8] He has recently finished translating and annotating Chitty, and since his youth, in his homeland and in exile, he has consecrated his life to the defense of his country's freedom, of which he gives noble proof when he moves aside the still warm body of his friend Varela, in order to occupy the dangerous position that had cost Varela his life.[9] The day after the murder of the honored writer, the following appeared in an article in *El Comercio del Plata* [The Commerce of the . . .]: "Its founder and editor Don Florencio Varela was treacherously murdered on March 20, 1848. It is now directed by Don Valentín Alsina, its principle editor." Hail, Alsina! With such sons, the Republic is not yet lost!

Doctor Gallardo, editor of *El Tiempo* and other newspapers of the Rivadavia period, now practices law with distinction in the port of Valparaiso, which honors his talents with a numerous clientele.

The Drs. Ocampo, residing in Santiago de Chile, in Copiapó, and Concepción. The surname alone is already recognized in Chile as testimony to the importance and depth of the studies that bear it.

Salvador M. del Carril, governor of San Juan, now living in Río Grande; Javier and Joaquín Godoy, the former having died in exile, the latter residing in Copiapó.

The Bedoyas, two of them in Copiapó, one of whom, in Santiago, tore from a person's breast and crushed under his foot the red rag that even in Chile could dare to flaunt the brutal injunction: "Death to the unitarian savages!"[10]

Dr. Zorrilla, an emigré in Bolivia for eighteen years, died six months ago while traveling, having been banished from Chuquisaca.

Subiría, a distinguished citizen of Salta, in exile for eighteen years.
Olañeta, from Chuquisaca.

Ellauri, from Montevideo, a Uruguayan envoy to France.

Lafinur, a celebrated poet and an outstanding musician, perhaps the first to introduce in these parts of America modern doctrines concerning points of philosophy, which he taught in Buenos Aires.

The Agüeros of Buenos Aires, and others of lesser political importance: Saravia, Orjera, Colinas, Villafañe, the Fragueiros, Allende, Cabrera, Urtubec, Aguirre, Dr. Vélez of Córdoba, Uriburu, Alvarado, Indebeirus, and Pinedo.

Of these Argentineans, the most illustrious ones, all those who have held public office, are in exile or have died in the slaughters and persecutions visited upon them by Don Juan Manuel Rosas, who had not studied under the direction of Dean Funes but who learned to read with Dr. Maza, whose throat was slit in the House of Representatives of Buenos Aires.

I am still forgetting two disciples of that teacher who, like one of the disciples of Jesus, split away from the school and came to agree with the Pharisees. Echagüe, doctor of theology, made a general by López, of Santa Fe, a man who squatted on his heels to chat, and is now governor of the village where there was once a city. As far as his theological learning is concerned, the following stylistic passage from one of his official notes can give you an idea: "The undersigned has read the contents of the *seditious, anarchistic, irritating* letter from the *stubborn, savage unitarian lodge member Sarmiento. . . .*"

The other is a Señor Otero, of Salta, who has been named special envoy to Chile and whom Rosas reprimanded in an official note for "using the Latin letter 'i' in cases where his government used the Greek letter 'y,'" ordering him to refrain from committing such an unpardonable lapse in the future!¹¹

But let us close this doleful page of losses the Republic has sustained from that crop of illustrious men that Córdoba produced under the inspiration of the learned Dean. Martyrdom, exile, and vilification have accounted for them all.

The resistance of the old ideas was made no less tenacious by the ousting of the Franciscans from the University and *Colegio* of Montserrat. The Middle Ages had taken cover in the numerous cloisters, and from there, dispatching its guerrillas, barefoot or shod, uniformed in black or white, it stirred up families and consciences, terrified as they were that

French was being taught in a *colegio*. In Spain itself, it wasn't until the middle, if not the end, of the seventeenth century that a quotation in that language appeared for the first time in a book. The venerable dean was accused, with absolute justification, of opening the way to Voltaire, D'Alembert, Diderot, and Rousseau, and the French Jacobins.[12] He was accused with even greater reason of marked preference for the study of law over that of scholastic theology, thereby leaving the souls of his disciples stripped of all defenses against feared and potential impiety. Not even mathematics was deemed deserving of indulgence, in view of its association with necromancy and magic, which still existed in some learned minds. Music was a worldly diversion that sent one singing and dancing down the primrose path to eternal perdition, and, what was more, a distinctly plebeian skill, inasmuch as only the slaves in the convents learned to play the violin, harp, and guitar. Lastly, Dean Funes, so gentle and easygoing in nature that his paternal indulgence relaxed school discipline, had allowed a fencing class to be organized, which led to squabbles and duels. But where was this saintly man heading, with all those innovations that were stirring up the tonsured and the long line of sanctimonious women who always hover about monasteries and convents? The dean kept the secret to himself and went on with his work. Doctor Don Leopoldo Allende, rector of the Colegio de Loreto, who was very influential in the city, officially forbade his students to attend the new classes of law, mathematics, French, geography, etc. The chancellor of the University called in the arrogant, fanatical rector to reprimand him and found, not to his surprise, that he was bragging publicly of his opposition to the reform, supporting his arguments in sacred texts that proved that a priest should know neither geography nor French, so as better to combat heresy. This time, Funes departed from his habitual meekness and had the rector arrested and sent back to his Colegio de Loreto, an order that affected the proud man so profoundly that he collapsed in a faint and had to be carried away. A few days later, Dr. Allende, in Bishop Orellana's house, while signing a certificate for an ordination exam being taken by Dr. Caballero of Córdoba, got as far as "*Doctor Leopoldo Al . . .*," and fell over dead. As was to be feared, this unfortunate accident, blown up and distorted, swelled the list of charges against the innovator, who had undermined the fatuousness of the ignorant doctor. The vacancy created in the rectorate of Loreto by that death was, however, filled by an able person, and reform was then introduced without difficulty.

Around this time (we are in the year 1809), slight rumblings were beginning to be perceived in the political world of Spain. The heated discussions were going on in Chuquisaca between the *audiencia* and its president Pizarro, regarding the rights of Carlota to the throne of Spain and
America during Fernando's captivity; and Monteagudo, Otero, Bustamante, Postillo, and other *porteños* or Argentineans could not obstruct
the revolutionary movements that were delaying plans already hatching
in Buenos Aires and that had ramifications in La Paz, Chuquisaca,
Lima, and other points in America.[13]* Many of the plot's threads, if not
all, passed through Córdoba under the gentle and knowing hand of the
doctor and dean. His reputation for wisdom, his influence with the
clergy, his relation with all the distinguished men of both viceroyalties,
the very confluence of so many students from so many different countries, made the celebrated dean the natural center of all the preparatory
movements of the revolution of independence.[14]

The first news to reach Córdoba of the Revolution of May 25th, 1810,
was received by the dean, a circumstance that seriously compromised
him in the eyes of the royal authorities. His friend Liniers, the former
viceroy, was in Córdoba at the time, and, as a consequence of the circulars that the new government was sending to all the provinces, a junta
was formed to deliberate on the change produced in Buenos Aires. This
junta was presided over by Linier and composed for the most part of
peninsulars, both Governor Concha and Bishop Orellana, themselves,
being Spaniards. Dean Funes was invited, as was his due, to cast his vote
on such a momentous deliberation, and in the presence of his bishop,
like Pope Sixtus V before the conclave of cardinals, he threw down the
crutches of dissimulation and declared himself an American, an Argentinean, a patriot, and a revolutionary. He could then say to his friend
Liniers, like Franklin to Lord Strahane: "You are a Member of Parliament, and one of that Majority that doomed my country to destruction. . . . You and I were long Friends: You are now my Enemy!"[15]

Not a single vote did the dean garner in favor of his idea of simply
recognizing the governing junta of Buenos Aires. Liniers, the bishop,
General Concha, Colonel Allende, Don Victorio Rodríguez, a government adviser and a man of great and merited influence, all of them
supported by all the Europeans of Córdoba and by the momentary

---

* An *audiencia* was a colonial appelate court with administrative functions.—Ed.

confusion of those minds unprepared for such a bold stroke, declared their opposition to the Buenos Aires government and war against the army that had set out to protect the provinces. But the damage was already done, and the arrow shot that left the Spanish system mortally wounded. As in all great revolutions, the instruments that prepared the events were neither decrees nor soldiers but moral sanctions, reputations, principles; the revolution was directed at the spirit, not the body, and the single vote of Dean Funes, the American sage, was the vote of the people. The dean sent copies of his vote to all the provinces, and even to Lima, the seat of the most powerful of the viceroyalties, and while Viceroy Abascal declared in his proclamations and official publications that the Buenos Aires revolution was the work of a few scoundrels, a clutch of creole *savages,* the voice of the people from one end of America to the other repeated the name of Dr. Don Gregorio Funes, chancellor of the University of Córdoba, who had educated a generation of athletes in the new ways of thinking.* Viceroy Abascal, as is often the case in these circumstances, ordered the confiscation in Peru of the property of the revolutionary Argentine *savages,* reaping a harvest of nearly four million pesos in securities belonging to those Argentineans who were residents in Lima and to those who were transients and who happened to be there at the time with large droves of mules. The dean took a loss of sixty thousand pesos in his assets, which his nephew Don Sixto was managing, and had to make good the credits he had drawn on in Córdoba and Buenos Aires. His brother Don Ambrosio, Don Domingo, and other relatives with interests in Lima were equally affected by these sudden punitive measures. One Señor Candiote of Santa Fe alone lost six hundred thousand pesos. As for the effect upon the dean, this coup of despotic knavery, while not deterring him for a moment from his purpose, since the thinking brain is not overly concerned with the quality of the food that enters the stomach, did, nonetheless, exercise an unhappy influence on the final days of his life.

The Spanish government of Córdoba brought pressure to bear upon the other towns in order to dissuade them from recognizing the governing junta of Buenos Aires. At that time, the cities of Santiago del Estero, Tucumán, and Catamarca were dependencies of Salta. The bishop of

---

*For a definition of "creole" (*criollo*), see Note 37, Introduction.—Ed.

that diocese was the same prebend Videla who had passed from Paraguay to Salta to wrest the miter from Funes's head. He decided, out of rivalry with the dean, in favor of passive obedience to the monarchs, and the rancorous bishop, supported by Governor Isasmendi, would have dragged those provinces along into the resistance, if Moldes, Gurruchaga, Castellano, Cordejo, and Saravia, friends and admirers of Funes, had not objected strongly to the discordant attempt, despite the Intendancy of Potosí, which had allowed itself to be dragged in by the overtures of Córdoba.

The army of Buenos Aires penetrated Córdoba at last, and Dean Funes's moral influence and principles began to prevail in the city, allowing, from that time onward, his doctrines to spread to all social classes without difficulty or interference, and to be disseminated in the other provinces, as well. Around this time, his nephew Don Juan Luis Funes, a member of the San Juan branch of the family, by means of a speech that, in his role as militia officer, he delivered to the civic troops, removed all the Spaniards still employed in public service. With this act, the revolution, initiated in Buenos Aires and now triumphant at last in Córdoba, was consummated in San Juan.

But there still remained more worthy terrain on which the dean could exercise his calming influence. The revolution inaugurated its triumph by abandoning itself to terrible onslaughts of rage, immediately singling out illustrious expiatory victims considered worthy of its cause, and Córdoba was chosen as the altar for their immolation. It is the dean himself who has preserved for us the details of the event.

"The Junta," he says, "had decreed that the revolution be founded on the blood of these misguided men, such that terror would impose a profound silence on the enemies of the cause. On the eve of this catastrophe, I realized what was going on. My surprise was equaled by my distress when I imagined how such respected victims must be trembling. For the good name of a cause that, being so just, was about to turn brutal, and even sacrilegious in the eyes of a people accustomed to kneel before their bishops; for fear that the patriotism of many worthy families might be stifled; in short, for all that the laws of humanity inspired in me, I felt I bore the obligation to present these arguments to Don Francisco Antonio Ocampo and Don Hipólito Vieytes, commanders of the expedition, and to plead with them to suspend the execution of such an odious sentence. The impression made by these arguments, and others that my brother Don Ambrosio Funes was able to add, had the desired effect a few hours before the execution."[b]

The prisoners were removed to Buenos Aires; but on the way, in an ill-fated spot, they were met by the dread representative of the people, who carried out the governing junta's implacable sentence against those who had dared to strike the first spark of civil war, as if from the beginning they had foreseen that there lay the cancer that would later devour the entrails of the Republic.

To sanction its acts, the governing junta had convoked a congress of provincial delegates, and Dean Funes went to Buenos Aires for the city of Córdoba, to lend the assistance of his learning and influence to the new government. What were the duties of this new congress to be? Would the governing junta continue as before, exercising power under the sanction of, but separately from, the incomplete congress that had just convened? This was an impasse from which they could not escape without suffering demoralization and without creating deep, open fissures in the harmony between the provinces and the capital. When the matter was raised for discussion, the delegate from Mendoza said: "that the delegates should join the junta to carry out the same duties as the members who had composed it until then."

The secretary of the junta, Doctor Don Juan José Paso, said: "that the delegates of the provinces should not join the junta, nor take an active part in the provisional rule it now exercised."

The president of the junta, Don Cornelio Saavedra, said: "that the incorporation of the representatives into the junta was not consistent with the law; but that he was acceding to it because it was in the public interest."

The secretary of the junta, Don Mariano Moreno, said: "that he considers incorporation of the delegates in the junta to be against the law and the general welfare of the State, in view of the future objectives of the great cause, of its constitution, etc."[c] On the basis of these differing opinions and the formal petition of the nine provincial delegates demanding "their right to be incorporated into the provisional junta and to take an active part in the governance of the provinces until such time as

---

[b] *Bosquejo de nuestra revolución* [Outline of Our Revolution], p. 491. [Author's note]

[c] *Acta de la Junta Provisional Gubernativa* [Record of the Provisional Governing Junta] of December 18, 1810. [Author's note]

the congress was convened," incorporation won the day, and an executive government of twenty-two members was formed, a government pregnant with impending storms, with provincial jealousies and, what is more, rife with naive inexperience in everything related to the practices of free governments: "Funes, the most influential of the delegates," says a contemporary author, "and the one who most contributed to this deficiency, expresses himself thus in his *Ensayo sobre la revolución* [Essay on the Revolution]: 'The decision to grant the delegates an active role in the government meant depriving it of secrecy in deliberation, promptness of action, and the vigor of its temperament.'"[d]

But even greater was the accumulation of evils that this measure and the blunders that produced and followed it were to create for the future of the Republic. The question scarcely broached in that indefinable junta was soon clearly articulated and delimited in public opinion, which split into bands of *provincialists* and *executivists,* already the embryonic form of the question of *federalists* and *unitarians* that was to engender the hybrid monster who has named himself the Hero of the Desert because, in effect, he has succeeded in the depopulation of his country. What is that government: federalist or unitarian? Let him respond, the stupid brute![16]

As was to be expected, the executive convention became rapidly demoralized, finding itself forced by its own impotence to dissolve, and delegating its undefined powers to a commission, until such time as a national assembly could convene. Public discontent aimed at the commission quickly erupted, and an attempt at subversion, attributed to Funes's influence, landed him in jail. It was then that Cordoba's longstanding animosity toward Buenos Aires reappeared, and with it, the learned central city's struggle for supremacy. The clergy of Córdoba, the University and the *Colegio* of *Monserrat,* in defiance of the *executivists* who constituted the government, sent their respective delegations to Buenos Aires to seek the freedom of the one they called their common father. The government of Buenos Aires turned a deaf ear on their plea, and so the city of Córdoba cast its lot with the counterrevolution, joining with and supporting any caudillo who sought to drown freedom in crime, from Artigas, the bandit of Montevideo, to Bustos, the deserter of Arequito. The struggle of ideas between the two cities spread and

[d] *Arengas del doctor Moreno* [Speeches of Doctor Moreno], Vol. 1, p. 170 of the preface; and Funes, *Ensayo histórico* [Historical Essay], op. cit. [Author's note]

passed from the city to the countryside, and today the last representative of Córdoba's academic pride is a cattleman turned federal governor.

Dean Funes, quickly forgotten by Córdoba and Buenos Aires, by *executivists* and *provincialists,* to whose abuses he refused to extend his support, consecrated himself to the study of his country's history, and in 1816, the publisher Gandarillas and Assoc., emigrés from Chile, brought out the *Ensayo histórico de la historia civil del Paraguay, Buenos Aires y Tucumán* [Historical Essay on the Civil History of Paraguay, Buenos Aires, and Tucumán], written by Doctor Gregorio Funes, dean of the Holy Cathedral of Córdoba, in three cuarto volumes, the publication of which was completed in 1817 by Benavente, now president of the Senate of Chile, for such is the way Chileans and Argentineans have always behaved in their respective emigrations.

This work, which he had been writing for thirty years, for he was approaching seventy when he published it, clearly shows that it was written in colonial times and was prepared with an eye to receiving the censor's seal unblemished. Nevertheless, there are concepts in his introduction that are worth remembering. "The day had finally to dawn," the illustrious patriot says, "when the tender and sublime sentiment of love for one's country would not be a crime. Under the former regime, thought was enslaved and the citizen's very soul was not his own. With tyranny always at large, the vices of those who have governed us will serve us as documents for distinguishing between good and evil, and for choosing the better." "The monarchs of Spain, under whose steel scepter we have lived, feared the *truth;* he who dared speak it would have been considered a bad citizen, a traitor. That grim period is now over. . . ."[e]

Ah! It is not yet over for your descendants, illustrious Funes! The dark clouds that hung over the colonies for three centuries broke one day to let the light of May 25th, Chacabuco, Maipú, freedom of worship, and the various Argentine Congresses shine forth, and then they closed again, grim, pestilent, bloody. Since then, as before, truth is feared, and he who dares utter its name is called a bad citizen, a traitor. Listen to your renegade disciple, Doctor Echagüe, to whose support the tyrant has appealed so that he may pretend there is a public opinion that condemns me, putting into deeds what your science of history had revealed to you when you said, "Let them not speak to us of ratification by the people;

[e] *Ensayo* [Essay], "Prologue," p. 10. [Author's note]

the power of the one in command and the *hypocrisy of the obedient* generally advance together step by step."[f] Ilustrious forebear of the revolution! I will follow, and others will follow your counsel. "Danger acts as a deterrent," you said, "only for cowardly peoples; the courageous equate the number of their efforts with that of their misfortunes; good fortune enters into the calculation of doubtful things; they trust in nothing but their righteousness."[g]

In 1819, Dean Funes surfaces again in public life as president of the Constitutional Congress. In the manifesto that recounted the work of the Congress that had sanctioned the Constitution of the United Provinces of South America, published on April 20, 1819, he said, among other things: "The meager population of the State justified that we should trace to its source an evil responsible for our common weakness. It is none other than the despotism of the former regime, the ravages of which are always *ignorance, sterility,* and *the absence of population in the countryside.* By authorizing the Supreme Director of the State to distribute uncultivated lands, the Congress gave the signal that it was guided by a spirit of reparation" . . . "Ignorance is the cause of the immorality that diminishes all virtues and gives rise to all the crimes that plague society. Congress listened with the greatest of interest, and approved the request of several cities for funds to establish primary schools and other beneficial institutions. There is nothing more reassuring to see than the propagation of public education. The efforts devoted by the Supreme Director of the State to fostering letters through education in this capital, and those expended in the other provinces, will in time serve to form men and citizens. Sympathetic to these laudable efforts, the Congress allocated all public funds derived from collateral inheritances to the employment of teachers."[h]

This was the last act of Dean Funes's public life. After the Constitutional Congress came that disintegration of the old society, that struggle among all the elements of organization, the frenzy that led to arguments at bayonet point in the streets of Buenos Aires, the favored solution of the most frivolous personalities, and that ended in 1820 with the victory

[f] *Bosquejo de nuestra revolución* [Outline of Our Revolution], Vol III *of Ensayo histórico* [Historical Essay], p. 500. [Author's note]
[g] *Bosquejo* [Outline], ibid., p. 502. [Author's note]
[h] Sessions of Congress. [Author's note]

of Martín Rodríguez, and the beginning of a new era of our history.[17] I had said at the outset that the men of Funes's time had two faces, two existences: one colonial, the other republican. From Martín Rodríguez on, this intermediate generation fades, overwhelmed in the presence of new men who appear to have had no knowledge of the colonies, who are pure future, if such can be said, since they take nothing of the past into account. From that point on, Dean Funes understands less of what is going on before his eyes, in the same way that he is no longer understood, nor respected by the new generation of literati and writers, philosophers, poets, and politicians that emerges. His stature, so grand and eminent in 1810, is diminished, obliterated in the face of the forgetful ingratitude of the next generation. And what could remain for the elderly chancellor of the University of Córdoba, the delegate to those first congresses, rehearsals bordering on the infantile of governmental inexperience? His religious condition distanced him from secular affairs, his age banished from his mind the thought that he could still depend on time for the realization of his every plan, and there are men whom nothing can save from death, because the atmosphere in which they had flourished has changed.

Moreover, incidental circumstances precipitated the decline of his spirits. The reaction of Córdoba, which, in 1812, had been prepared by him, in his name and for praiseworthy motives, had, in its subsequent vagaries, turned against him. Viceroy Abascal had confiscated his entire fortune, the Cathedral of Córdoba disowned its dean, and he, who had been the glory of its letters, its crown jewel, and the arbiter of the fate of so many men from 1809 onward, had, in order to survive, to sell one by one the books in his library, to dispose of his French encyclopedia, so very coveted and exceptional at the time, and to break up his collection of rare manuscripts, exchanging for bodily sustenance that which had been the food for his soul. That morality that had enabled him to lead the most difficult of all reforms, which is the one that, changing the object and idea of science, leaves an entire generation ignorant and without protection, weakened now in the struggles of a penurious life, without hope of rehabilitation, without object, and transplanted to another terrain. There is talk of amorous passions kindled in that heart which for sixty-five years had resisted their seductions, and when abject poverty had crossed his threshold, there came a woman to dispel from that strong spirit the despair that follows upon disillusionment. Human frailty! If such events be worth recording in the memory of those alive today, we must be thankful to you for having assailed the corpse of the illustrious reformer after the fruits of his high and noble mission had matured!

Still another factor contributed to the decline of his former reputation. The cosmopolitan republic that had throbbed with all the emotions of America, and had, for so long, found its blood and treasure put to equally good use in Chile as in Montevideo, in Lima as within its own borders, began at that time to concentrate on itself with an end to creating an Argentine nationality. Along the way, it had encountered a man great in glory, in service to the independence, who in terms of influence over America sought to overshadow and diminish it; that great man and that republic had begun to hate and to persecute one another.[18] The old dean understood nothing of these exclusions and of those antipathies, and, as though he were still in the golden age of the revolution, when the colonists were joined together in a single purpose, whether they resided in Charcas, Buenos Aires, or Santiago de Chile, he naively accepted a position as Bolivar's official agent in the Argentine Republic, and in recompense the income from a deanery in Charcas, seized by Bolivar from the territory of the United Provinces of the Rio de la Plata. These were more than enough justifications for the decline of his influence in the political domain.

Nor did his literary reputation escape the erosion of time and progress. We have a prejudice in America, which makes well-meaning men attach great importance to the study of our history as colonials. But that history has been repudiated by the American Revolution, which is the negation of and a protest against the legitimacy of the deeds and the rectitude of the ideas of the nation from which we came. North America separated from England without renouncing the history of its freedoms, its juries, its parliaments, and its letters. We, on the day after the revolution, had to turn our eyes in all directions in search of that which could fill the void left by the destruction of the Inquisition, the overthrow of absolute power, and the broadening of religious tolerance.

Thus, a history of the colonies that can be incorporated into our present-day life calls for a deep and rigorous study of our way of being, and the *Ensayo de la historia civil del Paraguay* [Essay on the Civil History of Paraguay] fell far short of fulfilling those conditions. With an author nourished on the reading of close to forty chroniclers who have dealt with those regions, his work suffered on the critical side, since it allowed itself to be influenced by the execrable taste of the old-time historians of America, for interpolating marvels, miracles, and fabrications, either of their own invention or collected from popular tradition, into the narration of events that, with their baseness and vulgarity, alienate all sympathy and tire the curiosity of the reader. Add to this that the author makes full use of his wealth of erudition in American chronicles, as well as in the classical books of Europe, which he almost alone possessed, while being totally oblivious to the fact that he was writing at the dawn of an epoch that was to make the very foundations of its knowledge available to everyone. And so, the reader began to notice in many of his works sentences and paragraphs that had rung pleasantly in the ear before, and pages that the eyes recognized as having already been perused. The accusation of plagiarism has been leveled against Dean Funes which, to us, rather than reproachable, clearly stands as a mark of merit. We still have in our American literature distinguished authors who prefer to cast a good concept of their own in the mold of the classical words of a renowned writer. García del Río is the most brilliant model of that erudite school that includes in its works encrusted like jewels bits of delightful literature and selected thoughts.[19] A layer prior to this beautiful alluvium of sediments of good reading has yielded the compilation, that is, the appropriation of the products of the talent of good writers to the manifestations of new trends in thought. Capmany, in Spain, belongs to this family of authors who translate pages of French and put them into circulation under the guarantee of their name and decked out in the raiment of pure Castillian language.[20] *El médico a palos* [The Doctor by Force] by Moratín was *Le médicin malgré lui* [The Doctor in Spite of Himself] by Molière.[21]

And so, that which today we call plagiarism was before erudition and enrichment; and I for one would prefer hearing for the second time an author worthy of being read a hundred times, to the incomplete rehearsals of an intellect and a style that are still in an embryonic state because our national intelligence has not yet developed sufficiently to compete with authors that the world considers worthy of being heard.

Dean Funes's writings prove that he could have survived without borrowing anything from anyone. That is how he was considered by competent judges, among them Bishop Grégoire who, in paying the highest tribute to his talent and vast knowledge, prompted with his criticism the dean's refutation regarding the role that Las Casas had played in the propagation of slavery; a literary polemic, carried on brilliantly and courteously from France and Buenos Aires, and that made Dean Funes's work, which had motivated the polemic, known in Europe.[22]

Nor, in the midst of so many profane interests, was his devotion to sacred matters neglected, and he dedicated to Bolívar his refutation of *Un proyecto de Constitución religioso* [A Draft Religious Constitution] proposed by Señor Llorente, a Spanish scholar, famous for his *Anales de la Inquisición* [Annals of the Inquisition].

He turned his hand to biography, taking as his subject the interesting life of General Sucre, insofar as it served his predilection for Bolívar.[23]

Rivadavia commissioned the aging dean to do the translation of the work of Daunou *Ensayo sobre las garantías individuales que reclama el estado actual de la sociedad* [Essay on the Individual Guarantees Demanded by the Present State of Society], and, in the prologue, in a translator's note, the dean took the opportunity to praise the solicitude on the part of a government to disseminate principles among the governed that serve as a support for liberty: "There is no tyrant so imprudent that he will open the eyes of those whom he tyrannizes and put weapons in their hands with which to fight him."[24] He added notes of his own to the work, many of exceptional merit. The observation inserted at the end of Note 2 seems intentional: "Fear of the law is healthy; fear of men is the fatal and fertile origin of crime." What bitter confirmation this apothegm has had in his own poor country, now that the will of a stupid brute is the supreme law of the land! The dean's tolerance in religious matters is set forth in Note 8 with such startling profundity that it deserves reproduction in full: "Emulation in all matters," he says, "is what creates a new being and a new life. It has always been the source of zealous fervor, and of those generous sentiments that elevate the spirit and fill it with noble pride and magnanimous trust. Who can doubt but that this would make itself felt in a State among followers of diverse beliefs?" And in Note 13, he adds in justification of the necessary reforms: "No need to fear those disturbances that shocked past centuries; the volcano of the Vatican is now inactive, and the days are over when a piece of paper could arouse the feelings of a state."

Doctor Anchoris, publisher of the second edition of the Daunou translation, once assured a respectable gentleman who sends us information about the Dean, that Funes had won the approval of the French author regarding the doctrines that he refuted in his translator's notes.

"Many of your opinions," he wrote him from Paris, "are splendid, and have induced me to rectify my judgements." In those times, the New World and the Old were joined together in their thinking. Rivadavia was a friend and correspondent of Lafayette and Bentham, whose legal principles were taught at the University of Buenos Aires; Dean Funes's stature had now risen to that of Grégoire and Daunou, with whom he debated on an equal footing.[25]

To earn a living, he also published *El Argos* in Buenos Aires for about four years, and the knowledgeable reader can find reflected in that collection of writings the concerns of the time and the special hues of the prism of his intelligence.

After those works, the illustrious patriot is eclipsed by the sorrows of old age, poverty, and oblivion. In the opinion of his contemporaries, Dean Funes had long been dead and buried, despite the fact that the colonies have perhaps produced no life that is longer nor one more fully realized. His literary works may be eclipsed by the progress of enlightenment; yet, to this day, his *Ensayo* [Essay] is the only history written about the colonization of the regions to which it refers, the only history that Europe has received from America, and this fact demonstrates how facile and pretentious criticism is that destroys without offering anything in its place. His political theories, like his historical times, belong to the past, and his labors in congresses and governments have been lost along with his name in the catalogue of so many other illustrious workers; but his reform of the curriculum at the University of Córdoba, the rare intelligence it revealed in an era when so few in America understood the new course upon which human intelligence had embarked, establish Dean Funes as the precursor of the American Revolution in its most beautiful aspect, as a reformer of colonial ideas; and in this sense, his place in history need not yield in the least to that of Bolívar, Moreno, San Martín, and so many other powerful levers of action.[26] Many can come to a stand in the middle of history's path to make it veer off in the direction of new ideas; very few, however, are those who have the foresight to inoculate intelligence itself with a great principle, and launch it into the world to give a new face to the masses; and the celebrated dean is among that number! What effort it must have cost him to bring his thought to fruition! What fortitude to have accomplished it! And whose was the glory but his of sowing the seed and watching the plant flower, even though his hands would be pierced by the thorns that surrounded it?

The year 1830 was a prelude to a new era in the history of the Argentine Republic, a history that is still as uncertain as the border that divides two distinct nations. The decade of independence, which lasted until the Congress of 1819, was followed by that of freedom, until 1829; after that came another decade pregnant with menace and danger. The detonations of partisan combat had subsided; now settled was the dense dust cloud raised by the masses of horsemen sent by Rosas against haughty Buenos Aires to compel her to receive him. On one of those sadly tranquil evenings that one can experience in defeated and occupied capitals, the octogenarian Dean Funes was strolling the winding alleys of Wauxhall, an English garden in the heart of Buenos Aires that had been established by a society as a recreational park and was at the time the property of Mr. Wilde, its creator. That space, cultivated with the elegance of British artifice, the flowers blending with bushes in bloom, the thickets in which the hand of man mimics the charms of Nature, were until then the best contrast to the deserted pampa that European culture could offer; it was a bit of Europe transported to America, to show how its countryside might one day look when the abandonment of wild nature has given way to the science and attentions of the intelligent tiller of the soil. To Wauxhall came the families of Buenos Aires to feel themselves civilized among the meticulously cultivated trees, fruits and flowers; to Wauxhall came tightrope walkers, equestrians, and acrobats from Europe, in search of an audience and an arena; to Wauxhall, in short, the octogenarian Dean Funes occasionally retreated to breathe the last fragrances of life, to deceive eyes and ears in that oasis of civilization that was slow to spread its ramifications over the wild, untilled spaces of the pampas; and in those sinuous paths that conceal from the eye an unanticipated enticement to the placid contemplation of nature, surrounded by that family that was posthumous to his public life, to the virtues of his state and even to the appointed age for the heart's most tender emotions, the dean, while breathing in the perfume of a flower, felt himself about to die, and thus he expressed himself to the tender objects of his affection, without surprise, as though it were an event he had long awaited. He died a few minutes later, in the last days of the Republic he had rocked in its cradle, in the bosom of nature, not as happy as Rousseau, who left the earth pregnant with a fertile seed he would never see destroyed. Funes died on the eve of Rosas's triumph, making out from afar the bloody fringe of the flames that announced the return of the ancien régime, rejuvenated, barbarized in the savage caudillo of the pampa, as if he had wished to exit the theater of life where such a horrible drama was about to unfold; as if he were shutting his eyes to avoid seeing his followers, the Carrils, Alsinas, Varelas, Gallardos, Ocampos, Zorrillas, in exile; the universities shut; science vilified; and a horrible page of shame added to the history he had written. One day, I shall go with deep religious reverence to seek out, among other patriots' tombs, the one that a decree erected to his memory.

12

The Bishop of Cuyo

José Manuel Eufrasio de Quiroga Sarmiento, son of Doña Isabel Funes and Don Ignacio Sarmiento, currently bishop of Cuyo and nearly seventy-three years of age, is one of the most modest individuals who can possibly be held up to the consideration of his fellow man.

In San Juan in the middle of the last century, the patronymic Sarmiento becomes extinct in the male line. As a consequence, the children of one Señora Doña Mercedes Sarmiento and of one Señor Quiroga, take the maternal surname, a tradition maintained by the present bishop of Cuyo, who calls himself de Quiroga Sarmiento. The name of a Señora Doña Tránsito Sarmiento appears in the public records for the year 1650; from that point on, this family line eludes me, and the most laudable efforts on my part have failed to establish a connection with the *adelantado* Sarmiento, founder of the colony of *Magallanes* [Magellan], of ill-fated memory, despite the local tradition that the Sarmientos of San Juan were Biscayans, just like him. I would have jumped with joy to have been able to trace to such a noble origin my own more recent efforts to repopulate the Straits.[*] I could then lay claim as family property to that imposing peak named Mount Sarmiento, which raises its majestic brow at the tip of South America, contemplating both oceans, desolated by the storms of the Cape, and bedecked with sublime

---

[*] An *adelantado* was a provincial governor.—Ed.

cascades that plunge from its heights to the sea. However, I should say, in all good conscience, that I do not consider my credentials sufficiently clear to justify such exalted and polar pretensions.

Bishop Sarmiento is simply an old soldier of the Church who has stood sentry for fifty years at the door of the Lord's house, without the disturbances to which he was witness having distracted him for a moment from his evangelical duties. Cleric, assistant priest, suffragan bishop, rector priest, dean and bishop of that mother church and later the cathedral of San Juan, he has been, above all, the administrator who is diligent in the conservation of the temple, the passive implementer of the advances initiated by others more audacious than he. His public life is entirely linked to the great calamities that have befallen San Juan; thus, the priest is the born representative of the people, the Church, the refuge of the persecuted, and the bishop, the shoulder for the suffering to cry on. When the First Chasseurs of the Andes rose up in rebellion, when Carrera invaded with his fearful *montonera*, when Quiroga made the square bristle with gallows, in all the days of conflict, the house of the priest or the bishop was the neutral camp where persecutor and persecuted, executioner and victim, could look on one another without fear or fury. That is the entire political history of this man, member and leader of every commission sent by the people before every oppressor to plead for mercy for the families; acting governor when there was none, on the morning after a defeat, on the eve of an enemy's arrival, in those sorrowful hours when the sunlight appears to dim, and the ear sharpens instinctively to catch the rumblings that one expects to hear at any moment, like the sounds of weapons, like galloping horses, like doors crashing in, like the screams of mothers who see their children being killed.

And yet, on the modest role of this timid servant there is in San Juan a history written in indelible characters, the only history unstained by the passions of the moment, the only one that survives the vicissitudes of opinion, which are more destructive than those of time itself. What is today the Cathedral of San Juan was formerly the church of the Company of Jesus, a beautiful structure of classical architecture, its interior stylistically perfect, while its facade, completed later, is less severe, though charming. All the old churches of San Juan have disappeared one by one, crumbling from neglect, deserted because of the natural death of the religious orders that once attracted worshipers with novenas, matins, and solemnities. All civil and religious construction in San Juan came to a halt on the same day, giving way to the rapid destruction that is everywhere wrought by the barbarism of those who govern. Jofre's *pyramid* was the last public work to be completed; the consistorial houses built in 1823 on the corner of the main square and left at the point of completion are now a stinking heap of ruins, a den of vermin; and public archives, printshop, hospitals, the School of the Fatherland, boulevards, have all perished in twenty years, demolished, robbed, razed. In the midst of this universal disintegration, of the destruction of everything that it is incumbent on the public authorities to preserve and improve, it would have taken great effort to resist the lethargy and indifference of the dominant spirit; but it is a shining example of devotion that one authority alone should advance, while the others tolerate destruction or even encourage it, and this is the unusual merit of Doctor José Manuel Eufrasio de Quiroga Sarmiento, whether as priest, dean, or bishop of the church entrusted to his care. In 1824, he set about to stucco the beautiful facade and erect the second tower, which had been left unfinished. In 1826 he ordered Don Juan Espada, a Spanish blacksmith and ironworker of exceptional merit, to build a great gate of forged iron for the baptistery, which is a work of art and the only one of which San Juan is able to boast. In 1830 he refitted with balustrades the galleries that the Jesuits had installed in the spaces between the Tuscan columns that beautify the faces of the temple walls at equal distances, and which, when filled with people for the grand solemnities, lend charm and vivacity to the spectacle. In the meantime, he gathered together an exquisite collection of ornaments embroidered with raised work such as few cathedrals in America can claim, including the vestments of a flamboyant cardinal in Rome that he was able to obtain. The columns were refitted with hangings in 1847, and not long ago, Italian artists were summoned from Buenos Aires to refurbish or complete the gold leaf of the altars that are of a most elegant design; and the cathedral today, in its embellishment, beauty, and freshness, is the sole oasis of civilization and progress in that unfortunate province, which is rapidly degenerating into a village unfit for habitation by men of refinement.

It is said that the elderly bishop's will leaves everything to the church, in the manner of those seamen who have grown old sailing their ships and make the hulk their universal heir; and I am at the point of condoning this seemingly witless charity on behalf of his lifelong companion, the instrument of his elevation and the object of his solicitude for half a century of his existence. Virtues of all sorts must be present in society, and it should not be insisted upon, though it be to our detriment, that he who practices a special virtue shall, at the same time, tend to all the others.[2]

The former Father Sarmiento has heard confession four hours a day for forty years; he has sung the mass of the Sacrament every Thursday, preached every Sunday despite his sometimes uncontrollable stammer, interspersing this daily routine, as regular as clockwork, with the commemoration of *Animas, Corpus,* Holy Week, and the celebrations of Saint John the Baptist, patron saint of the city, and the solemn service for Saint Peter, with its corresponding banquet given for the magnates of the city; and as if these tasks were insufficient to free him from further obligation, to the *School of Christ* that he had himself introduced, he later added the *salve,* sung on Saturdays, a tender devotion left abandoned by the Dominican brothers when they dispersed after the destruction of the temple, and which he took up and brought to his house to honor. He did the same with the *Way of the Cross,* which used to be celebrated in the church of Saint Anne and which had to be suspended because of the ruinous state of that building.

My uncle began teaching me to read when I was four years old; as a youngster, I was his altar boy, and during my last years in San Juan, his favorite nephew, an attribute I undoubtedly continue to possess to this day, if only the poor old man, on whose nerves fear plays so easily, were not continually upset to see me in danger of ending up impaled on the bull's horns, as has happened to so many others who paid dearly for being nobler in spirit than the fortunate tyrant on whose account I am obliged to relate all these things.

The bishopric created by his predecessor, His Grace Bishop Oro, has not increased much during the administration of the second bishop of Cuyo. The rebellion against the decrees of the Holy See instigated in 1839 by Doctor Don Ignacio Castro Barros continues to this day.[3] The provinces of Mendoza and San Luis do not recognize any circumscription on the map of Catholic geography. Separated by the pope from the diocese of Córdoba, they have refused to recognize the bishop of Cuyo as head of the Church. These quarrels are abetted and sanctified by the small-town spirit that makes belonging to the jurisdiction of Córdoba, rather than to that of San Juan, a matter of provincial self-esteem; and such is the subversion of ideas, that God-fearing people and even the clergy live in peace with their conscience in a schismatic and acephalous state for which there can be no justification. This matter has been a source of the endless sorrow and annoyance that have embittered the life of the old bishop.

Due to these puerile dissensions, the bishopric that promised so many benefits has become an apple of discord thrown among those towns. I understand that among the bishop's bulls there is a general one, as it were, inherent in the creation of the bishopric, for permitting mixed marriages, while, at the same time, freedom of worship is not permitted, a prohibition that violates the treaty with England, as Rosas pointed out to the governor of San Juan. His most illustrious Grace Oro, founder of the bishopric, indicated in 1821 to Canon Don Julian Navarro of the Cathedral of Santiago, from whose lips I heard this, his firm conviction that the Church could not oppose the laws of the state, which guarantee dissident Christians freedom of worship. Indeed, at that time His Grace Oro had provided Canon Navarro with information and a rationale on which to base his work entitled *El sacerdote Cristófilo. Doctrina moral cristiana sobre los funerales de los protestantes* [The Christophile Priest. Christian Moral Doctrine Regarding Funerals for Protestants], which that canon produced in defense of a decree by O'Higgins that permitted the establishment of cemeteries for Protestants in Santiago and Valparaíso.[4] It was against this same decree that thirty-nine priests from Santiago presented a formal appeal, determined, in their misguided zeal, to deny burial to persons who had not been born Catholics and who had the misfortune to die in Chile. I remember these antecedents because not long ago a dispensation was denied the only foreign Protestant in San Juan who has requested one, in order that he might marry a young woman from Mendoza without having to renounce his religion; and although this act is very much in keeping with the exclusionist sentiments bequeathed us by our parents, it is not for that reason any less baneful for the population of those countries, and for the establishment in them of industrious, moral, and intelligent Europeans. Señor Cienfuegos, later bishop of Concepción, cited the scarcity of population when he granted a dispensation in a similar case in 1818; and this shall always be a reason that will argue in favor of religious freedom in the countries of America.

13

The Story of My Mother

I feel an oppression in my heart as I set down the events I am about to relate. A man's mother is for him the personification of Providence, the living earth to which the heart attaches, like roots to the soil. All those who write about their family speak of their mother with tenderness. Saint Agustine praised his so much that the Church placed her at his side on the altars; Lamartine has spoken of his mother at such length in his *Confidences* that human nature has been enriched with one of the most beautiful examples of womanhood that history has known; a woman adorable for her physiognomy and endowed with a heart that resembles an unfathomable depth of generosity, love, and enthusiasm.[1] These qualities, however, have not compromised the gifts of supreme intelligence that have engendered the soul of Lamartine, that last scion of the old aristocratic society who is transformed under the maternal wing to become, soon thereafter, the angel of peace that will proclaim to a restless Europe the advent of the republic. For the effects of the heart there can be no mother equal to the one that fortune has given us; but when one has read pages like those of Lamartine, not all mothers lend themselves equally well to having their image sculpted in a book. However, as God is my witness, mine is worthy of the honors of apotheosis, and I would not have written these pages had I not been given the strength to do so by the desire, in the last years of her hard life, to vindicate her against the injustices of fortune. My poor mother! In Naples, the night I came down from Vesuvius, the fevers of the day's emotions brought on horrible nightmares instead of the rest that my trembling limbs required.[2] The volcano's flames, the blackness of the abyss that shouldn't be dark, were confused with I don't know what absurdity of terrified imagination, and upon awakening from dreams that sought to tear me apart, one single thought remained, tenacious, persistent like an actual event: My mother had died! I wrote to my family that night, bought a requiem Mass two weeks later in Rome, to be sung in her honor by the boarding-school girls of Santa Rosa, my pupils, and I made this vow and held true to it as long as I was under the influence of those sad thoughts, to appear in my land one day and say to Benavides, to Rosas, to all my torturers: You, too, have had a mother, I come to honor the memory of mine; suspend your brutal policies for a moment, then, and do not besmirch an act of filial piety.[3] Let me tell everyone who this poor woman was who no longer exists! And, by God, how faithfully I would have kept that vow, as I have fulfilled so many others, and am to keep so many more that I have made!

Fortunately, I have her by my side, and she instructs me in the things of other times, unknown to me, forgotten by all.[4] At seventy-six years of age, my mother crossed the cordillera of the Andes to say goodbye to her son before going to her grave! This alone is enough to give an idea of the moral force of her character. Every family is a poem, Lamartine has said, and the one about mine is sad, glowing, and useful, like the distant paper lanterns of the villages whose light, though pale, marks the way for those wandering in the fields. At her advanced age, few traces remain of my mother's austere, modest beauty. Her elevated stature, her accentuated and bony forms, her cheekbones especially marked in her physiognomy, an indication of decisiveness and energy, are all that is worthy of note in her external appearance, unless it be her forehead covered with irregular protuberances, since this is rare in her sex.

She knew how to read and write in her youth, having lost the latter faculty through disuse in her old age. Her intellect is little cultivated or, rather, devoid of all ornament, yet so clear that, in a grammar class that I was once giving my sisters, she was able, simply by listening at night as she carded wool, to solve all the problems that perplexed her daughters, giving the definitions of nouns and verbs, tenses, and later on, of irregularities in a sentence, with exceptional understanding and precision.

Apart from this, her soul, her conscience, were cultivated to a degree that the most advanced science, by itself, could never have achieved. I have been able to study this rare moral beauty while observing her under circumstances so difficult, so repeated and varied, without her ever giving in, without losing heart or temporizing, under circumstances that for others would have sanctified the concessions made to life. And here I must trace the genealogy of those sublime moral ideas that constituted the salutary atmosphere breathed by my soul as it evolved at the domestic hearth. I firmly believe in the transmission of moral aptitude through the organs, in the injection of the spirit of one man into the spirit of another by word and example. There are youths who never knew their parents, yet laugh, act, and gesture like them; the evil men who oppress peoples pollute the atmosphere with the rank breath of their soul, their vices and flaws reproduce themselves; there are peoples who reveal in all their actions those who govern them, and the morality of enlightened peoples who, through books, monuments, and education, preserve the maxims of the great teachers, would not have reached such perfection had not a particle of the spirit of Jesus Christ, for example, been introduced through education and preaching into each one of us to improve our moral character.

I have wanted to know, then, who taught my mother, and from her conversations, her references and recollections, I have extracted almost integrally the story of a holy man whose memory lives on in San Juan, whose teaching is perpetuated in more or less pure form in the hearts of our mothers.

At the end of the eighteenth century, a San Juan cleric, Don José Castro, was ordained, and from the beginning of his career in the priesthood, he displayed a singular dedication to his edifying ministry, the virtues of an ascetic saint, the ideas of a philosopher, and the piety of a Christian of the most beautiful of times. Besides being a priest, he was also a doctor, perhaps in order to combine spiritual aid with aid to the body, which is sometimes more urgent. In the fullest flower of his years, he suffered from insomnia, or feigned it, and spent the nights in the bell tower of the mother church ringing out the hours for the benefit of the sick; and so sure must he have been of his mastery of the art of curing that once, called upon to officiate at the burial of an important person, he uncovered the corpse's face as was his custom, and raising his hand, he signaled the singers to stop, immediately ordering the body to be placed on the ground in the open air, and praying from his breviary, until, seeing signs of life appear, he called out the man's name in a loud, deep voice, and said, "Arise, you have long years of life yet before you," to the complete stupefaction of the onlookers and utter consternation of the doctors who had treated him, at seeing the presumed corpse sit up and stare in horror at the lugubrious scene around him.

Don José Castro dressed carelessly and, such was his negligence, that his friends took pains to provide him with new clothes, pretending that they had come from a restitution offered in the confessional by a penitent, or some other equally acceptable reason. His charities exhausted his entire income; tithes, first fruits, and parish fees were distributed among the needy. Don José Castro preached six days a week; at *Santa Ana* on Mondays, at the *Desamparados* on Wednesdays, at the *Trinidad* on Thursdays, at *Santa Lucía* on Fridays, at *San Juan de Dios* on Saturdays, and at the mother church on Sundays.

But these doctrinal talks, in which he successively addressed the city's entire population, are of such a philosophical character that it makes me suspect that this holy man knew his eighteenth century, his Rousseau, his Feijóo, and his philosophers as well as he knew his gospel.[5]

Among Spanish populations, more so than among others of the Christian world, ridiculous, bloody, and superstitious practices have resisted the counsel of healthy reason. Processions abounded of saints and grotesque mummeries grimacing before the Holy Sacrament, and penitents with arms spread out during Holy Week, flagellants who scourged their backs with pitiless lashes, others, harnessed like animals, stepping on their reins as they walked on all fours, and other horrible practices representing the ultimate degree of human degradation. No sooner did Don José Castro become priest than he unleashed the whip of censure and prohibition upon these brutal practices and purged the observances of the faith of all indignities.

There existed then in popular belief such things as goblins, apparitions, ghosts, will-'o-the-wisps, witches, and other inventions of ancient religious beliefs, incorporated into those of almost all the Christian nations. The priest Castro made them all disappear, driven out by the ridicule and patient, scientific explanation, delivered from his pulpit, of the natural phenomena that gave rise to such errors. Children were swaddled, as is still the practice in Italy and other European countries rich in backward beliefs and traditions. The priest Castro, perhaps with *Émile* tucked under his cassock, taught mothers how to rear their children, about practices harmful to health, how to care for the sick, precautions that should be taken by pregnant women, and in private conversations with husbands in the confessional, he imparted considerations they should observe with their wives in special situations.[6]

His preaching was divided into two parts: the first, on the daily conduct of life, on popular customs, and their criticism, delivered without that insulting disapproval so common to ordinary preachers, had a more lasting corrective effect, the more it was accompanied by ridicule at once witty and spiritual, to the point that general laughter filled the temple, and he himself laughed till the tears flowed, only to come back with new jokes to interrupt the chat; until the vast conclave, drawn in by the delicious pleasures of this comedy, emptied their hearts of any bitter taste of ill humor, their spirits now soothed, and the priest would say, as he mopped his face; "Well, children, we've laughed enough; so pay attention to me now: by the Sign of the Holy Cross," etc.; and then came the gospel text for the day, followed by a flood of placid, serene enlightenment, of practical, easy, moral commentary applicable to all the situations of life. Oh! And what a pity it is that this Socrates, propagator in San Juan of the purest precepts of evangelical morality, has left nothing written on his interpretation of the spirit of our religion, there only remaining in the memories of the people of his time, unconnected fragments that require perspicacity, study, and discernment to give them the form of coherent doctrine. My mother's religion is the most genuine version of the religious ideas of Don José Castro, and I will have recourse to the practices of her entire life in order to explain that religious reform attempted in a remote province, where it is still preserved in many privileged souls. At times, my little sisters would say to my mother: "Let's pray the rosary" and she would answer, "I'm not in the proper mood tonight, I'm tired." On another occasion, she would say, "Let's pray the rosary, girls, I feel such a need for it!" And calling together the whole family, she would lead us in a prayer filled with reverence, with fervor, a true prayer directed to God, the purest emanation of what was in her soul, which overflowed with thanksgiving for the few favors He granted her, because divine munificence toward her was never generous. My mother performs few devotions, and those she does observe reveal the affinities of her spirit to certain allusions, if I may so express myself, of her condition with that of the saints in Heaven. Our Lady of Sorrows is her mother of God; Saint Joseph, the poor carpenter, is her patron saint;

and, on occasion, Saint Dominic and Saint Vincent Ferrer, Dominican friars both and linked, thereby, to the family predilection for the order of preachers; God himself has been, in all her anguished life, the true saint of her devotion, under the advocacy of Providence. In this way, God has entered into all the acts of that hard-working life and has been present each day watching her struggle against penury and fulfilling her duties. Providence has rescued her from her troubles through visible manifestations, which are completely real to her, and she has related countless instances to us for our edification, as proof of Providence's vigilance over his children. One time, on her way home from the house of one of her sisters who was poorer than she, disconsolate at not having found the means to relieve the hunger of a day that had dawned without providing its daily bread, she found a peseta on a bridge over a stream, out in the open and in plain view. Who could have left it there, if not Providence? On another occasion, when she and her children were suffering the pangs of hunger, the doors are suddenly burst open at twelve o'clock noon by a peon bearing a quarter of a steer sent by one of her brothers whom she hadn't seen in a year. Who but Providence had chosen that ill-fated day to cause the brother to remember his sister? And in a thousand difficult situations, I have seen this profound faith in Providence remain steadfast, stave off despair, mitigate anguish, and invest suffering and poverty with the august quality of a holy virtue, practiced with the resignation of a martyr, who never protests, who never complains, is always hoping, feeling herself sustained, supported, approved. I know no spirit more religious and, yet, I have never encountered among Christian women another more unconcerned with the rituals of worship than she. She confesses three times a year, and would frequent churches less often if on Sundays she didn't have to fulfil an obligation, on Saturdays commune with the Virgin, or on Mondays commend the souls of relatives and friends to God. The priest Castro advised mothers not to neglect the decorum of their social position when they left their homes to attend mass; for a family ought to appear in public at all times with the finery and propriety their status demands; and this precept my mother carried out in her times of need with a dignified modesty that has always characterized her every action.

All these lessons of such profound wisdom were but a tiny part of that seed sown by the holy man and made fecund by the common sense and moral qualities it encountered in my mother's heart.

To point out one of the strange combinations of ideas, I will add that when the revolution broke out in 1810, the priest Castro, still young, liberal, educated as he was, came out openly on the side of the king, fulminating from the pulpit, which had been his instrument of popular education, against disobedience to the legitimate sovereign, making predictions of war, demoralization, and disaster, which, unfortunately, time has proven true. The patriotic authorities were obliged to impose silence on the powerful counterrevolutionary; persecution was unleashed against him, his obstinacy brought him banishment to Las Bruscas, of sinister memory, from where he returned on foot to San Juan, mortally afflicted with the disease that ended his life.[7] He hid himself away in Angaco, and it was there that he died in penury and obscurity, abandoned and ignored by all, alternately kissing the crucifix and a portrait of Ferdinand VII, "the Desired."[8] My mother, weeping, once pointed him out to me as we passed close by him at the house of his retreat, and some years later, as a boy roaming about in public places, I saw his body being disinterred, skin and bones, intact, even his priestly vestments, almost immaculate. One of his sisters claimed the body, and for a number of years it has been exhibited to people who obtained such bountiful grace, in order that they might contemplate that placid countenance, on whose lips it seems that the chill of death has frozen a joke, or that some useful advice for mothers, some infallible prescription for a household remedy, or perhaps a sound Christian maxim, have remained trapped within its breast, since tongue and lips can no longer obey, hardened as they are by the effect of the grave, which has respected the body's physical forms, as it usually does with those that have housed the soul of a saint. I recommend to my uncle, the Bishop of Cuyo, that he recover these remains and have them deposited in a place of veneration so that the ashes may receive amends for the wrongs visited upon his person by the fatal demands of the times.

My mother's social position was sadly affected by the depleted inheritance that reached her. Don Cornelio Albarracín, the owner of half the Zonda Valley and troops of wagons and mules, after twelve years in bed, left only poverty to be divided among fifteen children, and a few tracts of uninhabited land. In 1801, Doña Paula Albarracín, his daughter, a young woman of twenty-three, undertook a task that was beyond not so much the strength but the very concept of what an unmarried girl could accomplish. There had been a great shortage of serge, a type of cloth in great demand for the habits of various religious orders, and from the product of her weaving, my mother had accumulated a little money. Together with a pair of slaves belonging to her aunts on the Irarrázabal side, she laid the foundation of the house that she would occupy in this world when she formed a new family. Since those few pieces of textile were insufficient for such an expensive project, she set up her loom under one of the fig trees she had inherited with the property, and from there, with the shuttle shooting back and forth, she oversaw the peons and artisans who were building the small house, and on Saturdays, she sold the cloth woven during the week and paid the workers with the fruit of her labor. In those days, an industrious woman, and they all were, even those born and raised in wealth, could depend on her own efforts to provide for her needs. Commerce had not yet introduced its goods into the interior of America, nor had European manufacturing brought down the cost of production to the extent that it has today. One vara of fine-quality finished raw textile was worth eight *reales*, ordinary quality, five *reales,* and four *reales* the *vara* of serge if the thread was supplied.* My mother wove twelve *varas* a week, the length needed for a priest's habit, for which she was paid six pesos, not without having had to stay up a little late each night to fill the bobbins with thread for the next day.†

The manual skills possessed by my mother are so numerous and so varied that to enumerate them would tax the memory with names that nowadays no longer have any meaning. She made silk suspenders, vicuña wool kerchiefs to send to Spain as gifts for the curious; and neckties and ponchos of that same soft wool. In addition to these textiles, there was drawnwork for albs, coverlets, lace, meshwork, and countless types of needlework for the adornment of ladies and of chalice cloths. Plain-stitch knitting in all its varieties and the complex art of dyeing were mastered to such a degree by my mother that even in recent years she was consulted on how to change a scarlet cloth to blue or to produce any of the dark half-tones fancied by European taste, and these feats she was able to perform with the practiced hand of the painter who, taking the primary colors from his palette at random, creates a half-tone to match the model. My family's reputation for industrial omniscience has survived up until my time; and the habit of manual work is in my mother an

---

* A *vara* measured about one yard.—Ed.
† One silver peso was worth eight reales.—Ed.

integral part of her existence. In Aconcagua in 1842, we heard her exclaim: "This is the first time in my life that these hands of mine are idle!" And to keep her, at age seventy-six, from fading into apathy, it is necessary to invent tasks for her within the limits of her tired vision, not excluding from among these, intricate handmade decorations that she still makes for petticoats and other superfluities.

With these elements, the noble worker entered into matrimony, soon after finishing her house, with Don José Clemente Sarmiento, my father, a handsome young man from a family which, like hers, was also in decline, and, as a dowry, she brought him the chain of privations and poverty with which she was to spend long years of her life. My father was a man of countless good qualities, which were undermined by others that, without being bad, worked in the opposite direction. Like my mother, he had been brought up on the rough labors of the time, a peon on the family hacienda *La Bebida,* a muleteer in the army; with a handsome face and an overriding passion for the pleasures of youth, he lacked the machinelike constancy upon which fortunes are built, and he had, along with the new ideas that came with the revolution, an irrepressible hatred for the material, unintelligent, and rough work on which he had been raised. The presbyter Torres once heard him say, referring to me: "Oh, no! My son will never put hands to a hoe!" And the upbringing he gave me showed that this was a fixed idea rooted in bitter and deepseated resentments. In the midst of poverty, I was raised as a gentleman, and my hands made no exertion beyond that required by my play and pastimes. One of my father's hands was permanently curled inward because of a callus developed at work. The revolution of independence broke out, and his imagination, so quick to cede to the excitation of enthusiasm, prompted him to squander in services to his fatherland the small savings he had been putting aside. Once, in 1812, he had witnessed the misery of Belgrano's army in Tucumán, and on on his return to San Juan, he took up a collection for the "mother fatherland," as he called it, which turned out to be a considerable sum, and at the instigation of the royalists, it was denounced to the municipality as a swindle. The authorities, after looking into the matter, were so well satisfied, that he himself was named to deliver in person his patriotic offering to the army. This earned him from that time on the nickname of "Mother Fatherland," which in his old age was the cause in Chile of a calumny that was intended to embarrass his son. In 1817, he went to Chile with San Martín as a militia officer in the army's service corps and was dispatched to San Juan from the battlefield of Chacabuco with the welcome news of the victory of the patriots.[9] San Martín recalled the incident very well in 1847 and was pleased to learn that I was his son.

With this background, my father spent his entire life in false starts involving projects that came to nothing at ill-advised moments; he would work intensively at something, only to end up deeply discouraged; he would regather his strength, and crash headlong into some sort of disappointment, dissipating his energy in extended trips to other provinces, until I reached manhood, when, from that time on, he followed his son's fate in the encampments, in exile, or in emigrations, like a guardian angel in an effort to shield him, if possible, from the dangers that could threaten him.

As a result of my father's ill fortune and lack of planning, support of the family fell, from the outset of the marriage, on my mother's shoulders, my father contributing only in periods of gainful activity with incidental windfalls; and under the pressure of the poverty in which we were raised, I watched my poor mother's equanimity of spirit shine forth, that trust in Providence, which was simply the last bulwark of her vigorous spirit against discouragement and despair. Winters approached that the fall had already forecast as ominous in view of the scanty stock of dried fruits and vegetables in the larder, and that helmsman of the dismantled vessel would ready herself with solemn tranquility to face the storm. The day of utter destitution would arrive, and her soul steeled itself, with resignation and ceaseless hard work, against that trial. She had wealthy relatives, two of her brothers were parish priests, and these brothers were unaware of her need. It would have belittled the saintliness of poverty combated by hard work, to alleviate it through outside intervention; this would have meant surrender in her mortal struggles against her ill fortune. The fiesta of Saint Peter was always accompanied by a sumptuous banquet given by the priest, our uncle; and it was understood that the children of the family both desired and deserved to take part in the lavish celebration. More than a few times, the priest would ask: "Why do I never see Domingo? And Paula . . . ?" And to this day, he suspects that this painful absence was due to a calculated plan of conduct on my mother's part. My mother had a childhood friend from whom death separated her at the age of sixty, Doña Francisca Venegas, who was the last person of that surname in San Juan, and a descendent of the families of the conquistadors, as I see in Mallea's list of questions.[10] Even without this evidence, a singular circumstance would attest to the long history of that family which, having settled in an outlying district, retained peculiarities of the old-time idiom. She and her daughters would use archaisms like *cogeldo, tomaldo, truje, ansina* and others that go back to the seventeenth century, which, for the untutored, was a motive for criticism.* The friends often visited together, devoting the day to the pleasure of fusing their two families into one, for the daughters were joined in the same friendship. Doña Francisca was quite wealthy, but my mother, on those days she was going to spend with her, would send her own servant to the kitchen to prepare all the food her family was to consume; twenty-seven years of protest against this practice of my mother's did not have the slightest effect on her firm and inalterable resolve that the ineffable pleasure of seeing Doña Francisca should not be tainted by the least suspicion that my mother might be sparing herself, for one day, the onerous duty of fending for her children, that she might be bowing her head to the inequalities of fortune. That is how, in the humble home of the family to which I belonged, the noble virtue of poverty was practiced. When Don Pedro Godoy, led astray by the passions of others, sought to disgrace me, he had the decency to place my family out of range of his poisoned darts, because the fame of those austere virtues had reached him, and I am grateful to him for that.[11]

When I responded that I had been brought up in an environment bordering on indigence, the president of the Republic, out of concern for me, deplored those confessions that can tarnish a man's reputation in the eyes of the common people. Those poor men who are favored by fortune, who are unable to conceive that old-fashioned poverty, the poverty of the Roman patrician, can be worn like the cloak of a Cincinnatus, an Aristides, when moral sentiment has conferred upon its folds the august dignity of a disadvantage borne without shame![12] Let them ask themselves how many times they saw the son of such poverty approach their doors without an invitation, and they will then appreciate the everlasting effects of that school of my mother's, in which need was an accident of fortune, not a disgrace. In 1848, I chanced to find myself at a house with President Bulnes and after a few moments' conversation, as we parted, I

---

* For *"cogerlo," "tomarlo," "traje,"* and *"así."*—Ed.

said to him mechanically, "I am honored to meet you, Your Excellency," an unconscious absurdity that caught his attention, and that on close consideration was not entirely unintentional, inasmuch as this was the second time in eight years that I had been in his presence.[13] Blesséd the poor who have had such a mother!

14

The Parental Home

My mother's house, the product of her diligence and skill, whose adobes and walls could so easily be computed in *varas* of linen woven by her hands to pay for their construction, has received some additions in recent years that make it appear now like other houses of a certain modest kind.[1] Its original form, however, is the one to which the poetry of the heart clings, the indelible image that stubbornly presents itself to my spirit, when I recall the pleasures and pastimes of childhood, the hours of play on coming home from school, the solitary spots where I have spent hours and weeks on end in ineffable beatitude, molding clay saints to worship as soon as they were finished, or troops of soldiers of the same material, which made me swell with pride at exercising so much power.

On the south side of the lot, which measured thirty *varas* wide by forty deep, was the only room of the house divided into two apartments; one that served as our parent's bedroom, and the other, larger one, as the living room, with its high dais and cushions, a survival of the Arab tradition of the divan that has been retained by the Spanish. Two indestructible tables of carob wood, handed down from the days when there was no other timber in San Juan save that of the carob trees in the fields, and some chairs of different construction lined the walls. These were adorned by two large oil paintings of Saint Dominic and Saint Vincent Ferrer, the products of an exceedingly poor but very devout brush, and handed down on account of the saints' Dominican habits. A short distance from the front door rose the dark-green branches of the patriarchal fig tree that in my childhood still provided shade for my mother's loom, whose moving bobbins, pedals, and shuttle would wake us up with their clatter before sunrise, announcing the coming of a new day, and with it, the need for hard work to stave off the privations it might bring. Some of the branches of the fig tree brushed up against the walls of the house and, being warmed there by the rays of the sun, anticipated the season by offering up for November 23rd, my father's birthday, their contribution of delicious early figs to the great delight of the family.

I dwell with pleasure upon these details, because later on the saints and the fig tree were protagonists of a family drama in which colonial ideas clashed obstinately with the new.

On the scarcely twenty *varas* of land that remained at the rear of the lot, there were other resources for habitual employment. Three orange trees yielded fruit in the fall and shade the year round; there was a small pond under a portly peach tree for the enjoyment of four or five ducks, who by multiplying, contributed to the minuscule but complex economy upon which the family's existence depended; and since all these means were still insufficient, surrounded by a fence to protect it from the voracity of the chickens, there was a vegetable garden the size of a scapulary, which produced all the vegetables customary in American cooking, and the whole place, adorned and brightened with clumps of common flowers, a purple rose bush, and various other flowering shrubs. And so, at a house in the Spanish colonies, a perfect economy of the soil was observed, and from it an inexhaustible production obtained, the way country people do in Europe. The chicken droppings and the manure of the horse my father rode were daily used to give new life to that piece of ground, which never tired of bringing forth varied and leafy plants; and when I have tried to suggest to my mother some ideas on rural economics, picked up carelessly from a few books, I have been deservedly put in my place as a pedant, in the presence of that science of cultivation which has been the pleasure and favorite occupation of her long life. Today, at seventy-six years of age, she still slips out of the house when we aren't looking, and she is sure to be found hoeing lettuces, responding quickly to our objections that the poor neglected lettuces would certainly die if not for her care and concern.

There was yet a little corner in that Noah's Ark where cloth was bleached in preparation for dyeing, and where there was a vat of bran that every week yielded a fair amount of fine white starch. In prosperous times, my mother would add a factory for handmade candles, some venture into bread baking that would always turn out badly, and a slew of other attempts at farming that it would be superfluous to enumerate. Such varied occupations did not interfere with there being a regular schedule for chores: The morning began by feeding the chickens, weeding the vegetable patches before they were scorched by the sun, and setting to work at the loom, for many years her primary occupation. I have the shiny, blackened carob-wood shuttle she inherited from her mother, who had it from her grandmother, a humble relic of colonial life that embraced a period of nearly two centuries in which noble hands wielded it almost without interruption; and although one of my sisters has inherited from my mother the custom and the need to weave, my greed has prevailed and I am the repository of this family jewel. It is a shame that I will never be sufficiently rich or important to emulate that Persian king who served himself in his palace from the same earthenware bowls from which they had served him in his childhood. He did this to keep himself from growing arrogant and looking down his nose at poverty.

To complete this menage, I must introduce two accessory personalities, La Toriba, a *zamba* raised in the family, the envy of the barrio, the close companion or *comadre* of all the *comadres* of my mother, the housekeeper, her mistress's right hand, the nursemaid who raised us all, the cook, errand boy, reseller, laundress, and helper in all the household chores.* She died young, overwhelmed with children, a kind of natural vegetation she was unable to do without, the sanctity of her ways notwithstanding; and her absence left a void that no one has ever been able to fill, not only in the domestic economy, but in my mother's heart; for mistress and servant were friends, two fellow workers, who together came up with ways to sustain the family; they would quarrel, argue, disagree, and then each would follow her own counsel, both leading to the same end. What fun for the children when they got home from school, to think of surprising the cook by entering as if to pay her a visit, but instead sopping up the fatty broth of the stewpot with their hidden crust of bread! If they should hit their mark, they had to be ready to break and run for the street without looking back, under threat of a whack from the

---

* *Zamba.* A female of mixed black African and Indian descent.—Ed.

most formidable wooden spoon there ever was, and which must have
landed a good thirty times on my not so substantial small-boy shoulders.
The other one was *Ña* Cleme, the pauper of the household; because my
mother, like Sue's Rigolette, who *never stinted on anything*, also had her
poor folk whom she helped sustain with her leftovers.[2] But the pauper of
the family was, like the servant, a friend, an equal, as well as a beggar.
My mother and *Ña* Cleme would sit on the divan and chat about hens,
fabrics, and onions, and when the poor thing was ready to ask for her
handout, she would invariably say, "Well, I'll be going now," which was
repeated until such time as some castoff garment, long since retired from
service, a tasty round bun, a pair of old shoes, a candle, if there happened
to be any in the house, and by some miracle, a half silver real, for lack of
a smaller subdivision of the coin, were forthcoming in response to the
ritual "I'll be going now," which, when first spoken, was no more than a
premonitory utterance.

As far as I have been able to surmise, that *Ña* Cleme, a full-blooded
Indian darkened by the years she calculated around seventy, an inhabitant of the outskirts of the barrio of Puyuta, had been the mistress of a
relative of mine on my mother's side, whose sinful past was given away
by the blue eyes and sharp, prominent nose of her daughters. The most
remarkable thing about this old woman is that people considered her a
witch, and, in talking to them, she did her best to give the impression
that this was true. What a strange human weakness of the human spirit,
which subsequently my knowledge of history has made me understand!
More than three thousand of the witches of Logroño, whom the Inquisition burned by the hundreds, and those of Maryland [*sic*], in North
America, confessed to being professional witches, making no bones
about it, corroborating the testimony of witnesses as to Witches' Sab-
bath, the black goat that brought them together, and the broomstick on
which they traveled through the air, and this they did, faced with the
torture to which the imbecility of the judges condemned them.[3] Certainly, we all have a need to draw attention to ourselves, and it is this
that impels those who can do no more, because of old age, brutishness,
and poverty, to become witches; the bold, without ability, to become
cruel tyrants; and me, perhaps, may God forgive me, to write these
pages. *Ña* Cleme told her tales in our house, my mother listened to her
indulgently, feigning agreement, so as not to hurt her feelings; we hung
on her mysterious words until, when she had left, my mother ridiculed

the old woman's stories and, with her good sense, dispersed any germs of superstition that might have lodged in our spirits; for this purpose, if it was necessary, she would have recourse to her favorite text, the sermons of the unforgettable priest Father Castro, who had attacked and discredited witches in San Juan, to the point where their activities were no longer of any concern. *Ña* Cleme was never persecuted for her religious beliefs in this respect, although later and not too long ago, several witches were persecuted in the barrio of Puyuta, which to this day is famous in the minds of the common folk as a hideout for a number of the devil's sectarians. In fact, as recently as twelve or fourteen years ago, the police (the *federales* were in power then) investigated a case of witchcraft, coming up with a confusion of stories that had the authorities puzzled. There was much talk in the town about a witch girl, and the police wanted to get to the bottom of it. To this end, they brought in the accused, and in the presence of many witnesses, she confessed to having an illicit relation with the devil; and, since they were about to flog her, whether for her brazen indiscretion or as punishment for her evil ways, the story does not tell, she broke into tears and said: "It's a good thing it's me you're punishing; I'm poor! For sure, you're not going to punish Doña Teresa Funes (my aunt), Doña Bernarda Bustamante . . . ," and other respectable old ladies whom she named, and who, according to her statement, went to the cemetery on Saturdays, where they practiced the customary rites of witchcraft. They must have been shocked and dumbfounded to hear such respectable names, and fearful of committing a serious injustice, they set the crafty girl free, leaving, in the opinion of many, the reputation of those matrons in very bad odor. What can we really know, really, when it comes to matters so obscure?

Such has been the domestic setting in which I grew up, and it is impossible, unless one were of a rebellious nature, for it not to have left on the souls of those who lived there, indelible impressions of morality, work, and virtue, received in that sublime school in which the greatest industry, the purest morality, dignity maintained amidst poverty, steadfastness, and resignation were taught every hour of the day. My sisters enjoyed the well-deserved reputation of being the most industrious girls in the entire province, and any feminine task that called for consummate skill was always entrusted to these supreme artificers of all that demands the greatest patience and ability and commands the lowest pay. Years ago, the confessed intention of a Chilean writer to denigrate me stopped short in the presence of those virtues, and he paid his tribute of respect to the honest industriousness of my sisters, but not without seizing the opportunity to make of me a contrast.

Our house remained as I have described it, until the time that my two older sisters reached marriageable age, at which point an internal revolution broke out that occasioned two years of argument and my mother's copious tears, at having to acknowledge defeat by a new world of ideas, habits, and tastes that were not those of the colonial life of which she was the last and most consummate example.

Trivial and unnoticed are the earliest symptoms with which the social revolutions that human intelligence engineers in the great centers of civilization, spread among peoples of common heritage, insinuate themselves into their ideas and infiltrate their customs. The eighteenth century had shone brightly upon France and undermined the old traditions, tempering beliefs and even arousing hatred and contempt for things long venerated; its political theories had upset governments, disconnected America from Spain, opened its colonies to new customs and ways of life. The time was to come when it would be thought necessary to look askance and with disdain upon the industrious life of American women, to propagate the French style, and to introduce into families a penchant for showing off wealth, by having an extravagant number and elaborate layout of rooms, or by advancing the dinner hour from twelve noon on the dot, to two, and even four o'clock in the afternoon. Who hasn't known one of those good old-timers who basked proudly in their opulence in a single large room with four dusty rattan chairs, the floor littered with cigar butts, and a table decorated with nothing but an inkwell bristling with duck, if not condor feathers, upon whose quills old age had deposited crystals of solidified ink? This was, nonetheless, the general aspect of the colony, these the furnishings of a time now past. One can find all of it described in the novels of Walter Scott or Dumas and still see the like in Spain and South America, the last among the old nations summoned to rejuvenate themselves.[4]

These ideas of regeneration and personal improvement, that impiety of the eighteenth century—who would have believed it!—entered the house in the heads of my two older sisters. No sooner had they reached an age when a woman feels that her existence is linked to society, that her existence has a purpose and an end, than they began to breathe in the particles of new ideas, of beauty, of taste, of comfort, which reached

them through the same atmosphere that had been stirred up and reno-
vated by the revolution. The walls of the common room were cleaned
and whitewashed again, something there was no reason whatsoever to
oppose. The mania that followed was to destroy the platform that occupied one side of the living room, with its *chuse*[a] and small cushions (the
divan, as I mentioned before, that has come down to us from the Arabs),
a privileged place where only women were allowed to sit, and in whose
ample space, reclining against *almohadones* (an Arabic word), they engaged with visitors and heads of household in noisy chatter, which
turned these platforms into seedbeds of conversation.[*] Why has the dais
been permitted to disappear, that poetic oriental custom, so comfortable
for sitting, so suitable for female leisure, by substituting it with chairs
that, one by one and in rows, like soldiers on review, stand at attention
in our modern parlors? But the divan signified that men could not approach young women in public, converse freely, nor mix with them as
sanctioned by our new customs, and so it was repudiated without objection by the very ones who had accepted it as their privilege. The divan,
then, gave up its place in the house to chairs, despite the weak resistance
on the part of my mother, who enjoyed sitting at one end of it to sip her
maté in the morning, with her brazier and kettle of water on the floor in
front of her, or to wind up her skeins of yarn, or to fill her spindles at
night for the next day's weaving. Unable to accustom herself to working
in a chair, she had to adopt the use of a carpet, instead of the irreplace-
able divan, whose loss she lamented for many years to come.

Borne on the wave of innovation, my sisters fell at once upon sacred
objects. I declare that I had no part in this sacrilege that they committed,
poor things, in obedience to the spirit of the times. Those two saints,
Saint Dominic and Saint Vincent Ferrer, so large and so old, looked decidedly ugly on the wall. If my mother were to agree to their being taken
down and placed in a bedroom, the little house would assume a new air
of modernity and elegant refinement, since it was in the seductive form
of good taste that eighteenth-century iconoclastic impiety was being introduced into the house! Ah! What harm has been wrought in the
bosom of Spanish America by that mistake! The American colonies had
been established in a period when Spanish fine art displayed with pride

[a] A Quechua word meaning carpet. [Author's note]
[*] *Almohadones* are large pillows.—Ed.

to the rest of Europe the prodigious brushes of Murillo, Velázquez, and Zurbarán, on a par with the swords of the Duke of Alba, the Great Captain, and Cortés.[5] Possession of Flanders added Flemish engraving to Spain's products, which represented in crude drawings and raw colors the religious scenes that were the substance of national poetry. In his early years, Murillo made images of virgins and saints for export to America; the lesser painters sent saints' lives for the convents, the passion of Jesus Christ in immense galleries' worth of paintings; and Flemish engraving, like French lithography of today, put within the reach of moderate incomes prints of the Prodigal Son, virgins, and saints, as varied as the types provided by the calendars. The walls of our parents' houses were covered with these images, and not infrequently the artist's practiced eye could detect the work of a master among so many poorly painted pictures. But the revolution came along, venting its spleen against religious emblems. Ignorant and blind in its antipathies, it had fixed its eyes on painting, which smacked of Spain, of colonialism, of things antiquated and incompatible with progressive ideas. Very devout families hid their pictures of saints, so as not to exhibit signs of poor taste by keeping them on display, and there have been people in San Juan and elsewhere who, by soaking them, put their partially bleached canvasses to use as breeches for their slaves. How many artistic treasures must have been lost in these stupid profanations, in which all of America has been complicit, because everywhere there was a year, or at least a time, in which all at once the fatal clearing began of that exuberant vegetation of the past artistic glory of Spain!

European visitors traveling throughout America during the last twenty years have rescued, for paltry sums, priceless works by the greatest masters, which they found among rummage, covered with dust and cobwebs; and now that the time has at last come for the resurrection of the arts in America, when the blindfold has fallen from people's eyes, the churches, the fledgling museums, and the rare connoisseurs have with luck discovered, from time to time, some painting by Murillo to put on exhibit, begging it pardon for the injustices it has suffered, rehabilitated now in the public eye, and reestablished in the exalted place where it belonged. In no different a way and for the same reasons, a future generation in our land will venerate the name of the unitarians, reviled today because of stupid politics, the vilification accepted because of one of those vertiginous errors that enthrall entire populations. But how many paintings of that cultivated school will have disappeared, and how few, damaged by the onslaught of time, will deserve the honors of apotheosis, in the resurrection of good sense and of the justice due them!

The best study that I made of the fine arts during my trip to Europe, that practical year-long course spent in the review of a hundred museums in succession, suggested to me the idea of writing to Procesa, the artist capable of translating my thoughts, so that, while taking every possible precaution not to reveal her objective, she might collect, little by little, the scattered paintings, and lay the foundation for an art museum.[6] A hopeless task! No sooner did she show interest in a canvas than those who had abandoned them in some dark room found them interesting, quite like the farmer who, unable to dispose of his grain, upon receiving an offer, raises the price on the assumption that since it is now in demand, it must be valuable. Both grain and canvases remain in the barn.

In the chapel of the Concepción there were six pictures of bishop saints, by good painters, that went up in flames not so long ago. In the Desamparados, there is one of the Virgin in the style and costume of the Middle Ages. In San Clemente, there was a large storeroom of paintings on various themes, among which one stood out, a Jesus in the orchard before the resurrection. Procesa cleaned and restored it, and, after she had varnished it at her own expense, the donor generously found it worthy of adorning his home and took it back. The Señoras Morales have a Magdalena sent from Rome by the Jesuit Morales. In the Oro home, there is a Saint Joseph of a good Italian school; in the Cortínez home, an excellent Saint John. What little there is in the way of portraits is nonetheless select: the Roman portrait of the Jesuit Godoy, companion of Father Morales; that of San Martín, an ugly daub, not as bad, however, as the one that hangs in the museum in Lima, but worth conserving as it was painted from the original; the portraits of Popes Leo XII and Gregory XV, both the work of a Neapolitan artist of considerable merit; one of Pius IX, by an unskilled hand and which I was unable in Rome to prevent from being sent to San Juan; and those of Bishops Oro and Sarmiento, the former by Graz, the latter by Procesa.

About all the best ones, and even others that I omit, I sent my sister details from Rome as to location and subject. As for the portraits of popes and bishops, I suggested to my bishop uncle the felicitous idea of forming a gallery of popes, contemporaries of the bishopric, and of the bishops of San Juan. A few years would have sufficed to enrich it with many dignitaries. There is still in San Juan something that would be worth examining. An American Michelangelo, if the comparison may be permitted, has left there many examples of the universality of his talent. Architect, sculptor, painter, he put his hand to everything. "San Pedro el Pontífice" [Saint Peter the Pontiff], "Nuestra Señora del Rosario del Trono" [Our lady of the Rosary of the Throne], as well as the "Virgen Purísima del Sagrario" [Immaculate Virgin of the Sanctuary], and the "Visitación de Santa Isabel" [Visitation of Saint Isabel], are works worthy of the chisel or the palette that he alternately employed; an altar at Saint Augustine, various others in the cathedral, I don't know if the main one, which is a work in good taste, and a tower or the frontispiece of the church, in quite bad taste, it is true, make up the works of Cabrera, from Salta, companion of Laval, Grande, and other *vecinos* of that city, artists and cabinet-makers, despite their excellent training. The bishop of San Juan can still bring together all those works of art in a gallery, the principal merit of which would lie in forming a collection and in fostering the nascent art of painting that numbers among the amateurs, two portrait painters: Franklin Rawson and Procesa.[7] A Virgin by the former, to replace Cabrera's very damaged one, and by the latter, a Belisario begging for alms, victim of a tyrant's envy, could eventually be added as studies. But the lack of spirit that reigns there, as in all places, will consign to the teeth of rats and the ravages of time, those poor remains of the old taste for painting that constituted part of the Spanish nation, and that we have repudiated out of ignorance, and like bad Spaniards, indeed like those who on the Peninsula have allowed themselves to be dispossessed of one of their clearest titles to glory.

The struggle at home began, then, between my poor mother, who loved her two Dominican saints as if they were members of the family, and my young sisters, who did not understand the sacred origin of that affection, and wanted to sacrifice the household gods to the accepted vogue and taste of the times. Every day, at any hour, on any pretext, the argument renewed itself; a threatening glance lighted on the saints as if to say to them, "Your days are numbered," while my mother, contemplating them tenderly, exclaimed, "Poor saints, what harm do you do them where you don't get in anyone's way?" But with such constant pounding, the ear grew accustomed to reproof, and day by day, resistance weakened; because, considering the matter carefully, as religious objects, it was not essential that they be in the living room, the bedroom being a more appropriate place of veneration, close to the bed, for commending oneself to them; as a family heirloom, the same reasons held; as a decoration they were in abominable taste; and with one concession after another, my mother started to soften up little by little, and when my sisters calculated that her resistance continued only because she wished not to have her arm twisted, one morning that the guardian of that fortress had gone to mass or was out on some errand, she was horrified upon her return at the sight of the blank walls where shortly before she had left behind two large black patches. My saints had already been settled in the bedroom, and to judge from their expressions, the snub had made no impression on them whatsoever. My mother knelt weeping before them, to beg their forgiveness with her prayers, and she remained in bad humor and grumbling all that day, sad the next, more resigned the following day, until finally time and custom brought the balm that makes our greatest misfortunes tolerable.

This singular victory emboldened the spirit of reform; and after the divan and the saints, glances lit one ill-fated day upon that fig tree that dwelt in the middle of the yard, discolored and knotty from lack of rain and the passage of time. Looked at from this side of the question, the fig tree was a lost cause in the public eye; it violated all the rules of decorum and decency; but for my mother, it was a question of economics, at the same time that it affected her heart profoundly. Ah, if only the maturity of my heart could have been reached sooner for her sake, since self-interest made me either neutral or only weakly inclined in her favor, because of the early-ripening figs! They wanted to separate her from one that had been her companion in the morning of her life and at the first test of her strength. Maturity in years links us to all the things that surround us; the domestic hearth is animated and enlivened; a tree that we have seen come into being, grow, and reach an advanced age, is a being endowed with life that has earned the right to existence, that reads our heart, that accuses us of ingratitude, and that would leave us full of remorse if we were to destroy it without good reason. The old fig tree's sentence was discussed for two years; and when its defender, tired of the eternal struggle, was about to abandon it to its fate and the preparations for the execution were getting under way, the repressed feelings in my mother's heart suddenly burst forth with new energy, and she stubbornly refused to allow the disappearance of that witness and companion of her labors. One day, however, when the withdrawal of the permission granted had lost all authority, the thud of an axe against the venerable tree trunk was heard, as well as the trembling of the leaves shaken by the blows, like the piteous moans of the victim. This was a moment of deepest sadness, a scene of sorrow and repentance. The blows of the figicidal axe shook my mother's heart as well, tears filled her eyes, like the tree's sap that oozed from the wound, and her sobs echoed the shuddering of the leaves; each new blow called forth a new cry of pain, and my sisters and I, full of remorse at having caused such intense sorrow, burst into tears, the only possible reparation for the harm now commenced. The work of destruction was ordered suspended, while the family prepared to go out and end the grievous repercussions of the axe blows on my mother's heart. Two hours later, the fig tree lay upon the ground revealing its hoary top, while the withered leaves exposed the knotty frame of the structure that for so many years had done its part in the protection of the family.

After these great reforms, our humble dwelling was slowly and unimpressively enlarged. It was my good fortune to be able to introduce a substantial reform. At the foot of our backyard, there was an ample plot that my father had purchased during a spell of prosperity. At the age of sixteen, I was a clerk in a small store. My first operational plan and the purpose of my earliest economies were to wall off that piece of property so as to make it productive. This aggregation of space made the family safe from indigence, without advancing it beyond the bounds of poverty. My mother now had a theater at her disposal worthy of her vast agricultural science; the slaughtered fig tree was replaced in her affection by a hundred little trees that her maternal eye encouraged to grow. More hours of the day were to be spent on the creation of that nursery, of that vineyard upon which a large part of the family subsistence was to depend from then on.

When I had finished this job, in my joy at having produced something good, I could say: *et vidi quod esset bonum,* and pat myself on the back.[8]

15

My Education

Here ends the colonial history, as I shall call it, of my family. What follows is the slow and arduous transition from one mode of being to another, the life of the nascent Republic, the struggle of the parties, civil war, proscription, and exile. The history of the nation, as the theater of the action and the setting, succeeds the history of the family. I succeed my progenitors; and I believe that by following my footprints, like those of anyone else on that road, the inquisitive person can pause to consider the events that shape the common landscape, accidents of the terrain that is known to all, matters of general interest, and for the examination of which, my *biographical* notes, of no intrinsic value in themselves, will serve as a pretext and a link, since in my life, which has been so bereft, so vexed, and yet so persevering in its aspiration to an elevated and noble *je ne se quoi*, I seem to see portrayed this poor South America, thrashing about in its nothingness, making supreme efforts to spread its wings, and at each attempt lacerating itself against the bars of the cage that keeps it imprisoned.

Strange emotions must have shaken the souls of our parents in 1810. The fresh perspective of a dawning epoch, liberty, independence, the future, new words then, must have sweetly played upon the fibers, excited the imagination, made the blood throb in our parents' hearts for minutes at a time. The year 1810 must have been fevered, filled with emotion, anxiety, bliss, and enthusiasm. A story is told of a king who would tremble like one poisoned with mercury at the sight of a naked dagger, the effect of the emotions that agitated him while still in the womb, when a man was stabbed in his mother's arms. I was born in 1811, in the ninth month after May 25, and my father had thrown himself into the revolution, and my mother had trembled each day with the news that arrived on the progress of the American insurrection. While I was still at the babbling stage, they began to familiarize my eyes and my tongue with the alphabet, such was the haste of the colonials, who considered themselves citizens, to educate their children, as can be appreciated in the decrees of the governing junta and the other administrations of the period. Filled with this holy spirit, the government of San Juan, in 1816, brought two men from Buenos Aires, worthy in knowledge and moral stature to be teachers in Prussia, and I went at once, when the School of the Fatherland opened its doors, to mix in with the mass of four hundred children of all ages and conditions, who rushed to receive the only solid instruction at the elementary level that has ever existed among us. The memory of Don Ignacio and Don José Genaro Rodríguez, sons of Buenos Aires, still awaits the recognition that their enormous, their saintly services deserve; and I will not die without my country having fulfilled this sacred duty.[1] The sense of equality was developed in our hearts through the requirement that we students address one another as *Señor*, regardless of race or status; and morality in conduct was stimulated by the teacher's example, the oral precepts, and punishments that were only severe and humiliating in the case of crimes. In that school, details of which I have presented in *Civilización y barbarie* [Civilization and Barbarism], in *Educación popular* [Popular Education], and which all of America now knows, I remained for nine years without a single absence for any reason whatsoever, for my mother saw to it, with a severity from which there was no appeal, that I did my duty of attending every day. At the age of five, I could read aloud fluently, with a tone of assurance in my voice that could have stemmed only from a thorough understanding of the subject matter, and such a precocious ability must have been so unusual in those days that I was taken from house to house to be heard reading, earning myself copious buns, embraces, and compliments that puffed me up with vanity. Apart from an innate facility for comprehension, there was a secret behind the scene of which the public was unaware, and which I must reveal so as to give credit where credit is due. My poor father, uneducated, but anxious that his children should not be, stimulated that incipient thirst for education at home by hearing my homework each day, and making me read, with no pity for my tender years, the *Historia crítica de España* [Critical History of Spain] by Don Juan Masdeu, in four volumes, *Desiderio and Electo,* and other abominable tomes, which I have never seen again, and which have left in my mind a confused jumble of history, allegories, fables, nations, and proper names. I owe to my father my fondness for reading, which has become the constant occupation of the better part of my life, and if later on he was unable to give me an education because of his poverty, he provided me instead, in his paternal solicitousness, with a powerful instrument with which I, through my own efforts, made up for everything else, thereby fulfilling his most constant, his most fervent desire.

While I was a pupil at the reading school, a high-backed chair like a canopied throne, with steps leading up to it, was built at one end of the room, and I was elevated to it with the title of *primer ciudadano* [first citizen]! Whether the seat was built for me is for Don Ignacio Rodríguez to say, for he is still alive; a youth by the name of Domingo Morón succeeded me in that honor, after which it was abandoned. This circumstance, the publicity received since then, the praise of which I was always the object and witness, and a series of subsequent acts, have inevitably contributed to lending my behavior a certain air of conceit, which has afterward been called to my attention. Ever since I was a boy, I believed in my talents, like a proprietor in his wealth, or a military man in his acts of war. Everybody said as much, and in nine years at school, not even a dozen among the two thousand pupils who passed through its portals outdid me in the capacity to learn, notwithstanding that school, and grammar, arithmetic, algebra, finally became distasteful to me, for having learned them several times over. My conduct as a student must have suffered under this perpetual life of going to school, for I remember that I fell into last place in the estimation of the teachers. The school introduced the system followed in Scotland of winning advancement by gradually moving up to the head of the class. A problem in arithmetic would be posed and those not sure of the answer would look at me. If the ones who stood up were going to lose out in the competition, I would make believe I was about to stand so the rest would stand up faster; on the contrary, if you were supposed to stand, I would slump back in my seat and then suddenly leap up to steal the place from those who had been watching me. Finally, I was given carte blanche to skip ahead in all the courses, and I always won the first seat at least twice a day; but my record was abominably bad, I had notes about my conduct, I had arrived late, I left class without permission, and other mischief that I got into as a way to fight the boredom, and they took away my first place and the silver five-centavo piece that one was supposed to hold onto throughout an entire day, which rarely happened to me.

Furthermore, my frequent reading of things that contradicted what was being taught, which developed my intellectual faculties to a degree not attained by the other boys, gave me a definite superiority. In the midst of my habitual abandon, I listened closely to the teacher's explanations, read profitably, and retained indelibly whatever entered my brain through my eyes and ears. Over a period of days, the teacher related the delightful story of Robinson, and I repeated the entire tale three years later, almost word for word, without mixing up a scene or leaving anything out, before Don José Oro and the whole family.[2]

From time to time, however, I was outshone by boys who were exceptionally gifted with the most brilliant intelligence and whose devotion to study was greater than mine. Among them, Antonio Aberastaín, José Alvarez, and a fellow of amazing ability named Leites, and others whose names I forget.

In that shipwreck of my moral qualities in the latter period of my schooling due to lack of mental employment, I did rescue one that it behooves me to make known. The Sarmiento family has an undisputed reputation in San Juan, passed on from father to son, for being, it mortifies me to say, liars. Nobody has denied them this quality, and I have seen them give so many convincing demonstrations of this innate and lovable inclination that I have no doubt as to its being a family trait. My mother, however, had taken precautions against the bane entering her house through my father, and we were brought up in holy dread of lying. I was always distinguished in school for my exemplary truthfulness, to the point that teachers rewarded it by proposing it as a model for the students, extolling it, thereby increasingly confirming my intention to be always truthful, a resolve that has become the keystone of my character, and which is borne out by all the actions of my life.

My apprenticeship in schooling ended on account of one of those frequent injustices, against which I have guarded myself whenever I have been in similar circumstances. Don Bernardino Rivadavia, that hapless cultivator whose carefully selected plants were to be trampled down by the horses of Quiroga, López, Rosas, and by all the other leaders of the barbarian reaction, asked for six youths of recognized talent from each province to be educated at the nation's expense, in order that they should return to their respective cities upon completion of their studies to practice their scientific professions and lend luster to the nation. It was requested that they be of decent, though poor families, and Don Ignacio Rodríguez came to the house to give my father the happy news that my name headed the list of favorite sons whom the nation was going to take under its wing. However, the greed of the wealthy had been aroused, wires were pulled, all citizens were to be considered eligible for the scholarship, and a complete list of candidates had to be drawn up; the winner was to be selected by lot, and since good fortune was not my family's patron saint, I was not one of the six lucky ones. What a sad day that was for my parents when we received the fatal news of the selection! My mother wept silently, my father kept his head buried in his hands.

Still, fortune, which had been unkind to me, was good to the province, even though later on the province did not know enough to take advantage of the benefits made available to it. Luck fell to Antonio Aberastaín, poor like me, and gifted with exceptional talents, an ironclad dedication to study, and a morality of conduct that has made him exemplary to this day. He attracted attention for those qualities at the School of Moral Sciences, where he learned English, French, Italian, Portuguese, mathematics, and law; he graduated from that school, and returned home, where, on the day after his arrival, he was obliged by the junta of representatives to take over the first judicial magistracy of the province. In 1840, he emigrated from his province never to return; he was appointed minister of the government of Salta because of the reputation for competence that he enjoyed, he left that province at the last minute among the lances of the *montonera*, went to Chile, was appointed secretary to the Intendant of Copiapó, and he resides in that province today, earning his living from the practice of law and enjoying universal respect. Nobody better than I has been able to penetrate the depths of his character, since I have been his friend since childhood, as an adult his protégé, when in 1836 we both came to San Juan at the same time, he from Buenos Aires, I from Chile, and shortly after getting to know me, he began to use his influence to put me back on my feet each time the malice of small-town envy plunged me into disfavor, each time the pervading vulgarity insisted on bringing me down to the common level.

Aberastaín, a doctor, chief justice of the Court of Appeals, was always there defending me among his own, against the crowd of wealthy or pampered youths who stood in my way. I have owed this man, generous to the marrow, forceful without appearing so, humble to the point of self-effacement, what I later owed another man in Chile, his high regard for me demonstrated by the many signs of respect he showed me; the two of them serving to elevate me beyond what good fortune alone would have done. The estimation of good men is a galvanism for analogous substances. A kindly glance from them can say to Lazarus: Rise and go forth. I have never loved so much as I loved Aberastaín; no man has left deeper impressions in my heart of respect and esteem.

From the time he left San Juan, the Supreme Court of Justice has been in the hands of men with no professional training, the poor fellows sometimes so inept, that even as muleteers they would be unfit. Recently, the honorable Chamber of Representatives has declared that, not even when no San Juan lawyer can be found, can a *foreigner,* that is, an individual from another of the confederated provinces, be a judge, and suffice it to cite this legislative act to show the depths of perversity to which the spirit of those people has sunk.

Don Saturnino Salas was another of the fortunate ones; he devoted himself to mathematics, for which nature had endowed him with one of those privileged organizations that produce the Pascals or the Ampères.³ He cultivated the discipline with passion, gave his schoolmates lessons to support himself, putting to use his manual skills to make his own shoes and mend his own clothes in the abject poverty and abandonment in which he was left by the destruction of the School of Moral Sciences, one of the thousand crimes committed by the reactionary party, by Arana and Rosas, in reprisal for the hatred that the students of that school justly professed for them, as the flame must abhor the candlesnuffer.⁴

That industrial talent is innate and organic in the Salas family. His father, Don Joaquín Salas, invented machines and all manner of apparatus, and lost an immense fortune inherited from Doña Antonia Irarrázabal, partly in those ventures of his ingenuity. His son, Don Juan José Salas, shows early signs of the same gift of inventiveness, which in San Juan, given the habits of Spanish routine, is wasted on unproductive curiosities. As for the Salas women, all unmarried, they live in modest respectability on the income from an industry that they have developed, perfected in its every detail, and elevated to the status of a fine art. The handmade artificial flowers of the Salas women are famous in San Juan, and it would be no exaggeration to say that they compare favorably in artistic beauty with the most beautiful flowers of Paris, samples of which they study to discover the manufacturing processes; and in terms of artistic beauty, they imitate nature herself, and not infrequently they could make her accept a rose or a branch of orange blossoms fashioned by their hands, such is the patience and skill they have invested in copying her down to the tiniest details. For many years, their brother Don Saturnino has pursued his vocation for studying mathematics, teaching it out of necessity, a member of the Buenos Aires corps of engineers, and content in his poverty, now the sole recompense in his fatherland for knowledge that does not end up in the service of crime and immorality. While this profound mathematician languishes in poverty, the San Juan government paid three thousand pesos a year to a shameless scoundrel who claimed to be a hydraulics expert, machinist, engineer, lawyer, and conversant in any subject that was mentioned. He handled lawsuits, was a theatrical producer, writer, colonel, *mazorquero,* public works director, water rights judge, federalist supporter, the terror of unitarians, and in fact, the vilest human being who ever disgraced the species, this ignoble farce having lasted for ten years to the shame of that city. Hail Federation! By its fruit shall ye know the tree!

The third was Don Indalecio Cortínez, who dedicated himself to medical science, to the applause of his entire class, and with such devotion to surgery that he received from the professors a special allotment of cadavers, to enable him to pursue, in his own room, his favorite studies of the human organism. He returned to San Juan to practice his scientific profession, after earning doctorates in three schools; he built a two-story house on the main square, having acquired the site of the ruined church of Santa Ana, and emigrated to Coquimbo, leaving behind everything he possessed, in order to escape the persecution that hung over the heads of all those who had the sense to anticipate the abyss of evils in which the Republic would be buried by the victory of the caudillos, who now have no idea how to get out of the morass they have gotten themselves into. To this day, Dr. Cortínez refreshes his knowledge and keeps up on scientific advances in Europe through the journals to which he subscribes; and San Juan has lost in him a skilled physician, and the fortune he is now accumulating in Coquimbo, the recompense for his achievements, has been diverted by his persecutors from San Juan.

I am waiting for the law to be passed at any moment that will prohibit *foreign* physicians from treating patients in San Juan, thereby giving preference, as in the courts, to charlatans born and raised within the province.

The other three were Don Fidel Torres, who has not returned to his province; Don Pedro Lima, who died; and Don Eufemio Sánchez, who, according to what I have heard, practices medicine in Buenos Aires. The one thing that is clear is that none of the six young men educated by Don Bernardino Rivadavia has remained in San Juan, the province being thus deprived of harvesting the fruits of that measure that by itself would have sufficed to atone for the government's many other faults.

Before embarking on more serious matters, I would like to cast a glance backward at the games of my childhood, for they reveal family customs that still affect me in my adult life. I never knew how to spin a top, bounce a ball, fly a kite, nor did I play a single one of those common childhood games, for which I never developed a fondness in my youth. At school, I learned to copy the knaves on playing-cards and later made a stencil for tracing a figure of San Martín on horseback like the ones storekeepers put on their paper lanterns, and with one accomplishment after another, during ten years of perseverance, I ended up unraveling all the secrets of making caricatures. On a family visit to the home of Doña Bárbara Icasate, I spent the day copying a face of Saint Jerome, and once I caught it properly, I turned to reproducing it in various ways in all ages and sexes. My teacher, tired of reproving me for this pastime, ended by resigning himself and respecting this instinctive mania. When later, because of my knowledge of the technique for teaching drawing, I was in a position to perfect my skills, I lacked the will to do so. On the other hand, in my province I later fostered interest in this graphic art, and under my direction or inspiration half a dozen artists have been trained in San Juan. But in my childhood play that natural inclination was turned into statuary, which took two different forms: I made saints and soldiers, the two great predilections of my boyhood fancy.

My mother raised me in the conviction that I would be a cleric and a priest of San Juan, following in my uncle's footsteps, while my father envisioned uniforms, military insignias, sabers, and the rest of such trappings. Through my mother, I was inclined toward the colonial vocations; through my father, I was infused with the revolutionary ideas and concerns of the time; and, in obedience to these contradictory influences, I spent my idle hours in pious contemplation of my clay saints, quickly abandoning them in their niches, however, to visit the house across the way and engage in a major battle between two armies that my neighbor and I had been planning for the past month, with a great hoard of bullets, to mow down the crudely painted ranks of formless clay soldiers.

I would not be recounting these trivia had they not later taken on colossal forms and provided me with one of the memories that make my heart pulse with glory and vanity to this day. As far as my priestly vocation is concerned, when I was a lad of thirteen I frequented a devout chapel, in the house of the hunchback Rodríguez, with a capacity for twenty persons, sacristy, bell tower, and the other necessities, as well as a supply of candlesticks, incense burners, and sonorous bells, made by Don Javier Jofré's slave, the negro Rufino, all of which we put to full use in our clanging and processions. The chapel was consecrated to our Father Saint Dominic, with me officiating for two years, by acclamation of the congregation, and to the great edification of the worshipers, in the august position of Provincial of the Order of Preachers. The priests of the Dominican convent would come to hear me sing mass, for which I parodied my uncle, the priest, who sang very well, and from whom, as an altar boy, I learned the entire mechanism of the mass, but not without marking the page in the missal where the gospel and the epistle of the day were, so that I could reproduce them in their entirety at my private mass.

On Sunday afternoons, the Provincial transformed himself into the commanding general of an army of boys, and, oh, woe to those who might choose to face the hailstorm of stones propelled by my phalanx!

As time passed, I had managed to ingratiate myself with a half dozen urchins who became my imperial guard, and with their support, I once reproduced the exploit of Leonidas with such verisimilitude that, when the reader hears about it, he will be unable to distinguish it from the deed of that celebrated Spartan.⁵ This is a serious matter that calls for bringing on the cast of characters, one by one, who performed most brilliantly on that memorable day.

At the house of the Rojos there was a chubby mulatto whose nickname was *Barrilito*,* a restless, daring lad, capable of mischief. Another of that ilk, of the household of the Cabreras, eleven years old, small,

*Little Keg.—Ed.

cunning, and so determined that when, as a man, having been promoted for bravery to corporal, he deserted Facundo Quiroga's ranks together with a few others, instead of fleeing, he fired on the army as it marched by, until he got himself caught and executed. This one was called *Piojito.**

The third one, going by the nickname of *Chuña,*† really stood out; he was an ungainly bird, a Chilean peon, twenty years old or more, somewhat retarded, and, so, quite comfortable in the company of children. The fourth was José I. Flores, my neighbor and boyhood companion, whose nickname was *Velita,*‡ which he has managed to live down by dint of being good-natured and jolly. The fifth was Gaucho *Riberos,* a splendid fellow and my classmate; joining later, Dolores Sánchez, brother of that Eufemio, whom we called *Capotito*§ because he wrapped his coat over his arm to protect himself from stones. This new recruit went through school with me and very soon proved himself worthy of the noble company in which he had enlisted. Then in the year of Our Lord I don't know what (children never know what year they're living in), we took part in three or four military expeditions with fair enough distinction, with a fair enough number of stones thrown and blows delivered and received, ending one Sunday with our routing an army and taking prisoner generals, drummers, and rabble, whom we paraded insolently through several streets of the city. Such humiliation imposed on the vanquished brought a reprisal, and no later than the next Wednesday or Thursday, we learned that preparations were under way in the Colonia and Valdivia districts, vast as they were and inhabited by shoals of boys, to pay us back the following Sunday. On Friday and Saturday, increasingly alarming reports poured in regarding the advances of the Colonia-Valdivia league, while I called up all my forces to be prepared to meet them properly. Sunday dawned, so eagerly awaited by some, so feared by others, then came afternoon, the hour was drawing close, and my soldiers did not appear, so frightened had the preparations and threats of our enemies left them.

Well, convinced that to engage the enemy was impossible, I and the

* Little Louse.—Ed.
† Booby.—Ed.
‡ Little Nuisance.—Ed.
§ Little Coat.—Ed.

six I mentioned, who would not have failed to show even if the sky had fallen, proceeded to the points from where it could be presumed the allied army would come, in order to have the pleasure of at least seeing them arrive. And so, with no fixed plan we headed for the *Pirámide*, where we could already hear the din of shouting and kids cheering, preceded by the noise of drums made of leather or gourds. A few moments later, the column appeared and poured into the neighboring open lot. My God! There must have been five hundred little devils carrying twenty banners, and wooden pikes and sabers that did not reflect the rays of the sun. We counted over thirty adults mixed in with the beardless mob, so great was the novelty of that uncommon crowd.

Instinctively, we fell back, fearful of being buried under that avalanche of boys eager to do mischief, above all in revenge for what had happened the Sunday before.

The seven of us took the cross street that led to the Torres mill, disconcerted and discouraged, and within a hair's breadth of taking to our heels. Before the bridge over the sluice gate of the mill, there is a solid terrain, clayey and smooth, while around the bridge there was a vast number of small stones dredged up from the bottom of the stream bed. An idea flashed into my mind, which Napoleon would have applauded, which the heroic Horatius Cocles would have disputed with me as being his.[6] It occurred to me that with the seven of us standing on that narrow bridge and having that blessing of stones right at hand, we could challenge the passage of the allied army of Colonia and Valdivia. I called my followers together, laid out the situation, delivered a harangue, and I concluded, drawing a hearty response from them of "sounds good!," crackling with enthusiasm. They swore absolute allegiance, and with two others, Riberos and *Barrilito,* I took the center of the bridge, distributed the rest, two on either side of the ditch formed by the stream, and we all set about diligently gathering stones to make up for our lack of numbers with the liveliness of our fire. Meanwhile, they had seen us, and the air rumbled with the shouts of the multitude that was advancing rapidly upon us. My plan was not to throw a single stone until we had them within range. The mob approached, and suddenly we let go such a hailstorm that ten or twelve boys in the multitude gave noisy proof that at least some of the stones had found their mark. The rabble broke ranks and fled, my forces spoiling to give chase, but the general had calculated everything, and seen that interposing the bridge was the only possible means of defense.

In stating that I had calculated everything, I was forgetting that the most important detail had failed to pass through my mind, which was that the very stones we threw, they could throw back at us, and that at its rear, the immense column had San Augustín Street, rich in stones to bruise the hooves of the horses that travel it. Once recovered from the shock of the initial encounter, the aggressors dispatched boys by the hundreds to fetch ponchos full of stones, giving rise to the fiercest battle ever recorded in the chronicles of street urchins. One of the boys, Pedro Frías, approached the ditch I was defending and proposed, in his role as parlimentarian, that we fight it out with sabers. We seven against five hundred! After careful consideration of the proposal, I rejected it flatly, and a minute later the air was filled with stones flying in both directions, to the point that there was even a danger we might swallow them. *Piojito,* his head cracked, pouring blood and snot from so much crying, and calling everyone the sons of whores, was throwing stones by the hundreds, like an ancient catapult; *Chuña* had already fallen faint into the ditch and was at risk of drowning; we were all of us bruised, and the fray grew ever fiercer; the distance was now some four *varas* and the bridge was not yielding, until Tomás, Don Dionisio Navarro's negro, who was in the enemy front line, shouted to his companions, "Hold your fire, look, the general can't move his arms!" That stopped the battle and the others who were closest immediately came over to me, silent, and happier about me than about their victory. The thing was that, in addition to the innumerable stones that had hit my body, so many had landed on my arms, that I was unable to move them, and the stones I was still throwing, out of pure patriotism, were falling harmlessly a few steps away. Of my hearties, two had cowered and fled, and I do not name them in order not to tarnish their reputations, since equal steadfastness cannot be expected from all. With Riberos still at my side, and *Piojito,* still sniffling and cursing, we pulled *Chuña* out of the ditch and ministered to our wounded. Some blackguards wanted me to come along as a prisoner; I put up as much resistance as I could with the little energy I had left, both arms hanging limp and numb; the men in the group intervened in my behalf, granting due merit and all honors of the encounter to the vanquished, and I went home, staggering with exhaustion, where, with utmost diligence for an entire week, I applied frequent compresses of salt water to myself to clear up the black and blue welts, which, had I stripped, would have made me look like a peibald colt, so numerous and repeated they were. Oh, you comrades in glory on that memorable day! Oh, you, *Piojito,* if you are still alive! *Barrilito, Velita, Chuña, Gaucho,* and *Capotito,* I salute you still from my exile as I pay tribute to the distinguished valor of which you gave proof! What a pity that no monument has been erected on that bridge to perpetuate your memory. Leonidas and his three hundred Spartans did no more at famed Thermopylae. The unfortunate Acha did no less in the ditches of Angaco, leaving so many idiots belly up in the sun, who didn't know how to appreciate the value of a well placed ditch when there are half a dozen rascals dug in on the other side.[7]

To return to my education, it can be said that fate intervened to block my way. In 1821, I went to the seminary of Loreto in Córdoba but had to return without being able to enter. Carita's revolution left me without a Latin teacher.[8] In 1825, I began to study mathematics and surveying under M. Barreau, engineer of the province. Together, we drew up the plan of the streets of Rojo, Desamparados, Santa Barbara, and from there all the way around to Pueblo Viejo; and I alone, because my teacher abandoned me, those of the Cathedral, Santa Lucía, and Legua. That same year, I went to San Luis to continue with the cleric Oro the education that had been interrupted by the revolution of the previous year. A year later, I was called by the government to be sent to the School of Moral Sciences, and I arrived in San Juan, after having been rejected once before, at the moment when the lances of Facundo Quiroga were entering like a dusty forest, waving their sinister pennants in the streets.

In 1826 I took a job as a humble clerk in a shop, I who had been educated by the presbyter Oro in the solitude that does so much to develop the imagination, dreaming of congresses, war, glory, freedom, in short, the republic. I was sad for days, and like Franklin, whose parents put him to work making soap, he who was to "snatch lightning from the sky and scepter from the hand of tyrants," I developed an aversion to the road that leads only to gain. In my meditations in the hours of idleness, I would hark back to that countryside around San Luis where I wandered through the woods, my Nebrija in hand, studying *mascula sunt maribus,* and interrupting the recitation to throw a stone at a bird. I missed that sonorous voice that had resounded in my ears for two full years, calm, friendly, touching my heart, educating my sentiments, elevating my spirit. Reminiscences of that oral precipitation that fell each day upon my soul, were to me like the plates in a book, whose meaning we understand from the expression of the figures. People, history, geography, religion, morality, politics, all that was already noted down as in an index; however, I lacked the book that contained the details, and I was alone in the world amid lengths of plain cotton and bolts of linen, which I measured out yard by yard for the customers. But, there must be books, I said to myself, that specifically take up these things, that teach them to children; and having a good understanding of what one reads, one can learn them without a teacher; and I immediately launched upon a quest for such books, and in that remote province and at that hour of resolution, I found what I was looking for, just as I had conceived it, prepared by patriots who loved America well, and who from London had foreseen South America's need for education, sending me in response to my clamors the *Catechisms* of Ackerman, which Don Tomás Rojo had introduced into San Juan.[9] "I've found them!" I could exclaim like Archimedes, for I had foreseen them, invented, unearthed those manuals which, later on in 1829, I handed over to Don Saturnino Laspiur for the education of his children. There was ancient history, and that Persia, and that Egypt, and those pyramids, and that Nile the cleric Oro had told me about. I committed the history of Greece to memory, and that of Rome, immediately thereafter, successively imagining myself Leonidas and Brutus, Aristides and Camillus, Harmodious, and Epaminondas, and this while selling maté and sugar, and scowling fiercely at those who dragged me out of the world that I had discovered so that I could live there.[10] Every morning, after I had swept out the store, I would settle down to read, and a Señora Laora, who passed by on her way to church and then back again, would see this immobile boy, insensitive to any distraction, his eyes fixed on a book, day after day, month after month, and so, shaking her head, she would remark at home, "That young fellow must be no good! If those were good books, he wouldn't be so eager to read them."

Another book occupied me for more than a year: the Bible! In the evenings after eight o'clock when the store closed, my uncle Don Juan Pascual Albarracín, by then a presbyter, would wait for me at home, and for two hours we would discuss what I had been reading, from Genesis to the Apocalypse, all the way through. How patiently he would listen to my objections, then proceed at once to tell me the doctrine of the Church, the canonical interpretation, and the legitimate and received meaning of the precepts, where it said white, even though I was reading black, and the divergent opinions of the holy fathers! *Natural Theology* by Paley; *Evidence of Cristianity,* by the same author; *True Idea of the Holy See,* and Feijoo, which fell into my hands at the time, completed that rational and eminently religious, but liberal, education, which came from the cradle, transmitted from my mother to the schoolmaster, from my mentor Oro to the commentator of the Bible, Albarracín.[11]

At that time, the canon Don Ignacio Castro Barros paid a visit to San Juan, and made his mission public by preaching for fifteen consecutive days by the light of the moon in the plazas, having for an audience as many people as could be packed into a square block of terrain.[12] I attended these talks assiduously, arriving early to get a good place. His reputation as a great preacher preceded him, and for many days he held me in a state of fevered excitation. He had succeeded in arousing in my spirit the rancorous fanaticism that forever poured from that mouth, frothing with rage, against the impious and heretics, whom he reviled in the most ignoble terms. Frenetic, ranting, he went from town to town, kindling popular passion against Rivadavia and the reform, and clearing the way for bandits like Quiroga and others, whom he called the Maccabees. I took general confession with him to consult myself in my doubts, to draw closer and closer to that source of light, which with the reason of my sixteen-year-old mind, I found empty, obscure, ignorant, and deceitful. The damage wrought in San Juan by that misguided soul can be inferred from the decree of July 28, 1827, issued by the government, enemy of Rivadavia and his partisans:

"An ill-fated experience," it says, "has shown how easily differences of opinion can lead to discord, and then to war. It is this very experience that has given rise to the government's conviction that, although every individual should be assured freedom to express his opinion in a decorous and legal manner, it is also necessary to prevent that he attempt to extend that freedom to attacking those who think differently, by censurable and highly dangerous means. When such license is involved, when certain sacred and venerable institutions have taken it upon themselves to speak out in favor of what is known to be political dispute, public tranquility is undermined. In view of these considerations and since it has become known that a certain minister of the sanctuary has spoken directly and even personally in the pulpit of the Holy Spirit on the very same political questions that have already caused bloodshed in San Juan, the government has seen fit to decree:

1. It is forbidden to discuss political questions in any public religious discourse conducted in the Lord's temple, where nothing should be heard but the blessed morality of the Gospel, the precepts of the Redeemer of the world, the consolation of divine religion and the pleas of the faithful.

2. Let the venerable clergy be notified and a copy be sent to the Official Registry.—*Quiroga*[a]—*José Antonio de Oro*, Secretary.[b]

I was made to question his sincerity by the spectacle of one of those farces that had given him fame. He was ending a sermon in the church by inveighing against Llorente, whom he called impious, a viper, for having slandered the holy court of the Inquisition, assuring the audience that he had died devoured by the worms in punishment for his sins.[13] I followed him avidly in such imprecations, as he spewed poison, blood, curses, and aspersions upon Rousseau and a string of others, whose names were unfamiliar to me, and his bile mounted in him, and the fury of one possessed came to his bloodshot eyes, and to his mouth, where dried spittle collected in the corners; when suddenly he stood up, and spreading arms and lifting his stentorian voice, to which the echoes of the church's vaults replied, he invoked the devil, ordering him to appear in his presence, assuring in positive, irrefutable terms that he possessed the power granted by Heaven to call him up, and that he was going to appear immediately; and his eyes shot about looking for him, and his clenched hands pointed to the darkest recesses of the church, and the uneasy women shifted and turned in readiness to flee, while I fixed my eyes on that convulsed and purple physiognomy of the priest, waiting to see there signs of bewitchment, for I dared not yet believe that it was all humbug. Afterward I have seen the actor Casacuberta play more difficult roles with the same passion, and I have felt my blood boil with indignation at that prostitution of the pulpit.[14]

The priest Castro Barros sowed in my spirit the first seeds of doubt that tormented it, the first disaffection with the religious ideas in which I had been brought up, knowing nothing of fanaticism and disdaining superstition. I later have learned the story of that madman. One of his favorite tricks in the countryside, among the uneducated, was to cast a little feather from the pulpit, calling it the soul of a condemned man and

[a] Don Manuel Gregorio. [Author's note]
[b] Brother of Bishop Oro. [Author's note]

declaring that the person upon whom it alighted was already predestined to eternal tortures; and the wretched women, whom he called to gather around the pulpit, with their wailing and their movements stirred up the air, and the errant bit of down fluttered and changed direction, spreading terror and despair over the heads of the crowd, which finally rose to its feet, maddened with fear, and ran shrieking from the church over the fields. I leave out a thousand horrible scenes of this sort, among them a skull and a crucifix, made to conduct dialogues, which might have been laughable if they hadn't been odious, between two such venerated objects, and his having the skull sing bawdy songs, and then describe its tortures in hell, and his taking pleasure in them, recalling to the skull its past sins, one by one. It is in this school of preachers that the political terrorists of the Spanish colonies are produced, and in their diatribes against the ungodly, the slogan of *"Death to the unitarian savages."* From there have arisen the sparks that incited the crowd, driving it to criminal acts, to the slaughter of which we have been victims. From the mouth of Castro Barros, as from that of the English Puritans, the Holy Scriptures always emerged soaked in blood, stirring up the brutal instincts of the mob. Fortunately for the glory of Castro Barros, he had the strength of spirit to reverse his direction, when he saw the crimes and barbarism that he had perpetrated in the guise of holiness. In 1829, he threw his enthusiastic support behind General Paz in Córdoba, won for him the sympathy of his fellow countrymen, and various *arrobas* of silver plate from convents and monasteries went, at his behest, to swell the depleted coffers of the army, as clear proof of his adherence.[*][15] In the newspapers of the period, Doctor Castro Barros published a statement to explain his reasons for changing parties and for turning against Facundo Quiroga and his followers the very same arms with which he had prepared the bloody struggle. Subsequently, he cast his lot with the unitarians, escaped being flogged by Quiroga, was thrown into one of Rosas's prison ships, where he was forced to man the pump every day for months on end in order to save his exhausted and unhealthy life. He arrived later in Chile, where, in his old age he lapsed once more into the fanatical excesses of the first period of his preaching, and heatedly supported the Inquisition and other extremist ideas until death gave rest last year to that

---

[*]One *arroba* is equal to approximately twenty-five pounds.—Ed.

life torn by so many passions. The *Revista Católica* [Catholic Review] found him saintly, and in passing, was kind enough to insinuate with evangelical charity that the dead doctor had emulators, alluding to me who had begun to write his biography, with other less equivocal but perhaps more injurious concepts.[16] May God forgive their arrogance, but the poor priest was not worthy of emulation.

From that time on, I set out to read every book possible that fell into my hands, in no special order, with no guide other than chance, or the news I received of its existence in the meager libraries of San Juan. The first was the *Life of Cicero* by Middleton, with excellent plates, and that book made me live for a long time among the Romans.[17] Had I possessed the means at the time, I would have studied law to become a lawyer and defend causes, like that illustrious orator whom I have always loved with such a predilection. The second book was the *Life of Franklin*, and no book ever did me more good. Franklin's life was for me what Plutarch's lives were for him, for Rousseau, Henry IV, Mme. Roland and so many others.[18] I felt like Franklin; and why not? I was dirt poor like him, studious like him, and by exercising my ingenuity and following in his tracks, I might one day develop as he had, become a doctor *ad honorem* like him, and make a place for myself in American letters and politics. The *Life of Franklin* should form part of the books read in elementary school. His example is so inspiring, and the course he pursued so well within everyone's reach, that there is no lad even moderately well-intentioned who would not feel inclined to be a little Franklin, prompted by that beautiful tendency of the human spirit to emulate the models of perfection that it envisions. To write a life of Franklin adapted for use in the schools has long been an ambition of mine; and now that I considered myself equipped to do so, M. Mignet, prompted by the same ideas and commissioned by the Academie Française, has done so with resounding success, although my plan was different, more popular and more adaptable to our conditions. Such as Mignet's book is, I ordered it from France and have had it translated into Spanish for dissemination, for I know from personal experience how beneficial this book is for children.[19] Blessed are the aspirations of the youthful spirit to beauty and perfection! Where is there among our books the type, the practical model, that is doable, possible, that can guide those youthful aspirations and lay out a course for them? The preachers propose that we emulate the saints in heaven in their ascetic virtues and mortification of the flesh; but no matter how well-intentioned the child may be, at an early age he renounces the pretension to perform miracles for the simple reason that those who advise it, themselves abstain from performing them. But the youth who with no support other than his reason, poor and deprived, works with his hands to survive, studies under his own guidance, examines his actions with a view to improving them, makes his name famous, serves his country, helping it loose itself from its oppressors, and one day, presents all of mankind with the gift of a simple instrument for taming the lightning of the heavens, and can brag of saving millions of lives with the device he gave to humanity, this man should be placed on humanity's altars, be considered greater than Saint Barbara, the protectress against lightning, and be called the People's Saint.

For Spanish-speaking peoples, learning a living language simply means learning to read, and at least one should be taught in the primary schools. The cleric Oro, in teaching me Latin, which I still do not know, had provided me a simple machine for learning languages that I have applied successfully to the few I do know. In 1829, having escaped execution by the friar Aldao in Mendoza, through the beneficent and spontaneous intercession of Colonel Don José Santos Ramírez, the weaknesses of whose judgement do not detract from the kindness of his heart, I had my house in San Juan for my prison and the study of French for recreation.[20] I got the idea of learning it with a Frenchman, a soldier of Napoleon, who did not know Spanish or understand the grammar of his own language. But my greed had been aroused by the sight of a French library belonging to Don José Ignacio de la Rosa, and with a borrowed dictionary and grammar, after one month and eleven days of having begun my solitary study, I had translated twelve volumes, among them, the *Mémoires* of Josephine.[21] Of my consecration to that task I can give an idea with concrete examples. I kept my books on the dining room table, pushed them aside to be served my lunch, after that for dinner, and at night for supper; the candle was blown out at two o'clock in the morning, and when I was carried away by my reading, I would sit for three days pouring over my dictionary. After that, I spent fourteen years learning to pronounce French, which I did not speak until 1846, after having arrived in France. In 1833, I was a clerk in a firm in Valparaíso at a salary of one *onza* per month, and of this I spent half on my English teacher Richard and two *reales* a week on the night watchman of the *bar-*

rio to wake me at two in the morning to study my English.* On Saturdays, I stayed up all night to make of them a single piece with Sunday,
and after a month and a half of lessons, Richard told me that all I had
left to learn was pronunciation, which to this day I still have not been
able to master. I went to Copiapó, and as an unworthy foreman of *La
Colorada*, which hid so much silver bullion from my eyes, I translated the
whole set of sixty novels by Walter Scott at a rate of one volume a day,
and many other works that I owed to the solicitousness of Mr. Edward
Abbott.²² Many people in Copiapó will remember the miner who was
always reading, and even in Lima, Señor Codecido reminded me, upon
my return from Europe, of something that had happened in those days.
For reasons of economy, amusement, and mischief, I had ended up fit-
ting myself out completely in the picturesque garb of the miners and had
accustomed the others to accept this disguise as my ordinary dress. I
wore slippers and woolen outer socks, blue trousers and a striped work
shirt, topping off this colorful outfit with the traditional red cap, in addition to a wide belt from which there hung a bag large enough to accommodate an *arroba* of sugar, and in which I always kept one or two
handfuls of Bolivian tobacco. In the afternoons, Don Manuel Carril
came up from the *Desempeño* mine, and he and I would repair to the
Manto de los Cobos, where, in the kitchen, we would join half a dozen Argentine overseers, bosses or peons, to discuss politics. To this smoky and
garrulous conclave, a young Parisian attached himself, to whom we gave
lessons in pure Castillian such that, on one occasion, when he was with
a group of ladies, he left them shocked, and we, his teachers, equally disconcerted at the advances our pupil had made in such a short time, and
thus we were forced to scold him afterward and explain to him all the
Castillian phrases, words, and interjections that would not be readily acceptable in any company other than that of the kitchen of the *Manto de
los Cobos*, of which he was a part.²³

In 1835, the judge who presided over the mines was Major Mardones,
who had fought in the Argentine Republic during the war of independence; his wife had social graces, manners, tidiness, and some pieces of
furniture that reconciled us with civilized life, and in the evenings we
used to go down to their residence, in the town of Placilla, and pass the
time agreeably. One night we met a new guest, Señor Codecido, a

*An *onza* is equal to 320 *reales*.—Ed.

fastidious, sybaritic, city type who complained of the inconveniences and hardships of the work. All greeted him courteously, I tipped my cap shyly, and slipped off into a corner to make myself as inconspicuous as possible, dressed as I was in my usual costume, nevertheless making a point, as I went by, of letting him see my ribbed leather gaucho belt, which is the *pièce de résistance* of the outfit. Codecido paid no attention to me, as was to be expected in the case of a miner whose boss allowed him into his house, and had I been closer by, he would have asked me for a light or some other such service. The conversation covered a number of topics, and disagreement arose regarding a point of fact in modern European history and several geographical place names, at which point, Carril, Chenaut, and the others automatically turned to me for the right answer. Thus prompted to take part in the gentlemen's conversation, I set them straight, but in such dogmatic terms and with such a wealth of details that Codecido's jaw dropped lower and lower as page after page of information poured forth from the lips of one whom he had taken for a simple miner. The reason for his mistake was explained to him, in the midst of general laughter, and from then on I remained in his good graces.

I entertained the miners in *Punta Brava* with drawings of animals and birds; gave French lessons to some young people, and met an overseer there who had such an extraordinary gift for retaining what he read, that he could recite entire books without omitting a comma. This person had bulging eyes, as is required by Gall.[24] My studies in Chañarcillo include a book I edited on *emigration,* from San Juan and Mendoza to the shores of the Colorado River toward the south, which not having found a publisher, I once recited out loud to Manuel Carril, keeping him so entranced for two hours with my story, that when I stopped to catch my breath, he said, "Go on, go on," and finally exclaimed enthusiastically, "I'd put up my own shirt to back this project"; since I was only asking for eighty thousand pesos, to enable a thousand lads of good will to go south with me and to found a colony on a navigable river, and make a fortune. I recall this because it pleases me to show how far back I can trace this obsession of mine to continue the task of occupying the land, which was brought to a standstill by the war of independence. In fact, today the land is being depopulated due to the ignorance and ineptitude of those governments.

In 1837 I learned Italian in San Juan, through my friendship with young Rawson, whose talents were already beginning to manifest themselves. Finally, in 1842, while editing *El Mercurio,* I familiarized myself with Portuguese, which does not need to be learned. In Paris, I shut myself in for two weeks with a grammar and a dictionary, and translated six pages of German to the satisfaction of the intelligent person I had asked to read them, the tremendous effort, however, having done me in, even though I felt I had already grasped the structure of that rebellious language.

I have taught French to many, out of a desire to propagate good reading, and to a number of good friends, without giving them lessons. Instead, in order to get them started on the road I had already traveled, I would first say to them: "It's clear to me you're not going to break your neck studying," and when I saw I had pricked their self-esteem, I would give them a few lessons on how to study on their own. Bustos, of the Normal School, and P . . . , my very young friend, informed me a month or two later that they already knew French, and, in fact they really had studied it.

How are ideas formed? I believe that in the spirit of those who study something happens that resembles the flooding of rivers, when passing waters deposit, little by little, the solid particles they carry in solution and fertilize the ground. In 1833, I was able to prove in Valparaíso that I had read all the nonprofessional works listed in the catalogue of books published by *El Mercurio.* These readings, enriched by the acquisition of languages, had laid out before my eyes the great debate of philosophical, political, ethical, and religious ideas, and opened the pores of my intelligence to absorb them. In 1838, my unfortunate friend Manuel Quiroga Rosas returned to San Juan, his spirit still inadequately prepared, but full of faith and enthusiasm for the new ideas that were shaking the literary world in France, and in possession of a choice library of modern authors.[25] Villemain and Schlegel, on literature; Jouffroy, Lerminier, Guizot, Cousin, on philosophy and history; Tocqueville, Pierre Leroux, on democracy; the *Revue Enciclopédique* as a synthesis of all the doctrines; Charles Didier and a hundred other names, unknown to me until then, fed my thirst for knowledge for a long time.[26] For two consecutive years, these books provided material for impassioned discussions at evening gatherings, where Doctors Cortínez, Aberastaín, Quiroga Rosas, Rodríguez, and I discussed the new doctrines, resisting them, attacking them, and finally ending up more or less won over by them.[27]

That is when, and in truth with good teachers, I did my two years of philosophy and history, and at the conclusion of that course of study, I began to feel that my own thinking, until then a mirror reflecting the ideas of others, was beginning to stir and want to move forward. All my ideas became clearly and distinctly defined, with the dissipation of the shadows and vacillations common in the young who are just starting out, and with the filling in of those lacunae that twenty years of disorganized reading had managed to leave. I began seeking the application of those acquired results to present-day life, translating the European spirit into the American spirit, with the changes that the different theater required.

In all these efforts, forever active was the organ of instruction and information that in me is the most expeditious: the ear. Instructed by means of the spoken word by the presbyter Oro, by the priest Albarracín, always seeking out the company of educated men, then and later, my friends Aberastaín, Piñero, López, Alberdi, Gutiérrez, Oro, Tejedor, Fragueiro, Montt, and so many others have contributed without knowing it to the development of my spirit, transmitting their ideas to me, or providing the support for mine that allowed them to develop on their own.[28] Thus prepared, I presented myself in Chile in 1841, mature, I can say, thanks to my years, my study, and my reflection, and the writings that the press put before me caused me to think, of course, that the men who had received a formal education had not stored up a greater amount of knowledge, nor had they digested it more slowly. Not at the beginning of my career as a writer, but later, there arose in Santiago a feeling of disdain for my inferiority, which was shared even by the boys in school. Today, I would ask, if it were necessary, all those young men of *El Semanario*, whether they had really done more serious studies than I.[29] Were they trying to hoodwink me, too, with their six years at the *Instituto Nacional* [National Institute]?[30] What, then? Do I, now a university examiner, not know what is being taught in the schools?[31]

16

Public Life

In the sixteenth year of my life I entered prison and left it with political ideas, the opposite of Silvio Pellico, whose imprisonments taught him the morality of resignation and self-abasement.[1] From the first time the book *My Imprisonments* fell into my hands, I was filled with horror at the doctrine of moral degradation that the prisoner went forth to preach in the world and that was so acceptable to those kings who felt threatened by the energy of the people. The human species would be considerably advanced by now if what man required in order to understand the interests of his country were eight years of spiritual exercises in the dungeons of Spielberg, the Bastille, and Santos Lugares![2] Woe to this world, if the czar of Russia, the emperor of Austria, or Rosas could teach morality to mankind! Silvio Pellico's book is the death of the soul, the morality of the dungeon, the slow poison of the spirit's degradation. He and his book have passed on, thank goodness, and the world gone forward, despite the maimed, the paralyzed, and the valetudinarian that political struggles have left behind. In 1827, I was a shopkeeper by trade, but, depending on whom I was reading, I couldn't say whether I was Cicero, Franklin, or Themistocles at the moment of the catastrophe, when I was notified for the third time to shut my store and go and stand guard as a second lieutenant in the militia, the rank to which I had recently been promoted.[3] I was annoyed by that duty, and on reporting to the government that I had been relieved of my watch without incident by the officer in charge, I added a protest in which I complained of such service, saying: "by which we are needlessly *oppressed.*" I was relieved of guard duty and summoned to appear before the former colonel of the Army of the Andes, Don Manuel Quiroga, governor of San Juan, who, at the moment I arrived, was sitting in the courtyard of the government headquarters, sunning himself.[4] Naturally, this circumstance and my extreme youth authorized the governor, while addressing me, to remain seated and keep his hat on. But it was the first time I had ever appeared before an authority, young, ignorant of life, and cocky by upbringing and perhaps by way of my daily contact with Caesar, Cicero, and my favorite characters; and since the governor offered no response to my respectful greeting, before I answered his question: "Is this, sir, your signature?", I removed my hat hastily, replaced it on my head deliberately, and replied, firmly: "Yes, sir!" The mute scene that followed would have left the on-looker perplexed, in doubt as to who was the official and who the subordinate, who was outstaring whom, the eyes of each fixed on the other, the governor trying to get me to lower mine before the bolts of anger that shot forth from his, I, with my eyes fixed, without so much as a blink, letting him know that his rage was crashing up against the parapet of an impregnable soul. I defeated him, and he, beside himself with anger, called for an aide and sent me to jail. Several friends hurried to visit me, among them Laspiur, now a minister, who was fond of me and advised me to do what he had always done: give way in the face of difficulties. My father came at once and when I told him the story, he said to me: "You did a foolish thing; but it's done; now suffer the consequences with dignity." An action was brought against me; I was asked if I had heard complaints against the government; I answered yes, many. Asked from whom, I replied that those who have spoken in my presence have not authorized me to report to the authorities what they said. They insist, I stand my ground; they threaten me, I stick my tongue out at them; and the action was dropped, I was set free, and made aware by the authorities themselves that there were political parties in the city, matters that divided the Republic, and that it was not in Rome or Greece where I must seek freedom and a country, but right there, in San Juan, before the broad horizon being opened up by events that were taking shape in the final days of Rivadavia's presidency. Even chance was pushing me into the partisan struggles of which I was still ignorant. During a fiesta of Pueblo Viejo, I set off a rocket at the feet of a group of horses, and from among the riders there appeared, to shout at me, none other than my Colonel Quiroga, by then ex-governor, attributing to intentional malice on my part what was no more than mere recklessness. We traded insults and began to close in on each other, he on horseback, I on foot. Fifty horsemen rallied round him, and I, keeping an eye on both him and his skittish horse to avoid being trampled, began to feel an object that was pressing on me from behind in an urgent, meaningful way. I reach back to identify it and touch . . . the barrel of a pistol being handed me! I, too, was at that moment the head of a phalanx that had formed in my defense. The federal party, headed by Quiroga Carril, was at the point of coming to blows with the unitarian party, for which I was just then unwittingly serving as a spearhead. The ex-governor withdrew, taken aback by the jeering, and perhaps astonished at coming up for the second time against a boy who neither provoked him with arrogance, nor backed down with timidity once he found himself in trouble! The next day I was a unitarian. A few months later, I was familiar with the issue of the parties, their essence, their people, and their aims, since from that moment on I was fully absorbed in studying the voluminous proceedings of opposing opinions.

When war broke out, I turned over the shop I was in charge of to my aunt Doña Angela, enlisted in the troops that had rebelled against Facundo Quiroga in Las Quijadas, took part in the campaign at Jachal, fought in the action at Tafín, avoided capture along with the wagons and horses I had taken in El Pocito, under the command of Don Javier Angulo; escaped with my father to Mendoza, where the same troops that had defeated us in San Juan had risen up against the Aldaos, and shortly after, together with Don J. M. Echegaray Albarracín, I was appointed aide to General Alvarado, who donated me to General Moyano, who took a liking to me and, one day, as a reward for a clever prank of mine, presented me with the golden-bay horse on which Don José Miguel Carrera had been defeated.[5] Afterward, I have been aide-de-camp attached to the Second Cuirassiers of General Paz; an approved instructor of recruits, to which Colonel Chenaut, under whom I served for fifteen days, can attest; later, I was declared assistant director of the military academy, in view of my extensive knowledge of cavalry tactics and maneuvers, which is easily explained by my devotion to study. But the war, with all the illusions it engenders, and the haze of glory that intoxicates even a company commander, have not left me with sweeter impressions, nor more unforgettable memories, than that campaign in Mendoza, which ended in the terrible tragedy of Pilar.[6] For me, that time was the poetry, the idealization, the realization of all my reading. A callow youth of eighteen, unknown to all, I have lived in a permanent ecstasy of enthusiasm, and although I did nothing worthy of note, since my position was that of an ordinary aide-de-camp with no soldiers at his command, I was or would have been a hero, ever disposed to sacrifice myself, to die wherever it could have been useful to obtain the slightest result. I was always the first one in the guerrillas, and at midnight the distant shooting would wake me up, and I would slip away, setting out through unfamiliar streets, guided by the powder flashes to the scene of the skirmish, to shout, create a racket, and to urge on the gunfire. Finally I had found myself a rifle with which, wherever there were guerrillas, I would fire a hellish barrage, until General Moyano took it away from me, the way one takes a top away from a child so that he'll do as he's told, when excitement interferes with obedience. My father, who followed me around like a guardian angel, would appear during these moments of intoxication to get me out of difficulties that, were it not for his foresight, might have proven fatal. Day by day, I made more and more friends in the division, and on the morning of September 29, the day of our defeat, after my vigilance and precautions had saved the camp from an attack, through a stretch of the wall that had been knocked down during the night, a young fellow named Gutiérrez lent me his platoon of twenty men to go skirmish with the enemy somewhere else. This time I was in command of an imposing force, and the street, with its walls long and narrow like a flute, saved the general from having to devise a complicated strategic plan. Advancing straight ahead and withdrawing straight back were the two principal, that is, *pivotal* operations of the engagement. Hand-to-hand combat was what the soldiers on both sides, generally militiamen, least desired, but this was for me my greatest curiosity, which I intended to satisfy. I ordered a volley that served as the introduction to the chapter; then, I advanced to provoke the enemy officer with words, calling him "coward," "ostrich" and other such niceties, while he, without advancing far, had me shot at by three or four of his men, who spent a good minute firing their guns at me. After taking fifteen rounds at twenty-five paces, I figured out the most respectable way to stop serving as a target. I gave the order to charge, we skirmished for a second, and then withdrew simultaneously, leaving the poor general alone on the transitory battlefield, disappointed because the game couldn't go on a little longer. I rejoined my men, and noticed in every evolution of my horse that a soldier kept me company. The others didn't recognize his face, and realized he was an enemy who had remained behind among us, for the poncho was the uniform for both sides; they attacked him, I defended him; they insisted on killing him, he bolted; I took off after him, and when he got back to his side, I managed to move in next to him, and swerving my horse, fetched him a clout in an appropriate place, sent him into the ditch alongside the street, and left his saddled horse at the disposition of my men, while I faced off those who were coming to his rescue. This was the deed most *contábile* that I have performed in my military adventures. Later on, I was a grown man, a captain of the line, and of necessity, circumspect.

I was often present at the discussions General Alvarado had with poor Moyano. Alvarado was never right, but he had the prestige of the war of independence and brought the force of inertia to bear against everything, which is the most fearful of powers. Moyano was executed, and Alvarado retired quietly to San Juan, after his defeat. Later he sent word to Señor Sarmiento, a writer in Chile, that in the *Vida de Aldao* [Life of Aldao] he made allusion to his conduct at that time, and that he, Alvarado, had already been cleared of those accusations. My reply came as a great surprise to Frías: "Tell the General that the young aide-de-camp he gave to Moyano and whom he once reprimanded for the close attention he paid to conversations between the commanders, is the Señor Sarmiento whom he now addresses." Oh! Ten times the Republic has been lost by honorable but ineffectual men, incapable of comprehending what was right in front of their faces! I was held in high esteem by Don José María Salinas, Bolivar's former secretary, and a fervent patriot, gifted with outstanding talents, whose throat was slit by Aldao and whose body, on Aldao's orders, was mutilated and disfigured with a barbarity unheard of until then. Finally, in the two days before the defeat at Pilar, in view of Dr. Salinas's friendship and the support of the Villanuevas and of Zuloaga, who had assumed command of the division, I was admitted to the senior officers' councils of war, despite my youth and because of my discretion; I must believe that they thought my judgement sound, for as to the sincerity of my resolve, there could be no doubt.

This episode concluded with incidents that are essential to the purpose of this narrative. All know the origin of the shameful catastrophe of

Pilar. The priest Aldao, drunk, unleashed a salvo of six cannons at the group of sixty of our officers that formed around Fernando Aldao, his brother, who had come into our camp, after a treaty had been made between the two warring parties. The disarray of our troops, scattered in view of the signed peace, was instantly converted into defeat, despite our useless efforts to reestablish our positions. Never before had human nature appeared more despicable to me, and only Rosas has exceeded in cynicism the wretches who thus prepared the way for him. I was stunned, blind with anger; my father came to take me from the camp, and I had the cruelty to force him to flee alone. Laprida, illustrious Laprida, the president of the Congress of Tucumán, came immediately and admonished me; he described to me, in the kindest terms, the danger that was mounting by the second.[7] Unfortunate man! I was the last of those who knew to value and respect his merit who heard that voice soon to be silenced forever! Had I followed him, I would not now have to deplore the loss of the man who most honored San Juan, his homeland, and before whom the most eminent figures of the Republic bowed, as one of the country's founding fathers, as before the personification of that Congress of Tucumán that declared the independence of the United Provinces. Shortly after that he was murdered, by people from San Juan, it is said, and for many years no one knew of the tragic fate that overtook him that afternoon. I abandoned the field at Pilar, after having seen the aide Estrella die at my side, and after one of our men killed an enemy soldier who was blocking my way, as we fought over the lance and the saber with which I had succeeded in wounding him. I made my way out through the enemy, through a series of sudden reverses and singular events, entering parts of the street where we were the victors, to pass on to others where we were prisoners. Farther along, two Rosas brothers, on opposite sides, were quarreling over a horse; then I met up with Joaquín Villanueva, who was soon run through with a lance, and his brother José María, who had his throat slit three days later; and all these changing situations were occurring as I slowly advanced on horseback, because the vertigo of victors and vanquished that seized us all for half a league's length of a street, precluded the idea of saving oneself by flight. Few knew what was actually going on in the rear, and I was one of those few. When my hour for reflection, anxiety, and terror came, was when having emerged from that labyrinth of death, by a route traced for me by my lucky star, I fell into the hands of the gangs who were on their way to loot the city, and one of them, after stripping me of my arms and clothing, turned me over to the commander Don José Santos Ramírez, who, to his honor, I must say, was carrying off the noble booty snatched from the field of battle: prisoners and the wounded, whom he was taking to his own home to save from the slaughter. Commander Ramírez saved my life then, and four days later, when the order arrived from San Juan to execute the young men from that town who had been taken prisoner, among whom were Echegaray, Albarracín, Carril, Moreno, and others, the majority from prominent families, who out of conviction had immediately taken up arms, Don José Santos Ramírez's replied to those who came to kill me: "That young man is a guest in my house, and only over my dead body will you lay hands on him." Shortly after, he turned me over to Villafañe so that one of my uncles could return me to my family. As for my father, saved at the beginning of the defeat, there is a deed worth recalling. Not knowing what had become of me, he was inconsolable, beside himself, as though ashamed at having saved his own life. He remained waiting for the last groups of fugitives, to see if his son was among them, until he was the last person in advance of the enemy contingents. When he reached haven, he chose not to follow those in flight to Córdoba, but remained for days prowling about the advance guards of the enemy until he was captured, like those tigresses whose cubs have been stolen and are impelled by maternal instinct to surrender to the implacable hunter. He was brought to San Juan, marked for execution, but escaped being shot by making a contribution of two thousand pesos.

I omit recounting the danger I escaped of being killed in the barracks in the revolution of Panta, Leal, and the Herreras, all professional bandits subsequently executed by Benavides, and the even greater risk I ran the next day of staining my hands with the blood of some few of those miserable rebels, a danger from which I was rescued by circumstances beyond my control. I also skip over other vicissitudes, military promotions, and sterile campaigns, until Quiroga's victory at Chacón, which in 1831 forced us to emigrate to Chile, and me to go from being the guest of a relative in Putaendo to schoolmaster in Los Andes, from there to shopkeeper in Pocuro with a tiny capital sent me by my family, a clerk in Valparaíso, a foreman in the mines at Copiapó, a gambler for eight days in Huasco, until in 1836 I returned to my province, suffering from a cerebral attack, penniless, and known only to a few, since with the political upheavals, the best class of society had emigrated, and to this day has not returned.[8] A complicated arithmetical calculation needed by the government soon drew attention to me, and as the days passed and I fed myself on privations, I was able, through the friendship of relatives, to join the circle of San Juan's most accomplished young men, later becoming the inseparable companion of my former schoolmates Doctors Quiroga Rosas, Cortínez, Aberastaín, men of value, talent, and culture, and worthy of distinction anywhere in America. Out of that association came ideas that were extraordinarily useful to San Juan: a school for women, another for men that ended in failure, a dramatic society, and a thousand other public pastimes aimed at the improvement and refinement of customs; and, as the culmination of all these preparatory activities, a newspaper, *El Zonda*, which criticized the small-town customs, fostered the spirit of reform, and would have produced incalculable benefits, if the government, which *El Zonda* did not attack, had not been in fear of the light that was growing stronger.[9] And that was what brought about my second imprisonment, for refusing to pay twenty-six pesos which, in violation of existing laws and decrees, the government was proposing to steal from me. Don Nazario Benavides and Don Timoteo Maradona, jointly *et in solidum*, owe me twenty-six pesos every day that dawns; and they will pay me, by God!, one or the other, sooner or later, the latter rather than the former, because a minister's job is to counsel the governor who is little versed in the laws of his country and too headstrong to be stopped by those fragile barriers to caprice, but which are nonetheless made insuperable by the respect that the rights of others deserve among cultured men. The province's law governing the press, since the only printing press in existence is public property, stipulates the means by which publications will be financed, assigning to the press the proceeds from the sale of all newspapers, in order to facilitate and promote their publication. The governor of San Juan, wishing to free the province from the serious dangers that could be occasioned by the circulation of a newspaper published by four highly competent men of letters, that is, in order not to have anyone examining the government's actions nor enlightening public opinion, had me advised that, starting with the sixth issue of *El Zonda*, each sheet of printed paper was going to cost twelve pesos. I ordered the printer to go ahead and print the issue in question, and *El Zonda* died like that, suffocated. One day, I receive a summons to appear before the government. "Have you liquidated the cost of the last issue of *El Zonda?*" "Liquidated? To whom?" "To the press." "To the press? Why?" "Because it is so stipulated." "Stipulated by whom? "Such an order was communicated to you." "To me? That is not so." "Send for the printer Galaburri." Galaburri arrives. "Did you not communicate to this gentleman the order that he pay twelve pesos per printed page of the sixth issue of *El Zonda?*" "Yes, Señor." "Then, how can you say, Señor Sarmiento, that this was not so?" "I repeat that I was not notified of such an order." "Yes, Señor, I did notify you." "I repeat that I received no order of any kind; Galaburri gave me a message from Don Nazario Benavides; Galaburri is in this case the same as His Excellency's cook, whom he surely does not want to make an intermediary between the government and its citizens. With respect to the press and public affairs, the government makes itself known through decrees, and as long as the laws in force are not replaced by other laws that amend them, I will have nothing to do with gossip brought me by Galaburri regarding what the Governor or the Minister says."

The Minister: Where are those laws that you invoke?

"It is shameful that a minister should ask me that; he who is in charge of enforcing them, let him go and check the archives."

The Governor: You will pay what was ordered.

"Your Excellency will permit me to assure you that I will not."

The Governor: Señor Aide-de-Camp Coquino, at four o'clock this afternoon you shall proceed to the home of the Señor to collect the amount he owes.

"At four o'clock in the afternoon, Your Excellency will be given the same answer. It is not the small amount of money that concerns me, but the manner of collecting it and the illegality of the fee. I stand on principle, I will not submit to the arbitrariness of the government that does not have extraordinary powers."

At four o'clock in the afternoon the aide-de-camp appears, and upon my negative, he orders me to accompany him to prison. At the jail, he says: "I have instructions to advise you that if you do not pay by six o'clock, be prepared to go into exile to the place that the government orders." "Very well." "But, what do I say to the government?" "Nothing." "But, Señor, you will lose." "I appreciate your interest." "But, what do I say?" "What do you have to say? That you have conveyed the order to me."

The official left saddened and dismayed; Benavides and Maradona soon passed by on horseback, also worried about the turn the matter was taking. A little later, my friends Rodríguez, Quiroga, Cortínez, and Aberastaín arrived; we consulted, and the majority decided I should capitulate, in view of the fact that it was necessary to save the school of which I was the director. Only steadfast, courageous Aberastaín supported me in my resolve to oppose this arbitrariness to the last. The aide-de-camp returned and received a bank draft against a tradesman, with which, and with his signature at the bottom, I would obtain a document that I could use in due time, in view of the laws and decrees violated to my detriment, to obtain reimbursement of the plundered amount, plus damages. Don Timoteo Maradona, now a presbyter! You who confessed every week, and now forgive the sins of others, examine your conscience, and if it does not tell you that you have stolen, seizing twenty-six pesos by force, which you owe every hour of your life, and if that does not weigh upon you conscience, I will say to you, Señor Presbyter, that you are a corrupt scoundrel!

My situation in San Juan toward the end of 1839 was becoming thornier by the hour, as the political horizon grew ever darker with threatening clouds. With no plan in mind, without influence, rejecting the idea of conspiracy, in cafes and salons, I spoke my mind with my usual candor, as if in the presence of Benavides himself, and the suspicion of the government surrounded me everywhere, like a cloud of flies buzzing in my ears.

An incident arose to complicate my situation. Fray Aldao was defeated, and his arrival in San Juan was expected at any moment. The few men who dared to challenge the government feared for their lives. Dr. Aberastaín was the only one who refused to flee. I convinced him; I asked him to go, and he relented. I alone among us knew Aldao firsthand. Only I had been witness in Mendoza to the atrocities visited on two hundred unfortunates, among whom twenty were my friends, my comrades. When I was approached to prepare for the intended flight, I gave the reasons of expedience and duty that obliged me to remain in San Juan, and they had to accept them.

Aldao did not come, but the fears of the government and the rage of the new men, upstarts whom the government had armed, sought their outlet in me. Aberastaín was defending a poor woman, whose drunken son had been killed by a property owner during an attempt to steal one of his sheep. The appeals court judge said to the mother: "Listen here, woman; thieves are to be killed and flung into the street." And with this formidable sentence, she was refused a hearing, and Aberastaín had been working for a year to gather evidence for a preliminary hearing on the case. Since her lawyer was absent, the judge handed down an interlocutory decree ordering the woman to present the accusation in due form within four days, or the case would be dismissed. On the second day, the hapless woman presented the necessary material, establishing the crime, on the one hand, and, on the other, recapitulating all the judge's wrongful actions, as evidenced by the case itself. The judge began to view the matter with some concern, and came to see me at my house to prove to me that the Carta de Mayo, that is, the political constitution, permitted killing an individual who entered a person's domicile!

The briefs became more pointed, the evidence of the property owner's crime more palpable, and the judge, should he lack the support of the government in power, a circumstance not impossible at the time, could be declared an accessory. An important federalist and friend of mine wrote me to say that I was defending a crime against property, and that from then on he would defend the homicide. I answered that it befitted him, a wealthy man, to defend property; that I was defending the right to life of us poor people, and hence we were each in his domain, and it depended on the outcome of the suits and the weight of the evidence to determine whether we were dealing with a thief or a murderer. A third brief from the woman set the judge to working out a settlement between the parties, on condition that the brief not be included in the case. The judge already saw himself convicted, confessed to complicity, and sentenced. The woman was destitute, her son could not be brought back to life. They flashed a little money before her eyes, and she agreed to a settlement. From that money, I took fifteen pesos for myself, for my three briefs that could have cost me my head, and sent fifty to Dr. Alberastaín in his exile; he had defended the poor woman for a year, and these fifty pesos were like a bag of gold to him, so welcome did they prove.

About that time I made a supreme effort. I saw Maradona, the former minister, the representatives of the legislature, every person who could bring any influence to bear on Benavides so that they might contain him, if possible, in the plunge down the steep slope that I saw he had already begun, toward despotism, *caudillismo,* the overthrow of all the foundations upon which societies rest. The fledgling tyrant summoned me to his home. "I know that you are conspiring, Don Domingo." "Untrue,

Señor, I do not conspire." "You are going about working on the representatives." "Ah! That's another matter! Your Excellency is aware that there is no conspiracy; I take advantage of my right to address the magistrates, the people's representatives, in an effort to stave off the calamities that Your Excellency is preparing for the country. Your Excellency is alone, isolated, stubbornly going your way, and I am interested in having those who can, who must, stop you in time." "Don Domingo, you will force me to take measures." "What does it matter?" "Severe ones!" "What does it matter?" "You don't understand what I am trying to say to you?" "Yes, I understand. To shoot me! What can it matter to me?" Benavides stood with his gaze fixed on me; and I swear that he was unable to see the slightest indication of bluster in my expression; I was at that moment possessed by the spirit of God; I was the representative of the rights of all, soon to be trampled on. I saw in Benavides's face signs of appreciation, of compassion, of respect, and I wished to respond to that movement of his soul. "Señor," I said to him, "do not besmirch yourself. When you can no longer tolerate me, banish me to Chile; meanwhile, Your Excellency, expect that I must work to restrain you, if I can, from deviating in the direction in which ambition is leading you, the unleashing of the passions." And with this I took my leave.

Some days later I was again called to the governor's house. "I have learned that you have received papers from Salta, and from Brizuela's camp." "Yes, Señor, and I was preparing to bring them to you." "I knew that you had received those papers," he said, then added sarcastically, "but I didn't know that you wanted to show them to me." "It's just that I hadn't made the clean copy of my own remarks with which I wanted to accompany them. Here you have the two of them, Your Excellency." "These proclamations were printed here." "You are mistaken, Señor, they were printed in Salta." "Hmm! You can't fool me." "I never fool, Señor. I repeat that they were printed in Salta. The printing press in San Juan does not have this small capital letter, this other type face, that. . . ."

Benavides insisted, sent for Galaburri, and was convinced of his mistake. "Let me have that manuscript of yours." "I'll read it to you, Señor; it is a rough draft." "Read it." I remained silent. "Well, read it." "Have the Señor Chief of Police leave the room, Your Excellency. I do not wish to share confidential information with him."

And when he had left, glaring at me with looks that kill, as though I were responsible for his bad manners in seeking to remain, I read my factum in a loud voice, with emotion, lingering upon each concept that I wished to emphasize, lending force to the ideas that I wanted to drive home more deeply. When I finished the reading, which had left me in a state of exaltation, I raised my eyes, and all that I read in the caudillo's face was . . . indifference. Not a single idea had ignited in his soul, nor any doubt stirred in him. His will and his ambition were an armor that defended his mind and spirit.

Benavides is a cold man; to this San Juan owes having been less abused than other towns. He has an excellent heart, is tolerant, envy hardly corrodes his soul, he is patient and tenacious. Afterward, I have reflected that reasoning is impotent at a certain cultural level of the spirit; its darts are blunted and slide off those flat and hardened surfaces. Like the generality of men in our countries, he has no clear concept of either law or justice. I have heard him say ingenuously that our province would not be well off until there were no more lawyers; that his colleague Ibarra lived peacefully and governed well because he decided cases by himself and in no time at all.[10] In Benavides, Rosas has his best support; he is the power of inertia in action, the call to quietism, to death without violence, without fanfare. Except for La Rioja, San Luis, and others, the province of San Juan is the one that has fallen the lowest; because everywhere Benavides has left the imprint of his materialism, his inertia, and his abandonment of all that constitutes public life, which is what despotism requires. Eat, sleep, keep your mouth shut, laugh if you can, and wait calmly, for in twenty years from now . . . your children will be walking on all fours.

Benavides was in a hurry to get rid of all encumbrances; he wanted to take part in military campaigns, to be the general of an army, and he employed all the means that Rosas had already put into play to gain his ends. He granted himself extraordinary powers, recruited men, and placed individuals of absolutely no distinction in command of them, without appointing a single federalist of any stature in the province to staff the army. He put a man by the name of Espinosa, from Tucumán, in command of his forces. This man had been a lieutenant or captain under Quiroga, a valiant young fellow, a habitual drunkard, and of no social standing whatsoever. One of the Herreras was released from prison, the last of three Chilean bandits of the same name, condemned to death for murder and highway robbery, two of them executed already, and this last one, later on by Benavides himself, when he relapsed into the practice of his former profession. The Indian Saavedra was called into service, a highwayman and murderer, later stabbed to death in a drunken brawl, and not executed, as, by mistake, I said when I was talking at the beginning about his family.[11] Mayorga, an actor from Lima, was a captain, who died drunk by General Acha's hand. Benavides called Juan Fernández to his side, as aide-de-camp to distribute levies. A young man of good family who had voluntarily fallen among the riffraff, with whom he lived, mired in drunkenness and gambling, he was the vilest and most vilified creature to be found then in all of San Juan. An Italian trickster, corrupt, uncouth, and ignorant, was made a major. Under the command of these leaders, the scum of society, there were many obscure young men called into the service who had the praiseworthy desire to improve themselves and rise in the world, all without education, most of them from families at the lowest rung of the social ladder. From among these, although in such a bad school, good soldiers and honest citizens have emerged. The United States is federal, and the equality of all men is, as it should be, the basis of its institutions; but the officers of the army are trained at the military academy of West Point, famous all over the world today for the science professed, and for the distinction of the cadets selected from the most influential families, children of the leading notables. Chile, itself, enjoyed no repose or prosperity until the day that it ennobled the army by calling to its ranks, precisely because of breeding, the sons of the most distinguished families. Thus in the Republic of Argentina, they have turned society upside down, by elevating what is debased and by humbling and pushing aside what is, in itself, elevated; thus the federation triumphed and thus it sustains itself, perpetually filled with fear, forced to survive by humiliating, by terrorizing, by committing new acts of violence and new crimes. Benavides had no minister by then, for all the federalists avoided him, and he alone, with his troops, carried out his mad design. Thus they take the name of the people to call themselves governments, after they have debased and despoiled them!

Finally, I was summoned a fourth time to the governor's residence. This time I had been warned; I knew that a terrorist coup was in the works and that I was the designated victim. It was a Sunday, and I had taken my leave of some friends at their home, half in jest, half in earnest, and had written once outside saying that my life was in danger. Nonetheless, I obeyed the summons, making sure that a servant accompanied me to spread the news of my imprisonment, if that should come to pass. On the way, I saw one of my friends, and I resisted his entreaties, his pleas, that I not go. "They are going to arrest you, it's all arranged." "Never mind. Benavides sent an aide-de-camp to notify me, and I would be ashamed not to attend the summons." They arrested me, and at prayer hour, when the escort appeared to take me to prison, the sound of the sabers made me shiver; my ears were buzzing, and I was afraid, terror-stricken. The death I felt imminent at that moment seemed to me sad, soiled, unbecoming; and I lacked the valor to receive it in that guise. However, nothing happened, and in my cell, they clamped a bar of shackles on me. The days passed, and like the eyes to darkness, the spirit grew accustomed to the shadows and the disenchantment. I was a passive victim, and with the exception of my family, nobody cared about my situation. My plight was mine alone. I was suffering because I had been imprudent, because I had sought to circumvent misfortune without possessing the means to do so; against material realities, I had pitted protest, isolated abnegation, and things followed their course.

On the night of November 17, at two o'clock in the morning, a group on horseback came to a stop in front of the prison, shouting: *"Death to the unitarian savages!"* So unmotivated was this manifestation, so cold and composed was that cry that issued from the mouths of those who pronounced it, that it was clear it was a calculated, concerted, and passionless act. I realized that something was afoot. At four o'clock, the same refrain was repeated as I sat, awake, writing some trifle that kept me busy. At daybreak, an Andalusian was brought into the prison who was putting on a show of being drunk, and between wisecracks and comical carryings-on to distract the guards, as he staggered by a prisoner close by me, he let drop in piecemeal phrases: "They're going to kill you all! Troops on the way to the square! Comandante Espinosa's gonna lance you all . . . ! Lance Señor Sarmiento . . . ! Try to escape if you can . . . !"

This time I was on top of the situation; I asked at home for a messenger boy, wrote to the bishop not to be frightened and to try to save me by his presence . . . , but the poor old man did just the opposite, he became so terrified he couldn't even get his legs to hold him up. Troops arrived and formed in the square. The boy who was at the prison door, acting as my telegraph, was communicating all their movements to me. Shouts could be heard in the square, galloping horses; I saw Espinosa's lance pass by, which he was calling for. Then, there was a momentary silence! And finally, a group of eighty officers formed below the prison, yelling, "Out with the prisoners!" The officer of the guard came up and ordered me to come out. "Who gave the order?" "Comandante Espinosa." "I refuse." So, he went to the next cell, took out Oro, and exhibited him. "Not that one! Sarmiento!" Well, then, I said to myself, there's no way out for me now; because I had already tricked my cellmate earlier into getting the heavier shackles by my lordly refusal to accept them on my delicate legs. I came out and was greeted with insults and a shout of "Hurrah! Kill him" from those men who didn't know me, except for two who had reason to hate me. "Bring him down! Bring him down! *Crucifige eum!*"* "I refuse to go down! You have no right to give me orders." "Officer of the Guard, use your saber and get him down here." "Go down," said the man, brandishing his saber. "I will not go down." I said, clutching the railing. "Go down," and he hit me repeatedly with the side of his weapon. "I'm not going down," I replied, calmly. "Give him the sharp edge . . . the son of a . . . ," yelled Espinosa, frothing with rage. "If I go up there, I'll run him through, Señor Officer of the Guard!" "Go down, Señor, for the love of God," said the goodhearted officer in a whisper, an executioner in spite of himself, and almost in tears as he struck me with the saber; "I'll have to put the edge to you now." "Do as you please," I said quietly, "I am not going down." The sight of that saber rising and falling brought shouts of horror at two windows on the square from people whose voices I recognized, and these shouts troubled me. But I wanted to die as I had lived, as I have sworn to live, without my will ever consenting to violence. Besides, there was chicanery in this on my part, which I humbly own up to. I had found out that Benavides was not in the square, and this fact made it possible for me to quickly develop my plan of defense. The railing of the top-floor balcony of the town hall was actually my life saver. I said to myself: The troops have come to the square; therefore, Benavides is involved in the charade; he isn't here so as to be able to blame it on federalist *enthusiasm,* and say,

---

* *Crucifige eum!,* "Crucify him." Since it is highly unlikely that the soldiers would have cried out in Latin, a more probable interpretation is that here Sarmiento takes license to dramatize himself as a Christ figure. Further on he refers to Benavides as Pontius Pilate. —Ed.

like Rosas on murdering Maza, that it was an act of "terrible license committed at a moment of tremendous and profound popular indignation."[12] Well, the prison is on a direct line, a block-and-a-half from Benavides's house. Sound travels at a speed of so many leagues per minute and so would need only a second to cover 225 *varas*. It would have been impossible for the governor to wash his hands of that anonymous outrage, for there I was, in a high and eminent place, to send back the crime to its source and origin. The servants of Benavides's household, one of his scribes, his aide-de-camp, ran at the sight of the saber flashing over my head, screaming frantically, one after the other, "Señor! Señor! They're killing Don Domingo!" And so, I had my wily gaucho caught in his own snare! Either he had to admit collusion or give orders to leave me alone, and Benavides did not then have the nerve to shoulder that responsibility; my blood would have been distilling over his heart, drop by drop, for the rest of his life!

When the frenzied wretches below were convinced that I did not wish to die under the hooves of their mounts, preferring to do so in a more respectable and open space, ten or twelve of them came upstairs, and seizing me by the arms, brought me down at the same time that a dozen chasseurs, summoned by Espinosa, arrived to finish me off. But Espinosa wanted to see my face and terrorize me. The actor from Lima, whom I jeered at in the theater for his ineptitude, made a captain of the Federation, had his sword at my breast, his eyes fixed on Espinosa, ready to plunge it in; the commander all the while brandished his lance, and pricked me in my heart, screaming blasphemies. I had my face composed, a copy of the expression I wished it to conserve after death. Espinosa then jabbed me harder, and my face remained impassive, which must have enraged him, for drawing back his lance, he made a fearsome lunge at me. The spearhead was half a *vara* long and a palm in width, and for many days I conserved the bruise that was left on my wrist when I knocked it away. Then, the brute readied to give vent to his frustrated ire, and I, emboldened by the instinct of self-preservation, and calculating that Benavides would now be sending his aide-de-camp, raised my outstretched hand and said to him imperiously: "Listen, *Comandante* . . . !" and as he heeded me, I turned round, got down below the corridor to skirt the group of horses, reached the end, they fell on me, I pushed aside a swarm of bayonets from my breast with both my hands, and the governor's aide-de-camp arrived, who ordered an end to the farce, agreeing to let them shave me, as he had done with others.[13] If, in fact, there was no permission for anything beyond that, Espinosa had already lost control of his criminal passions, and I would have had the nerve to knock off the mask with which Benavides sought to conceal himself. They put me into the lockup below, and then a scene took place that redoubled the peoples' fear. My mother and two of my sisters pushed past the guard and went up to the second floor; they were seen to go in and out of the empty cells; they went back down like wraiths to end up at Benavides's house demanding their son, their brother. Oh! Despotism also has its anguish! Various people know what happened right after that; and it was not I, to be sure, who begged, nor gave assurances, for I take pleasure every day that in the course of that test the severity of my principles did not deviate nor my spirit flag.

There is something more on the subject of this event and I would like to present it here, for the consolation of those who despair that the criminal acts committed with impunity a decade ago will ever receive their just punishment on earth. The perpetrators of that bloody farce, *all* of them, without exception, have met a tragic death. A bullet took Espinosa in Angaco. In the darkness of night, Acha, on the way from his parcel of land to the square, pumped a few shots into a shape he saw on the street, and the actor who had waited for the order to run me through fell dead off his horse; the Indian Saavedra, who had jabbed me, ended his career murdered. And if the gaucho Fernández, crippled, mired in drunkenness and debauchery, happens to be still alive, it is to demonstrate who the governor's assistant was during those days of vertigo and infamy. Like my mother, I believe in Providence, and Bárcena, Gaetán, Salomón, and all the members of the Mazorca, murdered within their own ranks, executed by the one who put the dagger in their hands, and eaten away by remorse, despair, delusions, and disgrace, tormented by epilepsy or consumed by pneumonia, make me wait even still for the end reserved for them all.[14] Rosas is now beyond recovery. His body is a trembling, emaciated cadaver. The poison in his soul is rotting out the vessel that contains it, and you will soon hear it burst so that the putrefaction of his existence may give way to the rehabilitation of morality and justice, to the nobler feelings so long repressed. Woe, then, to those who have not done penance for their past crimes! The worst punishment they can receive is to live, and I swear to bring my "influence" to bear so that all, without exception, shall be so punished.

My four-year residence in San Juan, and this is the only period in my adult life that I have resided in my country, was an unending and persistent struggle. I, too, like others, desired to advance, and the slightest concession on my part would have caused the doors of Benavides's administration and his army to open wide to me; he wanted that, and at the outset, held me in high esteem. But I wanted to advance without sinning against morality and without committing offenses against freedom and civilization. I always took the lead in organizing public dances, societies, masques, theatricals; to counteract the burgeoning fashion of ignorance, I established schools; to the threat of government without controls, I responded with a newspaper; to resist the rush to suppress it illegally, I surrendered my person to imprisonments; against extraordinary powers, I used my spoken and written word to exercise the right of petition to compel representatives to carry out their duty; against intimidation, rectitude and contempt; against the blade of November 18, an impassive countenance and patience to outwit scoundrels and ignoble roguery. I have been called everything in San Juan, some of the evil has been given credence; but nobody has ever doubted my patriotism, and I appeal on that score to the testimony of those who have chosen to style themselves my enemies. I lived honestly by acting as an expert surveyor, which I could do as I possessed the rudiments of applied geometry and mechanical drawing that I had acquired in my youth. Forced by the absence of lawyers, I defended several cases, and with Doctor Aberastaín as chief justice of the appeals court and my close friend, I lost the two of most importance before his tribunal. If this fact does not speak well for my legal skill, it does, at least, for the judge's incorruptibility.

17

Chile

On November 19, 1840, as I passed through the baths of the Zonda Valley on my way into exile, with my hand and arm covered in bruises from the previous day, I wrote beneath a coat of arms of the Republic: *"On ne tue point les idées* [One cannot kill ideas], and three months later in the Chilean press, speaking in the name of the first patriots: "All America is sown with the glorious champions of Chacabuco. Some have expired on the gallows; exile or estrangement from their country have removed the others, poverty debases many; crime has stained the beautiful pages of the history of several; one emerges from his long inactivity (I was alluding to *Cramer*) and dies in order to save the country from a despicable tyrant; another (*Lavalle*) struggles almost fruitlessly against the colossal power of a crafty despot who has sworn to exterminate every soldier of the war of independence because he himself never heard the whistle of Spanish bullets, because his obscure name, his name from yesterday, is not associated with the immortal names of those who won fame in Chacabuco, Tucumán, Maipú, Callao, Talcahuano, Junín, and Ayacucho."[a]

Those who have received a systematic education, attended classes, taken examinations, felt empowered by the acquisition of diplomas, are incapable of appreciating the emotions of novelty, of terror, of hope, and

[a] *El Mercurio*, February 11, 1841. [Author's note]

of fear that assailed me when I launched my first article in the Chilean press. If I had asked myself at the time whether I knew anything about politics, literature, economics, or criticism, I would have answered frankly, "No," and like the lone traveler approaching a big city who sees only the domes, roofs, and towers of the lofty buildings, I did not see a public before me, but only names, like Bello, Oro, Olañeta, and schools, chambers, courts, and other such centers of knowledge and opinion.² My obscurity, my isolation, unnerved me less than the novelty of the theater and this great mass of unknown men who presented themselves to my imagination as if all were waiting for me to speak so that they could judge me. On tenterhooks of misgiving, like the neophyte dramatist, I awaited the arrival of *El Mercurio* of February 11, 1841. Just one friend was in on the secret; I stayed home, hiding in fear. At eleven o'clock, he brought me good news; my article had been applauded by the Argentineans; this alone was already something. In the afternoon, it was being mentioned at gatherings, in the evening at the theater; the following day I heard that Don Andrés Bello and Egaña had read it together, and found it good.³ "God be praised!" I said to myself, "I'm safe at last." I took the liberty of dropping by the house of an acquaintance, and soon after I arrived, an individual comes in; "Well," he says to him, "What do you think of the article? The author is no Argentinean, for it even contains localisms from the provinces in Spain." Entering into the conversation, I ventured to observe with a timidity that could be construed as ill-concealed jealousy, that it was not bad, despite certain passages in which the interest wore thin. I was rebutted with academic indignation by my interlocutor who, as I later learned, was a Señor Don Rafael Minvielle, and out of politeness, I was finally obliged to agree that the article was irreproachable in its style, pure in its language, brilliant in its images, and rich in wholesome ideas embellished with a subtle gloss of sentiment.⁴ This is one of the few times I have allowed myself to be gotten the better of by Minvielle. The success was complete and my happiness indescribable, to be matched only by that of those French writers who, from a bare fifth-floor garret, toss off a book into the street and receive, in exchange, a name in the literary world and a fortune. If the situation was not the same, the emotions were. I was a writer by acclamation of Bello, Egaña, Olañeta, Orjera, Minvielle, all of them considered competent to judge. How many mistaken vocations had I tried out before finding the one that had, if I may say so, a chemical affinity with who I am!

In 1841, the Chilean parties were locking horns just like now on the eve of elections; just like now, and with greater reason, the government was being portrayed as a tyrant, as the sole obstacle to the country's progress. I had just emerged from the hell of the Argentine Republic; the bruises were still fresh that despotism had inflicted on me when it seized me in its claws. With my education in tolerance, with my thirty years of age full of virility, it is understandable that liberal ideas should have bewitched me, no matter who professed them. The *pipiolo* party sent a commission to induce me to defend their cause in the press, and, to ensure success, General Las Heras acted as an intermediary.⁵ I asked for eight days in which to reply, and in those eight days I thought a great deal, I studied the Chilean parties from a bird's-eye view, and I reached a conclusion, the correctness of which was confirmed by the 1841 elections, namely: that the old *pipiolo* party did not possess the necessary elements for victory, that it was a tradition and not a reality; that between its past existence and the present moment, a generation had appeared to represent the new interests of the country. At the end of the eight days I brought together several Argentineans whose opinion I respected, among them Oro, and after giving them a lengthy exposition of the way I saw the issue, I asked for their thoughts. In view of the fact that I was an Argentinean, there were other more weighty considerations to be kept in mind. We were accused by the tyrant of our country of being agitators, seditionaries, and anarchists, and in Chile they might take us for such, seeing us always in opposition to the government. We, on the contrary, had to prove to America that it was not in the name of some utopia that we were suffering persecution, and that, given the imperfection of American governments, we were disposed to accept them as facts, with the firm intention, on my part at least, of injecting them with progressive ideas; finally that, since the elections were about to decide the direction that politics would take in Chile, it would be fatal to our cause to have aroused the ill-will of the party then in power, if this party should win, and it was my deep-seated conviction that this was going to happen. Oro, who had been imprisoned and persecuted by that government, was the first to speak, and he agreed with my resolution, and so, supported by my compatriots, I turned down the invitation of the Chilean liberals.

Then, I could approach the friends of the government, to whom I was to be presented by that same Don Rafael Minvielle, who managed to find me in a bare room under the Arcade, with one chair and two empty crates for a bed. And so, I was introduced to Don Manuel Montt, then minister and head of the party, which, rejuvenated in its personnel and ideas, had gone from *pelucón* (conservative) to calling itself moderate.[6] It is a gift of talent and political acumen to be able to hit upon a remark as if by chance, and with it to break the ice in a conversation. "Ideas, sir, have no homeland," the minister said to me as he began the interview, and everything from that moment on was smoothed out between us, and the link forged that was to join my existence and my future to those of this man. By 1841, I was cured, or behaved as though I were, which is a tribute I render to the truth, of the ugly blemish of American prejudices, against which I have fought for ten years; and of which, until 1843, To-cornal, García Reyes, Talavera, Lastarria, Vallejo, and so many young Chileans gave no indication of having freed themselves, having printed this exclusive concept in *El Semanario:* "We, the contributors, are *all* Chileans, and we repeat, we are motivated by no other incentive than the good name and prosperity of the fatherland."[7] Let them now say whether *all* of them together have done more in the press for the prosperity of this fatherland than the *one* foreigner who also had no other incentive than the love of rightousness and whom they imagined they could deprive of his right to speak.

On one point, we argued stubbornly and at length with the minister, and this was the war against Rosas that I proposed to wage. We arrived at an accommodation that for the moment satisfied the interests of both parties, and cleared the way for me to educate the opinion of the government itself, and to steer it to accept freedom of the press straight out, as has subsequently happened.

What I did then in the Chilean political press, the principles and ideas with which I supported the government, were accepted by the very men whom I helped to defeat, and were even endorsed by old Infante, a judge impossible to accuse of partiality to the government.[8] *El Valdiviano Federal,* speaking of a newspaper of the period, said: "Among the multitude of newspapers that have been born since the beginning of the Republic, it would be difficult to find one that has expressed opinions more dangerous to the cause of freedom; in our next issue and with this in mind, we will make minor observations regarding some of its pages, even though there will be little to add to the sage and philanthropic impugnation found in *El Mercurio,* in various of the cardinal points that it argues." I claim for myself that glory of *El Mercurio* for having impugned, along side the government, those ideas that are dangerous to freedom. Nor am I less proud of having earned, at that time, the respect and support of the patriot Salas,[b] who had *El Mercurio* brought to his bedside where he lay dying, and inquired with interest about what I was doing, even though he did not know me, since I refused to visit him, in an act of discourtesy for which I do not forgive myself to this day because, in ignorance of his splendid record, I believed him to be some powerful figure who was sparing himself the trouble of seeking me out.[9]

To pick up the thread of events, I will return to Don Manuel Montt, first my support, now my friend. His name is one of the few to have been favorably received outside of Chile and, on becoming generally known in his own country, to have aroused diverse reactions of affection or ill will as a public figure, but with no fault laid to his personal character, which all acknowledge to be circumspect, upright, serious, forceful, and well-intentioned. To have met him along the journey of my life has added a new aspect to my existence; and should this life come to a praiseworthy end, it will be owing to his support given me when I needed it most. Certain affinities of character must have cemented our sympathies, confirmed by essential differences of spirit, which have made his serve as a counterforce to the impatience of my purposes, and perhaps I, on occasion, may have stimulated and expanded his willpower with regard to the adoption of improvements. The grave countenance of this man, who some people believe has never laughed, is sweetened by easy manners that charm and soothe all who approach him, finding him far easier to deal with than imagined. He speaks little, and when he does, expresses himself in terms that demonstrate a sure grasp of the ideas he is putting forward. He is more tolerant than he leads adversaries to assume, and I would be warier of giving free rein to my imagination before a poet or wild-eyed planner than before Don Manuel Montt, who listens to my novels without surprise, often with pleasure, touching them with the wand of his practical sense to make them evaporate with a word when he sees them floating in the air. He has a rare gift, which is that he is forever educating himself; the times, new ideas, events do not wash over him without leaving their traces on his brow. Don Manuel Montt pretends to know nothing, which enables those addressing him to express them-

[b] Don Manuel Salas. [Author's note]

selves openly, and to contradict him without provoking his pride to attack in reprisal. This differentiates him from most men with power and talent, who cling to an idea of their own, denying even the existence of adverse ones; and a cultured minister, or an orator who is not a pedant, is a rare blessing in these times when every man in the public eye is busy fashioning the apotheosis of his literary fame in speeches and decrees. For many years, we have communicated by signs, by meaningful glances, without the need for explanations on matters of vital importance, of the sort with which I was dealing in the press. He never discussed my literary feuds with me, and at most, a word would come to my attention by way of Don Ramón Vial that led me to suspect that he regretted I was going astray.[10] If he heard me praised by others, he remained silent; if his approbation was sought when I was being unjustly maligned, he would show a countenance that was blank, icy, impassive, and that disconcerted my detractors. Once, when I was beset by public opinion for being a foreigner, he sent me word with Don Rafael Vial to strike back at the public without mercy; and when I gave up and resigned as editor of *El Progreso* for the first time, he told me imperiously: "You must write a book, on whatever you want, and confound them!" If he had no faith in me, he behaved in such a way as to make me think that he did, and this set me back on my feet. It was on account of him that in 1843 I did not go to Copiapó to seek my fortune, because he showed me that such a selfish plan was unbecoming. In the presence of Don Miguel de la Barra, he has begged me, pleaded with me, that I not attack Rosas's agent, he, a minister, resigning himself to accepting my formal refusal to accede to his wish. Sometimes we would come to an understanding beforehand on how to deal in the press with certain points in the process of being aired; and, on one occasion, he negotiated for a month to get me out of a dangerous altercation I had entered into with the *Revista Católica,* in order that it back down without affronting me.[11] While I was complaining about an article in the *Revista,* that is, the way I complain through the press, which is going after my opponent as hard as I can, Don Manuel Montt wrote me: "Some clerics of the *Revista* have promised to drop the matter, and perhaps the article you refer to, which I haven't seen, came out before this promise was made." When in 1845 I resigned again from my position as public writer to escape the viciousness of the means being mobilized to wear me down, Don Manuel Montt said to me: "I'm sorry, but I would have done the same; one's reputation is not to be sacrificed in defense of any cause." When I told him about my idea of going to Bolivia, where the government had invited me to settle, he opposed it roundly: "That would seem a step down. Bolivia is very much out of the way. Weren't you thinking of going to Europe first?" And on my taking leave for that destination: "Given the way things are looking, you will probably be returning to your country; if you ever wish to come back to Chile, you will be whatever you want to be here. Don't be deceived; these hatreds that alarm you are all on the surface; nobody looks down on you, and many respect you."

A minister like that, can do as Deucalion: make men from stones.[12] In Europe, his letters reached me more regularly than those of my own family, and in each one some useful subject for study was noted in passing, or the hope that I would do a certain thing, which was an indication that in fact I should do it. Don Manuel Montt has all the qualities of the public servant, lacking the only one that is needed to make him perfect, resolute ambition, without which, acquired fame, prestige, and public respect are an injury to the country, a diversion of forces that recede from the central point to which they are summoned, and establish an external counterweight that can cause disturbance in the State, like those planets that divert others from their orbits, causing them to produce unjustifiable aberrations. The mistaken ideas attributed to him derive from national concerns, or rather, from the state of ideas in general, which is extremely bad, and which the inadequate philosophical and political studies at the educational institutions are unable to correct.

I believe I have studied the political conscience of those who have written in Chile and of the public figures to whom I have listened, and I could establish a scale on which to rate them in relation to each other, if that were to serve a useful purpose. Don Manuel Montt believes in popular education; and the discussions in the legislature in 1849 have shown with certainty that, among young and old, liberals and reactionaries, there is not a single statesman in Chile who is more advanced in this area. Lastarria, Bello, Sanfuentes, have been obliged this time to present themselves to the public as more moderate, less utopian, more practical, and more accommodating than Don Manuel Montt, which is indicative of the falsity of their position, and it may be that one day they will regret having assumed this role that so ill becomes their youth and their ultraliberalism.[13] On the subject of European immigration, he spoke to me in 1842, and since then we have not lost sight of the matter. Three or four simple, but paramount, ideas make up Don Manuel's political capital, and he happily leaves it to others to exploit the rest. Like all men whose vocation is to govern, he deplores the demoralization of the legitimate elements of force and stability in the government, although the harmful school of Louis Philippe, which held sway from 1830 to 1848 in all the cabinets of the world and was highly respected in Chile, paralyzed in him the expansion that should be given to progress, which is the only thing that renders the preservation of order virtuous and useful.¹⁴ The current world revolution has been beneficial to him in this respect. He possesses all the varieties of courage that confer those honors difficult to attain; the courage to speak rarely in the Chamber, despite the lucidity his enemies grant him; the courage not to court popularity, like those representatives intent on fine tuning their lies so they will play better to the public; the courage, in short, to be honest, the most difficult of all in these times when the vertigo of political cynicism runs, from Barrot on down, to the most wild-eyed of orators whom it disgusts me to name.¹⁵ Don Manuel Montt marches forward to rehabilitate in this Spanish America, rotten to the core, the dignity of the human conscience that has been so assailed and trampled on by the very powers meant to represent it. Cynicism toward the means has everywhere brought about crimes in the ends; and beardless tartuffes may be seen grimacing on the muddy path already followed by Rosas, likewise in the name of some honest end. Twice in this year's session of the Chamber, it has brought censurable proposals to the floor, which have only been defeated by the prestige of individuals of the sternest morality. Eloquence is still a useless weapon among hardhearted and thick-skulled populaces and men, when the stubborn will of the barbarian in coattails sets off in a particular direction. Would that heaven may light the way of my worthy friend, and give us, after the astute, petty tyrants supported in the name of the people by a mob of soldiers, *mazorqueros* or representatives, a school of honest politicians, which America is calling for to cleanse itself of the crimes, filth, and blood in which it has wallowed for the last forty years. It is the only revolution worth undertaking. Do they consider it a revolution to continue being the same rabble we have always been, everywhere, to this very day? There are men who believe that it is courageous to be immoral thieves and scoundrels in South America. Be virtuous if you dare!

In 1841, at the beginning of September, when the electoral campaign was over and we were assured that our candidate would win, I took leave of Minister Montt and the editorial staffs of *El Nacional* and *El Mercurio,* in order to return to my homeland. "What! You're going back? Oh, no! You have no guarantees! General La Madrid's situation is critical."[16] "That's precisely why I want to go back, Señor, to give him my support in Cuyo." My decision was irrevocable, and I left at once forearmed with this letter of introduction for General La Madrid: "September 1, 1841. To His Excellency the Director of the Coalition of the North, General in Chief of the Second Army of Liberation.—The Argentine Commission takes the liberty of recommending Señor Don D. F. Sarmiento to Your Excellency. In addition to his very satisfactory record, there is the circumstance of his having been one of its members, and having carried out his commissions with honor. A patriot devoted to the cause of freedom, his ability is another title that justifies his joining you and Your Excellency, giving him the opportunity to devote whatever service he can to our cause. He has the confidence of his compatriots here and is worthy of Your Excellency's. The Commission reiterates, etc.—J. Gregorio de las Heras.—Gregorio Gómez.—Gabriel Ocampo.—Martín Zapata.—Domingo de Oro."

On the afternoon of September 25, I and three friends thrust our heads, one after the other, over the main peak of the cordillera of the Andes. The difficult climb on foot for an entire day, plunging through the snow softened by the faint rays of the sun, had tired us out, and our legs demanded a moment's rest in that wasteland swept by the glacial wind coming off the thaw. To the east, the eye discovers a mountain chain that fringes and o'ershadows the horizon, white valleys like ribbons winding between black peaks that shine in the reflection of the sun; and below, at the foot of the eminence, like the head of a pin, the brick hut that offers shelter and repose to the weary traveler. "*Salud,* Argentina!" we each shouted, greeting her on the horizon and extending to her our arms full of longing.

In that narrow, white sea stretching out below, one of us noted the shapes of people walking, and this encounter with human beings, always so welcome in those solitary places, instinctively filled us all with misgivings, and we looked at one another not daring to communicate the fearful thought that entered our minds. We climbed down toward the Argentine side, less joyful than before, and as soon as we reached the hut, or even before, the word "defeat" made my ears throb in pain for a long time. The remains of La Madrid's army appeared a little later, making its way on foot, to take refuge in Chile.

Something had to be done. I immediately dispatched a messenger to Los Andes to have mules sent to the cordillera; and after talking to the first refugees, we returned to climb back up that mountain we believed we had left behind forever. When we reached Los Andes, I set up my office in the house of a friend; from one o'clock in the afternoon on, I was an executive with absolute public power to give aid to the unfortunate Argentineans who were still marooned in the cordillera.[17]* An old inhabitant of Los Andes, respected for his moral qualities, Don Pedro Bari, my close friend from the time I was twenty and he sixty, was my secretary general. These were the acts of that government consisting of twelve hours of labor: to find, hire, and dispatch to the cordillera that same afternoon twelve mountain peons to aid the exhausted. To purchase, gather, and dispatch six loads of sheepskins in which to wrap feet and legs that were naked and exposed, rope, jerked meat, chili peppers, coal, candles, tobacco, mate, sugar, etc., etc. To dispatch a courier to San Felipe, to advise the Intendant of the catastrophe and request protection for the needy. To appeal to the philanthropy of various inhabitants. An urgent message to the Argentine Commission to set it in motion. A letter to Minister Montt, calling for government aid, requesting doctors, and other assistance. A letter to the Viales and Señor Gana to kindle public charity; to the director of the theater to arrange a benefit performance for the victims. An article in *El Mercurio* of Valparaíso to arouse the entire nation and elicit sympathy. With all that done, assignments under way, and with my purse emptied to the last penny, I resigned my post, seeking the repose that my body required for having crossed and recrossed the cordillera as though on a bet, for having run all the way down from Ojos de Agua to Los Andes, in order to sit down and write without even so much as taking a pause. I received replies two days later from Sr. Gana and General Las Heras in terms that, I recall, did them honor.

---

*In the original Spanish, "with absolute public power" reads as "con la suma del poder público." This is an obvious irony on Sarmiento's part since Rosas in Argentina was in fact the executive who had demanded and received *la suma del poder,* an abuse for which Sarmiento constantly criticized him.—Ed.

Señor Don Domingo Sarmiento—*Santiago, October 1, 1841*—Fellow compatriot and friend: In response to your most estimable letter, I remit this draft, the proceeds of which you may apply to providing meat and bread to the unfortunate Argentineans who arrive. You must limit yourself to meat and bread, inasmuch as in providing this miserable aid we have exhausted all resources and overcome obstacles which you will not credit until you come and take over.

Right now, we are exhorting the people of Valparaíso to see how they can help us succor our unfortunate countrymen. The government has received our request, and it has promised us to issue the orders this same night that could serve to aid afflicted humanity.

A messenger has been dispatched before the time of arrival.

I cannot tell you how moving your account was of the horrors you did no more than mention. Let us leave that to the senses.

Embrace the brave and injured. We are Argentineans and they are Argentineans. One day, God will give us a homeland, and the meritorious shall receive due gratitude, or that country will be undeserving of such sons.

Goodbye, friend. Your obedient servant always,

J. Gregorio de las Heras.

The writer sends greetings to you and to all the unfortunate brave men.

Señor Don Domingo Sarmiento—Santiago, October 1, 1841.—Esteemed Señor: Shocked at the catastrophe you report to me, I went immediately to Orjera's house where I just learned of the disasters suffered in Mendoza. Deeply touched by such ill fortune, we were unable to think of anything we could do to alleviate the worst of it but to initiate a fund drive, appealing to the generosity of our fellow countrymen with respect to the unfortunate victims in the cause of civilization. The first steps have already been taken; and be assured that if success is commensurate with our efforts and concern, the most pressing needs will be covered. Never have I wished more intensely than at this moment to be a man of means and influence; but what use does it serve to throw our wishes into the scale? We are doing everything possible, which is all I am able to promise, together with my friendship. Your humble servant, *José Francisco Gana.*

October 2, 1841. The messenger you have sent us this day is returning. . . . The government has given us to understand that it will do its part regarding the purpose of the communication.

I also delivered your letter for Minister Montt and await his answer to forward to you. Some support is being elicited from among Chilean citizens. And I think the government will do something on its own here, too. Work is meeting with success.

At this very moment the government is going to dispatch another messenger with communications for the intendant. I am sending you a bundle of clothing I have gotten together from among my own and that of friends which you may put to use for those who arrive naked.

I am including a government communication for the intendant; deliver it to him immediately, for it concerns those unfortunates who are arriving ill.

Friend: I envy you your good luck on this occasion. Keep up your noble efforts; you are a hero; do not let up or flag for an instant. Courage, friend! *Martín Zapata.*

October 2.—Sarmiento: The Vials have behaved like great men. Don Antonio instructed me to head an appeal which is off to the printer right now; a number of leading persons chosen by him, and he himself, are going to circulate it among the clergy, businessmen, employees, ministers, etc., etc.

The entire theatrical company is ready to give the benefit performances Cascuberta wants. And the public is anxious to see him on stage. "Othello," "Marino Faliero," and I don't know what other piece, have been selected for this purpose and to show off the talents of that actor.[18]

The Vials are also helping to arrange a benefit concert for the emigration, to which the city's distinguished señoritas will be invited. If only Cascuberta would arrive as soon as possible. Inquire about my family and give me news of them, of Don Hilarión Godoy, of our friends, of Villafañe. Yours truly, *Quiroga Rosas.*

When I arrived later in Santiago, I had to respond in the press to the accusation of having complained of the hardheartedness of many, at the same time that I praised all those who deserved it; and later, of having embezzled those scanty funds earmarked for so many necessities. The individual who made the accusation was no countryman of mine, had contributed nothing to the fund, had no idea to what use I had put it, and purely out of arrant viciousness, invented that calumny to damage me. General Las Heras answered, vindicating me, and I remained shocked for a long time by that gratuitous, spontaneous act of depravity, and chilled as though a pail of cold water had been thrown at me.

Shortly afterward I returned to the editorship of *El Mercurio,* and from that point on began what was for me one of the most active, turbulent, and perhaps fruitful phases of my life, and perhaps for others, as well. Little by little, I was arousing concern, ill will, jealousy, hatred, I don't know if envy, until that volcano of passions that every day had been smoking and escaping through letters to the editor, erupted in some noisy event that had tempers flared up for two whole weeks. Now I have triumphed completely; the word "foreigner" is banned from the press; exiled and forgotten are the three who used it as a weapon with which to wound me in the deepest recesses of a man's being, that place that nobody has a right to touch, and now it is possible to remember those struggles that kept so many of us stirred up, hostile, and preoccupied. I leave out the many discourteous and offensive expressions that must have escaped from my pen, young man that I was, fervent in battle, sensitive to offense, mincing no words in telling the truth. Every day, every hour, there was a campaign that distilled its slow poison to aggravate my spirit and predispose it to harden itself against resistance. There is nothing that smoothes the rough edges of a journalist like contact with the society for which he writes. The courtier Voltaire enchanted the nobility among whom he moved and was caustic only toward the priesthood, with whom he had no contact. The solitary Rousseau, on the other hand, has spoken the crudest of truths and maintained his savage independence, amid the most frivolous society. I have kept myself isolated for six years to keep from being influenced by the ideas of others, and that is the severest sacrifice I have imposed upon myself. Furthermore, discourtesy was manifested even among certain young men who offered me their friendship by way of protection, some as noble and well-connected, others as wealthy, and even some as literati; they tried my patience and obliged me to conceal my displeasure. What really exasperated me, however, was that as a "foreigner" I had to be more circumspect, more measured than the native sons. Now, it seems to me an established fact that I have won the public's entire confidence as to the sincerity of my intentions and the ardent devotion to the common good that has always driven my pen; but, then, such was not the case. Criticism of matters that are the province of the press were attributed to envy, jealousy, a wish on my part to denigrate the country, and the public insisted on not wanting to read "*Mercurio*" where it said "*Mercurio*" but, rather, "Sarmiento," "foreigner," "Argentinean," "*cuyano*," and so forth; and I became greatly exercised about this public injustice, and went my way, daily, with increasing bitterness.* It was a Chilean newspaper talk-

---

* A "*cuyano*" is a person from the Argentine region of Cuyo.—Ed.

ing, and I always believed, and I continue to believe, that the public should not be able to tell from the pages themselves under what constraints an editorialist has been placed in writing about a particular situation. I have made this principle prevail *envers et contre tous*, and today the press follows it.

What a stubborn and bloody struggle that was! Exclusive patriotism was a hydra that sprouted ten new heads every time I thought I had blinded and burned that many others. It took on new guises at every step. In order to harm me, *El Desenmascarado* [The Unmasked] brought together all there is of rancor in the heart of man; baldfaced slander, filth, mud, obscenity flung in my face as weapons worthy of combat.[19] *El Desenmascarado* ended there, I moved on, and it is for the authors of that publication, now that their misguided passions have cooled, to say whether *El Desenmascarado* really hurt me and whether their own social standing was improved in any way. One of them was about to be named an intendant, and the other enjoyed a reputation as a writer until the appearance of *El Diario de Santiago*, which published so many lies about me.[20] Defamation is a poisoned double-edged sword, and each thrust it makes comes back to wound the hand that wields it, and the wound festers for many long years, giving off a foul odor. Those two men have been wiped from the list of public figures, with little chance they will recover from their fall, to which I have not contributed with a personal attack of any kind.

Literature also had its representative in *El Semanario*, and nobody can imagine the pleasure it gave me when I saw their authors bogged down in the slippery terrain of romanticism and classicism. I went to López's house, waving the inaugural issue, and together we hit on a combined plan of attack, in which I would take guerrilla action from *El Mercurio* and he, from *La Gaceta*, would advance with the heavy guns of erudition, to blast away at whoever was left standing.[21] García del Río was posted in the Valparaíso press, and when I wrote to Rivadeneira, shocked by the furor caused in Santiago by this battle, to tone down certain of the more incisive points in my articles, García del Río weighed them, measured their force, and sent them, as they were, sharp and pointed to Santiago.[22] The most formidable rival, however, to rise up in the press was Jotabeche, who was initially inspired by the passion of jealousy.[23] His attacks were so artful, his caustic wit so keen, that he would have overwhelmed my petulance had his articles not been weakened by a characteristic lack of general ideas and by the fact that justice was on my side. Jotabeche, a worthy example of national exclusivism, was a Viriato who had to end up in defeat.[24] He was defeated by the Argentineans of Copiapó, among whom he found enthusiastic and generous support for the founding of *El Copiapino;* I defeated him by taking on the defense of Señor Vallejo, victim of an abuse by a governor; and he was finally defeated for good by the well-deserved reputation that he earned, since the platforms of hate and persecution from which he launched his invective served him ill.[25] Today we are friends, and I could insert one of his letters here as an example of his laconic incisiveness and wit.

I choose to ignore the spate of letters to the editor in which *one Chilean, two Chileans, ten Chileans, a thousand Chileans* harassed me for over five years with the crudest of stupidities and nonsense. The Spaniards who were naive enough to believe that I held a grudge against them, the clerics who denounced me as an infidel, the students who rose up against whoever encouraged study and paved the way so they could better themselves by making the practice of letters feasible; all, some earlier, others later, for one reason or another: this one for my having invoked the name of the nun Zañartu, that one for my having said that the Constitution was a signboard written in pencil, another for my having spit in his face, when the only provocation was getting my hair pulled, all of them vilifying and torturing me, out of intolerance, laziness, and despotism.[26] One day exasperation reached the point of delirium; I was in a frenzy, out of my mind, and I came up with the idea, sublime in its misguidedness, of castigating all of Chile, of declaring it ungrateful, ignoble, and base. I wrote I know not what diatribe; I signed my name to it, took it to the printshop of *El Progreso,* and put it directly into the hands of the typesetters; having done so, I went home in silence, loaded my pistols, and waited for the explosion of the mine that was sure to blow me up but that left me feeling avenged and satisfied at having performed a great act of justice. Nations can be criminal, and they sometimes are, and there is no judge to punish them other than their tyrants or their writers. I complained of the president, of Montt, of the Viales, so that not a single one should escape my justice; and I excoriated the writers and the public *en masse* with awful, humiliating truths, enough to incite a city to riot, to drive it mad with fury, and to make it call for the head of the person who had the gall to injure it so.

I was saved from certain disaster by the kindness of Don Antonio Jacobo Vial, to whom the shocked typesetters showed the manuscript they were composing. Don Antonio Jacobo Vial came to my house, downcast, and spoke to me in the soft, compassionate tone that one uses to address the sick. There was not a trace of resentment or enmity in his mien. "Don Domingo," he said to me, "the printers have shown me the article handed in for tomorrow." "I am sorry." "Have you considered the consequences?" "Perfectly," indicating the pistols with my glance. "Useless." "I know it; leave me alone." "Has López seen this?" "No."

Don Antonio picked up his hat and went to López's house and to the ministry to tell Don Manuel Montt what was happening, and from that moment on he did not cease in his efforts until the mess had been resolved. López came, made me agree to his revising the text and removing some of the overly unbearable words, and I consented that he do so. This was at three o'clock in the afternoon; at midnight, Don Antonio brought me a brief note from López in which he told me he had desisted from deleting words, because it would show that concessions had been made; that if, notwithstanding my friends' disapproval, I insisted, I should immediately take a carriage and go to Valparaíso. López, with his customary sagacity, had touched the key to make me give in: first, not to contradict me openly, as one does with madmen; second, to disapprove of me, and this made an impression on me; third, to show me it was weakness to water down my words, and I would have shunned manifesting any sign of debility; fourth, to show me the road to flight, and that humiliated me. No; I did not see it in that light: I wished to wound them all mortally in their stubborn arrogance and to wait and suffer the consequences. The pillow soon gave me counsel, though it denied me sleep. Early the next day, the minister sent for me; he spoke of unrelated matters, of the normal school, of some current event or other.[27] Finally, he came around to touching the sore spot with caution, taking care to apply the balm, pointing out to me how many people honored and respected me as opposed to those insults of so little consequence. I began to talk, became excited, got to my feet, and at the moment I was about to lose all due respect toward the minister and friend, Don Miguel de la Barra opened the door, for whether by accident or design, he had arrived at just the right moment to prevent a scandal, guided by the adage of "*palabra y piedra suelta no tienen vuelta*" [No way to revoke a word spoke or a stone thrown]. And so, this Chile that I wished to condemn to the flames for its heresy, showed me at that moment virtues worthy of respect, infinite sensitivity and tolerance, and displays of sympathy and appreciation that rendered unjustifiable the suicide I had prepared. From that time on, public and writer have educated each other. The public has learned to be tolerant, has done justice to the soundness of my intention, and I have become accustomed to view it as an essential part of my existence, not to fear its fits of rage nor to provoke them, and now, by acclamation, I am declared a good and loyal Chilean. Woe to him who persists in calling me a foreigner! Such a one will have to expatriate himself to California.[28]

Of those struggles, nothing tangible has remained, and the writings that gave rise to them will grow less and less meaningful with each passing day, because such is the condition of human progress. What comes at the beginning is imperfect, looked at in hindsight, when those ideas have become part of common sense, and new writers better prepared have left those behind who did no more than show the way. However, since 1841, the Chilean press has gained a better reputation in the Pacific, and Chile has greatly benefited from this, because of the liveliness of the polemic and the battle of ideas that drew everyone into the discussion. *El Mercurio* expanded its columns; the literary issues defended in it and in *La Gaceta* prompted the appearance of *El Semanario*. *El Semanario* led to the idea of founding *El Progreso* in Santiago, which until then had no daily paper. From those struggles, there came poets, to prove the flimsiness of the charges; there came Jotabeche, successfully vindicating the national aptitude for writing with a light touch.

The normal school, the institutions that have sought to foster elementary education, cannot be completely separated from that common origin, which heated up all the debates and lent tangible and necessary force to things that were in the minds of everyone, as a desideratum, as things possible but not immediately feasible. Because this should be noted: It is a rare case when a writer can impose his own thinking on a society, but it is the nature of the press to draw from society ideas that are in embryo, and to incubate them, encourage them, and clear the way for their advancement; and the editor of *El Mercurio*, of *El Nacional,* of *El Progreso,* of *La Crónica*, could point to the trail of many ideas that have been thus advanced, until they became public concerns.[29] From 1842, *El Mercurio* chose the roads as subjects for satire and lampoonery, traces of which remain in "Un viaje a Valparaíso" [A trip to Valparaiso], and other writings of the period.[30] Minister Irarrázabal called in the ed-

itorial staff of *El Progreso* to complain that they were treating him un-
fairly. Today, Chile's roads are the best in South America. *El Mercurio*
and *El Progreso* took on the municipalities, one after another; when Valparaíso's showed signs of life, it was used as a goad for Santiago's; when
the matter was going to be legislated, *El Progreso* formally threatened to
wage an open battle against the government's plans. Who can forget that
annoying rustic "Aaaveee Maaría" of the night watchman; those broken
and wobbly fire wagons that never got where they were needed; those
streets without names or numbers? All the improvements can be traced
back to the press, which has done as much for the public good as the authorities themselves. The occupation of the Straits of Magellan was
prompted by the articles in *El Progreso*, just as the vindication of Chile's
titles of possession came about after the investigations of *La Crónica*.
The *Congreso Americano* was sentenced to death by *El Progreso*, and in
vain the governments of the Pacific all tried to set it on its feet.[31]

Were it permissible for a writer to draw attention to his own character, I would not hesitate to single out the main features of my work in
the daily press. Hailing from an inland province of the Argentine Republic, I, not without surprise, had discovered in my study of Chile the
similar nature of all of Spanish America, which the remote spectacle of
Peru and Bolivia did nothing but confirm. At the beginning of 1841, I
wrote these concepts in *El Nacional:* "Thirty years have elapsed since the
American revolution began; and although the war of independence
ended in glory, there is so much inconsistency in the institutions of the
new states, so much disorder, so little personal security, and so little if
any progress in the intellectual, material, and moral development of the
people, that the Europeans . . . regard the Spanish race as condemned to
consume itself in internecine wars, to foul itself with every kind of crime,
and to offer up a depopulated, exhausted land, as easy prey for a new European colonization." This sad concept constitutes the basic philosophical premise of my writings and is reprinted in *El Mercurio, El Progreso,
Viajes por Europa, La Crónica,* etc.; and surely no one will dispute with
me in America the sad distinction of being the writer who has most assailed the pretentiousness, arrogance, and immorality of Hispanic
America, persuaded that it is essential to bring about in America a profound revolution, less in its institutions than in its national ideas and
sentiments. This is so if we are to spare ourselves the death that already
sounded its rattle in Paraguay, that gasps its last breaths in Mexico, and

that now waits at the bedside of Argentina and Bolivia. In that same early article, and indicated with equal foresight, is to be found the double remedy of European immigration and popular education. This would be a sure antidote, were it not that it must be administered to the sick by the sick themselves, who rob it of its effect by turning away their faces in disgust, even though they are persuaded of its efficacy.

This is who I am in terms of transcendent politics, for in terms of the politics of circumstance, which is linked to persons and parties, my position in the Chilean press has been clear from the start, associating me both spontaneously and deliberately with the party in Chile in which Montt, Irarrázabal, García Reyes, Varas, and so many other distinguished young men are active, and to which Aldunate, Blanco, Benavente, and other politicians are not hostile. Movement in ideas, stability in institutions, order to be able to agitate all the better in politics, the government in preference to the opposition, this is what may be deduced from my writings with respect to my predilections. I can flatter myself that I have never courted vulgar passion of any kind to ingratiate myself to the public, nor have I supported anything in politics that healthy morality could reproach, compromises that no few writers have allowed themselves in the name of liberal ideas.

In concluding this quick review of the acts that constitute my public life, I feel that the interest of these pages has already evaporated, even before my work is done; and I would conclude them here if, in having to respond in these pages to the systematic detraction practiced by a government, it were not necessary for me to submit my service record, as it were, which consists of the various publications of my ideas and thoughts in the press. The spirit of an author's writings, when he has a strongly defined character, is his soul, his essence. The individual is eclipsed by this manifestation, and the public already has less interest in his private acts than in the influence those writings have been able to exercise on others. Here, then, is the meager index that may serve as a guide for whoever wishes to submit my thoughts to more rigorous scrutiny.

18

Daily Newspapers and Periodical Publications

Periodical publications are in our time like daily respiration; neither freedom, nor progress, nor culture is conceivable without this vehicle that links societies to one another, and makes us feel at every moment members of the human species, due to the influence and repercussion of events in certain countries on others. It is for this reason that despotic and criminal governments must, if they are to exist, seize possession of the newspapers and persecute those in neighboring countries that expose their iniquities. Rosas, at the expense of the taxes paid by the poor Argentine people, has established a network of newspapers throughout the world that are funded to whitewash and defend his atrocities. *El Defensor de la Independencia Americana* [The Defender of American Independence] in Oribe's camp, *O americano* [The American] in Brazil, *Le Courrier du Havre* and *La Presse* in France, these four newspapers and *La Gaceta* Mercantil, cost the Republic of Argentina over forty thousand pesos a year.[1] All the persecution of which I am currently the victim stems from the fact that with the appearance of *La Crónica*, I made it necessary for the editorship of *El Progreso*, which was under the influence of Rosas, to pass into other hands and change its perspective.[2] Rosas is more afraid of the press than he is of conspiracies; a conspiracy can be drowned in blood, but a book, a revelation of the press, even if a dagger should appear like the one that killed Varela, lives on forever; because what is printed remains printed for all time, and if at the moment it is useless and ineffectual, it is not so for posterity, which, basing its judgement on a study of the facts and free from any personal consideration and from any intimidation, hands down its sentence, which admits no appeal.³

1839—Together with educated and capable young men, I founded *El Zonda*, in San Juan, which ceased publication because of abuses and extortion by Benavides, who put me in jail, as already mentioned, notwithstanding that the newspaper was only concerned with social customs, public education, the cultivation of the mulberry bush, mining, literature, etc.

1841—Under the pseudonym "Un Teniente de Artillería" [An Artillery Lieutenant] I published an article in Chile, which won me an invitation to edit *El Mercurio*, where I remained until *El Progreso* was founded. On topics such as literature, roads, townships, and political affairs relevant to their moment, there are articles that can still be read with interest today, despite the advancements that the periodical press has made in Chile.

In the same period, I was made editor by the friends of General Bulnes, then a presidential candidate, of *El Nacional*, in Santiago, a newspaper that was extremely influential in the fusion achieved at that time between the leaders of the *pipiolo* party and the party of General Bulnes.

1842–1845—The capital of Chile had, until this time, remained without a daily newspaper. I successfully launched the first, under the name of *El Progreso*, as editor along with Don Vicente F. López. The first period, which lasted eight months, was of great importance due to the seriousness of the subjects it dealt with, such as the colonization of the Straits of Magellan. Problems with the management caused us to resign as editors, but the paper soon fell into discredit, and I was asked to return to put it on its feet, which I succeeded in doing.

At the same time, in order to combat Rosas, I edited *El Heraldo Argentino* [The Argentine Herald], the publication of which I abandoned when news came of Rivera's defeat at Arroyo Grande, for I believed that the struggle was over.⁴

1846 and 1847—In the course of my travels, I wrote in *El Comercio del Plata* a series of articles defending Argentineans residing in Chile against the libelous attacks of Rosas; in Río de Janeiro in *Le Courrier du Bresil*, on Americanism; in *Le Courrier de la Gironde*, in Bordeaux, I published a description of bullfighting in Spain; in Madrid, various articles against the expedition of General Flores, which were reprinted throughout America and with a very laudatory article in *La Gaceta de Buenos Aires,* which cast its net my way, finding me a good American, with nothing savage or revolting about me, because from Paris they had made Rosas conceive the hope that I might submit to his system of iniquities.[5] People spoke well of me publicly in Buenos Aires and at Manuelita's soirée, until *La Revista de Ambos Mundos* arrived, and the praises showered upon me changed anew into anger and resentment.[6]

1849—I published *La Crónica,* in which I sought to call public attention to immigration, public education, silk cultivation, and, generally, all matters of American concern for which I have not ceased agitating since 1839. The collection of documents on immigration contained in *La Crónica* is unique in America and worth consulting. *La Crónica* has closed down after its first year, to avoid the need of answering all the stupidities that Rosas writes against me in his notes to the government of Chile, and all the insolence of the provincial governments that form a chorus to repeat the rubbish.

The importance of the questions raised by *La Crónica* is implicit in this fact, that in response to every one of its campaigns—education, currency, immigration, passports—a law has been either passed or established.

19

Pamphlets

Programa de un colegio de señoritas en San Juan [Program for a Girls' School in San Juan]. Description of the need, advantages, and overall aspect of the education of women in the remote provinces of the Republic of Argentina. My first piece, full of reflections that are not lacking in insight. The province of San Juan listened to my advice, and strongly supported my effort.

Método de lectura en quince cuadros [Reading Method in Fifteen Tables] by Bonifaz, a young Spaniard living today in Montevideo; I published it *at my own expense* in 1841, to make it known in this country, and it was successfully adopted by the schools for elementary education.

Análisis de las cartillas, silabarios y otros métodos de lectura conocidos y practicados in Chile [Analysis of Primers, Syllabaries, and Other Reading Methods Known and Used in Chile], 1842. A study commissioned by the government, the purpose of which was to demonstrate the imperfection of the methods in use, and to help "elicit the observations of intelligent men in order to develop a simple and rapid reading method; to arouse everyone's interest in improving the schools by introducing new methods of instruction."

Memoria leída a la Facultad de Humanidades [Report Presented to the School of Humanities], 1843. After a lucid discussion in the University and in the press, this report produced a ruling on the subject of orthography and an accord in favor of the author. In *Educación Popular,* this question is finally dealt with extensively. The author's studies in the field of *Castillian orthography* are new in the Spanish language. Their purpose was to simplify the teaching of reading and writing, and, having seen all the rules of etymology broken by the Academy, to make spelling subject to pronunciation, as has been the wish of all Spanish orthoepists. If the result has not been commensurate with his efforts, the usefulness of the purpose and the unassailable logic of his arguments shield him from attacks of ridicule. He has submitted his most recent papers to the Spanish Academy, requesting and advising that it clarify its position on the matter.

Método de lectura gradual, adoptado por la Facultad de Humanidades y mandado seguir por el gobierno en las escuelas públicas [Gradual Reading Method, Adopted by the School of Humanities and Ordered by the Government for Adoption in the Public Schools]. This is a new system for teaching reading in Spanish, based on the study of the problems that children encounter and the analogies they use to overcome them. Señor Arbau in Spain has reached the same conclusions as the author.

Instrucción a los maestros de escuela [Instruction for School Teachers] for the purpose of making the *Método de lectura gradual* accessible.

Método sobre la cría del gusano de seda [Method for Raising Silkworms]. Sent from Paris to the Agricultural Society of Santiago de Chile and published in *El Agricultor* [The Farmer]. Several advances in this industry have been prompted by this paper.

Sociedad Sericícola Americana [American Sericulture Society]. Contains a statement by the author on the advisability and timeliness of generalizing this industry, and the by-laws of the society established for this purpose.

Mi defensa [My Defense]. Collection of autobiographical writings in which the author, libeled as at present, answered the attacks by making known the principal aspects of his life.

Programa de estudios del Liceo de Santiago [Program of Study of the Santiago Lyceum]. Prepared together with Don Vicente F. López; contains some new ideas on the order and selection of subjects, placing Latin where it belongs. The public and the young people of the schools accepted our reform with interest; but the clergy and certain school principals undermined us with their calumnies, and we did not wish to fight against such underhanded and treacherous enemies.

Discurso pronunciado en Francia al recibirse de miembro del Instituto

Histórico [Speech Delivered in France upon Induction into the Historical Institute], published by the *Investigateur*. Its subject is a consideration of the motives and consequences of the interview between Bolívar and San Martín in Guayaquil.

Memoria sobre emigración alemana al Río de la Plata [Dissertation on German Emigration to the River Plate], 1846. Published in German by Dr. Wappäus, Professor of Geography and Statistics, University of Göttingen, accompanied by notes and comments by the editor, with whom the author left the work of the Argentine engineer and geographer Arenales, and other papers and books for further background on the subject. Dr. Wappäus expresses himself in these terms in the introduction: "The following dissertation on the provinces of the Río de la Plata is an addition made by the author, Señor Sarmiento, to a small pamphlet I published in 1846 on German colonization and emigration. . . . The author's desire to make the advantages of those countries known in Germany motivates this supplementary paper."

Dr. Wappäus added 179 pages to the *Memoria* consisting of illustrative annotations on the extensive regions of whose riches, were they to be populated in proportion to their wealth, it would scarcely be possible for me to present an abridged idea. To judge the value of those notes, suffice it to list the authors consulted by the German scholar to support his opinion on the subject: Arenales, the *Diario* [Diary] of Matorras, *Colección* [Collection] of de Angelis, Arredondo, Azara, *Viaje* [Travel] by Soria, Sir Woodbine Parish, Nuñez, Félix Frías, Lozano, *Viaje en la América del Sud* [Travel in South America] by Lindau, Thaddeus Haenke, Walkenaer, *Viaje al Paraguay* [Trip to Paraguay] by Rengger and Longchamp, D'Orbigny, *Vientitrés años de residencia en la Republica Argentina* by King [Twenty-three Years of Residence in the Argentine Republic], *Cartas sobre el Paraguay* [Letters on Paraguay] by Robertson, Baralt, Codazzi, Gay.[1]

Publication of this work would be of the utmost importance for the Republic of Argentina, since it contains most valuable details on the topography of the provinces, their trade routes, their rivers, and the advantages that their navigation would signify for world trade and the nation's wealth. But it is impossible to publish it in Chile, where there is no interest, my writings being currently banned in the Argentine Confederation, and those who read them liable to discretionary punishments.[2]

Let the need to counter Rosas's libel with the opinions with which I have been honored by learned Europeans serve as my excuse for the sad necessity of inserting here what Dr. Wappäus says about me in his work: "We cannot give our readers a more complete idea of this than by quoting the very words of Señor Sarmiento, a profoundly educated Argentinean endowed with wide-ranging knowledge, who, pursuing with all the ardent passion of the South American the history of his country, from which he was banished by political persecution, presents in his every word and deed, and in his view of the world, the idea of the true republican of South America, who aspires to the full realization of liberty. We owe to him, beyond the *Memoria* with which this study begins, plentiful and varied instruction on the Republic of Argentina, for which we give him our sincerest thanks, especially for his lively oral explanations. We have extracted the following outline from the works of this writer, who, in order to gain an intimate sense of Europe, has recently visited Italy, France, Germany, etc. . . ."

20

Biographies

A *puntes biográficos* [Biographical Notes]. Under this title was pub- lished a life of the priest Aldao, an apostate and general allied with Rosas; a small study well received by discerning readers as a literary com- position. At a later date, the author intends to collect, under the title *Vidas americanas* [American Lives], the various biographies he has pub- lished of Chilean and Argentine figures worthy of recollection. The bi- ography is the most original book that South America can produce in our time, and the best material that one can provide for the writing of history. *Apuntes biográficos* was translated into French by M. Eugène Tandonnet, twice candidate to the National Assembly, who, though a supporter of Rosas due to personal friendship with Oribe, explains him- self regarding the author in these terms: "With no pretension to literary perfection, he has sought only to put into relief some of the more force- ful figures of the period of independence, and to give us a glimpse of the general physiognomy of the Argentine provinces, customs, concerns, passions, in a word, the life of a people who are both warriors and herds- men. In this sense, Señor Sarmiento's *Apuntes biográficos* is unquestion- ably of superior merit. It is certainly a study au naturel, although written with spontaneity and passion. In the forward march of the style and the general development of the ideas, one finds the melancholic abandon and the violent outbursts characteristic of the inhabitants of the Argen- tine provinces. . . . Señor Sarmiento's lofty spirit and his careful studies, separate him entirely from the principal leaders of the unitarian band. . . . But when memories of the homeland are called up in the exile's imagination; when he reflects upon the brilliant and useful role that his attributes would have assured him in that beloved homeland, then the rage brims over in his heart and spills out in burning imprecations against the fortunate adversary, whose victory has provoked his exile."[1]

I have published other biographies in the newspapers, namely, that of the presbyter Balmaceda, that of the presbyter Irarrázabal, that of Colonel Pereira, an Argentinean, founder of the Military School of Chile, that of Senator Don Manuel Gandarillas, that of Don José Dolores Bustos, of San Juan, Inspector General of Schools in Chile.

Facundo, or *Civilización y Barbarie* [Civilization and Barbarism] and these *Recuerdos de Provincia* [Recollections of a Provincial Past] belong to the same genre.

21

Books

Civilización y Barbarie [Civilization and Barbarism]. I wrote this
book, which should have been a thoughtful work enriched with historical data and documents, in order to make the politics of Rosas
known in Chile. Every page betrays the haste with which it was written:
Originals were still being composed as the book was being printed, and
manuscripts were lost that I could not replace. Nevertheless, this book
has won me a respectable reputation in Europe, as a consequence of the
compte rendu of the *Revue des Deux Mondes*.[1] It was published by *El Nacional* of Montevideo; it has been translated into German, illustrated by
Rugendas, and has provided European publicists the explanation of the
struggle of the Argentine Republic.[2] *Rosas y la cuestión del Plata* [Rosas
and the Question of the River Plate], and many other European publications are based on the data and viewpoint of *Civilización y Barbarie*. This
book contains the germ of many other writings and is aimed at destroying Rosas in the estimation of the enlightened world. He himself has felt
that it was a mortal blow to his politics, and in five years of diatribes
against me, *La Gaceta Mercantil* has not once mentioned this book, despite the fact that there is not in Buenos Aires a federalist of any importance who does not own it or has not read it, and that over 500 copies are
circulating in the Republic, there being no single book that has been as
eagerly sought after and read there. Rosas only pretends not to know
that such a book exists, for fear of drawing attention to it.

The *Revue de Deux Mondes*, in an article "On Americanism and the Republics of the South, Argentine Society, etc.," said with respect to the book and the author: "During his sojourn in Santiago, which has preceded his travels through Europe, Señor Sarmiento has published this work full of charm and novelty, instructive like history, interesting like a romance, glowing with images and color. *Civilización y Barbarie* is not only one of those rare testimonials that reaches us from the intellectual life of South America: it is a precious document. . . . Undoubtedly, passion has dictated more than one of those vigorous pages; but there is in talent, even when it shows itself exalted by passion, a *je ne sais quoi* of impartiality of which it cannot divest itself, and with the aid of which, it gives characters their true personality, and things their natural color. . . .

There would be no less interest in subjecting South America to the same analysis as North America. This would be the work of the philosopher and the traveler, of the poet and the historian, of the genre painter and the publicist. Señor Sarmiento has tried to achieve this in a book published in Chile, which proves that if civilization has enemies in those regions, it can also count on eloquent spokesmen."

Viajes por Europa, Africa y América [Travels in Europe, Africa, and America]. The Chilean press has passed favorable judgement on this work, which reveals the intimate thoughts of the author and the impressions made upon him by the spectacle of the countries he visited. It was my good fortune to touch, from close up, all the strings of European politics on the question of the Río de la Plata, and to marvel at the pettiness of the outlook, the ignorance of the background, and the ineptitude of the men who have played the most prominent roles in that matter. Travel is the complement of a man's education, and if contact with eminent figures elevates the spirit and perfects ideas, I can brag of having been fortunate on my trip, since I was able to approach, not without having been favorably introduced, the most eminent men of the time. I met M. Guizot through the recommendation of the government of Chile, Sr. Rosales having been my sponsor; M. Thiers, through the agent of Montevideo; the celebrated Cobden and Marshal Bugeaud, in Africa, through M. de Lesseps, who has been Ambassador to Spain and later representative in Rome; Alexandre Dumas, through Blanchart and Girardet, well-known painters; Gil de Zarate, through Colonel Sesé; Bretón de los Herreros, Ventura de la Vega, Aribau, and other Spanish literati, through the recommendations of French literati and of

Rivadeneira.[3] The renowned Baron von Humboldt, and the ministers of the king of Prussia, who lavished endless favors upon me as a representative of the Chilean government, through Doctor Wappäus and the head of the office of statistics, Mr. Dieterice; Pius IX, by recommendation of my being the nephew of the bishops of Cuyo, Oro and Sarmiento, he having met the former in America; M. Mérimée, by the painter Rugendas; Mme. Tastu, through M. Laserre; San Martín, by Argentineans who had recommended me highly to him; Mr. Mann, in the United States, by a senator of the Congress, to whom Mr. Ward of Valparaíso gave a most favorable report; and a hundred others, whom it would be tedious to enumerate, with whom I spent many hours discussing the most serious of matters, having been deemed worthy by all of the most flattering distinctions, and with many of whom I enjoyed the closest intimacy.[4] Two provincial governors, a certain Tamayo, a Minister Laspiur, and other names I do not remember, are welcome to call me "vile," "evil," "foul", and all such filth worthy of their authors, with complete assurance that if we meet one day, I will bear them no ill will.[5] On the contrary, I am sure that more than eight of them hold me in high regard, and Rosas can recognize them in the virulence of their language. The higher their estimation of me, the more extravagant the epithets, in order that their master should not suspect their loyalties.

Educación Popular [Popular Education]. This is the book I most esteem. Every page is the fruit of my diligence, visiting cities, talking with professionals, gathering data, consulting books, reports, and pamphlets, looking and listening. It is the matured fruit of that seed that appeared in my childhood in the school of San Francisco del Monte, in the semibarbarous countryside of San Luis. From there, I advanced in teaching from school to school, until I reached the Normal School of Versailles and the seminaries of Prussia, which are the pinnacle of the humble profession of teaching. I have had to invent for myself the science and the professional study of elementary education, and despite the general indifference, I have brought to South America the entire program of popular education. I do not know which critic it was who deplored my not having indicated the means for putting into practice the observations and doctrines accumulated in this work. A single word would suffice to complete and satisfy this desire. Give me a homeland where I am allowed to work, and I promise to transform every syllable into deeds, and this in a very few years. That book, barely intelligible to ordinary people, more than any other book of mine, is the one to which I would grant custody of my name. The highest praise this book has earned me is the reapplication to me of these words originally addressed to the author of a French work in praise of civilization: "Your book attests not only to painstaking research and study carried out with conscientiousness, but it also reveals the soul of an honest thinker and the heart of a good citizen." If the friend who addressed these words to me sought to please me, he shows in his choice that he knows the most intimate recesses of my heart. In the demoralization of ideas and feelings perpetrated by our tyrant, "honest" is the most difficult but most necessary of reputations, and it is the only one that can stand up to the cunning of the executioner and the dissemblance of the victims.

2 2

Translations

The object of all the translations I have done is to provide useful treatises for primary education, outstanding among them being books
that have an eminently moral and religious spirit. There are in Chile
naive people who fear my ideas, a bit free in terms of philosophical issues, a fact that, far from hiding, I make it my duty and a question of
honor to let everyone see, because the very thought of dissimulation
makes me indignant. Never will I accept subjection imposed by the stupid concerns of the mob, or by the intolerance of Spanish clerics. But,
when it comes to primary education, I am guided by other principles.
Lofty philosophical, religious, political, and social questions belong to
the realm of developed reason; children should only be taught that
which touches the heart, contains the passions, and prepares them to
enter into society. This is the explanation I gave the bishop of San Juan
to allay his fears in an analogous situation, and the result justified my
assertions.

Among these books are: *Conciencia de un niño* [A Child's Con-
science], a delightful book of morality and religion for awakening in the
hearts of children the first notions of the awareness of God and of the
duties of man.[1]

La Vida de Jesucristo [The Life of Jesus Christ], which did not exist in
Spanish, is a simple story and, at the same time, a luminous exposition of
the teachings of the Gospel.[2]

Manual de la Historia de los Pueblos [*Manual of the History of Peoples*]. Excellent elementary treatise by Levi Alvarez, which contains the core of all subsequent historical developments.³

¿Por qué? o la física popularizada [Why, or Popular Physics], which, if correctly understood, would be sufficient to engage the child's intelligence, revealing to him the natural causes of all the phenomena that present themselves for his consideration at every step.⁴

Vida de Franklin [Life of Franklin]. I arranged with a friend for its translation, in order to popularize knowledge about this extraordinary man, because I know what a beneficial effect the example of his virtues and his accomplishments can have on the impressionable souls of children.⁵ If the fourteen governors of the Argentine provinces think they should ban the circulation of this book, they can assign Angelis to write a life of Don Juan Manuel Rosas, from the time he ran away from home, until he became a horsebreaker, and all the lovely aspects of that life, and have it adopted by the schools, so that their own sons can emulate that sublime model.⁶

23

Institutions of Learning

Rosas's first administrative act was to strip the schools for both boys and girls in Buenos Aires of the financial support guaranteed them by the State; doing the same thing for professors at the University, having no shame in putting down in writing that those worthy citizens continued to teach out of patriotism and with no remuneration whatsoever.[1] The destruction wreaked in the Republic of Argentina by that stupid villain will not be remedied in half a century, for not only did he slit the throats of the country's enlightened men or force them to emigrate, but he closed the doors of the institutions of learning, because he has a keen sense of smell and knows that enlightenment is not the surest support of tyrants.

Natural instinct led me from the very beginning to take a road in the opposite direction. Ever since I was a boy, I have taught what I knew to as many as I could induce to learn. I have created schools where there were none, improved others that already existed, founded two secondary schools, and the Normal School owes me its existence.[2] It has produced a multitude of distinguished young graduates who have made teaching into a religious calling, and who promise Chile new and surer advances on the highroad of civilization.

Such is the modest picture of my small efforts in favor of liberty and progress in South America, and of universal education and European immigration as their powerful auxiliaries. Efforts, it must be said, made at the same time that I was struggling with life's difficulties to survive, that I was fighting against the instruments of Rosas to have a homeland, that I was educating my spirit to refine my ideas; efforts that in South America are not common either for their constancy, tenacity, or uniformity; efforts that from the first day to the last, from the first article in a newspaper to the last page of a book, make up a coherent whole, infinite variations on a single theme, change the face of America, and above all the Republic of Argentina, by substituting the European spirit for Spanish tradition; and, for brutality as the driving force, cultivated intelligence, study, and the remedy of want.

In these formless essays in which good intentions and perseverance are uppermost, I have reached the final stage of youth, have married after seeing the world, and have succeeded, by means of study, the discussion of ideas, the spectacle of events, travel, contact with eminent men, and my relations with the political leaders of Chile, in completing that education for public life that began in 1827, in prison cells and dungeons.[3] Though I have clearly arrived at the virility of reason, my heart has lost none of its fortitude, and this keeps me from sliding into indolence at the first moment that I overcome my obstacles, like that tyrant who has himself authorized not to *administer* public affairs *for many years,* when in fact he has managed, during eighteen years of violence, to nullify every other will but his own. Our lot is otherwise: to struggle to give us access to the homeland, and when we have achieved that, to work to accomplish in her the good that we conceive. This is the most fervent and most constant of my vows.

This small work, then, is the prologue to a larger one barely begun. The first volume is entitled *Viajes por Europa, Africa y América* [Travels in Europe, Africa, and America]. The second volume is still in the hands of Providence. Don Juan Manuel Rosas claims that it must not be published without his authorization and that he knows the way to undo books at their source. Florencio Varela! Are you in on the secret, too?[4]

Editor's Notes

1. Juan Facundo Quiroga (1788–1835), at one point one of the richest men in Argentina, belonged to a powerful family of rural property and livestock owners in La Rioja, the province contiguous with the eastern border of San Juan. He fought for independence, and by 1816 was supplying Belgrano's patriot Army of the North with cattle and troops. In 1820 he was named Military Commander of the Militias of the Llanos (the plains of La Rioja), and soon became warlord of his province, acquiring through personal charisma a legendary status among the rural population, reflected in numerous popular songs that portrayed him as a hero with supernatural powers. Initially sympathetic with the unitarian, or centralist cause, he opposed Buenos Aires's unitarian constitution in 1826, and especially the designs of the central government to exploit the mines of La Rioja for its own gain. Capitalizing on widespread provincial opposition to the national government's anticlerical religious reforms, Facundo rose up in arms under the banner of "Religion or Death," and after a series of military victories became the effective federalist leader of Cuyo, as well as of the north central provinces of La Rioja, Córdoba, Santiago del Estero, and Tucumán. However, after two defeats by unitarian armies, the federalist block of the interior fell apart, and in 1830 Facundo sought refuge in Buenos Aires, where Rosas was now in power. Subsequently, the unitarian League of the Interior disintegrated, and Facundo, again in arms, defeated the remnants of its army. Once more in Buenos Aires, Facundo was asked by Rosas to mediate in a conflict between Salta and Tucumán. Near Córdoba, while returning from his mission, he was assassinated at Barranca Yaco in 1835.

2. Sarmiento is referring here to his 1845 biography of Quiroga, *Civilización i barbarie. Vida de Juan Facundo Quiroga i aspecto físico, costumbres i ábitos de la República Arjentina* [Civilization and Barbarism, Life of Juan Facundo Quiroga and the Physical Aspect, Customs and Habits of the Argentine Republic]. Sarmiento considered this book an international success after it was favorably reviewed in 1846 in the prestigious French journal *Revue des Deux Mondes* [Review of Two Worlds] by Charles de Mazade, and although he never directly names this earlier book here in his preface to *Recuerdos*, he clearly constructs this inaugural scene of repetition (the two letters, the two famous and powerful enemies) in order to remind his readers that the person writing is the author of the celebrated *Facundo*.

In 1851, the year after publishing *Recuerdos*, Sarmiento brought out a second edition of the *Facundo* with a new prologue in which he wrote, "Facundo died physically in Barranca-Yaco; but his name in History was able to escape and survive a few years, without the exemplary punishment it deserved. The verdict of History has now been pronounced, and the suppression of his name and the scorn of nations protect the repose of his tomb." Thus, in 1851 Sarmiento returns to the assertion he has already made a year earlier, albeit obliquely, in "To My Compatriots Only," that is, that it was his 1845 biography that defined history's judgment of Facundo as a villain. In the *Facundo*, Sarmiento had also accused Rosas of being the instigator of the conspiracy to assassinate Facundo, an accusation that, to my knowledge, has never been proven.

3. Juan Manuel de Rosas (1793–1877) belonged to an old, well-connected, and rich family of landowners in Buenos Aires. Early on he mastered all the roles associated with cattle ranching, from overseer to cowpuncher. An astute businessman, he helped lead the dramatic expansion of the domestic cattle industry that began in the second decade of the nineteenth century, and he personally amassed an enormous fortune and vast landholdings. In 1820, when what little national unity as had existed since independence collapsed into anarchy, Rosas emerged as an important military and political power, organizing a disciplined militia mainly from his own ranch hands with which he helped secure Buenos Aires from outside intervention as well as from internal disorder. He supported the unitarian provincial government established in September of that year as long as it represented and protected the interests of the *estancieros*. However, Rosas's disaffection with the unitarians came to a head during the shortlived presidency of Rivadavia, who led a briefly centralized country between February 7, 1826, and June 27, 1827. Certain of Rivadavia's policies were unacceptable to the *estancieros;* for example, he pushed through the federalization of the city of Buenos Aires as national capital, which meant that from now on the revenue from customs on goods passing through the port would belong to the national government to spend as it wished and would no longer be for the exclusive benefit of the

province of Buenos Aires. When Rivadavia failed to gain support for his new centralizing constitution from the most powerful *caudillos* of the interior, he resigned as president, and the provinces, including Buenos Aires, once more became autonomous. A period of violence ensued in Buenos Aires between unitarians and federalists, which led to the election of Rosas as governor with extraordinary powers to impose order, in December of 1829. He ended his term in 1832, but accepted the governorship once again in 1835, in exchange, this time, for full dictatorial powers granted him by the legislature. Over time he spread his rule virtually throughout the entire country, by means of his monopoly of the port of Buenos Aires and his control of foreign affairs handed him by the other provincial governors. His authoritarian regime, punctuated in 1840 and 1842 by bloody reigns of terror, lasted until 1852, when he was easily overthrown by a large coalition of forces led by the rebellious governor of Entre Ríos, Justo José de Urquiza. During the Rosas years, Argentina was known as the Confederation of the River Plate, or the Argentine Confederation.

—Sarmiento's letter, dated May 26, 1848, was addressed to the federalist general José Santos Ramírez, the same man who had saved his life in the battle of El Pilar nineteen years before. (This earlier episode is narrated here in *Recuerdos,* in Chapter 16.) Recently returned from abroad in February of 1848, Sarmiento used the occasion of the letter to inform the general, whom he perceived as disgruntled with Rosas, that when the time came, he would repay his old debt by taking up arms to help him overthrow the tyrant. Ramírez forwarded the letter to Rosas, calling its author "the lunatic, fanatic, savage unitarian Domingo F. Sarmiento." On this letter and the exchanges it occasioned, including Sarmiento's ensuing journalistic attack against Rosas in his newspaper *La Crónica,* which he began publishing in January of 1849, in Santiago, see Paul Verdevoye, *Domingo Faustino Sarmiento, Educar y escribir opinando (1839–1852)* (Buenos Aires: Plus Ultra, 1988), 340–44.

4. Both sides, that is, Rosas, in his official documents and in the press under his control, as well as his exiled opposition, in their press, cultivated a rhetoric of insult and sensationalism.

5. The "various Argentine governments" are, of course, the governments of the fourteen provinces that make up the Argentine Confederation during the Rosas regime. Sarmiento's "response, which is registered in No. 19 of the *Crónica,*" dated June 3, 1849, is titled "Circular Regarding My Letter to General Ramírez" [Circular sobre mi carta al general Ramírez]. Sarmiento's "protest, in No. 48," dated Dec. 23, 1849, is literally titled "Protest" [Protesta]. Both are reprinted in Domingo Faustino Sarmiento, *Obras completas,* VI (San Justo, Buenos Aires: Universidad Nacional de la Matanza, 2001).

THE GENEALOGY

i. This genealogy is partial and highly selective. In it, Sarmiento has privileged those ancestors who would have been recognized by contemporary Argentine readers from Cuyo, and perhaps from Buenos Aires, as distinguished by their public service or philanthropy. This criterion is consistent with the author's desire to present his own record of public service as part of a long family tradition.

ii. Domingo de Oro. Born October 3, 1810. Sarmiento's cousin and oldest son of José Antonio de Oro, who was a first cousin of Sarmiento's mother. He is the subject of Chapter 10.

iii. Miguel de Oro. Also known as Juan Miguel de Oro. Originally from Buenos Aires. We learn in Chapter 8 that he had a brother and a daughter who were both insane.

iv. José Antonio de Oro. Son of Miguel de Oro and Elena Albarracín. Brother of the Presbyter José de Oro, Fray Justo de Santa María de Oro, and Tránsito de Oro, and first cousin of Sarmiento's mother.

v. Presbyter José de Oro. Born 1775; died 1836. Son of Miguel de Oro and Elena Albarracín, and first cousin of Sarmiento's mother. He is discussed at length in Chapter 8.

vi. Fray Justo de Santa María de Oro. Born 1772; died 1836. Son of Miguel de Oro and Elena Albarracín, and first cousin of Sarmiento's mother. He is the subject of Chapter 9.

vii. Elena Albarracín. Sister of Cornelio Albarracín, Sarmiento's maternal grandfather, and aunt of Sarmiento's mother. She is married to Miguel de Oro and is the mother or grandmother of the remaining five members of the Oro family named here.

viii. Tránsito de Oro. Born 1789; died 1856. Daughter of Miguel de Oro and Elena Albarracín, and first cousin of Sarmiento's mother.

ix. Master Fray Remigio Albarracín. Brother of Sarmiento's maternal grandfather, Cornelio Albarracín. A Dominican priest active toward the end of the eighteenth century and the beginning of the nineteenth.

x. Master Fray Justo Albarracín. Brother of Sarmiento's maternal grandfather. At the beginning of Chapter 9, we learn that in 1772, when his grandnephew Justo Santa María de Oro was born, Fray Justo Albarracín was "the shining light of the monastery of Saint Dominic" in San Juan.

xi. Fray Miguel Albarracín. Brother of Sarmiento's maternal grandfather. We learn in Chapter 7, where he is discussed at some length, that his work *Los Milenarios* appeared a few years before the outbreak of the wars of independence in 1810.

xii. Bernardino Albarracín. Sarmiento's great grandfather, through his maternal grandfather, Cornelio. Born in Salta, he moved to Cuyo at the beginning of the eighteenth century. In 1724 he served on the town council of San Juan. José S. Campobassi, *Sarmiento y su época. I. Desde 1811 a 1863* (Buenos Aires: Editorial Losada, 1975), 23.

xiii. Pédro Albarracín. Brother of Sarmiento's maternal grandfather.

xiv. Paula Albarracín. Sarmiento's mother (1778–1861), daughter of Cornelio Albarracín and Juana Irarrázabal (called "Antonia" in this genealogy) and sister of Juan Pascual Albarracín and of numerous other brothers and sisters not named here; however, in Chapter 13, we learn that Cornelio Albarracín was survived by fifteen children. Paula Albarracín married José Clemente Sarmiento in 1801, and she bore fifteen children, five of whom grew to adulthood and are named in this genealogy. Sarmiento's mother is the subject of Chapters 13 and 14.

xv. José Manuel Eufrasio de Quiroga Sarmiento. He is the subject of Chapter 12.

xvi. Raymond Quinsac Monvoisin (1790–1870). French historical painter and portraitist who trained in the workshop of Pierre-Narcisse Guérin, successful and influential neo-classicist painter during the French Revolution and the Napoleonic Empire, as well as teacher of Delacroix and Géricault. In 1842 Monvoisin was invited to Chile by the government to establish an Academy of Painting. He arrived in Santiago in January of 1843, after having passed briefly through Buenos Aires, where he painted a portrait of the dictator Rosas. In March of the same year, he organized the first public art exhibit in Chilean national history, an exhibition of nine of his own paintings brought with him from France. Sarmiento enthusiastically reviewed this exhibition in his article "Cuadros de [Pictures by] Monvoisin," published in *El Progreso* on March 3, 1843, and reproduced in Sarmiento, *Obras*, II. With a few short interruptions, Monvoisin remained in Chile until 1857, when he returned to live in France. During his years in Chile, he was much solicited as a portraitist by the Chilean rich, of whom he executed between five and six hundred portraits.

xvii. José Clemente Sarmiento. Sarmiento's father (1778–1844/1848?). According to some sources, i.e., Horacio Videla, *Historia de San Juan, IV* (Buenos Aires: Academia del Plata, 1962–76), 725, he died in San Juan in 1844; according to others, i.e., Campobassi, *Sarmiento y su época*, 276, he died in San Juan on December 22, 1848.

xviii. Re. Chacabuco, see Note 5, Chapter 4.

xix. María Antonia Irarrázabal. Sister of Sarmiento's grandmother Juana (Antonia) Irarrázabal. In 1785, she helped found a Home for Orphans and Wayward Women in San Juan. She is apparently included in this genealogy because of her civic-minded philanthropy. In the first and second editions of *Recuerdos*, her name is placed below that of Antonia (Juana), creating the mistaken impression that she was married to Cornelio Albarracín.

xx. José Ignacio Sarmiento. Sarmiento's paternal grandfather, also known as José Ignacio de Quiroga Sarmiento. At the beginning of Chapter 12, Sarmiento explains the origin of the surname "de Quiroga Sarmiento," which his father's brother José Manuel Eufrasio used but which his father, José Clemente, did not. There we also learn that, to the best of the author's knowledge, the Sarmientos of his family did not descend from the Sarmientos of distinguished lineage.

xxi. Abbot Don Manuel Morales. Jesuit, born in San Juan in 1731. After the expulsion of the Jesuit Order from all the realms of the Spanish crown in 1767, Morales lived in exile in Italy, where he wrote his *Historia de Cuyo*, in Bolognia. He died in Florence in 1790. Videla, *Historia de San Juan*, II, 212.

xxii. This text by the Chilean abbot Juan Ignacio Molina, which first appeared in 1776, is cited again by Sarmiento in Chapter 1. According to Videla, *Historia de San Juan* I, 286, between the founding of the city of San Juan in 1562 and the creation of the Viceroyalty of the Río de la Plata in 1776, that is, during the 214 years in which San Juan was under the administrative jurisdiction of the Captaincy-General of Chile (created in 1546), the most complete accounts of San Juan de la Frontera were produced by Spanish and Chilean Jesuits.

xxiii. Gregorio Funes (1749, Córdoba, Argentina—1829, Buenos Aires) was born into an elite family of Córdoba and never resided in San Juan. A member of the secular clergy, he was named rector of the University of Córdoba in 1808. He is the subject of Chapter 11.

xxiv. Re. Pierre Claude François Daunou, see Note 24, Chapter 11.

—*El Argos de Buenos Aires*. In 1823 Funes was named the editor-in-chief of this newspaper (founded in 1821), which disseminated general news and current debates. While not openly political in nature, the *Argos* was published by the local Literary Society and reflected the sentiments of the provincial government of Buenos Aires, which had been created in 1820 with the dissolution of the centralist Directory and the victory of provincial self-government nationwide.

CHAPTER 1: THE PALM TREES

1. This poem is a *romance*, or typical Spanish ballad, with eight-syllable verses and assonant rhyme at the end of every second verse in the original. Abd-al-Rahman was the name of three important Omayyad rulers of the Arab emirate and later the caliphate of Córdoba, in Spain. Abd-al-Rahman I (731–788) turned Córdoba into an independent emirate when he broke relations with Damascus in 773. In 929 Abd-al-Rahman III (891–961) broke away from Baghdad and assumed the title of caliph of Córdoba; under his rule the city reached its zenith as one of the most culturally vibrant in all of western Europe. Algarve is a region at the extreme southern point of Portugal, where the town Faro is located.

2. The Boston oak to which Sarmiento refers is most likely the "Great Elm," which was already a mature tree when Governor Winthrop arrived from England with the charter of the new colony in 1630. Shortly thereafter, the land on which the elm stood was declared the property of the people, a "Common Field" upon which no house could be built nor garden plot established. This land became the Boston Common, which remains today in the center of the city proper. However, the Great Elm, still standing in 1847 when Sarmiento first visited Boston, was finally destroyed by a storm in 1876. Sarmiento may have confused the famous elm in Boston with another equally famous tree on the Cambridge Common, the Washington Oak, under which George Washngton is said to have taken command of the Continental Army. I am indebted to Nicholas Graham, reference librarian at the Massachusetts Historical Society, for helping me clear up this confusion.

CHAPTER 2: JUAN EUGENIO DE MALLEA

1. Pedro de Valdivia (1497–1553) was a Spanish conquistador and colonizer. Maister of the Campe under Pizarro in Peru, he prepared an expedition to Chile in 1539. He was responsible for opening up Chile's fertile Central Valley to European colonization, and in 1541 he founded the city of Santiago, which became the capital of the new colony. In 1548, when the Captaincy General of Chile was created, Valdivia was named its first governor and captain-general. He subsequently continued his explorations southward to the Straits of Magellan, founding the towns of Concepción, in 1550, and Valdivia, in 1552. 1553 marked the first great uprising of the Araucanian Indians, who would successfully resist the Spaniards in southern Chile during the entire colonial period, and who, during the national period well into the final quarter of the nineteenth century, would continue hostilities (especially raids) against Hispanic settlements in the southern portions of both Chile and Argentina. In the year 1553, Valdivia and his forces were defeated at Tucapel, a locality to the south of the Bío Bío River, long to be considered the frontier and entrance into Araucanian territory. Valdivia was captured at Tucapel, tortured, and put to death by the Araucanian victors.

—Francisco de Villagra, another Spaniard, on expedition from Peru to Chile in 1551, got as far as Cuyo in May and was then forced by the winter's snows to wait until October to cross the Andes. Based on the time he stayed in the region besieged by the weather, he is considered by Euro-centric historians to be the discoverer of Cuyo. Villagra became the third governor of Chile, between 1561 and 1563, the period during which the towns of Mendoza and San Juan were founded.

2. The abrupt switch from the past verbal tense to the present occurs in the

original Spanish and is characteristic of Sarmiento's prose. Many, but not all, such switches in the verb tenses have been maintained in the translation.

—Don García Hurtado de Mendoza was the son of Don Andrés Hurtado de Mendoza, viceroy of Peru (1555–1561), who in 1557 named Don García the second governor of Chile, a position he held until 1561. Don García himself subsequently became the viceroy of Peru, from 1589 to 1597.

3. Eastern Chile was, at the time, the land to the east of the Andes that fell within the jurisdiction of the Captaincy of Chile and that included Cuyo. Sarmiento writes that Pedro de Castillo founded Mendoza in 1560. Others, i.e., the historian Videla, claim that the same person, Juan Jufré (or Jofré), founded both Mendoza, in 1561, and San Juan, a year later in 1562. In 1563, the Argentine northwest, including the settlements of Tucumán and Córdoba, was removed from Chilean jurisdiction, but Cuyo remained subject to the captain-general of Chile until 1776. See David Rock, *Argentina, 1516–1987: From Spanish Colonization to Alfonsín* (Berkeley: University of California Press, 1987), 15.

4. The Huarpes were the indigenous population that inhabited Cuyo upon the arrival of the Spaniards. At that time the Huarpes, an agricultural people, were in the process of being acculturated into the Andean civilization of the Incan empire. Since colonial Cuyo was to remain part of Chile until late in the eighteenth century, very soon after the founding of Mendoza and San Juan, the *encomerderos* there began to send large numbers of their Indians to the Central Valley of Chile to compensate for the ever dwindling native population north of the Bío Bío River. By 1620, this forced migration, along with ethnic mixture, contributed to the near disappearance from Cuyo of the Huarpes as a distinct cultural group. See Rock, *Argentina, 1516–1987,* 18.

5. Cuzco, in the Peruvian highlands, was the capital city of the Incas, associated in the minds of Spaniards everywhere with the enormous wealth that the Spanish invaders found when they conquered and sacked the city in 1533. The opulence of Cuzco's great Temple of the Sun, the interior walls of which were covered with sheets of gold, quickly became legendary. When the Spaniards sacked the temple, they tore down what remained of its decoration and melted most of it into bars of gold that they shipped back to Spain. Only the king's fifth was sent back in its original form.

CHAPTER 3: THE HUARPES

1. Pedro Carril was one of the richest landowners in San Juan and the father of Salvador María del Carril. See Note 2 below.

2. On Fray Miguel Albarracín, see Note xi, "Genealogy."

—Francisco Narciso de Laprida (1786–1829) was a lawyer from San Juan who collaborated with General San Martín in organizing the Army of the Andes. He was also San Juan's representative to the Congress of Tucumán, over which he presided and in which Argentina's independence was declared, in 1816. Subsequently, as San Juan's delegate to the Constituent Congress in 1824, he voted in favor of the centralist constitution of 1826. After Rivadavia renounced the national presidency in 1827, Laprida left Buenos Aires and returned to San Juan, where he continued to defend unitarian ideals. Jailed and subsequently freed, Laprida fled to Mendoza, but there in September of 1829, at the Battle of Pilar, which Sarmiento describes in Chapter 16, he was killed by Aldao's troops.

—José Ignacio de la Rosa (1788–1839), born into a rich and influential family in San Juan, graduated in law from the University of San Felipe in Chile, and was introduced to the cause of the revolution in Buenos Aires, where he practiced law from 1809 to 1814. De la Rosa was lieutenant governor of San Juan from 1815 to 1820, a close friend of Laprida, and an active collaborator with General San Martín in organizing the Army of the Andes when, between late 1814 and early 1817, San Martín was governor of Cuyo and used Mendoza as his civil and military headquarters. During De la Rosa's five years in office as lieutenant governor, Sarmiento's boyhood school, the public *Escuela de la Patria* [School of The Fatherland], was founded (in April 1816), San Juan's mail service was improved, and an additional public irrigation ditch was built.

—Salvador María del Carril (1798–1883) was a member of the San Juan elite who was trained as a lawyer at the University of Córdoba and, from 1816 to 1819, received further training in Buenos Aires. He was governor of San Juan from 1823 to 1825. As a governor who was also an ardent supporter of Rivadavia's liberal reforms, he suppressed both the military and ecclesiastical *fueros* (corporate privileges that gave the military and the clergy immunity from civil jurisdiction), and imposed severe restrictions on the religious orders, closing some of the convents and confiscating much of their property. According to historian David Bushnell, "No other interior province imitated the work of Buenos Aires reformers quite so closely as this. . . ." David Bushnell, *Reform and Reaction in the Platine Provinces, 1810–1852* (Gainesville: University Press of Florida, 1983), 39. In 1824 Del Carril also encouraged the local legislature to purchase the province's first printing press. (Córdoba had acquired its first printing press in 1765; Buenos Aires, in 1780; and Tucumán and Mendoza, both in 1820.) (Carmen P. De Varese and Héctor D. Arias, *Historia de San Juan* [Mendoza: Ed. Spadoni, 1966], 146). Temporarily ousted from office by a conservative and proclerical uprising on July 26, 1825, Del Carril was soon reinstated, at which time he abdicated in favor of an interim governor of similar politics. After one more short-lived liberal and pro—Buenos Aires government, the federalists and the federalist caudillos would control the provincial government of San Juan from the beginning of 1827 until the end of the Rosas period in 1852. Upon leaving office in San Juan in 1825, Del Carril returned to Buenos Aires, where he became Rivadavia's minister of the treasury in 1826. When Rosas came to power in 1829, he emigrated to Uruguay and was active in anti-Rosas emigré politics.

3. A motif that structures this whole chapter is the lament, which also appeared in the *Facundo,* regarding the contemporary decadence of San Juan and its inhabitants. Sarmiento begins with an *ubi sunt* motif about the once numerous Huarpes, but he fails to enter into any discussion of why the Huarpes disappeared. Indeed, he constructs his portrait of the Huarpes with the rhetoric of romanticization, suggesting that in some ways they were superior to the whites of present-day San Juan. Elsewhere, however, both during the 1840s and '50s as well as toward the end of his life, whenever he spoke of the contemporary and unsubjugated marauding tribes of the Argentine and Chilean south, Sarmiento expressed himself like an Indian hater of Jacksonian proportions. (See Elizabeth Garrels, "Sobre indios, afroamericanos y los racismos de Sarmiento," *Revista Iberoamericana* 63, nos. 178–179 [January–June 1997]: 99–113.) In fact, his portrait of the Huarpes is so uncharacteristically benign that one is tempted to speculate that this is because they were agrarian and sedentary and thus easier to force into *encomienda,* and, what is more, they belonged to the past.

It is interesting to reflect on the complete absence of Indian violence in this chapter, since Indian raids, the destruction of creole lives and property, and the taking of creole captives are themes that during these years (1840s-50s) preoccupy the writer Sarmiento. According to Fernando Operé, between the mid-seventeenth and eighteenth centuries, Indian tribes from Chile conducted frequent and destructive raids across the Andes against the frontiers of Cuyo. Fernando Operé, *Historias de la frontera: el cautiverio en la América hispánica* (Mexico: Fondo de Cultura Económica, 2001), 84. Although the province of San Juan had no Indian frontier in the early decades of the nineteenth century, Mendoza to the south did; in fact, according to Halperín Donghi, Mendoza experienced a recrudescence of Indian incursions after 1820 (Tulio Halperín Donghi, *Politics, Economics and Society in Argentina in the Revolutionary Period,* trans. Richard Southern [Cambridge: Cambridge University Press, 1975], 327).

CHAPTER 4: THE SONS OF JOFRÉ

1. Osuna, Joinville, Orleáns. From the seventeenth century onward, these three families were recognized as belonging to the earliest established nobility in Europe, who claimed the ability to count their lineage backward by twenty-nine generations.

2. William Pitt (1759–1806) became prime minister of Great Britain in 1783 at the age of twenty-four and directed British policy toward France during much of the French Revolution. He resigned as prime minister in 1801 but was recalled to office in 1804, and died shortly after hearing of Napoleon's victory at Austerlitz.

—George Washington (1732–1799), first president of the United States and commander in chief of the Continental Army in the American Revolution.

—François Arago (1786–1853), French physicist, astronomer, and politician. Minister of War and the Navy, he abolished slavery in the French colonies in 1848.

—Benjamin Franklin (1706–1790) was an American statesman, scientist, printer, and writer. He helped draft the Declaration of Independence and negotiate the peace with Britain that ended the American Revolution. He was author of perhaps the most popular and widely influential modern autobiography ever written. It served as a model for such disparate writers as Frederick Douglass and Domingo F. Sarmiento.

—Alphonse de Lamartine (1790–1869). French romantic poet, prose writer, and statesman. Son of an aristocrat who was imprisoned during the French Revolution's Reign of Terror, Lamartine became head of the provisional government when the Second Republic was proclaimed in Paris, after the revolution of February 24, 1848. By June 24 of the same year, however, the revolution was crushed, and Lamartine was thrown out of office. Among his prose works, he authored the autobiographical text *Les Confidences,* which first appeared serially in 1845 in the French daily newspaper *La Presse.* Sarmiento refers to Lamartine's *Confidences* at the beginning of Chapter 13, "The Story of My Mother."

—Alexandre Dumas (1802–1870). An exceptionally prolific French novelist and playwright, known as *Père* [Father] to distinguish him from his son, also a writer. He was most famous for his novels *The Three Musketeers* (1828) and *The Count of Monte Cristo* (1844). In 1843 Sarmiento serially published a novella by Dumas in the daily newspaper *El Progreso* [Progress], which he had founded in Santiago, Chile, the year before. In October of 1845, the month he relinquished the directorship of the paper to leave on his trip to Europe, *El Progreso* began the serialized publication of a Spanish translation of *The Three Musketeers,* which continued into 1846.

3. Lautaro was an Indian probably from the area of Santiago. It is believed that he was captured by Pedro de Valdivia and subsequently escaped, but not before learning a great deal about Spanish behavior. He became an Indian leader and a gifted military strategist who plotted the capture and execution of Pedro de Valdivia, and then led a general uprising that lasted four years, ending with his death in the battle of Peteroa in 1557. Praised by the Spanish poet and conquistador Alonso de Ercilla in his epic poem *La Araucana* (three parts, 1569–89), Lautaro was thereafter considered an Araucanian by Chilean historians during the postcolonial period and turned into a hero of Chilean nationalism.

4. "Santiago" is the Spanish form for Saint James the Greater, one of the apostles of Jesus. Since the Middle Ages, Santiago has also been the patron saint of Catholic Spain.

5. Sylvia Molloy identifies this type of sentence as characteristic of many Spanish American autobiographies. In the original Spanish, this sentence begins with "Yo alcancé," which means "I was just in time" to know, experience, or see something or someone before it disappeared forever, something or someone that belonged to a time now irrevocably gone. Molloy explains that it is not surprising that "the autobiographer should adopt this particular stance," given "the constant changes and frequently violent upheavals that characterize Latin America as a continent." Molloy, *At Face Value: Autobiographical Writing in Spanish America* (Cambridge: Cambridge University Press, 1991), 162.

6. This was the Army of the Andes organized by General San Martín to liberate Chile from the royalists. In January of 1817, the army of 5,000 moved out of Mendoza to cross the Andes, a feat that historian John Lynch calls "one of the greatest . . . of the revolutionary wars" (John Lynch, *The Spanish American Revolutions, 1808–1826* [New York: W.W. Norton, 1986], 141). On February 12, 1817, San Martín's army defeated the royalists on the plains of Chacabuco outside of Santiago, and then entered the Chilean capital. San Martin's decisive victory against the royalists, however, was not won until the Battle of Maipo, also a plain outside Santiago, on April 5, 1818.

7. Between July 20 and August 25, 1839, Sarmiento directed a weekly newspaper in the city of San Juan entitled *El Zonda*. He claims to have done most of the writing for the newspaper and was also its printer; briefly, between June 28 and August 2, 1839, he actually held the official position of director of the printing press owned by the provincial government, then under federalist control. The article "La Pirámide" appeared anonymously in the newspaper's final issue, on August 25.

CHAPTER 5: MALLEA

1. On the possible motives for such revenge, see the first two Footnotes in Chapter 2.

2. On the racial prejudice to which Sarmiento alludes—that in San Juan it was considered worse to be mulatto than mestizo—consider the following information on the racial composition of San Juan. When the Spaniards arrived in the sixteenth century to conquer and settle the Argentine territory, roughly two-thirds of the area's indigenous population resided in the northwest (Rock, *Argentina, 1516–1987*, 6). By the time of the royal census of 1777, the city of San Juan had a total population of 6,141, as compared to the larger Mendoza, with 7,478; nonetheless, the numerical distribution of the various racial groups within the two populations was significantly different. For San Juan, the census recorded 1,569 whites, 2,990 mestizos, 718 Indians, and 837 blacks; for Mendoza, 4,344 whites, 565 mestizos, 446 Indians, and 2,125 blacks (Videla, *Historia de San Juan*

II, 130–31). If one assumes that the category "blacks" included mulattos, one can conclude that not only had there been considerably more racial mixture between whites and Indians in San Juan, but there were also many fewer blacks than in Mendoza and consequently less racial mixture between whites and blacks, producing fewer mulattos than presumably existed in the neighboring city not far to the south. Also, in the remaining northwest, the two cities of Tucumán (fd. 1685) and Córdoba (fd. 1573) each had populations that were recorded as up to 30 percent black, comprised of both slaves and blacks who had bought their freedom, with Tucumán having the largest concentration of blacks of any city in the interior. (See James R. Scobie, *Argentina: A City and a Nation* [New York: Oxford University Press, 1971], 49, 56.) In the eighteenth century these cities were connected by well-established trade, and comparisons of a defensive and competitive nature no doubt constituted an important part of each city's local self-image.

3. The "personage" was reading an official document sent by the government of Rosas to the government of Chile. See Note 4, "To My Compatriots Only."

4. Slavery was abolished in the Argentine republic in 1853. However, since the province of Buenos Aires did not join the republic until 1860, it did not formally abolish slavery within its territory until this later date. In continental Spanish America, only the region of the Río de la Plata continued to import significant numbers of slaves after independence. Until 1839, this illegal slave trade was openly tolerated by the Buenos Aires government, especially by Rosas, who himself was a slave owner and did not question slavery as an institution. Only in 1839, during the French blockade of the port of Buenos Aires (March 1838–October 1840), when Rosas especially needed to court British favor, did he sign a comprehensive treaty to end the trade. See Tulio Halperín Donghi, "Economy and society," and John Lynch, "The River Plate Republics," in *Spanish America after Independence, c.1820–c.1870*, ed. Leslie Bethell (Cambridge: Cambridge University Press, 1987), 24, 43,338–39.

5. Francisco de Quevedo (1580–1645), Spanish author of the picaresque novel *Historia de la vida del Buscón* (1626), and one of the most important satirists and poets of the Spanish Golden Age. Here we most likely have another case of Sarmiento quoting from memory, in which the evoked citation is reworded in the process of recollection. Sarmiento may be thinking of a fairly well-known *romance* by Quevedo entitled "Pintura de la mujer de un abogado, abogada ella del demonio" [Painting of the wife of a lawyer/advocate, she being the advocate of the devil]. Portraying the "*viejecita*" [little old woman] of the poem's initial verse, Quevedo writes of a "nariz a cuyas ventanas/ está siempre el romadizo,/ muy juguetón de moquita,/ columpiándose en el pico" [nose at whose windows/a head cold is always present,/ very playful with snot,/ swinging from its tip]. I thank Professor Jim Iffland of Boston University for directing me to Quevedo's poem.

6. Nazario Benavides (1805–1858), was born into a San Juan family that was not part of the provincial elite. Like the young Sarmiento, he attended San Juan's public School of the Fatherland, founded in 1816, but received no further formal education. He grew up working on his family's farm and around the age of sixteen became a muleteer. In 1831, he was called into military service by Facundo Quiroga and fought with the victorious federalists at the Battle of the Citadel (*Ciudadela*) in Tucumán. His rise to power as federalist governor of San Juan, a position he would maintain, with brief intervals, until 1854, illustrates the point made by historian Halperín Donghi when he writes that after independence, but especially after the collapse of national unity in 1820, the political equilibrium inherited from the colonial period in which the same elite held power and administered it, shifted, so that now those holding social and economic power often sought the political and administrative collaboration of individuals from different social backgrounds. Echoing a point made by Sarmiento in the *Facundo*, Halperín writes that, "Especially after 1835, when Juan Manuel de Rosas was trying to rebuild on tougher and more solid foundations the hegemony of Buenos Aires, his ascendancy over the Interior was to favour the rise of figures who, even in the new political hierarchy born of the dual process of militarisation and ruralisation, occupied a secondary place" (Halperín, *Politics*, 387). Such a figure was Nazario Benavides.

Elsewhere, though with a different emphasis, Halperín makes a similar point about the crisis of the colonial elite in the new social arrangements of the post-independence era. He states that by the middle of the nineteenth century, "a new criterion for social differentiation was emerging: wealth. . . . In Argentina in the 1840s, wealth and enlightenment did not necessarily go together: in the interior, the enlightened classes lost their economic predominance. . . . Nazario Benavides was now the richest man in San Juan" (Tulio Halperín Donghi, "Sarmiento's Place in Postrevolutionary Argentina," in *Sarmiento: Author of a Nation*, ed. Tulio Halperín Donghi, Iván Jaksic, Gwen Kirkpatrick, and Francine Masiello [Berkeley: University of California Press, 1994], 22–23). Benavides, who had accumulated his fortune through his own efforts as well as through marriage, was a relative upstart who had inherited neither his wealth nor his values from the colonial elite. As for his wealth, although "not to be sneezed at, given the times and the environment," it was far from being "extraordinary" in the way that Sarmiento, at the beginning of Chapter 3 ("The Huarpes"), suggests that the aristocratic Pedro Carril's had been just a generation before. (The quoted characterizations of Benavides's wealth are from De Varese and Arias, *Historia*, 227 [my translation]).

In *Recuerdos*, Sarmiento presents an idealized vision of the colonial elite as combining economic power with an enlightened commitment to public service. By upbringing, in Sarmiento's vision, even the poor relations, who, according to

Halperín, were never lacking in the "surprisingly large" colonial aristocracy of San Juan, shared in the enlightened commitment of their class (Halperín, "Sarmiento's Place in Postrevolutionary Argentina," 22). Thus, in the rigid social hierarchy of the colony, "breeding," rather than individual wealth, was apparently what mattered most, although the socially valued kind of breeding was only available to those with class affiliations to the wealthy.

7. Sarmiento refers to the chapter entitled "Roma" [Rome], in his book *Viajes*, which he published in Chile in two parts in 1849 and 1851, respectively. The chapter "Roma" appeared at the end of the first volume, in 1849. Like all the chapters in this book, "Roma" is written in the form of a letter; it is addressed to the Bishop of Cuyo (Sarmiento's paternal uncle José Manuel Eufrasio de Quiroga Sarmiento; see Chapter 12) and dated April 6, 1847, when Sarmiento was in Rome during his first trip to Europe. In this letter, Sarmiento asks his uncle to go see their mutual cousin (who is still alive in 1847 but who dies the following year) and to make him read the writer's epistolary account of his visit to the ruins of Pompeii. Sarmiento never names cousin Fermín Mallea outright, but refers to him as "our cousin M***"; the anecdote that follows is narrated comically as an "old offense" perpetrated years before by Mallea against the precocious child Domingo: "I don't know how or when it was that I read an account of the discovery of Pompeii, but here you have me, unable to contain myself with the surprise and novelty, going out into the street to search for passersby to whom I can narrate the portentious history, complete with the bits about the oil and the bread that had been found; I tell the story to M***, and instead of responding with an open mouth as I had imagined, he laughs at me right in my face; and every time we are around other people he makes me tell the story of Pompeii, for purposes of general amusement" (my translation). Domingo Faustino Sarmiento, *Viajes por Europa, Africa y América, 1845–1847, y Diario de gastos* (Buenos Aires: Colección Archivos, 1993), 241.

8. The twentieth-century Argentine writer Jorge Luis Borges considered the story of Don Fermín Mallea "the most memorable" of all the vignettes in *Recuerdos*. In his prologue to an edition of the book, he wrote that this story is a "page that would be easy to expand into a long psychological tale, without having to add anything essential" (my translation). "Prólogo," in *Recuerdos de provincia*, by Domingo F. Sarmiento (Buenos Aires: Emecé, 1944), 10.

It should be noted that this is the first story of some length in this book that Sarmiento tells about a relative. It is also a story of failure, excess, obsession, and insanity—in short, a tale told about an idiot (that is, a *loco*, a crazy man). This tale fits into the theme of insanity that is introduced by the book's inaugural epigraph and that resurfaces on various other pages. It is also related to the book's subterranean Oedipal themes in that it is a story about a basically good man whose character flaws bring harm to the younger man he views and treats like a son.

CHAPTER 6: THE SAYAVEDRAS

1. Juan Lavalle (1797–1841), who began his military career under San Martín in 1812, became one of the most important generals of the unitarian forces in the 1820s and '30s. In 1827 he joined the short-lived national army to fight in the war against Brazil (1825–28). When the federalist governor of Buenos Aires, Manuel Dorrego (who had nullified the national constitution in 1827 after Rivadavia's resignation), negotiated a peace with Brazil, which, among other things, recognized Uruguay as an independent state, Lavalle returned to Buenos Aires with his troops and overthrew Dorrego, in what was subsequently known as the December 1st Revolution, of 1828. During the revolt, Dorrego was captured and summarily shot. This unpopular act, coupled with the repressive policies Lavalle proceeded to impose on Buenos Aires, formed the basis for the epithets "savage" and "assassin," which were to become part of the official anti-unitarian rhetoric during Rosas's years in power. Finally, in 1829, when Lavalle could no longer withstand the pressures from the militia led by Rosas, he and other remaining unitarian leaders left Buenos Aires for Montevideo. Lavalle once more became militarily active in 1839, when in the company of 430 men, he disembarked on the coast of the littoral province Entre Ríos to initiate a campaign to overthrow Rosas. The dictator survived the challenge, and Lavalle was finally killed in October of 1841 by federalists in the province of Jujuy, in the extreme northwest of Argentina, effectively ending this most recent round of unitarian resistance and civil war.

2. Here Sarmiento alludes to the assault in which he was almost killed by a federalist mob on the day before he left San Juan to begin his decade-long exile in Chile. The author will provide an extended narration of this scene in Chapter 16. It is the same scene he had already reproduced at the beginning of the *Facundo* of 1845, placing it between the "Advertencia" [Foreword] and the "Introduction." The scene corresponds to the *topos*, or rhetorical commonplace, in Sarmiento's prolific writing of the "frequently repeated story." These stories get retold throughout the complete works in a way that some have judged obsessive and others have seen as rhetorical staples of the hurried writer-journalist's "writing machine," that is, the fixed repertoire that allowed him to write so fast and so very much.

3. This chapter gives the impression of being a preliminary draft that Sarmiento never completed. It is not only disproportionately short and completely lacking in narrative development, but the first sentence has no logical connection to the rest of the paragraph. The first sentence, about the aged pine,

appears to be picking up the book's leitmotif of associating trees with important families. The second sentence abandons the theme of the tree altogether, and jumps to "I met the last two descendants of . . . ," a variation of the motif "*Yo alcancé*" (see Note 5, Chapter 4). Sarmiento does not claim to be related to the Sayavedra family, nor does he clarify who the original Sayavedra was, beyond identifying him as "the soldier with this last name." Reading backward to Chapter 2, one can discover that Hernán Daría de Sayavedra is mentioned in passing as one of the witnesses who signed Mallea's *probanza*, so we can conclude that the soldier Sayavedra was one of the original *vecinos* of San Juan. The elliptical nature of the text here suggests a hastiness in its elaboration. In fact, later on in Chapter 16, "La vida publica," Sarmiento confesses to carelessness in the preparation of this chapter, when he acknowledges and corrects a factual error contained here. Noteworthy about his method of composition is, of course, the fact that once he realizes he has made a mistake, he does not go back and correct it in the place where it occurred.

CHAPTER 7: THE ALBARRACÍNS

1. M. Beauvais. In *Viajes,* in the letter from Paris dated September 4, 1846, Sarmiento writes, "I make sidetrips to all the famous outskirts, and to Mainville, where I am studying the art of cultivating silk, under the direction of M. Camille Beauvais, in case one day in America, in Mendoza, in Chile, they should think about the industrial future of the temperate countries of South America, so obscure, so insecure" (Sarmiento, *Viajes,* 118; translation mine). According to P. Verdevoye, Sarmiento spent most of the month of June 1846, as a student of M. Beauvais, taking a free course in silk cultivation at the Magnanerie des Bergeries, a sericultural farm founded by Beauvais in 1826. For more details, see Paul Verdevoye, "Viajes por Francia y Argelia," Sarmiento, *Viajes,* 684–89.

—Montmorency. About this reference, Sylvia Molloy writes, "Sarmiento's attitude towards aristocracy is notoriously ambiguous. . . . [W]hen tracing his maternal family back to a twelfth-century Saracen chieftan, he pointedly compares the Albarracines to the Montmorencys—not by chance one of the most distinguished families in France." Sylvia Molloy, *At Face Value: Autobiographical Writing in Spanish America* (Cambridge: Cambridge University Press, 1991), 153.

2. On his cross-Atlantic trip from 1846 to 1847, Sarmiento visited northern Africa after touring in France and then Spain. He was in Algiers and Oran between December of 1846 and January of 1847, and writes about this experience in the chapter "Africa" of his *Viajes.* In Oran, the Argentine traveler tells us, he donned a burnoose for a ride on horseback across the desert to visit a group of Bedouin tents, in order to see the tribes people "in their normal state" ("en su estado normal"). Although it is clear from his description that Sarmiento enjoys

playing the role of "Argentine gaucho as Bedouin," his judgments in *Viajes* about both Bedouin culture and Islam are generally damning. For Sarmiento's visit to the Bedouin tents dressed in a burnoose, see Sarmiento, *Viajes*, 187–94.

In the *Facundo* of 1845, Sarmiento had already developed an Orientalist analogy between the Argentine gaucho and the Arab tribesman, but there the analogy was intended to discredit both as barbarians. Here in *Recuerdos*, in an opposite rhetorical move, Sarmiento identifies the gaucho and the Arab through a positive analogy: He is "pleased and gratified" that he is "a presumptive relative of Mohammed." This same kind of affective reversal, which positively romanticizes what in earlier texts was condemned, can also be appreciated in the *Recuerdos*'s treatment of American Indians (the Huarpes) and of the Spanish colonial past. In the *Facundo*, the latter is consistently damned as a time of fanaticism and backwardness, whereas in the *Recuerdos*, the fanaticism is distanced from provincial San Juan by projection onto the faraway Inquisition in the viceregal capital of Lima, Peru, while local backwardness is recast as a healthy and benevolent simplicity of customs.

3. The house of Alba is one of the most famous aristocratic families of Spain. The title of Duke of Alba has been in the family since the fifteenth century.

4. Sarmiento refers to the well-known character from the play *Le bourgeois gentilhomme* [The Bourgeois Gentleman] (1671) by the seventeenth-century French writer Molière. In the play, the comical M. Jourdan discovers that all along he has been speaking prose without knowing it, that is, "speaking" and not "writing," as in Sarmiento's incorrectly remembered, or purposefully revised, version.

5. Fray Justo de Santa María is the subject of Chapter 12.

6. As part of the religious reforms enacted by unitarian Governor Salvador María del Carril (see Note 2, Chapter 3), an 1823 decree ordered the closure of the convents of Saint Dominic and of Saint Agustin, as well as the Convent of La Merced. Sarmiento writes that the Convent of Saint Dominic was closed in 1825; perhaps he has in mind the year that Del Carril's *Carta de Mayo* [May Charter], a kind of provincial bill of rights, was approved. Shortly after the federalists gained control of the provincial government in 1827, they reversed a number of Del Carril's liberal reforms, reestablishing the ecclesiastical *fuero* and restoring the confiscated convents to their respective orders.

7. Saint Vincent Ferrer (ca. 1350–1419) was a missioner, born in Valencia, Spain. He joined the Dominican friars in 1367, and soon became a powerful preacher, especially among the Jews and the Moslems. In the papal schism that divided the church from 1378, he supported the Avignon claimant, but in 1416 withdrew his support. He was an apocalyptic preacher, and his sermons drew large crowds and inspired groups of penitents who followed him from place to place.

8. The Mazorca was a paramilitary group that formed part of the larger *So-*

ciedad Popular Restauradora [Popular Society of the Restoration], which first emerged in Buenos Aires in the period 1832–33 and was composed of ardent supporters of Rosas. The elite of the larger organization were members of the upper class, but the *mazorqueros* were recruited from the lower classes, and it was their job to physically intimidate, torture, and often murder members of the opposition, their preferred methods being slitting the throats of their victims or beheading them. They were the principal actors during the Terror unleashed in Buenos Aires by Rosas in 1840–41, as a response to serious challenges to his power that unfolded in 1839–41. The Mazorca was disbanded in 1846. For more on the Society, the Mazorca, and terrorism under Rosas, see John Lynch, *Argentine Dictator: Juan Manuel de Rosas, 1829–1852* (Oxford: Clarendon Press, 1981), 201–46.

—Camila O'Gorman (1823–1848) was a young woman of the Buenos Aires elite who fell in love with a priest. The two of them fled northward and lived together for a while on the western border of the littoral province of Corrientes. Recognized, they were arrested and taken back to Buenos Aires, where they were executed for creating a public scandal. Camila was in an advanced stage of pregnancy when she was put to death. Not only was her treatment at the hands of the Rosista state denounced by the opposition in exile, but her story became an enduring part of national culture, retold by liberals to demonize Rosas, and more recently by feminist filmmaker María Luisa Bemberg. Her well-known film *Camila*, which opened in Buenos Aires theatres in 1984, was clearly meant to suggest historical antecedents to the routine practice of state-sponsored violence against women's bodies, and more generally against all expressions of freedom and nonconformity during Argentina's recent military dictatorship, which lasted from 1976 to 1983.

9. José Gaspar Rodríguez de Francia (1766–1840). Dictator of Paraguay from 1814 until his death, in 1840. Established a rule of political and economic autarchy, prohibiting foreign trade and suppressing individual liberties. He nationalized all rural property, industry, and commerce. Presiding over an absolutist paternalist state, Francia quadrupled Paraguay's national revenue, diversified its agricultural production, and is said to have eliminated unemployment and illiteracy. His policies were anathema to both liberals and free-trade capitalists, and consequently he joined liberalism's crowded pantheon of demonized historical figures.

—José G. de Artigas (1764–1850). Born in Montevideo into an upper-class family, Artigas was a defender of federalism and a major political and military player in the Río de la Plata during the second decade of the nineteenth century. Uruguayans consider him the founding father of their nation (fd. 1828), although he withdrew from political life in 1820 and opposed the separation of the Banda Oriental (an earlier name for Uruguay) from the United Provinces of the River

Plate. Argentine liberals of the nineteenth and twentieth centuries, however, have traditionally demonized Artigas. Sarmiento considered him a barbarian caudillo, placing him squarely in the federalist tradition of Facundo Quiroga, Estanislao López, and even Rosas. However, unlike these men, rich *estancieros* who mobilized the rural masses but did not want to empower them, Artigas is considered by many to have "sought full political participation for the lower classes," to have opposed the concentration of land by powerful *estancieros*, and to have pursued an egalitarian racial policy of inclusion. Nicolas Shumway writes that Artigas was "the first to articulate basic notions of Argentine populism," and the "first major political leader to recognize the dangers free trade posed for South America's fledgling industries." See Shumway's useful discussion of Artigas in *The Invention of Argentina* (Berkeley: University of California Press, 1991), 52–67.

10. This is probably José Santos Ramírez, identified in Note 3, "To My Compatriots Only."

11. Jean de La Bruyère (1645–1696). French satirist and moralist, best known for *Les Caractères de Théophraste traduits du grec avec Les Caractères ou les moeurs de ce siècle* [The Characters, or the Manners of the Age] (1688). Sarmiento quotes the entire passage corresponding to 2(1) from the section entitled "Du souverain ou de la République" [The Sovereign or the Republic].

12. St. Thomas Acquinas (Italy, c. 1225–1274). Canonized in the fourteenth century and named a doctor of the church in the sixteenth, Acquinas was the great systematizer of medieval western Christian theology. A member of the Dominican order, he taught, preached, and wrote voluminously. His most famous works are the *Summa contra Gentiles* (1259–73) and the *Summa theologica* (1266–73). In 1879 Pope Leo XIII proclaimed Aquinas's scholastic system the official philosophy of the Catholic Church.

—Duns Scotius, or John Duns Scotus (1266–1308). A Scottish scholastic theologian who adapted Aristotelian thought to Christian theology but who opposed the theological thinking associated with Acquinas. A Franciscan, he was known as the "Subtle Doctor."

13. Esteco was a town founded by seditious soldiers in what was to become the province of Salta in Argentina's extreme northwest. Legally recognized in 1567, it was destroyed by an earthquake on September 13, 1692.

14. It is no coincidence that the detail used to describe Doña Antonia's jewels and clothing is reminiscent of the genre of fashion reportage. In their early writings from within Rosas's Argentina, Sarmiento, in *El Zonda* of San Juan, and certain of his liberal contemporaries in Buenos Aires, in the journal *La Moda* (1837–38), cultivated the prose of the fashion review, in part as a subterfuge to speak publicly about politics without appearing to do so. For a discussion of this strategic feminization of discourse, see Francine Masiello, *Between Civilization*

and Barbarism: Women, Nation, and Literary Culture in Modern Argentina (Lincoln: University of Nebraska Press, 1992), 23–27.

15. Already in the *Facundo* of 1845, Sarmiento had briefly criticized slavery as an economic institution inimical to the advancement of capitalism and the social well-being of Argentina. Throughout his long career, he would never really abandon this position, articulated in 1776 as a general principle in Adam Smith's classic defense of laissez-faire capitalism *Inquiry into the Nature and Causes of the Wealth of Nations*. The reactionary romantization of slavery in this passage of *Recuerdos* is exceptional in Sarmiento's writing, but it is consistent with the equally mild treatment that Spanish colonial life receives throughout this book, in comparison to its usual derision elsewhere in Sarmiento's works. See Garrels, "Sobre indios, afroamericanos y los racismos de Sarmiento," 99–113.

16. *"Restaurador de las leyes"* and *"Héroe del Desierto"* were two of the several titles of the dictator Rosas. Both of his governments (December 1829–December 1832, and April 1835– 1852) were preceded by periods of social disorder, and in both cases, he presented himself as the one leader capable of restoring order and the rule of law. He received the second title of *"Héroe"* or *"Conquistador"* of the "Desert" (that is, Indian territory) as a result of his Campaign of the Desert, which he had begun planning during his first term in office. In January of 1833, no longer governor but newly appointed Commander General of the Countryside and Chief of the Left Division of the National Army, Rosas set out to secure and expand the frontier, through the continuation of his earlier policy of making alliances with friendly Indians but now also waging war against hostile ones. In 1830, only a third of what is now the province of Buenos Aires was owned or legally occupied, but in one year of military operations (1833–34), Rosas "had effectively added to Buenos Aires an area extending 100 leagues west to the Andes and south beyond the Río Negro, thousands of square miles in all" (Lynch, *Argentine Dictator,* 17, 54). This, of course, was a boon to the expanding *estancia* economy, which by 1830 had reached "the limits of profitable expansion" (ibid., 51). On Rosas and his complex dealings with the Indians (a mixture of alliances and negotiated peace, gifts and government subsidies, and all-out war), see Note 36, Chapter 10, as well as Lynch, *Argentine Dictator,* 17–20, 23–26, 29–31, 35, 51–56, 59.

17. Richard Cobden (1804–65). A British politician who had made a fortune as a calico printer, Cobden was also one of the major figures in the Manchester School, a group of economists who advocated free trade and minimal intervention by the state in economic matters. Sarmiento greatly admired Cobden for his advocacy of free trade, and even purchased a reproduction of his portrait in Manchester, when he visited the city in August 1847.

—On Lamartine, see Note 2, Chapter 4.

—Louis Adolphe Thiers (1797–1877). Center-left French statesman, journalist, and historian, who became first president (1871–73) of the Third Republic. His historical works include a ten-volume *Histoire de la révolution française* [History of the French Revolution]. Thiers was one of the principal political figures during the July Monarchy (1830–48). He served as government minister until 1840, when he was replaced by his rival Guizot, and between 1840 and the Revolution of 1848, Thiers remained in the opposition. In 1843, on a mission sponsored by the government in Montevideo, the unitarian Florencio Varela visited Thiers in Paris and persuaded him to attack Guizot's policy of nonintervention in the River Plate. On May 29, 1844, Thiers delivered a speech in the French Chamber of Deputies claiming that Rosas had failed to respect the Mackau Treaty, which in 1840 had ended the two-year French blockade of the port of Buenos Aires. Thiers reasoned that therefore France should intervene on behalf of the Argentine unitarians exiled in Montevideo. His rival Guizot responded two days later that the opposition had exaggerated its charges against Rosas, and that Rosas had respected the treaty. (However, in September of 1845, the French, in conjunction with the British, imposed another blockade on Buenos Aires, and in November, they launched a joint expedition up the River Paraná to allow direct trade with the littoral provinces. Neither venture proved effective.) In September of 1846, when Sarmiento visited Paris, he was taken to meet Thiers, who asked after Varela. Sarmiento writes in the chapter "Paris," in his *Viajes,* that Thiers listened with great interest to what he had to say about the River Plate: "the precise words in French came easily to me." When Sarmiento started to leave, Thiers asked him to stay longer: "after so much suffering I had the pleasure, so important for men who are just beginning and who lack prestige, to see myself encouraged, approved of, applauded by one of the foremost intellectuals in the world." *Viajes,* 109.

—François Guizot (1787–1874). Leader of the conservative constitutional monarchists during the July Monarchy in France, and from 1840 foreign minister and the government's real, if not official, policy maker in foreign affairs. A prolific historian like his rival Thiers, he wrote such works as the three-volume *Histoire de la civilisation en Europe* [General History of Civilization in Europe], and the five-volume *Histoire de la civilisation en France* [The History of Civilization in France]. In the Introduction to the *Facundo,* Sarmiento criticizes Guizot for his refusal to allow the French residents of Montevideo to fight against Rosas with the exiled unitarians (*Facundo o civilización y barbarie* [Caracas: Biblioteca Ayacucho, 1977], 11–12). On Sarmiento's first trip to Paris, in 1846, he interviewed Guizot, as he did Thiers. From 1832 to '37, Guizot had been minister of education, and in his interview with Sarmiento, he spoke with him about primary education and offered him the cooperation of the French government to fulfill his mission, which was to report on foreign public education systems to the government of Chile.

—"Absolute power" is a reference to the *"suma del poder"* (absolute or dictatorial power) that Rosas demanded (and received) from the Buenos Aires legislature as a condition for accepting the governorship in 1835.

CHAPTER 8: THE OROS

1. The Great Captain (*el Gran Capitán*) refers to Gonzalo Fernández de Córdoba (1453–1515), commander of the Spanish armies against the French in Italy (1502–1504), who succeeded in establishing Spanish dominion over the realm of Naples.

2. Near the end of his life, Sarmiento compiled a list, titled "Los emigrados," of eminent Argentineans who went into exile at some point during the Rosas dictatorship. In his entry on Juan Apóstol Martínez, he wrote:

From Santa Fe. General in the War of Independence. Turbulent military officer with a unique character. San Martín said he was a rabid dog whom it was necessary to keep tied up until the day of combat. But if in the garrison he was unbearable, on the battlefield he knew no rival, famous guerrilla, he has performed feats that surpass all consideration. The very eccentricity of his character gave him the bravery of a madman. [Translation mine.]

Sarmiento goes on to say that Martínez's military career began in 1806 in the local defense of Buenos Aires (which successfully ended the British occupation of the port city that had lasted from June 27 to August 12). Martínez died, between 1839 and '40, when he returned from exile to Argentina to fight in the armed resistance against Rosas. Domingo Faustino Sarmiento, "Los emigrados," *Obras completas,* XIV (San Justo, Buenos Aires: Universidad Nacional de la Matanza, 2001), 264.

3. José de Oro's youthful extravagances, which Sarmiento describes in the first paragraph of this chapter, amount to the portrait of the young José as a gaucho priest, a figure that resonates with Sarmiento's earlier portraits of both the caudillo priest José Félix Aldao, in the brief biography that Sarmiento dedicated to him in early 1845, and the gaucho as typified in the *Facundo,* of the same year. José de Oro is a secular priest who loves weapons and who fights in the war of independence, who normally dresses like a *paisano* (see Fourth Editor's Footnote, Chapter 8, 49), who, like the *gaucho malo* described in Chapter II of the *Facundo,* is drawn to public dances and abducts young women (but, unlike the author's portraits of Aldao and Facundo, is merely wild but not licentious), and whose skill at taming horses matches that of the best roughrider and horse

tamer in the country, the dictator Juan Manuel de Rosas. However, in stark contrast to the criminalization of both Aldao and Facundo in their respective biographies, José de Oro, cast primarily as a mentor for the young Sarmiento, is portrayed here with indulgence and affection.

4. This chapter presents José de Oro as the young Sarmiento's "Teacher" par excellence, and the apprenticeship with him as one of the definitive experiences of the author's youth: "I emerged from his hands with my mind fully formed at the age of fifteen." In Sarmiento's autobiographical works, age fifteen is repeatedly privileged as an important milestone in his life. Among other things, it is narrated as the beginning of a new period of the author's existence, one in which he will have to do without teachers and instead rely on teaching himself. In *Recuerdos,* in the chapter "My Education," Sarmiento will describe how, at this point in his life, he began to search for the books that would allow him to learn on his own. In his earlier autobiography, *Mi defensa,* of 1843, Sarmiento had written that "From the early age of fifteen, I have been the head of my family. Father, mother, sisters, servants, everyone has been subordinate to me. . . . I have never recognized any other authority than my own, but this subversion is founded on justifiable reasons. From that age the responsibility for the subsistence of all my relatives has weighed upon my shoulders. . . ." (Translation mine). In *Obras de D.F. Sarmiento,* III (Buenos Aires: Félix Lajouane, 1885), 20–21.

5. See Note 17, Chapter 7.

6. Antonio de Nebrija (Spain, 1441–1552), author of the first grammar of a modern European language, the *Arte de la lengua castellana* [Art of The Castillian Language], published in 1492. In its famous prologue dedicated to Queen Isabel, Nebrija referred to "language as the companion of empire."

7. The Council of Trent (1545–63) was an ecclesiastical council that met to define and purify the dogma of the Catholic faith. The ideological centerpiece of the Counter-Reformation, the work of the council was a defensive measure to combat the spread of Protestantism and other religious beliefs competing with or seen to be threatening orthodox Catholicism. (Martin Luther had supposedly tacked his famous ninety-five dissenting theses on the castle church door of Wittenberg in 1517; his excommunication in 1520 marked the beginning of the Protestant Reformation.)

8. This newspaper article appeared on December 28, 1842, and is reproduced in Sarmiento, *Obras,* II.

9. The reconquest of Chile. Without openly declaring independence, an extraordinary town council (*cabildo abierto*) in Santiago de Chile followed the example of the earlier May revolution in Buenos Aires, and established a governing junta on September 18, 1810. From 1810 to 1814, though legally a part of the Spanish realm, Chile functioned with relative independence and had its own govern-

ment and instititutions. (This four-year period was later known as the *Patria vieja* [The Old Fatherland]). At the beginning of 1814, however, the Viceroy of Peru, considering that Chile had exceeded its authority, sent royalist forces that ultimately defeated the revolutionaries in the battle of Rancagua (October 1–2, 1814). The patriots' military leaders Bernardo O'Higgins and José Miguel Carrera fled across the Andes to Mendoza, in Argentina.

The month before, in September of 1814, San Martín, governor of Cuyo since August, had set up his headquarters in Mendoza, where he was undertaking the organization of the Army of the Andes with which to liberate—or *reconquer*—Chile from the royalists (see Note 5, Chapter 4). In February of 1816 Bernardo O'Higgins (1778–1842) joined San Martín in Mendoza, and O'Higgins quickly became San Martín's choice for future head of the Chilean government. Indeed, after the decisive battle of Maipú, in 1818, O'Higgins became Supreme Director of a sovereign Chile, a position he held until January, 1823, when he agreed, under pressure, to abdicate. He died in exile in Peru in 1842.

10. On Chacabuco, see Note 5, Chapter 4.

11. "In France, I was never able to get San Martín to discuss. . . ." Bearing a letter of recommendation from Juan Gregorio Las Heras, an Argentine general in the wars of independence who in the 1840s formed part of the exile community in Chile, Sarmiento was able to visit General San Martin (1778–1850) repeatedly during his stay in Paris in 1846. In part based on his discussions with San Martin, Sarmiento subsequently wrote a study on the general's fateful interview with Bolívar at Guayaquil, which, in order to be admitted as a member, he then read before the French Academy of History. This study was published both in France and in Chile in 1848.

Sarmiento writes about a visit with San Martín in the chapter entitled "Paris" in his *Viajes.* He begins by referring to the general as "the first and the most noble of the emigrés who have abandoned their native land" (118), alluding to San Martín's permanent relocation to Europe in 1822. However, he ends by portraying the general as a confused old man, no longer able to understand the Americas clearly. This is because in 1838, during the French blockade of Buenos Aires, San Martín had become a defender of Rosas, whom he considered a champion of Argentine sovereignty in the face of European aggression.

The Carreras. When, after the patriots' defeat at Rancagua (October 1814), José Miguel Carrera (1785–1821) and his two brothers fled to Mendoza, they refused to bow to the authority of San Martín. As a result, the brothers were disarmed and briefly imprisoned. Already bearing a strong grudge against his archrival O'Higgens, José Miguel, along with his brothers, spent his time in Argentina trying to raise a force with which to return to Santiago to regain his lost position as Supreme Director of the revolutionary government. At the age of twenty-six, José Miguel, son of a powerful landed and military family, had returned from Spain a veteran of the peninsular war, and had carried out a coup against the Congress in Santiago (November 15, 1811). He acted as Supreme Director, with interruptions, and carried out two more coups until 1814, when the Spaniards put an end to the *Patria vieja* (1810–14). Transformed into feared and bloody montoneros in Argentina, the Carreras were eventually captured and shot by formal order, José Miguel in 1821 and his two brothers, Luis and Juan José, earlier in 1818. In Chile, José Miguel Carrera is considered one of the major figures of the struggle for national independence.

    12. On Salvador M. del Carril, see Note 2, Chapter 3.

    13. On Del Carril's *Carta de Mayo,* see Note 8, Chapter 7.

    14. Women did not get the vote in Argentina until 1947, nor in Chile, until 1949.

    15. On the Battle of Las Leñas, see Videla, *Historia de San Juan* IV, 659, and Note 21 below.

    16. On the uprising of July 26, 1825, in San Juan, see Note 2, Chapter 3, and Note 21 below.

    17. On the December 1st Revolution, in Buenos Aires in 1828, and the fate of that city's unitarian party in 1829, see Note 1, Chapter 6.

    18. The revolution of which Sarmiento speaks refers to the anti-Rosas resistance between 1838 and the end of 1841, a period during which the dictator's regime was seriously challenged on multiple fronts. On March 28, 1838, the French began a naval blockade of Buenos Aires. Later that year, when Uruguayan caudillo Fructuoso Rivera overthrew President Manuel Oribe, Rosas's ally in the fledgling neighboring state, the French proceeded to form an alliance with Rosas's enemies within Montevideo. Historian John Lynch writes, "With the fall of Oribe and the intervention of France, thousands of *porteños* [residents of the city of Buenos Aires], especially the student population and the professional and educated youth of Buenos Aires, crossed to Montevideo, where they had a free press and an outlet for their politics and propaganda. By now, of the 30,000 inhabitants of Montevideo, 20,000 were Argentine *émigrés,* together with some French and Spaniards" (*Argentine Dictator,* 203). These *émigrés,* including the unitarian General Lavalle (see Note 1, Chapter 6), conspired with Rivera and the French to contribute to a three-pronged attack against the Rosas regime. Lavalle was supposed to disembark with troops at the port of Buenos Aires, at the same time that conspirators within the city, and disgruntled *estancieros* in the southern part of the province (whose economic interests had been particularly hurt by the blockade) would rise up to oppose the dictator. Things went awry, however. The urban conspiracy was infiltrated and suppressed in June of 1839, the rebellion of the South was defeated within five days of its inception on October 29, and in September of the same year, Lavalle chose not to disembark in Buenos Aires but to do so in Entre Ríos. (Lavalle's plan was to seek the support of dissident fac-

tions in the littoral and the interior. This he did with partial but short-lived success, as at least six provinces subsequently declared themselves against Rosas.) Almost a year went by before Lavalle and his troops finally entered the province of Buenos Aires, on August 5, 1840, and then, on September 5, in an action that still confounds historians, he retreated to the north, without ever having launched a direct attack against the port city and Rosas.

19. Sarmiento is referring to Carril's *Carta de Mayo.* See Note 6, Chapter 7.

20. On Laprida, see Note 2, Chapter 3.

21. The battle of Las Leñas. Governor del Carril was originally ousted from office, on July 26, by a conservative uprising known locally as the Revolution of 1825, of which Sarmiento's uncle José de Oro was one of the organizers. The deposed governor and a number of his unitarian supporters repaired to the city of Mendoza, governed by unitarians, to plan a return to power in San Juan. With an expeditionary force mobilized by the government of Mendoza, Del Carril advanced on San Juan, and in a place called Las Leñas to the immediate south of the city, he defeated the defending army in a battle on September 9, and was then reinstated as governor (see Note 2, Chapter 3).

—Regarding his abandoned "engineering studies," Sarmiento gives us more information in Chapter 15, "My Education." In 1825 he was briefly employed as an assistant and apprentice by the French engineer Victor Barreau, whose job it was to survey San Juan and draw up a map for the city.

22. *De la educación popular* [On Popular Education] is the title of a book that Sarmiento wrote and published in the Press of Julio Belín and Co., in Santiago in 1849. The book is based on the report he had submitted to the government of Chile the year before, outlining the findings of his state-sponsored mission to study the educational systems of Europe and the United States. The book was heavily influenced by the ideas of Horace Mann, whom Sarmiento visited in 1847 when Mann was secretary of the Massachusetts State Board of Education.

CHAPTER 9: FRAY JUSTO SANTA MARÍA DE ORO

1. Justo Santa María de Oro was born in 1772 and died the same year as his younger brother, José de Oro, in 1836. Cuyo remained subject to the captain-general of Chile until 1776; at that time, it was integrated into the new Viceroyalty of the River Plate. However, the pattern of ecclesiastical administration was different from that of the political. Horacio Videla writes that Cuyo was subordinated to the diocese of Santiago de Chile until 1809, at which time it was transferred to the diocese of Córdoba, in Argentina (*Historia de San Juan* III, 762). This latter administrative organization remained in place for a good two decades, and as a separate vicariate, San Juan enjoyed relative autonomy. It is unclear whether Sarmiento has in mind the political-administrative or the

ecclesiastical capital when he writes that Santiago was the capital of the provinces of Cuyo at the time that Justo was sent there to continue his studies.

2. See Note 9, Chapter 8.

3. On Laprida and the Congress of Tucumán, see Note 2, Chapter 3.

4. In 1828 Pope Leo XII had recommended that Fray Justo de Oro be made bishop *in partibus infidelium*, under the title of *Thaumaco* (a place in what was at the time part of European Turkey). In 1831 Gregory XVI replaced Leo XII as pope, and it was he who in 1834 ratified the creation of the bishopric, or episcopate, of Cuyo, with Justo de Oro at its head. Videla, *Historia de San Juan*, III, 762–73.

5. On Saint Vincent Ferrer, see Note 7, Chapter 7.

6. In 1767, the reform-minded Bourbon monarchy in Spain, as part of their attempt to increase the power of the state over the Church, expelled the Jesuits from America. Indeed, the Jesuits were expelled from the majority of Catholic countries between 1759 and 1768 but were reestablished as an order by Pope Pious VII in 1814. However, they did not return to Argentina until 1836, when they were invited by Rosas, who hoped they would prove themselves forces of order and actively support his regime. When they resisted turning their schools and churches into centers for pro-federalist propaganda, Rosas withdrew his support and expelled them once again from the province of Buenos Aires in 1843. By 1852, when Rosas fell from power, there were no Jesuits anywhere in Argentina. See Lynch, *Argentine Dictator*, 178.

7. Pierre Jean de Béranger (Paris, 1780–1857). French poet and songwriter, Bérenger wrote liberal and patriotic songs and produced some of the most effective propaganda to promote the Napoleonic legend.

—Nueva Granada, or New Granada, was originally the name given to a Vicerealm that was created in the Spanish colonies in the early eighteenth century and that included present day Colombia, Venezuela, Ecuador, Panama, and part of Peru and Brazil. In 1831, after the breakup of Bolívar's Republic of La Gran Colombia in 1830, the name Nueva Granada was resurrected for the new independent republic that, starting in 1858, would be renamed several times until, with the Consitution of 1886, it acquired its contemporary name of the Republic of Colombia. Thus, in 1850 when Sarmiento published *Recuerdos*, the country of Colombia was known by the name of Nueva Granada.

8. By this time the reader will have noticed that Sarmiento uses a number of direct quotations to construct the present chapter. The use of long quotes by other authors or even by himself, from others of his own texts, is characteristic of Sarmiento's writing. See Sylvia Molloy's persuasive explanation of her assertion that for Sarmiento, "[q]uoting lies at the origin of writing," in *At Face Value*, 30–35.

9. Sarmiento published an incomplete biography of Pedro Ignacio de Castro

y Barros (La Rioja, Arg., 1777-Chile, 1849) in *La Crónica,* Santiago de Chile, on May 13 and 27 and June 10, 1849. This is reproduced in Sarmiento's *Obras,* III. Castro Barros had emigrated to Montevideo in 1833 and then to Chile, in 1841, where he died eight years later.

10. Vitruvius was a Roman architect and engineer in 1 b.c. He was the author of a treatise *De Architectura,* which influenced neoclassicism in Europe and the Americas.

11. Manuel J. Quiroga Rosas was a contemporary of Sarmiento's who had studied in Buenos Aires and returned to his native San Juan with his head full of the ideas and his trunk full of the books with which the Young Generation of 1837 (Echeverría, Alberdi, Vicente Fidel López, Juan María Gutiérrez, etc.) had ardently communed until, one by one, they were forced into exile between the critical years of 1838 and 1840. Quiroga Rosas died young and in exile, in Santiago de Chile, in 1844.

—Here we have an example of Sarmiento quoting himself, except that, in this case, the modesty perhaps prescribed for such an act is protected by its insertion in another primary quote, so that Sarmiento is able to quote his deceased friend Quiroga Rosas in the act of quoting Sarmiento.

12. On Sarmiento's ideal of motherhood, see Elizabeth Garrels, "Sarmiento and the Woman Question: From 1839 to the *Facundo,*" in *Sarmiento, Author of a Nation,* ed. Tulio Halperín Donghi, Iván Jaksic, Gwen Kirkpatrick, and Francine Masiello (Berkeley: University of California Press, 1994), 272–93.

13. "Tancredo" is the madrigal "Il Combattimento di Tancredi e Clorinda," by the Italian Baroque composer Claudio Monteverdi (1567–1643). The "Tancredo," as it is often referred to in Spanish, was composed in 1624 and published in Monteverdi's eighth book of madrigals, in 1638.

CHAPTER 10: DOMINGO DE ORO

1. Simón Bolívar (1783–1830). Born in Caracas, the son of a wealthy plantation and slave-owning creole family of Venezuela, Bolívar is considered by many the greatest military leader of the wars of independence. Known as "The Liberator," he personally secured the independence of Venezuela, New Granada (Colombia), Quito (Ecuador), and Peru.

—Diego Portales (1793–1837), owner of a commercial house in the Chilean port of Valparaíso who became the real power behind the conservative political settlement of the 1830s that produced the Chilean Constitution of 1833 (which endured, ammended, until 1925) and that set the scene for three decades of conservative control of the Chilean presidency (1830–61). Never president himself, Portales served as minister of war and the interior for two brief periods (1830–31 and 1835 until his assassination in 1837 by dissident elements in the military).

Nonetheless his influence was crucial in defining the authoritarian elite order and strong presidentialist rule that characterized Chile during the long period of relative national stability under conservative rule.

—On Rosas, see Note 3, "To My Compatriots Only."

—On Facundo Quiroga, see Note 1, "To My Compatriots Only."

—José María Paz (1791–1854). Born to an elite family in Córdoba, Argentina, Paz began his long military career in the wars of independence. In 1829 he was named minister of war by the unitarian Lavalle briefly in control of Buenos Aires (see Note 1, Chapter 6), and placed in command of the unitarian armies in the Interior, which he successfully led until his capture in May, 1831. Escaping imprisonment in 1840, he fled to Uruguay to resume his part in the war against Rosas and in 1845 was asked to take charge of the armed resistance within Argentina. A year later, in 1846, he was defeated by the federalist governor of Corrientes (Urquiza) and fled Argentina, only to return after the fall of Rosas. Nonetheless, the prestige of his leadership in 1845 accounts for the great hope Sarmiento placed in him at the end of his *Facundo* of the same year. In the posthumous text "Los emigrados," Sarmiento called him "The General reputed to be the best strategist and the best student of military science in all of the Americas" ("Los emigrados," *Obras*, XIV, 267).

—General José Ballivián, a member of an elite family from La Paz, became president of Bolivia when in November of 1841, he defeated the Peruvian army headed by General Gamarra, then president of Peru, whose design was to annex its neighbor to the south. Ballivián was overthrown in December of 1847 and permanently banished from his country. He died in Rio de Janeiro in 1852. His presidency saw the creation of the country's first daily newspaper, *La Epoca*, which included articles by Argentine exiles, i.e., Domingo de Oro and Bartolomé Mitre, who had sought asylum in Bolivia.

2. Raphael (1483–1520), one of the greatest painters of the High Renaissance in Italy and widely imitated far into the nineteenth century.

—Emile Jean Horace Vernet (1789–1863), an immensely popular military painter in nineteenth-century France reputed to possess extraordinary artistic facility.

3. *Robert le Diable*, an opera in five acts by German composer Giacomo Meyerbeer (1791–1864), debuted in 1831 at the Paris Opéra, with a monumental set. Meyerbeer's first Parisian opera, an instant success, is said to have defined French Grand Opera for the rest of the nineteenth century. Indeed, a season without an opera by Meyerbeer became almost unthinkable in the major opera houses of Western Europe and the Americas up until the early twentieth century. In his *Viajes* (I, 1849), in the letter dated May 9, 1846, from Rouen, France, Sarmiento had written, "Who in America has not heard of the marvels of the opera *Robert the Devil*, by Mayerbeer [sic]?" (Sarmiento, *Viajes*, 91). That same

month, two weeks after arriving in Paris, Sarmiento bought himself a ticket to see this renowned opera. (Paul Verdevoye, "Notas Aclaratorias," in Sarmiento, *Viajes,* 435).

4. Estanislao López (1786–1838), became federalist governor of the littoral province of Santa Fé in 1818 and held power for the next twenty years until his death from tuberculosis. In 1831, along with the leaders of the other three littoral provinces, López signed the Federal Pact and declared war against the unitarians, who between February 1830, and May 1831, briefly controlled nine interior provinces. Upon General Paz's untimely capture, López, Quiroga, and Rosas formed a victorious triumverate of federalist caudillos. With the deaths of Quiroga in 1835 and López three years later, Rosas was able to consolidate his power over the entire country.

5. Corpus fiesta. An annual Catholic celebration in honor of the Eucharist, it takes place in June during the week after Trinity Sunday. One of the more important religious and popular festivals of the Catholic liturgical calendar, it was observed throughout the Spanish colonies and the fledgling nations that replaced them. In San Juan, Corpus (or Corpus Christi) involved a mass in the morning attended by the town's dignitaries, followed by a procession through the decorated streets of the city that brought together all the castes of society.

6. Mendizábal revolt. Occurring on January 9, 1820, this was the first revolt of the First Battalion of the Chasseurs of the Andes, that battalion of the Army of the Andes (see Note 5, Chapter 4) that San Martín had left quartered in San Juan. The revolt was led by Captain Mariano Mendizábal and had the support of a number of groups, among them the financially neglected soldiers and the conservative faction of the city's elite, to which the Oro family belonged. The revolt successfully overthrew San Juan's lieutenant governor of five years, José Ignacio de la Rosa (see Note 2, Chapter 3). Following the revolt, Mendizábal governed for two and a half months, during which time San Juan ceased to be subordinate to Mendoza, as the seat of the Intendancy of Cuyo, and became an autonomous province.

7. The second revolt of the No. 1 of Chasseurs of the Andes, led by his earlier military collaborator and now his rival, deposed Mendizábal in March. Meanwhile Domingo de Oro had gone to solicit the approval of Colonel Domingo Torres, San Martín's personal representative in Mendoza, of a pact to grant general amnesty to the rebels and recognition to the new government in San Jan, in exchange for the commutation of De la Rosa's death sentence and subsequent exile. Apparently, when Oro returned, he found a new governor in Mendizábal's place.

8. On Don José Miguel Carrera, see Note 11, Chapter 8.

9. Francisco Ramírez (1786–1821). As a lieutenant of Artigas (see Note 9, Chapter 7), he fought to expel the Spaniards from Entre Ríos and later, in 1817,

to defeat troops sent by the governing Directory in Buenos Aires. As governor of Entre Ríos, he had joined the League of the Free Peoples of the Littoral under Artigas, but broke with him, after he and López of Santa Fé (see Note 4 above) defeated Buenos Aires at the Battle of Cepeda in February, 1820, and forced the port city to accept the principle of federalism. Buenos Aires's defeat by Ramírez and López marked the collapse of a centralized national authority, which is referred to by Sarmiento in this book as the disaster of 1820.

10. Sir Henry Morgan, a famous seventeenth-century pirate on the Spanish Main.

11. Río IV refers to a battle that took place on the shores of the Cuarto River, near the village of Concepción, on July 8, 1821.

12. Colonel José María Pérez de Urdininea was a Bolivian officer who had participated in the revolt of the patriot Army of the North (see Note 3, Chapter 11) against its acting commander at a post called Arequito, in the Argentine province of Santa Fé, on January 9, 1820, the same day as the revolt of the No. 1 of Chasseurs of the Andes, in San Juan. The revolt in Arequito had left part of that force still in the Argentine Interior in August of 1821. Thus Urdininea was able to come to San Juan and quickly organize a local defense against Carrera, although ultimately the feared Chilean never attacked, and was soon after betrayed by his own officers, handed over to the authorities in Mendoza, and executed on September 4, 1821. The historian Videla reports that Carrera's left arm was sent to San Juan to be put on public display (*Historia de San Juan*, III, 590).

13. Possibly a Bolivian lieutenant named Manuel Rodríguez, who formed part of Urdininea's rapidly assembled defensive force in San Juan.

14. Duke d'Enghien. The French Duke d'Enghien (1772–1804), last of the house of Condé, a collateral branch of the royal house of Bourbon, was captured in Germany and executed by order of Napoleon, to weaken the possibility of a Bourbon restoration.

15. Pedro José Agrelo. A pro-independence journalist and political figure in the city of Buenos Aires, active during the decades of 1810 and 1820, Agrelo was an early member of the Patriotic Society founded in 1811, the author of an autobiographical text, director of the newspaper *El Independiente* (1816–17), and for a time of *The Gaceta de Buenos Aires* (which appeared between 1810 and 1821). In 1824 he became the first professor of political economy at the University of Buenos Aires, founded in 1821.

—All four littoral provinces (Corrientes, Entre Ríos, Sante Fé, and Buenos Aires) had similar terrains and shared a common cattle culture.

—Lucio N. Mansilla (1792–1871) served in the Army of the Andes from 1814 to 1820 and became governor of the littoral province of Entre Ríos (not Corrientes) between 1821 and 1824. A unitarian and supporter of Rivadavia, he became a federalist when he married Rosas's sister. He belonged to Rosas's intimate circle, serving him in important military and political positions, including that of chief of police. As commander of Rosas's army, he capituled to Urquiza after the Battle of Caseros in 1852.

16. Harun ar-Rashid. The fifth caliph of the 'Abbasid dynasty (786–809), Harun (766–809) ruled Islam from Baghdad at the height of its empire. His reign was marked by many revolts, and he is not remembered for his statesmanship but rather for the lavishness of his court, which was romanticized in *The Thousand and One Nights*, where Harun appears as a character in numerous tales. This collection of stories in Arabic, of uncertain date and presumed to be, in its origins, the work of many oral storytellers, received its first European translation—in French—in the early eighteenth century. This translation was subsequently added to, both in French and English, and the tales, also known as *The Arabian Nights*, were popular reading in Europe and the Americas in the nineteenth century.

17. On Bolívar, see Note 1 above. The Argentine legation arrived in Bolivia in October of 1825 to mend tensions that had arisen over Buenos Aires's disagreement with the *Libertador* over the recent constitution, in August, of that country as an independent nation, and to solicit Bolívar's support against the expansionist pretensions of Brazil.

—General Carlos María de Alvear (1789–1852). Like San Martín, the Argentine-born Alvear began his military career in Spain and in 1812 returned with him to Buenos Aires to participate in the revolutionary movement. He led the Buenos Aires army that forced Montevideo to capitulate in June 1814. Supreme Director in Buenos Aires (January–April, 1815), he later distinguished himself in the war against Brazil (1825–28).

18. Antonio José de Sucre (1775–1830). An official in the Venezuelan independence army from 1810, he became next in command under Bolívar in 1818. In 1824 he successfully led the patriot forces against the royalists in the Battle of Ayacucho in Peru, which ended the South American wars of independence.

—William Miller (1795–1861) was a British officer who became a commissioned captain in San Martín's Army of the Andes in 1817. He continued to serve in the patriot armies, reaching the rank of brigadier-general by 1823, and was rewarded for his military service in Peru with the post of governor of Potosí in 1825.

—General Mariano Necochea (1792–1849), an Argentine officer who distinguished himself under both San Martín and later Bolívar in the wars of independence.

—On Lavalle, see Note 1, Chapter 6.

—Colonel Isidoro Suárez (1797–1841), an Argentinean who fought in the independence campaigns in Chile and Peru and later in Argentina's war against Brazil. He died in exile in Uruguay.

—Colonel Juan Pascual Pringles (1795–1831), an Argentinean who fought under Bolívar and Sucre in the Battles of Junín and Ayacucho and who was killed in the Argentine civil wars by one of Juan Facundo Quiroga's officers.

19. On Facundo Quiroga, see Note 1, "To My Compatriots."

20. The Aldaos were three brothers who achieved considerable political and military power in the province (and city) of Mendoza, to the south of San Juan. The most famous, José Félix Aldao (1785–1845), about whom Sarmiento wrote and published a biography (see Note 3, Chapter 8), was a priest and chaplain in San Martín's Army of the Andes. Later, upon returning to Mendoza, he fought in the civil wars on the side of the liberals until 1828, when he allied himself with the federalist caudillo Facundo Quiroga. In 1832 he would become commander general in Mendoza, and in 1842, governor.

21. Here Sarmiento refers to Rivadavia's renunciation of the presidency of the nation on June 27, 1827. See Note 3, "To My Compatriots Only."

22. For Manuel Dorrego (1787–1829), see Note 1, Chapter 6, Note 35 below, and Note 7, Chapter 11.

23. Fructuoso Rivera (1788–1854) was twice president of Uruguay: 1830–1834 and 1839–43. See Note 18, Chapter 8.

24. December 1st refers to the December 1st Revolution of 1828. See Note 1, Chapter 6.

25. Plaza de la Victoria. Since the definitive establishment of the city of Buenos Aires in 1580, a large open space for a Plaza Mayor, to be flanked by a cabildo (home of the municipal council) and a cathedral, was designated for the site where the Plaza de Mayo now stands. In 1803 the plaza was divided into two mutually accessible plazas on an east/west longitudinal axis. In 1807 the western plaza was named the Plaza de la Victoria, and after independence the plaza to the east became known as 25 de Mayo. In 1884 the Plaza de la Victoria ceased to exist when the two plazas were rejoined to form today's Plaza de Mayo. The Plaza Mayor and its early nineteenth-century reincarnation functioned both as a marketplace and as the political and ceremonial center of Buenos Aires. Nearly all important public events, including executions, proclamations, parades, and celebrations, took place there.

—On Salvador M. del Carril, see Note 2, Chapter 3.

26. At the Battle of Puente de Márquez (April 1829), Rosas, with a militia of *estancia* workers and gauchos and in alliance with Estanislao López of Santa Fé (see Note 4 above), defeated the unitarian troops commanded by Lavalle (see Note 1, Chapter 6), thereby ending the latter's brief rule of Buenos Aires. Later that same year, Rosas became governor of the port city for the first time.

27. Pedro Ferré (1788–1867) was three times governor of Corrientes: 1824–1828, 1830–1833, and 1839–1842. He resisted Buenos Aires's monopoly of the

port and advocated opening the Paraná and Uruguay Rivers to trade, but did not break definitively with Rosas until 1839. In 1842 he was defeated by the Uruguayan Oribe (see Note 18, Chapter 8) and emigrated to Brazil, but later returned to fight with Urquiza against Rosas.

—Manuel Vicente Maza (1777–1839), a supporter of Rosas who in 1834 became the president of the chamber of representatives in Buenos Aires. He was assassinated by the *Mazorca* (see Note 8, Chapter 7) when his son was found to be conspiring against the dictator.

28. On Portales, see Note 1 above.

29. The *Gaceta Mercantil,* founded in 1823, became the most important newspaper published in Buenos Aires during the Rosas regime; it ceased publication the day that Rosas was defeated by Urquiza's army at the Battle of Caseros and boarded a British ship to begin his twenty-five-year exile in England—February 3, 1852. See Note 3, "To My Compatriots Only."

30. On General Mansilla, see Note 15 above; on Maza, Note 27 above.

31. On the Campaign of the South, also known as the Campaign of the Desert, see Note 16, Chapter 7.

32. Andrés Santa Cruz (1792–1865) was president of Bolivia from 1829 to 1839. In 1836 Santa Cruz united Bolivia and Peru in a new confederation, which Chile and Argentina both saw as too powerful a neighbor. First Chile and then the government of Buenos Aires declared war against Santa Cruz. The confederation was dissolved after a Chilean expedition, led by General Bulnes, defeated Santa Cruz at the Battle of Yungay, in Peru, on January 20, 1839.

33. José Martín Yanzón was federalist governor of San Juan between 1834 and 1836.

—Colonel Lorenzo Barcala (1795–1835) was a freed mulatto slave born in Mendoza who distinguished himself in the war against Brazil and later served under the unitarian General Paz in the city of Córdoba between 1829 and 1831. Captured by the federalists, he then served under Facundo Quiroga. After Facundo's death, Barcala retired to San Juan and conspired against Aldao, who controlled Mendoza. Sarmiento admired Barcala, and praised him in both the *Aldao* and the *Facundo.*

34. *La Puerta* was identified in the second edition of *Recuerdos,* by its Chilean editor Luis Montt, as a mining establishment belonging to Mariano Fragueiro. Fragueiro, an Argentinean from Córdoba, was one of approximately 10,000 Argentineans who emigrated to Chile during the Rosas regime.

35. San Nicolás. En 1820, after the Battle of Cepeda in February and the dissolution of all central national authority, Buenos Aires experienced a period of anarchy during which the victors at Cepeda (López and Ramírez; see Notes 4 and 9 above) tried to impose upon the chaotic province a government of their own choosing. The leaders in Buenos Aires called on the estancieros in the south

to organize rural militias in an attempt to reestablish order. It was at this time that Rosas organized his own laborers to form a regiment of 500 men for the defense of the province and the interests of property owners like himself. With this regiment he fought in two battles won by the forces of Buenos Aires, San Nicolás (in the north of Buenos Aires province on the border with Santa Fé) and Pavón, but by September, Rosas favored a negotiated peace with López and supported Martín Rodríguez for governor. On October 5, Rosas and his militias put down an uprising in the port city by supporters of Dorrego (who had recently been governor himself), and confirmed Rodríguez in power. His support for Rodríguez was short-lived, but when he returned to private life on his estancias, he had become a known name in politics and a power to be reckoned with. (For more on Rosas, see Note 3, "To My Compatriots Only.")

36. After the Campaign of the Desert, the Indians from whom Rosas had seized thousands of square kilometers of territory entered into treaties with him, whereby they became "friendly," promising not to enter the province of Buenos Aires without permission and agreeing to perform military service when asked. In exchange, each chief received, at regular intervals, a certain number of horses and a small allotment of provisions. On the other hand, Rosas had no mercy with "unfriendly" Indians, such as the Araucanians of Chilean origin, and in 1836 he had eighty of them, captured when they raided Bahía Blanca to the far south of the province on the Atlantic coast, brought to Buenos Aires, and executed in public.

37. Tiberius (42 B.C.–37 A.D.). Emperor of Rome from 14 to 37 A.D. and known for his inscrutability. Suffering a change in behavior at the end of his life, he was thought by many around him to have always been wicked but, through dissimulation, to have long succeeded in hiding this fact.

38. On La Bruyère, see Note 11, Chapter 7.

39. On General Ballivián, see Note 1 above. The "disorganizing" and "sad revolution" to which Sarmiento here refers was the presidency of Manuel Isidoro Belzú. The mestizo general who overthrew the white plutocrat Ballivián, Belzú himself became president of Bolivia from 1848 to 1855. He actively sought the support of the country's large Indian population by attacking the interests of the landowning elite. He also appealed to the urban artisans, hurt by Ballivián's free-trade policies, by limiting imports and putting restrictions on foreign merchants.

CHAPTER 11: THE HISTORIAN FUNES

1. Charles III, a member of the Bourbon royal family and an exponent of enlightened despotism, was king of Spain from 1759 until his death in 1788. His reforms included the establishment of free trade between multiple Spanish and

Spanish American ports, by a series of decrees from 1765 to 1778. He is also known for having expelled the Jesuits from all of Spain's realms in 1767.

2. Later in the chapter the reader learns that Dean Funes was wont to reproduce the words of other authors without citing sources.

3. Juan Bautista Bustos (1779–1830), a powerful rural property owner in Cordoba, supported the 1810 revolution and fought in Belgrano's Army of the North. He occupied the position of chief of the general staff in this army, when he was sent by the national government to Cordoba to protect its border with Santa Fe against forces loyal to Artigas. Upon arriving at Arequito, in Santa Fe, Bustos rebelled against the central government for using an army charged with defending the northern frontier against royalists to engage in civil wars. He then marched to Cordoba and became provincial governor, a position he held for eight years. An ardent defender of federalism, he fought against the unitarian General Paz in 1829 and was defeated. He then allied himself with Juan Facundo Quiroga and fought with him at the battle of La Tablada, in Cordoba, in June of 1829, in which Quiroga was defeated, also by General Paz. Bustos then retreated to Santa Fe, and died in 1830. In 1821 or 1822, the ten- or eleven-year-old Sarmiento had accompanied his father to the city of Cordoba, where his father had unsuccessfully tried to enroll him in the Seminary of Loreto.

4. Santiago Liniers (1753–1810). 1806 and 1807 each witnessed a separate British invasion of Buenos Aires, and each time the British were forced to capitulate by the colonial militia under the command of Santiago Liniers, a French naval officer in the service of the Spanish crown. As a result of the port city's successful resistance, its principal citizens elected Liniers viceroy to replace the former one, whose response to the invasion had been to flee to the interior city of Cordoba. Liniers proved a liberal viceroy (1807–9) but was shot as a counterrevolutionary in August 1810.

5. Juan Cruz Varela (1794–1839). Born in Buenos Aires, Varela received a doctorate of theology from the University of Cordoba in 1816. Back in Buenos Aires, he became a prominent unitarian, worked as a government official, and supported the centralist politics of Rivadavia. He emigrated to Montevideo shortly after Rosas's election as governor in July of 1829. Probably the most important Argentine neoclassical writer of the 1820s, he composed two tragedies based on classical themes, *Dido* (1823) and *Argia* (1824).

6. Manuel José Quintana (1772–1857). A Spanish neoclassical writer of poetry and prose, he was crowned "National Poet" by Queen Isabel II in 1833.

7. Martín Rodríguez, governor of the province of Buenos Aires from 1820 to 1824 See Note 35, Chapter 10.

—General Juan Gregorio de Las Heras was elected governor of Buenos Aires in 1824 and served in this position until Rivadavia became president of a short-lived centralized Argentine republic in February of 1826. Also see Note 11, Chapter 8.

—Bernardino Rivadavia (1780–1845), son of a rich colonial functionary, was secretary of war, government, and foreign relations under the first executive triumvirate that held power in Buenos Aires between September 1811, and October 1812. Like the triumverate, he espoused liberal economic and institutional reforms but held conservative social attitudes, strongly opposing the egalitarian and federalist ideas of Artigas (see Note 9, Chapter 7) and favoring a constitutional monarchy to govern the River Plate. Away in Europe between 1815 and 1821, he returned to Buenos Aires to become minister of government and foreign relations under Rodríguez, and once more began to institute a number of liberal enlightenment reforms. The most visible leader of the unitarians in the 1820s, he left the country after resigning from the national presidency in June 1827, and spent the rest of his life in exile. Also see Note 3, "To My Compatriots Only."

—Manuel Dorrego (1787–1828), son of a rich businessman of Buenos Aires, fought during the independence in the Army of the North. In 1816, he was exiled to the United States (where he remained until 1820) for his articles in the Buenos Aires press in favor of federalism and against the Directory's monarchist project. Upon his return, he was named governor of Buenos Aires (July–September 1820). In 1827 he again became governor of Buenos Aires, with the strong support of the popular sectors in both the city and the countryside. He was overthrown and executed by the unitarian General Lavalle in December of 1828. See Note 1 of Chapter 6, and Note 35 of Chapter 10.

8. A reference to the courts of law in both Buenos Aires and Montevideo.

9. Probably Edward Chitty (1804–1863), British legal reporter and author of several works on equity law.

—Sarmiento is referring here to Florencio Varela (1807–1848). Although a contemporary of the Generation of 1837, Florencio, along with his older brother, Juan Cruz Varela (see Note 5 above), was an *unitario* and a supporter of Rivadavia. He and his brother emigrated from Buenos Aires to Montevideo in 1829, and there Florencio became one of the most active political figures in the the anti-Rosas movement organized from abroad, founding, in 1845, the important daily *El comercio de la Plata* [The Commerce of La Plata], an explicitly anti-Rosas newspaper. At the time of his death, he had become probably the most respected journalist among the broad community of Argentine exiles and was seen by many as the likely opposition candidate to replace Rosas as leader of a new Argentine government upon the dictator's fall from power. He was assassinated in front of his house on March 20, 1848, and people were quick to define his murder as a political crime, instigated by Oribe and Rosas. It is to Varela's recent assassination that Sarmiento explicitly refers here.

10. Sarmiento refers here to the red insignia that people in Buenos Aires were

obligated to wear to show their loyalty to the Rosas regime. The insignia bore the words "Long live the federalists; death to the filthy unitarian savages." Red was the regime's official color, as opposed to light blue and green, which, associated with the unitarians, were prohibited for everything, from clothing to furniture to exterior house paint. From the time of the Terror of 1840–41 (see Note 8, Chapter 7) to the fall of Rosas in 1852, the entire city of Buenos Aires was apparently painted red.

11. Both Sarmiento and Andrés Bello (see Note 2, Chapter 17) advocated substituting the letter "i" for "y" when "y" functions as a vowel, in order to simplify the Spanish language's orthography and thus make it easier for people to learn to read and write.

12. Voltaire was the pseudonym of Francois-Marie Arouet (1694–1778), the famous enlightenment French writer known for his satirical wit and his liberal, rationalist, and anticlerical ideas. Considered anathema during much of the nineteenth century by conservative Catholics the world over, he cultivated all the literary genres. His short novels *Zadig* (1747) and *Candide* (1759) are still read today.

—Jean Le Rond d'Alembert (1717–83). French *Philosophe*, mathematician, and writer of the Enlightenment. He was Diderot's main coeditor of the *Encyclopédie* project between 1746 and 1758, but thereafter limited his commitment to the project to writing articles on mathematics and science. The first volume appeared in 1751 and the last in 1772.

—Denis Diderot (1713–1784). A French *Philosophe*, who between 1745 and 1772 served as chief editor of the *Encyclopédie*. This work became known throughout the western world as a radical compendium of enlightened thinking on the arts and sciences. At one point publication of the *Encyclopédie* was offically forbidden because of its materialist perspective, but Diderot remained in France and continued to publish it covertly. It eventually constituted seventeen volumes of text and eleven volumes of plates.

—Jean-Jacques Rousseau (1712–1778). Born in Geneva, Switzerland, Rousseau arrived in Paris at the age of thirty, where he became friends with Diderot and the other French Philosophes. Never an athiest like the Philosophes, he remained a Christian but espoused, in his enormously influential work *The Social Contract* (1762), a simple civil religion, focused not on the afterlife but on teaching individuals to be virtuous republican citizens in the here and now. He also wrote that true republican liberty would be based on the collective will of the people, though codified by an enlightened lawgiver. His proto-romantic novel *Julie: or, The New Eloise* (1761) was the most widely read of his works during his lifetime and was not the object of censorship and bookburning as were *The Social Contract* and his educational treatise *Émile* (1762). Rousseau was one of the most important transitional intellectuals bridging the Enlightenment and early romanticism. On *Émile*, see Note 6, Chapter 13.

—The French Jacobins. A club or society of radical bourgeois democrats during the French Revolution of 1789, which, under the leadership of Robespierre, was responsible for the Terror that began September 1793, and ended with the fall and execution of Robespierre in July 1794.

13. Chuquisaca. Sarmiento is referring to a preamble to political independence that occurred in May 1809, in Chuquisaca (one of the colonial names for the city known today as Sucre, capital of the department of Chuquisaca, Bolivia). Between 1776 and 1810, Alto Peru (today's Bolivia) formed part of the viceroyalty of the Río de la Plata. Within Chuquisaca's colonial bureaucracy composed of *peninsulares* (Spaniards born in Spain), conflict broke out over how to proceed in the power vacuum created by Ferdinand VII's imprisonment. The judges of the *audiencia* deposed the president-intendant and assumed his powers, while pledging their continued allegiance to Ferdinand. Although these men were not creoles, their action was supported by a small group of Argentine creoles, one of them Bernardo de Monteagudo (Tucumán,1785–1825), who then went on to agitate in the rest of Alto Peru. Two months later a much more radical junta, headed by a mestizo, was established in La Paz.

—Carlota Joaquina, sister of Ferdinand VII of Spain, had fled to Rio de Janeiro with her husband, Dom João, prince regent of Portugal, after Napoleon's invasion of Portugal in September 1807. From Brazil, following Ferdinand's imprisonment by the French in 1808 (see Note 8, Chapter 13), Carlota had offered to rule the suddenly orphaned Spanish colonies on her brother's behalf. A faction of creole businessmen and professionals in the Río de la Plata were drawn to her offer in the hope of establishing an enlightened constitutional monarchy. However, Carlota herself was an absolutist, and the monarchist project in the Río de la Plata failed for this and numerous other reasons.

14. The viceroyalties of the Río de la Plata and of Peru.

15. Sarmiento is referring to Franklin's letter, dated July 5, 1775, to his friend William Strahan, M. P., who was a printer, and not a lord. The letter can be found in Benjamin Franklin, *Writings*, ed. J. A. Leo Lemay (New York: Library of America, 1987), 4. The fact that the text mistakenly identifies Strahan as a lord is consistent with Sarmiento's documented habit of writing quickly and often citing from memory. However, the Spanish version of the English original is sufficiently accurate that it has been rendered here by reproducing Franklin's own words. Both the mistaken title of "Lord" and the addition of the final "e" to Strahan's name appear in the first and second Spanish editions, and are reproduced, without comment, in all the many other Spanish language editions consulted for the preparation of the present translation. However, without consulting the original handwritten manuscript of *Recuerdos*, which we, the translators, have not been able to do, we cannot be sure whether these particular errors are the fruit of the writer's pen or of the original typesetter's and proofreader's care-

lessness. These errors, nonetheless, belong to the text as it is commonly printed and read, and for this reason, they, as well as other errors of fact that standardly appear in the text, have been maintained in the translation (although an effort has been made to identify them in the notes). To do otherwise, that is, to "correct" them within the text, would be to falsify the historical and material reality of Sarmiento's text as one that circulates in published form. Finally, the editor would like to take this opportunity to thank Franklin scholar Leo Lemay for indicating to her the identity of the addressee of the letter to which Sarmiento is referring.

16. On Rosas's title "Hero of the Desert," see Note 16, Chapter 7.

17. On Martín Rodríguez, see Note 7 above and Note 35, Chapter 10.

18. The great man that Sarmiento is referring to is Bolívar, whose image as a military dictator made the government of Buenos Aires increasingly uncomfortable, especially after 1820, when the unitarians wished to promote civilian institutions rather than strong individual leaders and the use of force. Funes had accepted the position as agent of Bolívar in 1824, and shortly thereafter had been made the dean of the Cathedral of La Paz.

19. Juan García del Río (1794–1856). Born in Colombia and educated in Spain, García del Río was an important writer and diplomat who, when sent to London as General San Martín's envoy in 1822, became a close collaborator of Andrés Bello (see Note 2, Chapter 17). (García had begun his journalistic career in 1818 in Chile, while serving as Bernardo O'Higgins's minister of foreign relations.) In London, he and Bello were the principal writers for the important journals *Biblioteca Americana* [American Library] (1823) and *El Repertorio Americano* [The American Repertory] (1826–27). García del Río eventually returned to Chile where he was one of the directors of the newspaper *El Mercurio,* and where in 1842 he published the weekly magazine *Museo de Ambas Américas* [Museum of Both Americas], which at the time was highly praised by Sarmiento in three articles of his own.

20. Antonio de Capmany (1742–1813). A historian and philologist from Barcelona, Spain, Capmany was the author of the *Filosofía de la elocuencia* [Philosophy of Eloquence] (1777), which was reprinted several times in the nineteenth century and was influential in Chile, although less so than the *Lectures on Rhetoric* by the Scotsman Hugh Blair, which were translated into Spanish between 1798 and 1801, and, starting as early as the 1820s, used in Chilean secondary education throughout the nineteenth century.

21. Leandro Fernández de Moratín (1760–1828). Energetically defended the introduction of neoclassical comedy on the model of Molière in Spain. His most important original play of this type was *El sí de las niñas* [The Young Girls' Yes], which debuted in Madrid in 1806. He adapted Molière's *Le médicin malgré lui* for the Spanish stage as *El médico a palos,* which debuted in Barcelona on December

5, 1814, where Moratín had fled from Madrid, via Valencia, out of fear of reprisals for his support of the French invasion and his service to the occupying government of Joseph Bonaparte. An *afrancesado* (supporter both of Enlightenment reforms on the French model and later of French intervention), he had been protected and promoted by influential liberal reformers Jovellanos and Floridablanca during the period of Charles III and then by Godoy under Charles IV. When "El médico a palos" was presented in Barcelona at the end of 1814, Ferdinand VII had already been restored to the Spanish throne (March 1814), and the Spanish Inquisition, the target of nationalist liberals and *afrancesados* alike, had been reestablished (July 1814) after being suppressed (December 1808), under the French occupation.

—On Molière, see Note 4, Chapter 7.

22. Bishop Henri Grégoire (1750–1831) was a French revolutionary who was constitutional bishop of Blois until 1814 when, on the eve of the French Restoration (1815–30), he was forced to retire as bishop due to his liberal ideas. The polemic between Grégoire and Funes was published in Paris in 1822.

—Bartolomé de Las Casas (1474–1566). A Spanish priest who arrived in the New World in 1502 and spent the rest of his long life championing the indigenous peoples of America and denouncing the abuses of Spanish colonization.

23. On Bolivar and Sucre, see Chapter 10, Notes 1 and 18, respectively.

24. On Rivadavia, see Note 7 above.

—Pierre Claude François Daunou (1761–1840). Ordained a priest in 1787, Daunou was an enthusiastic supporter of the French Revolution of 1789 and was associated with the Girondists. During the Restoration (1815–30), he lost his post as archivist of the Empire, but regained that position under the July Monarchy. From 1819 to 1830 he held the chair of history and ethics at the Collège de France and was famous for his lectures. The original title of the book Funes translated was *Essai sur les garanties individuelles que reclame l'état actuel de la societé.*

25. Marie Joseph, Marquis de Lafayette (1757–1834). A French aristocrat, he was commissioned as a major general by the Continental Congress and fought in the North American Revolution. In the French Revolution of 1789, he was made commander of the National Guard and later of the army of the center, but he opposed the Jacobins (see Note 12 above), and fled France in August of 1792 after trying to persuade his army to march on Paris. During the July Revolution of 1830, he led the moderates.

—Jeremy Benthan (1748–1832). Famous British utilitarian philosopher, jurist, and political theorist.

26. Mariano Moreno (1778–1811) was a secretary of the patriot junta proclaimed on May 25, 1810, in Buenos Aires, and led the radical faction within the revolutionary leadership. In the pages of the junta's official newspaper, *Gaceta*

de Buenos Aires (see Note 15, Chapter 10), of which he was director, he serially published his own translation of Rousseau's *Social Contract,* and although he left out the parts on religion, this still upset the conservatives (see Note 11 above). When conservative provincial deputies were admitted to the junta, Moreno resigned and accepted a diplomatic mission to England. He died en route in March 1811.

CHAPTER 12: THE BISHOP OF CUYO

1. Sarmiento had been interested in the southernmost region of South America since his arrival in Chile in the early 1840s, and in 1842 had published a series of unsigned articles in the daily newspaper *El Progreso,* in which he argued that it was in Chile's interest to occupy the Straits before another European or American power did so. He also emphasized the need for Chile to colonize the southern region and to undertake the exploitation of its natural resources.

In 1847 the Argentine government of Rosas claimed sovereignty over the Straits of Magellan, even though Chile had maintained a fort and a penal colony there since 1843. On March 11, 1849, Sarmiento inaugurated a series of articles in his journal *La Crónica* in which he defended Chile's right to ownership of the Straits and attacked Argentina's claims. This gave the Rosas government an opportunity to brand him a traitor to his country.

—The *adelantado* Sarmiento to whom the autobiographer refers is Pedro Sarmiento de Gamboa, who attempted to found a Spanish colony in the Straits during the sixteenth century.

2. This chapter, about this "most modest" individual who was Sarmiento's paternal uncle, repeatedly finds ways to express, albeit discreetly, the nephew's disappointment in the second bishop of Cuyo. A later reference to the bishop in *Recuerdos,* found in Chapter 16, relates how in November of 1840, when the imprisoned Sarmiento was almost killed by a mob, the "poor old man" had such an attack of fright upon learning that his nephew's life was in danger that he became physically incapable of heeding his nephew's urgent request that he come at once and try to save him with the authority of his presence. Verdevoye writes that José Manuel Eufrasio, who became bishop in 1837, was a federalist in good standing with the Rosas regime. He swore allegiance to Rosas in the presence of the provincial governor Benavides in 1840, and in 1841 sent the dictator a letter in which he congratulated him on his victories over "the revolting horde of the savage unitarians," signing off as a "friend of Your Excellency, and the person most loyal to the sacred cause of the Federation." Paul Verdevoye, *Educar y escribir,* 27.

3. On Castro Barros and the rebellion against the Holy See, see Chapter 9.

4. On Bernardo O'Higgins, see Note 9, Chapter 8.

CHAPTER 13: THE STORY OF MY MOTHER

1. On Lamartine and his *Confidences,* see Note 2, Chapter 4.

2. Sarmiento includes a detailed description of his ascent to the mouth of the crater of Vesuvius, in March of 1847, in the chapter "Roma," in his *Viajes.* See Note 7, Chapter 5.

3. The boarding school of Santa Rosa was founded by Sarmiento in San Juan in July 1839. Sarmiento was the school's director until he was ordered to leave the province by the authorities in November 1840; his school, however, continued to operate until around August 1841, when it was closed. In 1851, Benavides, governor of San Juan, ordered the school reopened with a new director and teaching staff, but there was no Colegio de Santa Rosa in March of 1847, when Sarmiento bought a requiem Mass in Rome to be sung in his mother's honor by his former pupils. Many if not most of these pupils would probably still have been living in San Juan and presumably could have been persuaded to sing at his mother's funeral had there been one at that time. Here in *Recuerdos* at the conclusion of Chapter 9, Sarmiento discusses the Colegio and remembers his students singing the "Tancredo" to him in prison in 1840.

4. Actually, shortly after Sarmiento's marriage to Benita Martínez Pastoriza in May of 1848, his mother traveled to Chile, accompanied by the author's sixteen-year-old illegitimate daughter, Ana Faustina, whom she had reared since the child's infancy. The two of them came to live with Sarmiento and his wife and adopted son, Dominguito, in the comfortable house on the outskirts of Santiago left the wife by her deceased first husband.

5. Fray Benito Jerónimo Feijóo (1676–1764), a Spanish Benedictine monk and a prolific rationalist critic of society's foibles. He wrote abundant articles attacking superstition, prejudice, and false religious beliefs, and disseminating information about contemporary European science and philosophy. Always remaining within the bounds of orthodoxy (i.e., he criticized both Voltaire and Rousseau), his writings nonetheless generated fierce opposition (and energetic praise) within Spain; for example, when the Inquisition opened an investigation into his writings, these were publicly defended by the Spanish monarch Ferdinand VI. Feijóo's articles were published in two multivolume series, *El teatro crítico* (1727–39) and *Cartas eruditas y curiosas* (1742–60).

6. *Emile.* Sarmiento refers to the novel by Jean Jacques Rousseau (1712–1778) *Emile ou de l'education,* first published in Amsterdam in 1758. This novel, which presents Rousseau's notion of the ideal citizen and a program for educating the male child in accordance with nature and by tapping his natural susceptibility to religion and to God, exercised an enormous influence on pedagogical methods worldwide. However, it was ordered burned by the French parliament and caused Rousseau to leave France to avoid arrest. Rousseau was considered dan-

gerously radical by the Catholic Church and, in general, by conservatives in the Hispanic world; this explains why the priest Castro might have hidden his copy of *Emile* under his cassock. For more on Rousseau, see Note 12, Chapter 11.

7. Las Bruscas was a prison in the province of Córdoba. José María de Castro Hurtado (1776–1820) was banished from San Juan in 1814 because of his prorealist ardor but was allowed to return in 1817.

8. Ferdinand VII of Spain, "the Desired," was absolutist king of Spain from 1814 until his death in 1833. In March of 1808, widespread opposition to his father, Charles IV, and to the pro-French prime minister Manuel de Godoy forced the old king to abdicate in favor of his son, who, because he had been seen as the alternative to the unpopular Godoy, was already called by many "the Desired" (*el deseado*). Ferdinand had to wait another six years to rule, however, because Napoleon, whose troops already occupied parts of northern Spain, refused to recognize either him or his father and instead placed his brother Joseph Bonaparte on the Spanish throne. Ferdinand spent the ensuing years under surveillance in France, during which time his epithet "the Desired" was used by the Spanish populace to invoke their absent king. Finally, in March of 1814, Ferdinand was allowed by Napoleon to return to Spain as monarch. In the meantime, the independence movement had begun in Spain's American colonies in 1810, and when Ferdinand finally assumed the Spanish throne, many creoles were unwilling to recognize him as their king or to continue as subjects of Spain. Not so the priest José Castro of San Juan, however, who remained an outspoken loyalist to the Spanish crown and was expelled from the province by the end of October in 1814. When Castro died a sick and ostracized man in 1820, Ferdinand the Desired was still on the Spanish throne and would remain there until his death thirteen years later. See also Note 13, Chapter 11.

9. On the battle of Chacabuco, see Note 5, Chapter 4.

10. Sarmiento is referring to the witness who answered a list of questions in the *probanza* of Juan Eugenio de Mallea, in 1570. This *probanza* is described here in Chapter 2, although curiously Venegas is not one of the surnames that Sarmiento reproduces there in his enumeration of the witnesses.

11. Don Pedro Godoy. Sarmiento is referring to the episode in 1842–43 in which the Chilean Godoy conducted a libelous campaign against him and prompted his writing *Mi defensa*. See Part III of the editor's "Introduction."

12. Cincinnatus (5 B.C.). A historical figure of ancient Rome but much embellished by tradition, he is remembered as a farmer who heeded the call of civic duty and accepted the reigns of power to defeat a foreign invasion and then relinquished power and returned to his farm when the danger was past.

—Aristides (5 B.C.), an Athenean general and statesman known by his contemporaries as Aristides the Just. Plutarch, whose *Lives* Sarmiento knew well, wrote on Aristides, praising him as an exemplum of justice as well as a man of ordinary birth and little fortune who never allowed himself to profit from public service and who died poor.

13. President Manuel Bulnes (1799–1866). A popular general from Concepción who had won an important military victory against Bolivia in the 1830s, Bulnes became Conservative president of Chile for two consecutive terms, between 1841 and 1851. His government was more conciliatory than either that of Portales had been or that of his successor, Manuel Montt, would be. As a consequence, the Liberal opposition was treated relatively well during most of his administration. Toward the end, however, in response to the emergence of a small but outspoken group of radical liberals, he declared a state of siege, shut down the opposition press, and arrested and exiled several prominent liberal figures.

CHAPTER 14: THE PARENTAL HOME

1. This house still stands and has had the status of a national monument since 1911. The original structure, along with later additions, including the rooms added by Sarmiento himself when he occupied the house as governor of San Juan in 1862, can be visited in person as well as virtually on the website maintained by the staff and curators of the Casa Natal de Sarmiento, Museo y Biblioteca [House of Sarmiento's Birth, Museum and Library] http://www.casa natalsarmiento.com.ar/defaulta.htm. August 17, 2004.

2. Sarmiento is referring to a female character in Eugene Sue's novel *Les Mystères de Paris* [The Mysteries of Paris], first published serially in the *Journal des Débats* [Journal of Discussions] from June 9, 1842, to October 15, 1843. Immensely popular, it is considered perhaps the most widely read novel of the nineteenth century. Only five months after its final installment in the French newspaper, Sarmiento published several translated chapters of the novel in *El Progreso* of Santiago (On *El Progreso*, see Note 62, Introduction). Serving as an indication of how quickly bestseller French novels could be translated into Spanish and published in Latin America, a full Spanish translation of *Les Mystères* was published in eighteen installments for special subscribers by the press of *El Mercurio* [The Mercury], of Valparaíso, Chile, between August 1844, and June 1845. (*El Mercurio*, which was founded in 1827 as a biweekly and then became a daily publication two years later, preceded *El Progreso* as the first daily newspaper in Chile; in addition to the newspaper, the press of *El Mercurio* published books, pamphlets, etc.)

3. The auto de fe of Logroño, in northern Spain, took place in 1610, during the most intense period of witch hunts in Europe (1580–1630). Contrary to perceptions common from the eighteenth through the twentieth centuries, witch prosecutions and executions occurred far less often in Spain, Portugal, and southern Italy than in western Germany, the Low Countries, France, northern

Italy, and Switzerland, where three-fourths of the European witch hunts took place. In fact, recent scholars credit the Inquisition with actually having restrained and reduced the occurrence of witch trials in the areas where its influence was strong, and view the trial in Logroño as an exception rather than the rule in Spain.

Nonetheless, in 1811, when the pro-French Spanish writer Leandro Fernández Moratín (see Note 21, Chapter 11) annotated and published a second edition of the *Relación* of this auto de fe, originally published in Spain in 1611, the reedited text was intended as a contribution to the lively contemporary anti-Inquisition propaganda generated within Spain by both enlightened Catholics and active supporters of the Napoleonic occupation (1808–1814). In 1811, even though the French controlled the royal court in Madrid and had abolished the Inquisition, Moratín still published his annotated edition under the pseudonym Ginés de Posadilla. Given the subsequent history of the Spanish Inquisition (briefly reestablished during the periods of 1814–1820 and 1823–1834), the Logroño trial proceedings were again republished in 1812, 1813, and 1820, and then once more as part of Moratín's works included in Rivadeneira's *Biblioteca de Autores Españoles* [Library of Spanish Authors], in 1846. Since the Inquisition had been formally and definitively suppressed in Argentina by measures passed in Buenos Aires in 1813, and since many of the ideas and publications of eighteenth- and nineteenth-century Spanish liberals were approvingly received by creole liberals in Hispanic America before, during, and after the American independence movements, one can be fairly confident that Sarmiento knew about the Logroño trials as a result of the notoriety they had received from Moratín's publication. (See "Withcraft," *Encyclopaedia Britannica*, 2003. Encyclopaedia Britannica Online, available at <http://www.search.eb.com/eb/article?eu=115001>, accessed July 11, 2003; and René Andioc, "Las reediciones del Auto de fe de Logroño en vida de Moratín," available at <http://cervantesvirtual.com/serlet/SirveObras/05701668788545062987857/p0000001.htm#1>.

I have also consulted several Spanish-language websites on witches in Logroño for recent non-scholarly perceptions of the numbers of victims at the Logroño trials; these vary (from 6 to 12 executed), but they differ dramatically from Sarmiento's claim that hundreds were burned.

—Maryland. The first, second, and all subsequent editions of *Recuerdos* that I have consulted all say "Maryland," which makes no sense; whereas it would have made sense for them to say "Massachusetts." Whether the origin of "Maryland" in Sarmiento's text is due to his own carelessness or to that of his original typesetter and/or proofreader, I cannot say. This is one of several instances I have encountered in which an error in information or diction that appeared in the first edition has been routinely maintained in subsequent ones. In this particular case, I have chosen to respect the misnomer because it is characteristic of what I and others have referred to as the "factual unreliability" of Sarmiento's prose. Regarding errors in diction, in those extremely few cases where the existing Spanish editions have not provided me with any reasonably acceptable meaning, I have reconstructed the meaning that makes the most sense given the immediate context, even if I have had to ignore the exact wording of the original in order to do so.

4. Sir Walter Scott (1771–1832), prolific Scottish author of the historical novel. Until his death, his books were, along with those of James Fenimore Cooper, of the United States, the most widely read contemporary novels in the world. His titles include *Rob Roy* (1817), *Ivanhoe* (1819), and *Quentin Durward* (1823).

5. Bartolomé Esteban Murillo (1618–1682), of Andalucía, was the most popular religious painter of seventeenth-century Spain and its colonies, and his works were copied and imitated throughout the realm.

—Diego Rodríguez de Silva Velázquez (1599–1660). Born in Seville, he became court painter for Philip IV in Madrid at the young age of twenty-four. He would continue in this position and as a trusted member of the royal household until his death thirty-seven years later. A true connoisseur of the arts, Philip IV appreciated and encouraged Velázquez's artistic genius, and *Las Meninas* [The Maids of Honor] (ca. 1656), the painter's most radically innovative painting, which looked forward to nineteenth-century impressionism, was immediately considered his best work by his royal patrons. Despite the exceptional success of his career, he left behind few pupils or imitators, and, unlike Murillo, was not widely known beyond Spain until the beginning of the nineteenth century. He is now considered one of the masters of Western painting.

—Fernando Alvarez de Toledo, 3rd Duke of Alba (1508–1582), the most famous member of this Spanish aristocratic family titled in 1469. He led the army of Spain's Charles I to victory against the German Protestants at the Battle of Mühlberg in 1547, became Viceroy of Naples in 1556, and was governor general of the Netherlands between 1567 and 1573.

—On the Great Captain, see Note 1, Chapter 8.

—Hernán Cortés (1485–1547), famous Spanish captain who conquered the Aztec Empire of Mexico (1519–21).

6. Procesa Sarmiento (1818–1899), sister of Domingo. In Chile, where she lived during part of her brother's exile, she studied drawing with the French neoclassical painter Raymond Quinsac Monvoisin. On Monvoisin, see Note 16, "Genealogy."

7. Franklin Rawson (1819, San Juan–1871, Buenos Aires). A prolific portraitist and also a student of Monvoisin's, Rawson painted portraits in Chile of both Sarmiento (in 1845) and of Sarmiento's wife, Benita Martínez Pastoriza de Sarmiento. He also painted the historical canvas, *Salvamento operado en la Cordillera por el joven Sarmiento* [Rescue in the Andes by the Young Sarmiento],

on the theme of Sarmiento bringing aid in 1841 to Lamadrid's defeated troops in the Andes.

8. *Et vidi quod esset bonum* is Sarmiento's ironic variation on the biblical "And God saw that it was good," referring to God's satisfaction with his creation of the world at the beginning of Genesis (1:12).

CHAPTER 15: MY EDUCATION

1. On the School of the Fatherland (*Escuela de la Patria*), see Note 2, Chapter 3, on José Ignacio de la Rosa.

2. This is a reference to the story told in Daniel Defoe's novel *Robinson Crusoe*, originally published in 1719. This novel was a great favorite of Sarmiento's.

3. Blaise Pascal (1623–62), a famous writer, philosopher, scientist, and mathematician, whose contributions to mathematics include founding the modern theory of probability and contributing to the advance of differential calculus.

—André-Marie Ampère (1775–1836) was a French physicist and mathematician who in the 1820s produced a law of electromagnetism, known as Ampère's law. The basic unit of electric current, the ampere, is named after him, as well.

4. The School of Moral Sciences [Colegio de Ciencias Morales] had been in existence since 1823, when Rivadavia had changed the name of an existing secondary school and altered its curriculum, turning the new establishment into a university preparatory school that would not only serve the youth of Buenos Aires but would educate, with the help of government scholarships, select deserving youth of the provinces. This was the school for which the young Sarmiento was denied a scholarship in 1823 when the local competition, originally based on merit, was changed into a random draw by lots. The school was closed in late 1830.

—Felipe Arana, a wealthy *estanciero* of Buenos Aires, was an intransigent federalist and a close associate of Rosas. He held the post of minister of foreign relations in Rosas's government between 1835 and 1852.

5. Leonidas, King of Sparta (490–480 B.C.), who died defending the pass of Thermopylae in central Greece against the huge invading army of the Persian king Xerxes. After commanding the bulk of his troops to fall back, Leonidas, vastly outnumbered, resisted the Persians with his royal guard of 300 men, but in the end all perished. This resistance "against overwhelming odds" has become an emblem of Greek heroism and has been recalled throughout Western history as proof of the claim that "Spartans never surrendered." From "Leonidas," *Encyclopaedia Britannica Online,* available at http://www.search.eb.com/bol/topic?tmap=_id=119010000&tmap=_typ=dx&pm=1, accessed March 29, 2002.

6. Horatius Cocles was held up to generations of Romans as an example of dedication and quick thinking. According to legend, when in 509 B.C. an

Etruscan king attacked Rome, the Romans hid inside the city walls and counted on the walls and the Tiber River to protect them. "Horatius the one-eyed" was a soldier on guard at the single bridge over the river. When the enemy appeared and his fellow soldiers started to flee, Horatius convinced two of them to remain and destroy the wooden bridge while he stood alone to delay the advancing troops. After hesitating, the Etruscans attacked, and the bridge collapsed. Horatius jumped into the river, in full armor, and either drowned or survived, depending on the version consulted.

7. General Mariano Acha (1799–1841), a *porteño* officer in Lamadrid's unitarian army, entered the capital of San Juan with an advance column of about 500 men on August 13, 1841. Acha controlled the city for nine days, was then captured by the federalists, taken to Mendoza, and executed. On August 16, due to the superiority of the unitarian artillery, Acha's severely outnumbered troops defeated the combined federalist forces of Cuyo under the command of José Félix Aldao, at the Battle of Punta del Monte, in Angaco, close to the capital city. The battle is reputed to have been so bloody that the irrigation ditches filled with dead bodies, allowing the survivors to use them like bridges to cross from one side to the other.

8. Carita's revolution was an episode in the Revolution of 1825 in San Juan (see Note 21, Chapter 8). "Carita" was the nickname of a federalist sergeant who led a barracks uprising, freed the prisoners from the local jail, and issued an edict proclaiming that the May Charter would be burned in public and that the local theatre and café, denounced as gathering places where libertines could speak out against religion, would be closed at once.

9. Rudolf Ackermann was born in Germany but by 1810 was a successful publisher in London of books in English with colored prints. Between 1823 and 1828, in collaboration with a group of exiled liberal writers from Spain (including José Blanco White and José Joaquín de Mora) who in London were all close associates of Andrés Bello, Ackermann published a number of magazines and books in Spanish for the Spanish American market. Among these were the *Catechisms*, elementary books and often primers on such varied topics as commercial arithmetic, natural history, mythology, rhetoric, political economy, ancient history, modern history, astronomy, and algebra.

10. On Leonidas, see Note 5 above.

—Brutus was the name of at least two famous Romans: Lucius, a legendary figure who expelled the last Roman monarch and became one of the first two consuls of the Republic around 509 A.D., and Marcus, a Roman politician who conspired with Cassius to assassinate Caesar.

—On Aristides, see Note 12, Chapter 13.

—Marcus Furius Camillus (ca. 114–365 B.C.), a Roman politician and general who reputedly liberated Rome from the Gauls around 390 B.C.

—Harmodious. An Athenian youth who, with his lover Aristogiton, attempted to kill the tyrant Hippias and his brother Hipparchus. They managed to kill the brother but not the tyrant. Harmodius was killed on the spot, and Aristogiton was subsequently executed. The two would-be tyrannicides were made heroes of Athens after the expulsion of Hippias in 510 B.C.

—Epaminondas, born in Thebes, was considered one of the greatest military tacticians of ancient times. He defeated the Spartans at the battle of Leuctra in 371 B.C., dealing a severe blow to Spartan power.

11. William Paley (1743–1805), an English Anglican priest who wrote influential books on Christianity, ethics, and science, including *A View of the Evidence of Christianity* (1794) and *Natural Theology* (1802), a work that made a strong impression on Charles Darwin. "Paley, William," Encyclopaedia Britannica Online, available at http://www.search.eb.com/bol/topic?eu=59551&sctn=1&pm=1, accessed March 29, 2002.

—On Feijóo, see Note 5, Chapter 13.

12. On Castro Barros, see Note 9, Chapter 9.

13. Juan Antonio Llorente (1756–1823), a liberal Spanish priest and historian who sided with the Bonapartists in 1808 and worked with the occupying regime to close down the monastic orders. Upon the restoration of absolutism in Spain in 1814, he was forced into exile. From 1789 to 1801 he had been the secretary general of the Spanish Inquisition in Madrid, and during his exile in France he authored the *Historia de la Inquisición de España* [History of the Inquisition in Spain] (Paris, 1815–1817), which was translated into English and published in London in 1826. In 1818 he published his autobiography, *Noticia biográfica* [Brief Biographical Review], in Paris.

14. Juan A. Cascuberta (1798–1849) was, in Sarmiento's opinion, "the most notable dramatic actor that America has produced" (Sarmiento, "Los emigrados," *Obras*, XIV, 254). Born in Buenos Aires, Cascuberta established his acting career in Montevideo during the 1820s, arrived on the stage in Buenos Aires in 1830, where he reigned as the most celebrated and admired leading man until 1840. That year he abandoned Buenos Aires, never to return, and acted briefly on the stage in Córdoba until this city was occupied by a federalist army in December. Cascuberta then signed on as a regular foot soldier in the unitarian army of La Madrid and crossed the Andes into Chile with La Madrid's defeated troops after their resounding defeat in September 1841. Thus began the final Chilean period of Cascuberta's career (1841–49), spent touring various cities in Chile (Santiago, Valparaíso, Copiapó) and Peru (Lima, Arequipa, Tacna). His repertory included mostly famous neoclassical tragedies and comedies and romantic melodramas from Europe; his acting style particularly suited the French melodramas of Ducange, Dumas, and Hugo, which gained popularity in the federalist Buenos Aires of the 1830s.

15. On Paz in Córdoba, see Note 1, Chapter 10.

16. The *Revista Católica* was founded in Santiago de Chile in 1843 by the newly appointed Archbishop of Santiago, the ultramontane Rafael Valentín Valdivieso Zañartu. It was intended mainly for the clergy, its purpose being to unify the opinion of parish priests with respect to religion and their proper relationship to the State. Beyond the church hierarchy, its circulation was limited, but it was read and often reacted to by the more combative liberal press. Sarmiento, for one, sustained a spirited polemic with the *Revista* from December 1844, to February 1845, regarding whether or not women should be allowed to *read* the French writer Louis Aimé Martin's saccharine book *De la education des mères de famille* [On The Education of Mothers of Families] (1834).

17. Conyers Middleton (1683–1750), an English clergyman who took the rationalist and enlightened side in the numerous polemics he provoked, published a *Life of Cicero* in 1741.

18. The famous autobiography of the American statesman and scientist Benjamin Franklin (1706–90) was written off and on during the final eighteen years of the author's life. It was first published posthumously (1791) in a pirated French translation of Part I only; followed by an English version (1793) based on the French and expanded with information taken from a posthumous 1790 American condensation of all four parts. It was not until 1868 that all four parts, based on the original holograph, first appeared in English.

—Plutarch (circa 45–125 A.D.) wrote his *Parallel Lives,* in which he paired the biography of a famous Greek with that of a famous Roman, in Attic Greek. The *Lives* were rediscovered in the Renaissance and became enormously popular. The first Spanish translation appeared in 1491.

—Henry IV (1553–1610) became the first Bourbon monarch of France in 1589 toward the end of a long series of civil wars between the Roman Catholics and the Hugeunots that began in 1562. A Hugeunot himself when he acceded to the thrown, he was not able to enter Paris and put an end to the war until 1594. A year earlier he had abjured Protestantism, allegedly remarking that "Paris is well worth a Mass," but once in control, he established religious tolerance.

—Madame de Roland (1754–1793), an influential woman of letters whose important salon in Paris was a gathering place for the Girondists during the French Revolution. When the Girondist government was overthrown in early June 1793, her husband, a Girondist politician, fled to Rouen, and she was imprisoned. There she wrote her *Memoires,* which were published posthumously in 1795, the same year the Girondists were reinstated in the Convention and proclaimed "martyrs of liberty." Madame de Roland was guillotened on November 8, 1793. Sarmiento greatly admired her, and his writings refer to her *Memoires* on a number of occasions.

19. On Mignet's Franklin and Sarmiento's commissioned translation by Gutiérrez, see Note 5, Chapter 22.

20. This is the same "former benefactor" who handed Sarmiento's letter over to Rosas, and thus provoked the diplomatic reaction that Sarmiento cites, in his dedication "To My Compatriots Only," as prompting him to write *Recuerdos* in his own self-defense. See also Note 3, "To My Compatriots Only."

21. On José Ignacio de la Rosa, see Note 2, Chapter 3.

—Josephine de Beauharnais (1763–1814), whose first husband was guillotened during the Terror, became Napoleon's first wife in 1796, and was crowned Empress of France in 1804. Their divorce in 1810 was the first under the Napoleonic Code. Her two children from her first marriage both wrote memoirs, but she is not known to have done so, although letters exchanged between her and Napoleon have survived.

22. Edward Abbott was an Englishman who lived near the mine *La Colorada* (see Note 23 below) and who lent Sarmiento books to read in English.

23. Manto de los Cobos—and Punta Brava, mentioned further on—were other mines near the northern Chilean city of Copiapó. In Chañarcillo (also mentioned further on), in the same general area and the site of a spectacular silver discovery in 1832, Sarmiento was employed in the silver mine *La Colorada*, owned by General Nicolás Vega, under whom he had served in the Battle of Niquivil, in 1829. (Vega employed a number of exiled Argentineans.)

24. Franz Josef Gall (1758–1828), a German doctor who created the discipline of phrenology.

25. On Manuel Quiroga Rosas, see Note 11, Chapter 9.

26. Abel François Villemain (1790–1867). French politician and man of letters. While professor of French eloquence at the Sorbonne, he delivered a series of lectures on literature that were extremely influential on the French generation of 1830. These were published in five volumes as the *Cours de la litterature française* [Course on French Literature].

—August Wilhelm von Schlegel (1767–1845), one of the first German theoreticians of romanticism.

—Theodore Simon Jouffroy (1796–1842), a French philosopher, was an effective popularizer of other peoples' ideas and in 1835 published a *Cours de droit naturel* [Course in Natural Law] that was widely disseminated.

—Jean Louis Eugène Lerminier (1803–1857), who in his youth associated with the Saint-Simonians, abjured his liberalism in 1836. However, in 1828, he delivered a series of public lectures in Paris that were published the following year as the *Introduction générale à l'histoire du droit* [General Introduction to The History of Law]. This text was very influential in the Río de la Plata, as was the series of lectures he gave at the Collège de France in 1831, published the same year as the *Philosophie du droit* [Philosophy of Law].

—On Guizot, see Note 17, Chapter 7.

—Victor Cousin (1792–1867) delivered a set of enormously popular lectures on philosophy at the École Normale in Paris in 1828–29; after that Cousin dominated the field of French philosophy for the next twenty years. The 1828–29 lectures, published as the *Cours d'histoire de la philosophie moderne* [Course in the History of Modern Philosophy], were enthusiastically received by the Argentine Generation of 1837. Lecture X, on "Great Men," influenced Sarmiento in his writing of the *Facundo*.

—Alexis de Tocqueville (1805–1859) was the French author of *De la démocratie en Amérique* [Democracy in America], published in two volumes, in 1835 and 1840, respectively. Sarmiento greatly admired this book, and with his *Facundo*, aspired to do for South America what de Tocqueville had done for the United States.

—Pierre Leroux (1797–1871), son of an artisan, was briefly associated with the Saint-Simonians in Paris but broke with them in 1831. A romantic utopian socialist, he was a literary critic and a philosopher openly antagonistic to the positions of Victor Cousin. As a socialist thinker, he enjoyed considerable international popularity among his contemporaries.

—The *Revue Enciclopédique*, a periodical that started to appear in Paris in 1829, published the writings of Saint-Simonians and other utopian socialists. Beginning in 1832, Pierre Leroux (see above) was its co-director. This French journal exercised a strong influence on both *La Moda*, of Buenos Aires, and *El Zonda*, of San Juan.

—Charles Didier (1805–1864), largely forgotten today, was born in Geneva and arrived in Paris in 1830. Influenced by Saint-Simonianism, he authored novels and travel books.

27. Idalecio Cortínez received one of the local scholarships to study at the School of Moral Sciences in Buenos Aires. He practiced medicine upon his return to San Juan and settled in Coquimbo, Chile, when he went into exile.

—Antonio Aberastaín (1810–1861) was one of Sarmiento's closest friends. Recipient of a scholarship to study at the School of Moral Sciences in Buenos Aires, he trained as a lawyer and became Appeals Court judge in San Juan under Governor Benavides, but toward 1840 went into exile and relocated first in Salta, Argentina, and then in Copiapó, Chile. On December 30, 1860, in the midst of extreme local instability, he became governor of San Juan, but was put to death fifteen days later after the defeat of San Juan's troops by the joint forces of Mendoza and San Luis, whose governors refused to recognize Aberastaín's legitimacy in office.

—On Manuel Quiroga Rosas, see Note 11, Chapter 9.

—Dionisio Rodríguez also belonged to the group of close male friends with whom Sarmiento collaborated on a number of projects during his five years in

San Juan between 1835 and 1840. At the end of this period, Rodríguez, like the others, found his way to Chile.

28. On Aberastaín, see Note 27 above.

—Possibly Miguel Piñero, a lawyer from Córdoba, who died in Chile in 1846. In the second edition of the *Facundo* (1851), Sarmiento writes in a footnote that, while writing the *Facundo,* he received details about the caudillo's death from the "untimely deceased Dr. Piñero" (then in Chile), who had learned them from his relative Señor Ortiz, Facundo Quiroga's personal secretary. Ortiz had been present at Facundo's assassination.

—Vicente Fidel López (1815–1903), *porteño,* graduated from the University of Buenos Aires in 1839 with a degree in law. He was part of the Salón Literario and Echeverría's May Association, of which he founded a branch in Córdoba during his brief stay there in 1840 after leaving Buenos Aires. That same year he went on to Chile, where he would become a close collaborator of Sarmiento, joining with him in the polemic on romanticism in 1842 and, the following year, in opening a private school for the sons of the wealthy. He published numerous articles in the local press, in both Santiago and Valparaíso, as well as several longer academic studies on history and letters. He left Chile for Montevideo shortly after Sarmiento left for Europe in October 1845. During his time in Chile, he also published his historical novel *La novia del hereje* [The Heretic's Sweetheart] as a serial in a local newspaper. He and Mitre (see Note 1, "Introduction") would become the two major nineteenth-century historians of Argentina; the ten volumes of his *Historia de la República Argentina* [History of the Argentine Republic] would appear between 1883 and 1893.

—On Juan Bautista Alberdi, see VII, "Introduction."

—On José María Gutiérrez, see Note 64, "Introduction."

—Sarmiento is referring to Domingo de Oro, the subject of Chapter 10.

—Probably Carlos Tejedor, from Buenos Aires. In the 1840s he was in Chile and published articles in *El Progreso* (see Notes 62, "Introduction," and 2, Chapter 18).

—Possibly Mariano Fragueiro. See Note 34, Chapter 10.

—On Manuel Montt, see VI, Note 61, "Introduction."

29. *El Semanario de Santiago* [The Weekly of Santiago] was published between July 14, 1842, and February 2, 1843, reaching a total of thirty-one issues. At Andrés Bello's recommendation, the newspaper, which aspired to provide a forum where young Chilean writers could prove themselves, welcomed the collaboration of a broad cross-section of intellectuals, including Sarmiento's liberal Chilean friend Lastarria, some of the elder Bello's more conservative students, and others of various political stripes. The paper made a point of only allowing Chilean collaborators, and among these, Salvador Sanfuentes, A. García Reyes, and José Joaquín Vallejo early on took jabs at romanticism, in the defense of

which Sarmiento and his fellow Argentinean Vicente Fidel López responded with a series of now famous articles. During this polemic, concluded with the *Semanario*'s fourth issue, Sarmiento felt that the attacks on romanticism were really directed at him personally, and that both his intellectual credentials and his right as a foreigner to express opinions were being questioned.

30. The *Instituto Nacional* was founded in Santiago in 1813, the same year as the national library. It was financed by the government and intended to be the nation's flagship secondary school. Tuition was free, and in a study of Chilean public education that Sarmiento wrote in 1855, he pointed out that the institute, though public, was in fact only educating the children of people in the capital and the provinces who, in the absence of the state's largesse, could have afforded to pay for their sons' education themselves. Simon Collier writes that the *Instituto* "is popularly believed to have educated three-quarters of all Chile's leaders between 1830 and 1891" (Simon Collier and William F. Sater, *A History of Chile, 1808–1994* [Cambridge: Cambridge University Press, 1996], 101).

31. Sarmiento was one of the eighty-six professors originally named to the newly founded University of Chile in 1843. Until the death of the University's first Rector (Andrés Bello) in 1865, it held no classes of its own, but was exclusively dedicated to research, deliberation, and the supervision of the country's educational system. Thus, evaluating the performance of local schools would have been consistent with Sarmiento's faculty appointment.

CHAPTER 16: PUBLIC LIFE

1. Silvio Pellico (1789–1854) was a romantic Italian poet and playwrite, who in 1819 joined the Carbonari, a secret political association formed in Italy to fight for unification and establish a republic. He spent eight years in prison for his political activities, and in 1832 published his memoirs *Le mie prigioni* [My Imprisonments], an account of his hardships as a prisoner. Translated into both French and English in 1833, this work was widely read and generated international sympathy for the cause of Italian nationalism.

2. Spielberg was an infamous fortress in Brunn, Austria, used by the Hapsburgs for political prisoners, including Silvio Pellico. The Bastille, a state prison in Paris, was stormed and destroyed on July 14, 1789, a pivotal event in the French Revolution. Santos Lugares, about 15 kilometers to the west of Buenos Aires, was the general military headquarters of the Rosas regime, as well as a political prison for dissenters; Rosas had it built toward the end of the 1830s.

3. On Cicero, see Note 16, Chapter 15.

—On Franklin, see Note 2, Chapter 4.

—Themistocles (ca. 525–ca. 460 B.C.), was an Athenian statesman, general, and brilliant military strategist, whose defeat of Xerxes and the Persian navy at the Battle of Salamis made Athens the great naval power of the Helenic world. A strong advocate of democracy, he was disliked by the upper classes, and spent the last part of his life in exile.

4. Manuel Gregorio Quiroga Carril was the first federalist governor of San Juan (mid-January 1827, to the end of November 1828). As Facundo Quiroga was advancing with an army against San Juan, the province's unitarian governor José Antonio Sánchez fled to Mendoza, and Quiroga entered the city on January 11, 1827. Days later, Quiroga Carril, from a well-known federalist family, was elected governor with the approval of Facundo, who remained with his troops in the provincial capital until March 20. In the *Facundo* ("Guerra social: Ciudadela"), Sarmiento narrates his version of Quiroga Carril's ignominious death at the hands of Facundo, after the Battle of Ciudadela in November 1831.

5. Las Quijadas, a place near the San Juan border where ex-governor Quiroga Carril's federalist forces from San Juan, en route to join the army of Facundo, rebelled against their commander and returned to San Juan in early June 1829, to support the local unitarians. According to Bunkley, Jachal was a unitarian military encampment about fifty leagues to the north of San Juan (Allison Williams Bunkley, *The Life of Sarmiento* [(Princeton: Princeton University Press, 1952], 73). Tafín refers to an armed encounter won by the Aldao brothers' federalist forces; these same troops subsequently revolted against the Aldaos on their return to Mendoza. El Pocito was a unitarian camp outside of San Juan. These particular clashes between federalist and unitarian armies all occurred in 1829. On the Aldaos, see Note 20, Chapter 10. On José Miguel Carrera, see Notes 9 and 11, Chapter 8.

6. The tragedy of El Pilar occurred on September 21–22, 1829.

7. On Laprida, see Note 2, Chapter 3.

8. Facundo Quiroga's victory against the unitarian governor of Mendoza, General Videla Castillo, at the Battle of Chacón took place on March 28, 1831. As a result of this battle, Facundo gained control over all of Cuyo and La Rioja. Sarmiento narrates this battle in "Guerra social: Chacón" in the *Facundo,* and describes the city of Mendoza, before Facundo's occupation, as "an eminently civilized town, rich in enlightened men and in possession of an entrepreneurial spirit without equal in the Republic of Argentina: it was the Barcelona of the interior" (*Facundo,* 162; translation mine).

9. *El Zonda* was a weekly newspaper directed and largely written by Sarmiento in San Juan. Six issues appeared between July 20, 1839, and August 25, 1839.

10. Juan Felipe Ibarra (1787–1851), caudillo and federalist governor of the Argentine province of Santiago del Estero between 1820 and his death in 1851.

11. See Chapter 6. It is worth noting that Sarmiento points out his earlier error here, but neither in the first nor in the second edition does he go back to Chapter 6 to correct it.

12. On June 27, 1839, Manuel Maza, president of the House of Representatives and the Supreme Court in Buenos Aires, was assassinated by the Mazorca. The next day his son, Colonel Ramón Maza, arrested for conspiring to overthrow Rosas, was murdered in prison.

13. A popular form of federalist harassment toward unitarian males was to forcibly shave their side burns, which often joined together in a beard at the chin to form a "u."

14. Julian González Salomón, the owner of a general store and bar in Buenos Aires, was the president of the *Sociedad Popular Restauradora* [Popular Restauration Society]. Captain Manuel Gaetán was a *mazorquero* who was executed after the notorious assassination, in 1839, of Manuel Maza.

CHAPTER 17: CHILE

1. Sarmiento's biographer Allison Williams Bunkley provides the following translation of a description of the various meanings of "Zonda" in the province of San Juan in 1839. He quotes from the cover article, probably written by Sarmiento, of the first issue of the local newspaper *El Zonda* (see Note 6, Chapter 4).

Zonda is a delicious and happy valley surrounded by wild and monotonous hills. . . . Zonda is an embracing, impetuous wind that destroys all that is not firmly rooted. . . . Zonda is a cooling bath whose healthful waters alleviate a thousand pains, where youth enjoys the most varied pleasures, where pastimes, the graceful dance, the happy song, the merry revelry goes on uninterrupted for four months of the year, where etiquette is exiled, families are mixed, and social bonds are extended. (*Life of Sarmiento*, 114)

—Sarmiento had earlier reproduced this quote on the title page of the first edition of the *Facundo* (1845), where he had attributed it to the French writer Hippolyte Fortoul (1811–1852). (On the much contested origin of this quote, see Paul Verdevoye, Note #62, *Educar y escribir*, p. 80.) The same quote had then reappeared on the next page of the first edition, followed by a brief first-person narrative not only about how Sarmiento had written it on a wall with a piece of coal the day he left San Juan to go into exile at the end of 1840, but also about how the Argentine authorities had reacted to this graffiti, in a foreign tongue. Sarmiento's laconic allusion to the episode in the first sentence of Chapter 17 here in *Recuerdos* seems to assume that the reader will already be familiar with the earlier, more lengthy account of the episode in the *Facundo*.

—Ambrosio Cramer was one of the *estancia* owners who led the Rebellion of the South (see Note 18, Chapter 8). Rosas had him executed for his role in this intraclass revolt.

—On Lavalle, see Note 1, Chapter 6.

—Chacabuco, Tucumán, Maipú [Maipo], Callao, Talcahuano, Junín, and Ayucucho were all scenes of important military actions during the wars of independence. See Notes 5, Chapter 4; 9, Chapter 8; and 18, Chapter 10, and Note 5 below.

2. Andrés Bello (1781–1865) is one of the towering intellectual figures of nineteenth-century Hispanic America. Born the son of a minor official in the Spanish bureaucracy in Caracas, he studied arts, law, and medicine at the University of Caracas, gave private lessons on geography and literature to the young Simón Bolívar, and in 1800 joined Alexander von Humboldt on the latter's research expedition in northern South America. He became an administrator in the local colonial government, but in 1810 he was named to the Ministry of Foreign Relations of the first patriot government in Caracas. That year he accompanied Simón Bolívar on a mission to England in a failed attempt to procure the recognition of the British government. He remained in London, where he was active in support of the independence movement until its conclusion in 1824. In 1829 he arrived in Chile, where he would live for the remainder of his life. He immediately began serving in what would become a series of important positions in the Chilean government, became Rector of the recently founded secondary school *Colegio de Santiago* in 1830, and that same year began collaborating in the local newspaper *El Araucano*. He became a Chilean citizen in 1832 and was subsequently elected senator in 1837, 1846, and 1855. He was founder and rector of the University of Chile in 1842. In 1847 he published what remains today one of the most famous and authoritative of Spanish grammars, *Gramática de la lengua castellana destinada al uso de los Americanos* [Grammar of the Castillian Language for Use by Americans]. He was also the author of Chile's Civil Code, which became law in 1855. See also Note 11, Chapter 11, and Notes 29 and 31, Chapter 15.

—On Domingo de Oro, see Chapter 10.

—Casimiro Olañeta was a Bolivian diplomat representing his country in Santiago when Sarmiento arrived.

3. Mariano Egaña (1793–1846) was secretary of the interior in the patriot government of the *Patria vieja* (see Note 9, Chapter 8). In 1824 he was sent by the Chilean government to England in a thwarted attempt to gain British recognition of the independence. There he contracted Andrés Bello to emigrate to Chile to work for the state. A Conservative, he was one of the authors of the Chilean Constitution of 1833 (see Note 1 on Portales, Chapter 10), which established a strong executive, and he was also a longtime Conservative senator.

4. Rafael Minvielle. Originally from Spain, Minvielle was a member of Lastarria's Literary Society (1842–43; see Note 7 below), who, in 1842 wrote and staged a play entitled "Ernesto," about which Sarmiento, on the occasion of its second presentation in February, 1843, wrote and published a very positive re-

view. Sarmiento called it "one of the lovely flowers with which our young [Chilean] literature has adorned itself," as well as "one of the few [works] that are truly of national and American interest." ("Ernesto: drama de don Rafael Minvielle," *El Progreso*, February 15, 1843, in *Obras*, II [Santiago de Chile: Gutenberg, 1885], 107, 112; translation mine.)

5. The Pipiolo Party was another name for the Liberal Party in nineteenth-century Chile.

—General Gregorio Las Heras (1780–1866), from Buenos Aires, distinguished himself fighting with General San Martín's victorious Army of the Andes in the Battle of Maipú, which took place outside Santiago de Chile on April 5, 1818, and guaranteed Chile its independence from Spain. Las Heras returned to Buenos Aires in 1821 and became governor of the province from 1824 to 1826. An enemy of the Rosas regime, he went to live in Chile, where he lent his active support and the prestige of his name to the resistance campaign organized by the younger generation of Argentine exiles in Chile—Sarmiento, López, Mitre, etc.

6. On Manuel Montt (1804–1880), see Section IV and Note 61, "Introduction."

7. Manuel Antonio Tocornal (1808–1878) was a student of Andrés Bello who formed part of the group of young Chileans who brought out *El Semanario de Santiago* between 1842 and '43 (see Note 29, Chapter 15). By 1849, Tocornal and Sarmiento were allied as supporters of President Bulnes against interior minister Manuel Camilo Vial, and the two of them, along with Antonio García Reyes, founded the paper *La Tribuna* to oppose him. In 1857 Tocornal defected from President Montt and led the Conservatives in the creation, along with the Liberals, of a new National Party, also known as the Liberal-Conservative Fusion. In 1863 Tocornal became president of the Chamber of Representatives, and upon the death of Andrés Bello in 1865, rector of the University of Chile.

—Antonio García Reyes was a Conservative lawyer and congressman who also published in *El Semanario de Santiago* (see Note 29, Chapter 15). Later he would collaborate with Sarmiento and Tocornal on *La Tribuna* (see Note on Tocornal above).

—Manuel Talavera was another of the eleven writers on the staff of *El Semanario de Santiago*.

—José Victorino Lastarria (1817–1888) was an important liberal writer and political figure of nineteenth-century Chile. Born to the south of Santiago in Rancangua and of modest origin, Lastarria studied with the famous Spanish liberal expatriot José Joaquín de Mora, who lived in Chile between 1828 and 1831 (when he was expelled by the conservative government), and then subsequently with Andrés Bello, toward whom later on he often reacted combatively. A lawyer and a teacher, he helped found the Literary Society in Santiago in 1842, which was intended to enlighten young Chilean intellectuals and to encourage them to study their national reality and to found a truly national literature. (The society met weekly between 1842 and '43.) He was instrumental in founding *El Semanario de Santiago* (see Note 29, Chapter 15), and several other journals in the 1840s, and is credited with having written the first Chilean modern short story, "El mendigo" [The Beggar] in 1843. He served as a Liberal deputy numerous times, including the periods 1843–46 and 1849–52 (interrupted by a brief political exile in 1850), as well as a senator, and was minister under several Liberal presidents. He published widely on history and law, and was the author of the important memoir *Recuerdos Literarios* (1878), which has been translated and published in the Library of Latin America Series as *Literary Memoirs* (2000).

—José Joaquín Vallejo (1811–1858) was born in the north of Chile in Copiapó, and moved to Santiago in 1829 to study in the *Liceo de Chile* under the Spanish liberal Mora (see Note 7 on Lastarria above). He remained in Santiago for twelve years, returning to his birthplace Copiapó in 1841. However, as a correspondent, he published in *El Mercurio* of Valparaíso, where he was probably paid the most per article of any of its writers. He also published in *El Semanario* in 1842 (see Note 29, Chapter 15), where he was one of Sarmiento's detractors. Known by his pseudonym Jotabeche, with which he signed his articles starting in the early '40s, he became so popular among his Chilean contemporaries for his witty *costumbrista* articles that a selection was published in book form in 1847.

—On *El Semanario*, see Note 29, Chapter 15.

8. José Miguel Infante (1778–1844) was a Chilean lawyer who supported the independence and was a member of several of the patriot juntas during the *Patria vieja* as well as Minister of Finance under O'Higgins (see Note 9, Chapter 8). He was an ardent defender of federalism, and in 1827 founded the newspaper *El Valdiviano Federal* to argue his point of view. (This paper would exist until Infante's death in 1844.) By the mid-1820s he was enormously influential and was crucial in drafting the federalist constitution of 1826, which was in force for about a year. He was also an abolitionist: In 1811 he fought to pass a law abolishing the slave trade in Chile, and in 1823 he spearheaded the final abolition of slavery, at a time when some 4,000 slaves remained in the country. After the conservative victory in 1829, he became an outspoken opposition figure. In 1843 he refused to accept an appointment as professor of law at the University of Chile.

9. Manuel de Salas (1754–1841), born into one of the most aristocratic families in Chile, began his career of public service as mayor of the Cabildo de Santiago in 1775. He was an enlightened reformer in the late colonial period and an ardent promoter of the first patriotic junta in 1810. During the *Patria vieja*, he held several important political positions and wrote for the first daily newspaper in Chile, *El Aurora de Chile* [The Dawn of Chile], founded in 1812. In 1818 he was named head of the National Library (est. 1813). Like Infante, he supported the

abolition of slavery. In 1838 he made a first attempt to found the National Agricultural Society to promote the introduction of new technologies from Europe.

10. The Vial family owned the newspaper *El Progreso*. See Note 62, "Introduction."

11. On the *Revista Católica*, see Note 16, Chapter 15.

12. Deucalion, a mythical Greek figure, son of Prometheus. He and his wife, Pyrrha, as the only survivors of a great flood sent by Zeus to punish the living for their wickedness, were allowed to repopulate the world by throwing stones behind their backs. When the stones landed on the ground, they took on human shape, and were known as the Stone People, whose descendents became the human race.

13. On Lastarria, see Note 7 above.

—Probably a reference to Andrés Bello's son Juan (1825–1860). In 1849, at the age of twenty-four, he was elected to Congress, where he soon joined a new liberal opposition to the Bulnes government. He was in office when the barracks revolt of April 20, 1851, took place and was put down by President Bulnes himself, on horseback. Two hundred men were killed in the mutiny, including its leader, Colonel Pedro Urriola. The young Bello delivered a speech at Urriola's funeral and was promptly exiled, first to Copiapó and then to Lima, by the conservative government, causing his father, a Bulnes supporter, considerable consternation.

—On Sanfuentes, see Note 29, Chapter 15.

14. The "harmful school of Louis Philippe" reflects Sarmiento's judgment on the political experience of the constitutional monarchy of Louis Philippe (1830–1848) from the vantage point of 1850. Louis Philippe had walked a middle road between the reactionary monarchists on the right and the republicans and socialists on the left. He alienated the lower bourgeoisie by refusing to grant them suffrage, thus pushing them into a short-lived alliance with the proletariat during the Revolution of 1848. About Sarmiento's positive response to the French Revolution of 1848 and the abdication of Louis Philippe, see Section IV, "Introduction."

15. Camille Hyacinthe Odilon Barrot (1791–1873), French politician who took part in the July revolution of 1830 and supported the idea of liberal but nonrepublican government. Both within France and without, he was criticized for compromising his political beliefs to gain favor with the crowd.

16. General Gregorio Aráoz de La Madrid (or Lamadrid) (1795–1857), from Tucumán, fought for the independence and against López in 1818 (see Note 4, Chapter 10) and Ramírez in 1820 (see Note 9, Chapter 10). Between 1826 and 1831 he fought four battles against Facundo Quiroga (all memorably described in the *Facundo*). In 1838, the unitarian officer was reconciled with Rosas, but returned to the unitarian fold in 1840, was named governor of Tucumán in 1841

and then was defeated by federalist troops at the Battle of Rodeo del Medio that same year, after which he retreated with his defeated army across the Andes into Chile. In 1852 he fought with Urquiza at Caseros.

17. Los Andes is a town in Chile at the same latitude as the Argentine city of Mendoza, and near the border with Argentina.

—On the *"suma del poder,"* see Note 17, Chapter 7.

18. On Cascuberta, see Note 14, Chapter 15.

—The *Othello* that was one of Cascuberta's war horses was not Shakespeare's play but an eighteenth-century neoclassical French recasting of the English tragedy. The French version had then been translated into Spanish and suffered further changes along the way. On several occasions Sarmiento criticized this eighteenth-century version as grossly inferior to Shakespeare's original, although he praised Cascuberta's rendition of the lead role. The benefit performance of this play was presented in December 1841, in the Teatro de la Universidad [University Theatre] of Santiago.

—The benefit performance of the tragedy *Marino Faliero,* by Casimir Delavigne (1793–1843), was presented in the Teatro de la Universidad in November 1841. The French poet and playwrite Delavigne, elected to the Académie Francaise in 1825, modestly departed from the unities of neoclassicism but opposed the innovations of Victor Hugo's romantic theater. Delavigne's plays were among Cascuberta's favorites.

19. *El Desenmascarado* was a newspaper published by Pedro Godoy, the sole purpose of which was to attack Sarmiento. Only one issue appeared, on February 7, 1843. On Pedro Godoy, see Note 11, Chapter 13.

20. *El Diario de Santiago* [The Santiago Daily] published 208 issues in 1845.

21. Vicente Fidel López published six of his articles on romanticism in the newspaper *La Gaceta de Comercio,* of Valparaíso. On López, see Note 28, Chapter 15.

22. On García del Río, see Note 19, Chapter 11.

—Manuel Rivadeneira (1805–1872) was a Spanish publisher who lived in Chile between 1839 and 1842. Early in 1841, just as Sarmiento was arriving in Santiago, he purchased the newspaper *El Mercurio* of Valparaíso and its press. In 1842 he returned to Spain and sold *El Mercurio* to another Spaniard, Santos Tornero, who, in Valparaíso in 1840, had opened the first real bookstore in the country (*La Librería Española* [The Spanish Bookstore]). (Before that time, what books there were for sale, mostly expensive foreign imports, were sold with miscellaneous other merchandise at general stores.)

23. On Jotabeche (José Joaquín Vallejo), see Notes 29, Chapter 15 and 7 above.

24. Viriato (d. 139 B.C.), an Iberian who led the guerrilla struggle to defend Lusitania from the Romans. After his assassination, the Romans were able to

conquer Lusitania, which today corresponds to Extremadura and Portugal south of the Duero River.

25. *El Copiapino* was a newspaper that Jotabeche founded in Copiapó in 1845; he sold it shortly after, although the paper continued to be published until 1876.

26. The nun Zañartu was the protagonist of a well-known story in Chile about an eighteenth-century woman from the Zañartu family who had been forced by her father to join a convent against her will and who died cloistered and in despair. In his review of a play published in *El Progreso* in 1843, Sarmiento had referred to this popular story. The archbishop of Santiago, whose mother was a Zañartu, wrote to the paper in protest, accusing Sarmiento of calumny. Sarmiento defended himself, and this irritated the Godoys, who also claimed to be related to the nun. Thus began the smear campaign that the brothers Godoy conducted against Sarmiento in 1843. See Note 19 above, and Note 11, Chapter 13.

27. In 1842, Manuel Montt, minister of public education, charged Sarmiento with establishing a Normal School. This teacher-training school in Santiago, for men only, was the first of its kind in Hispanic America and the second founded in the western hemisphere, the first being the normal school founded in Lexington, Massachusetts, in 1839. (Chilean women had to wait until 1854 for their first normal school.)

28. Sarmiento is writing in 1850. The California Gold Rush of 1848 had already had an enormous impact on Chile's export of wheat as well as on emigration. Simon Collier and William Sater write that, "At the height of the rush there were thousands of Chileans in California." Collier and Sater, *History*, 81.

29. Sarmiento is the editor to whom he refers here.

30. "Un viaje a Valparaíso," is a *costumbrista* article in five installments that Sarmiento published in *El Mercurio* between September 2 and 7, in 1841. In it, he assumes the fictional persona of a young Chilean gentleman who travels from Santiago to Valparaíso, in a two-passenger coach, along the only road that connects the capitol and the nation's major port.

31. On "the occupation of the Straits of Magellan," see Note 1, Chapter 12.

—From December 1844, to January 1, 1845, Sarmiento published a series of articles in *El Progreso* in which he argued against the wisdom of having an inter-American congress. Rosas of Argentina would be interested in having such a congress take place because, according to Sarmiento, Rosas would like nothing better than to have the countries of Hispanic America united behind him in his conflicts with England and France. Within Chile, Sarmiento was fairly alone in maintaining this position, but eventually the Congress proved too difficult to organize, and it never took place.

CHAPTER 18: DAILY NEWSPAPERS AND PERIODICAL PUBLICATIONS

1. Manuel Oribe (Montevideo, 1772–1857). From 1828, when Uruguay becomes an independent nation, until 1851, Oribe will define his career in opposition to fellow Uruguayan Fructuoso Rivera (see Notes 18, Chapter 8 and 23, Chapter 10) and in alliance with Juan Manuel de Rosas (see Note 3, "To My Compatriots Only"). One-time president of Uruguay in the mid-1830s, he renounces the presidency and goes to Buenos Aires, where Rosas not only recognizes him as the legal head of state of the Banda Oriental, but puts him in charge of the Army of the Argentine Confederation. Under his military leadership, this army defeats the Interior League (the armed anti-Rosista resistance in the Argentine interior) and then goes on to defeat the dictator's enemies in the Littoral. In 1843 he returns to Uruguay and lays siege to Montevideo, until his capitulation in 1851. It is in Oribe's encampment outside Montevideo that the pro-Rosas newspaper *El Defensor de la Independencia Americana* is published.

2. Publication of the weekly *La Crónica*, founded by Sarmiento, began on January 28, 1849, and was interrupted on January 20, 1850; it was not resumed until November 12, 1853, and it ended shortly after, on January 7 of the following year. Sarmiento founded *El Progreso* in 1842 and was its editor in chief, with a few brief interruptions, until October, 1845, when he left Chile to travel abroad. This daily newspaper continued to appear until 1852, but not under the direction of Sarmiento.

3. This is a reference to the assassination of Florencio Varela in Montevideo, in 1848. See Note 9, Chapter 11.

4. *El Heraldo Argentina* only appeared twice, on December 23 and 30, 1842.

—With Rivera's defeat by Oribe at Arroyo Grande (1842), the anti-Rosista resistance of the Littoral, organized by the governments of Uruguay, Santa Fe, and Corrientes, was temporarily liquidated, causing the Argentine immigration in Chile to despair of overthrowing Rosas in the near future. On Fructuoso Rivera, also see Notes 18, Chapter 8 and 23, Chapter 10.

5. *El Comercio del Plata* appeared in Montevideo on October 1, 1845. It was a daily newspaper under the direction of the Argentine unitarian expatriot Florencio Varela (see Note 9, Chapter 11). After a brief interruption, when, in March, 1848, Varela was assassinated (perhaps to silence his—by then—internationally influential newspaper), the paper continued under the directorship of the Argentine unitarian Valentín Alsina. Read in Europe (as well as in Argentina, where almost two hundred copies a day were imported by foreign businessmen), the paper reached an edition of four hundred copies a day, an exceptionally large edition for a Spanish American daily at that time. See Félix Weinberg, "El periodismo en la época de Rosas," *Revista de Historia* (Buenos Aires), no. 2 (2nd trimester, 1957): 91–92.

—Sarmiento was in Spain between the middle of October and the middle of December 1846. General Juan José Flores (1800, Venezuela– 1864, Ecuador), three times president of Ecuador (1830–34, 1839–43, 1843–45), was forced to give up power in June 1845, and left for Europe for two years. In 1846 he attempted to organize an expedition, from Europe and with the collaboration of France, Spain, and England, to return to America and regain control of Ecuador. This plan was frustrated when the British cabinet withdrew its support. Flores finally returned to Ecuador in 1860, where he supported President Gabriel García Moreno until his death in military action in 1864.

6. Sarmiento is referring to Manuelita Rosas (1817–1898), the daughter of Juan Manuel de Rosas. Rosas did not remarry after the death of his wife in 1838; from this time on, until the end of his regime in 1852, Manuelita served as his official hostess and also exercised considerable political influence.

—The *Revue des Deux Mondes* was probably the most important cultural review in nineteenth-century France. It was published in Paris in 1829 and then from 1831 to 1944. (After 1948 it was published under a different name until 1982, when it resumed its original title; it continues to appear today.) In 1846 it published a favorable review of Sarmiento's *Facundo*, of 1845. Sarmiento must be referring to the arrival in Buenos Aires of the 1846 issue that contained the review of his book. See also Note 2, "To My Compatriots Only."

CHAPTER 19: PAMPHLETS

1. A number of the Spanish titles that Sarmiento employs here refer to books that were originally published in English or German; for example, the study by Rengger and Longchamp, published first in German in 1827, was subsequently translated into English. To the best of my knowledge, this book was not translated into Spanish until 1883. King's original title in English was *Twenty-four Years in the Argentine Republic*, not as Sarmiento translates it. Sarmiento's indiscriminate mix here of author's names and book titles covers a range of mostly eighteenth- and nineteenth-century texts on Latin America by naturalists, historians, paleontologists, metalurgists, geographers, explorers, and travelers of various nationalities.

2. One year later, however, in 1851, Sarmiento did publish *Emigración alemana al Río de la Plata* in his own publishing house Julio Belín y Cía., in Santiago de Chile. He had the work translated from German into Spanish by a certain Guillermo Hilleger.

CHAPTER 20: BIOGRAPHIES

1. Sarmiento had met Tandonnet in 1846 during his Atlantic crossing to Europe; he describes their conversations at sea in the chapter "Ruan" in *Viajes*. Tandonnet published his translation of *Apuntes* in Bourdeaux in 1847.

—On Oribe, see Note 1, Chapter 18.

CHAPTER 21: BOOKS

1. On the *compte rendu* of the *Revue des Deux Monde,* see Notes 2, "To My Compatriots Only," and 6, Chapter 18.

2. *El Nacional* was a newspaper published in Montevideo that represented the point of view of the Argentine Generation of 1837. It appeared in 1838 under the direction of the Uruguayan Andrés Lamas and the Argentinean Miguel Cané.

—Johann Moritz Rugendas (1802–1858), German artist who in 1821 joined an expedition into the interior of Brazil but soon went off by himself to paint the local landscape, people, flora, and fauna. In Paris in 1823, he met and became a friend of Alexander von Humboldt, who encouraged him to return to South America in 1831. He made numerous drawings and watercolors of the landscapes and peoples of Mexico, Chile (where he lived from 1833 to 1845), Argentina, Peru, and Bolivia. On his return to Europe, he eventually became court painter to Maximilian II of Bavaria.

3. All in all, in this single sentence Sarmiento drops fifteen names and apparently expects his contemporary readers to recognize at least most of them: M. Guizot, Sr. Rosales, M. Thiers, Cobden, Marshal Bugeaud, M. de Lesseps, Alexandre Dumas, Blanchart, Girardet, Gil de Zarate, Colonel Sesé, Bretón de los Herreros, Ventura de la Vega, Aribau, Rivadeneira. Frequent name-dropping is characteristic of Sarmiento, whose egocentrism has often been commented on by his biographers. Some of the names included here are identified in the Editor's Notes to this edition.

4. Alexander von Humboldt (1768–1859), the famous German naturalist who reported on his travels (1799–1840) in Mexico, Central and South America, and Cuba, in thirty widely read volumes, published between 1805 and 1832. Sarmiento visited him in Potsdam in 1847.

—Prosper Merimée (1803–1870) was the French author of the novella *Carmen* (1845), upon which Bizet based his famous opera of 1874. Both works contributed to the nineteenth-century romantization of Spain beyond its own borders.

—Amable Tastu (1798–1885) was a French female writer who published almost thirty volumes during her lifetime, including collections of poetry, pedagogical treatises, and travel accounts.

—Horace Mann (1796–1859) was an important nineteenth-century educational reformer in the United States, who was to have considerable influence on Sarmiento. Among other things, Mann founded the first public normal school in the western hemisphere, in Lexington, Massachusetts, on July 3, 1839. Sarmiento fails to mention here that on that same trip he also met Horace Mann's wife, Mary Peabody Mann, who would be the first English-language translator of *Facundo* and of parts of *Recuerdos de provincia.* See also Notes 22, "Introduction," 28, Chapter 8, and 27, Chapter 17.

5. Here Sarmiento refers to some of his Argentine detractors.

CHAPTER 22: TRANSLATIONS

1. Sarmiento translated this book from French, and published it in 1844, with the press of the newspaper *El Progreso*.

2. Also published in 1844, by *El Progreso*.

3. Published in 1849, by the Julio Belín y Cía.

4. Ibid.

5. The book translated was not Benjamin Franklin's autobiography but rather a popularized biography written in French by M. Mignet, and published in Paris in 1848: *Vie de Franklin: a l'usage de tout le monde*. The translator was Sarmiento's friend and the original proofreader of *Recuerdos*, Juan María Gutiérrez. Gutiérrez's Spanish translation was published in 1849, by Julio Belín y Cía.

6. Pedro de Angelis (1784–1859). An Italian intellectual who emigrated to Buenos Aires at the invitation of the unitarian Bernardino Rivadavia. After Rosas came to power, he placed his journalistic talents at the service of the dictator, and from 1843 to 1851 he edited the regime's official newspaper, *Archivo Americano y Espíritu de la Prensa del Mundo* [American Archive and Spirit of the World Press], published in Spanish, English, and French, and aimed at presenting a positive image of Rosas to readers abroad.

CHAPTER 23: INSTITUTIONS OF LEARNING

1. It was in 1838 that Rosas withdrew state funding from primary and secondary schools in the city of Buenos Aires as well as from its University, which had been recently founded in 1821.

2. See Note 27, Chapter 17.

3. This is the only time in the book that Sarmiento makes any reference to a wife. He was married for the first and only time on May 19, 1848. He never mentions in this autobiography that he is a father, twice over.

4. It is to Varela's recent assassination that Sarmiento refers here at the conclusion of his autobiography. On Varela, see Note 9, Chapter 11.